The Complete
Anti-Inflammatory
Cookbook for Beginners

1200 Quick & Simple Anti-Inflammatory Recipes and 4-Week Meal Plans for Beginners and Advanced Users

Lisa Sadler

CONTENT

Introduction

Welcome to the anti-inflammatory diet cookbook! This cookbook will guide you in understanding and following an easy anti-inflammatory diet. The immune system of human causes inflammation in response to an injury or the presence of foreign pathogens to fight off infirmity and heal. The anti-inflammatory diet can be easy, delicious, and affordable. Best of all, it is an excellent investment in your long-term health. To understand the anti-inflammatory diet, it is critical to know what inflammation is and how it works. Inflammation can cause pain and anxiety, and it is an essential part of healing. When you get an injury or infection, you'll feel swelling, warmth, pain, and redness around the distressed area. The seasonal flu is a perfect example of the body's response to internal inflammation. There is another type of inflammation, and it is called chronic inflammation. The symptoms of long-term inflammation include high blood pressure, abdominal pain, digestive issues, emotional distress, weight gain, pain, chronic fatigue, loss of weight, high blood sugar level, etc.

An anti-inflammatory diet is not complicated or restrictive to follow. There are two types of inflammation; chronic (long-term over months or years) acute (short-term over a brief period). Inflammation can be caused by environmental toxicity, poor diet, genetics, stress, limited physical activity, and reliance on medication. Inflammation is the root of many diseases. Any condition that ends with "itis" involves inflammation such as laryngitis, appendicitis, bronchitis, endocarditis, arthritis, colitis, etc.

Many diseases can cause chronic inflammation. It can be a driving factor for type-2 diabetes, heart disease, cancer, autoimmune diseases, and gastrointestinal problems, including inflammatory bowel diseases, chronic infections, fibromyalgia, etc. An anti-inflammatory diet can reduce the risk of these diseases.

This cookbook will get simple-to-make and delicious recipes prepared with healthy spices and ingredients. Nutrition is an essential part of healing, whether you have inflammation from heart, diseases, cancer, diabetes or blood sugar issues, autoimmune disease, or other diseases. Good food can be a pillar of your healing. Eating proper food, stay hydrated, less inflammation, and living a healthier and happier life!

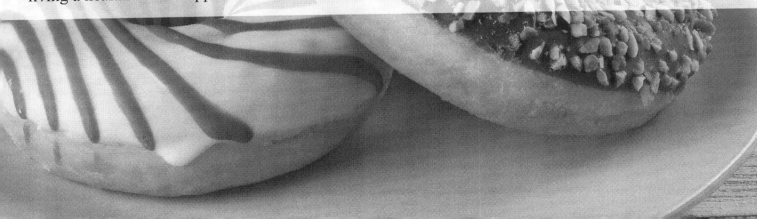

Fundamentals of Anti-Inflammation Diet

What is Anti-Inflammation Diet?

Inflammation is a natural healing response by the body and there are types of inflammation – chronic and acute inflammation. Chronic inflammation is long-term over years or months. Acute inflammation is a short-term and it goes away slowly over a few days as healing occurs. Chronic inflammation is not healthy and it continues long-term for months or even years.

	Acute Inflammation	Chronic Inflammation
What is this?	Healthy or short-term immune system response to a stimulus	Long-term inflammation, low-level immune system response to an unresolved stimulus
Causes	Injury, toxin, Harmful bacteria, sprain, allergic reaction, burn, cut bruise, etc.	An acute inflammation is not being completely resolved, foreign bodies or continuously irritant (lack of sleep, stress, autoimmune system, sedentary lifestyle, diet)
Signs	Pain, redness, and swelling, heat	Symptoms increase in severity as inflammation builds.
Immune response	Immediately, within seconds to minutes.	From months to years or delayed
Health impact	Inflammation slowly removes with healing usually within a few days to weeks. The body returns to normal healthy state.	Inflammation may be encouraged the foreign bodies to initiate damage or disease at a higher rate than normal.

Symptoms of Chronic Inflammation:

♣ Lack of energy
♣ High blood pressure
♣ Abnormal changes or mutations in healthy cells
♣ Atherosclerosis
♣ Accelerated aging
♣ Insulin resistance
♣ Constipation
♣ High LDL, low LDL, cholesterol level
♣ Bloating and gas
♣ Weight gain
♣ Stiffness
♣ Inability to lose weight
♣ Joint pain
♣ Depression
♣ Memory loss

Causes of Chronic Inflammation:

Many people don't know the initiation and development of chronic inflammation. People don't know what to eat or what lifestyle they should be adapted. The food and lifestyle habits both play an important role in discouraging and calming inflammation.

Top Inflammatory Foods:

♣ Processed food
♣ Fried food
♣ Refined, low-fiber starches
♣ Added sugars
♣ Artificial sweetener
♣ Trans and saturated food
♣ Drinking alcohol or caffeine in excess amount
♣ Excessive carbohydrate intake
♣ Artificial colors and flavorings
♣ Excessive calories intake
♣ High-fat meats and processed meats
♣ Excessive omega-6 intake

Top Anti-inflammatory Foods:

♣ Environmental pollutants
♣ Lack of sleep
♣ Inactivity
♣ Stress
♣ Gut permeability
♣ Excess body weight

There are many symptoms that may indicate inflammation in the entire human body.

Normal Symptoms:

Heat	Redness	Swelling	Pain

Silent Symptoms:

Many people don't realize the symptom when they are experienced to inflammation. Some common silent symptoms are followings:

Disease	Possible Symptoms
Inflammatory bowel diseases	Night sweats, blood or mucus in stools, diarrhea, constipation, poor appetite, nausea
Obesity	Sweating, excess weight, imbalance of blood sugar, and snoring
Heart disease	Fluttering the chest, high blood pressure, fatigue, dizziness, sweating
Osteoarthritis	Stiffness in the morning
Rheumatoid arthritis	Weakness, joint stiffness, fatigue, weight loss
Lupus	Anemia, fever, hair loss, light sensitivity, and fatigue,
Asthma	Mucus, coughing
Allergies	Watery eyes, runny nose, bedwetting, acne, digestive issues, mental fogginess, food intolerance, dizziness
Hashimoto's disease	Cold sensitivity, fatigue, thin hairs, dry skin, depression, weight gain
Skin conditions	Ache, digestive problems, family history of allergies
Brain disorders	Behavioral changes, memory loss, decrease cognitive function, insulin resistance, anxiety
Multiple sclerosis	Weakness, tingling, blurred vision, dizziness
Headache	Dull ache, nausea, blurred vision
Diabetes	Thirst, urination, and increase hunger
Cancer	Fatigue, fever, weight loss
Celiac disease	Greasy stools, digestive issues, weight loss, fatigue

Eat More Vegetables/Plants:

Encourage yourself to eat more plants or vegetables because they are good source of fiber. High fiber food is good for your health. They also provide antioxidants and other essential nutrients to support good health. These low-calories food fight cellular damage, promote digestion, and help maintain a healthy weight.

Enjoy Nuts and Seeds:

Nuts and seeds are good source of healthy fats and proteins, as well as fiber and micronutrients. Nuts and seeds enhance the flavor of meals.

Choose Healthy Fats:

The anti-inflammatory diet is related to plant-based option such as olive oil and it is good source of healthy saturated fats that support immunity. These are good to pro-inflammatory Trans fats and saturated fats from animal products such as butter. Choose omega-3 fats such as fish and walnuts, these are good source of omega-3 and it directly reduces the inflammation.

Eat Fresh Spices and Ingredients:

Garlic, ginger, and turmeric are anti-inflammatory ingredients. They add good flavor in each meal. They provide essential nutrients.

Discover Whole and Ancient Grains:

Ancient grains are those that predate modern varieties created through selective breeding and hybridization such as quinoa, oats, barley, chia seeds, sorghum, and bulgur. These whole grains retain fiber, anti-oxidants, and other essential nutrients that encourage a health immune response.

Top Ten Anti-Inflammatory Ingredients:

We all have the expression "food is a best medicine." When it comes to managing inflammation, true words have never been spoken. To reduce the inflammation, it is important to note that what to eat or not. It is well established that we should strive to eat a healthy and balanced diet that includes whole grains, fresh vegetables, fruits, lean protein, and fish that is abundant in good fats. It is also known that we should avoid processed food that are loaded with added sugar, refined grains, preservatives, stabilizers, hydrogenated fats, and high carbohydrates. When it comes to anti-inflammatory ingredients, we collect some foods that are good for your health.

Mushrooms: Edible fungi like Portobello, cremini, shiitake mushrooms are good sources of vitamin D, selenium, and antioxidant. These are essential minerals that help prevent inflammation.

Salmon: Fatty fish like salmon, anchovies, sardines, and mackerel contain high level of omega-3 fatty acids. It improves cardiovascular health and fight with inflammation.

Cayenne oil: Cayenne oil has chili peppers and it has both analgesic and anti-inflammatory properties that make it useful for topical and edible uses.

Broccoli: Vegetables like broccoli, Brussels sprout, cabbage, and cauliflower has large amount of disease-fighting phyto-chemicals such as sulforaphane which helps in reducing inflammation.

Blueberries: Blueberries are loaded with antioxidant and have strong anti-inflammatory qualities.

Turmeric: Ground or fresh turmeric has anti-inflammatory properties. It has a lot of health benefits.

Bone broth: Bone broth has lot of benefits. It boosts the immune system and reduces the inflammation.

Ginger: Ginger is aromatic ingredient which helps to alleviate pain and inflammation.

Avocado: Avocado is packed with powerful antioxidant and heart-healthy monounsaturated fats that help in reduce the inflammation.

Walnuts: Nuts like walnuts, pecans, cashews, and almonds are rich in antioxidant, high in fiber, low in carb, and inflammation-busting omega-3 fatty acids.

What to Eat?

In this diet, you need to choose fresh ingredients only. If you want to stay healthy and active, you should follow these ingredients. Consume fresh fruits, vegetables, gluten-free grains, nuts, seeds, lean meat, and fish, and avoid the junk, fast, and processed food. Take 8 hours of sleep per night. Drink eight glasses per day. Take regular exercise and go for a walk. Take less stress and enjoy a simple life.

Fresh Vegetables:

Artichokes	Bok choy	Fennels	Onions	Swiss chard
Carrots	Cauliflower	Green beans	Pea shoots or sprouts	Watercress
Cabbage	Celery	Green peas	Squash (summer, zucchini, acorn, and winter)	White potatoes
Broccoli	Corn	Lettuce	Sugar snap peas	
Beets	Endive	Kale	Sweet bell pepper	
Asparagus	Cucumbers	Napa cabbage	Sweet potatoes	

Fresh Fruits:

Apples	Blackberries	Blueberries	Coconut	Grapes	Melons
Apricots	Pears	Cherries	Cranberries	Mangoes	Peaches

Grains:

Amaranth	Corn (cereal no malt, organic, non-GMO-chips, starch, flour)	Garbanzo bean flour	Oats	Quinoa	Rice (cereal, crackers, black, cakes, noodles, flour)
Arrowroot flour	Millets	Masa harina (organic, non-GMO)	Potato starch	Noodles (gluten-free)	Tapioca starch

Nuts and Seeds:

Chia seeds	Flax seeds	Macadamia nuts	Pumpkin seeds	Sunflower seeds	Sesame seeds

Dairy:

Cream cheese	Farmer's cheese	Cream	Milk (pasteurized)	Fresh mozzarella
Butter	Goat milk	Mascarpone	Ricotta cheese	

Note: Use less amount of dairy. Excessive amount of dairy can be inflammatory

Fresh Fish:

Salmon	Trout	Cod	Haddock	Halibut

Note: Use fresh fish. Fish frozen at sea is processed almost immediately, which lessens the time that bacteria can grow on it. Don't defrost it in the refrigerator overnight. Cook from frozen or defrost in the microwave right before cooking.

Fresh Meat, Legumes, and Eggs:

Beef (organic, grass fed), less amount	Chicken	Navy beans(cooked from dry)	Turkey
Chickpea (cooked from dry)	Eggs (cooked)	Pinto beans (cooked from dry)	
Black beans (cooked from dry)	Duck	Split peas (cooked from dry)	

Note: Select organic if possible and make sure that meats are neither injected with broth nor marinated.

Beverages:

Coffee (small intake, except if you have tachycardia)	Herbal teas (peppermint, holy basil, and rooibos	Fruit juice (100 percent natural)
Espresso (small intake, if you have tachycardia)	Milk (coconut, nut, rice, oat, and cow)	Water (infused with recommended fruits)

Condiments, Spices, And Baking Ingredients:

Citrus acid	Ascorbic acid	Garlic	Sage	Oregano	Sweet paprika
Cardamom	Baking powder	Flaxseed oil	Rosemary	Olive oil	Stinging nettle
Black cumin	Holy basil	Dill	Pectin	Mint	Thyme
Basil	Ginger	Cumin	Peppermint	Lemon juice/lime juice	Turmeric
Baking soda	Gelatin	Cream of tartar	Parsley	Salt/sea salt	Vanilla extract

Sweetener:

Coconut sugar	White sugar	Honey
Brown sugar	Maple syrup	Stevia

Note: Avoid any artificial coloring, flavoring, or preservatives

Gluten:

Gluten is protein, and it is present in wheat germ, rye, wheat, spelt, bulgur, Kamut, farro, semolina, triticale, and farina. Gluten is hard to digest, and it may cause digestive problems. Celiac disease has a specific immune response to a protein in gluten, and it is called gliadin. Gluten may cause more than digestive distress. It may also cause skin conditions, joint pain, and imbalances of hormones, blood sugar imbalances, and many more. Focus on gluten-free foods such as fresh fruits, vegetables, gluten-free grains, nuts, seeds, beans, lean meats, and fish. Skip gluten-free cookies and bagels. A healthy diet will provide you with good and essential nutrients.

Vegetables:

Avocados	Red beans	Tomatoes
Chili peppers	Eggplants	Spinach

Fruits:

Banana	Pineapple	Strawberries
Kiwi	Raspberries	Citrus (except small amounts of lemon or lime juice for cooking)

Grain:

Rye	Wheat germ	Buckwheat	Whole-grain wheat flour

Nuts:

Walnuts	Pecans	Almonds	Cashews

Dairy:

Blue cheese	Milk (unpasteurized)
Parmesan cheese	yogurt
Cheddar cheese	Sour cream
Processed cheese	Buttermilk

Fish:

Canned tuna or other shelf-stable fish, smoked salmon, etc.	shellfish	crab	lobster

Meat and Legumes:

Aged meats, deli, marinated, dried, smoked	ham	Salami	Tofu
pork	Sausages	Soybeans	

Beverages:

Alcohol	Tomato juice	Black tea
Processed or added-sugar drinks or juices	Citrus juices	Green tea

Sweeteners:

Malt extract	Corn syrup – high fructose	Artificial sweeteners

Spices, Condiments, And Baking Ingredients:

Allspice	Cocoa	Pepper	White wine vinegar
Chocolate	Mustard seeds	Balsamic vinegar	Walnut oil
Bouillon	Cinnamon	Red wine vinegar	Nutritional yeast
Anise	Marinades	Soy sauce	Red wine vinegar
Caraway	Cloves	Nutmeg	Yeast extract

Inflammation Linked to Health Conditions

Studies have proven that chronic inflammation is the root of many diseases. Inflammation is especially suspected in diabetes, heart diseases, Alzheimer's diseases, and cancer. Health conditions connected to inflammation are followings:

Heart Disease:
Chronic inflammation is a long-term disease, and it leads to the formation of plaque in the arteries, which leads to heart attacks and strokes.

Asthma:
Asthma is one lung disease caused by shortening of breath, chest tightness, and coughing. Asthma can result from the airways being attacked by chronic inflammation, and it is also close to allergies.

Diabetes:
The immune system allows regulating blood sugar levels throughout the day. It may lead to an inflammatory response during periods of high blood sugar, which may increase diabetes.

Inflammatory Bowel Disease:
Inflammatory bowel disease may lead to inflammation of the stomach and intestines, which may cause bleeding and abdominal pain. It also includes colitis and Crohn's disease.

Cancer:
Research suggests that inflammation in the body may hike the cancer attacks such as breast cancer, prostate, colon, etc.

Alzheimer's Disease:
The connection between inflammation and Alzheimer's disease is not completely understood. Studies say that people at risk for Alzheimer's commonly have chronic inflammation before developing the sickness.

Allergy:

Allergic reaction contains immune system hypersensitivities. When an allergic reaction appears, the body releases histamines that may cause eyes to water, throat or chest tighten, etc.

Lupus:

Lupus disease affects the entire human body. The symptoms include muscle and joint pain.

Rheumatoid Arthritis:

This condition may cause pain, stiffness, swelling, muscle weakness, and reduced mobility.

Celiac Disease:

This condition affects the small intestine and may lead to chronic inflammation in the body. It may be caused by an inherited protein which is called gliadin. When gluten enters the bloodstream, it affects an immune response that damages the small intestine and may cause inflammation.

Skin Disease:

Inflammation occurs on the skin in various diseases such as ache, eczema, psoriasis, etc.

Brain Disorders:

Chronic inflammation may affect the brain, weakness, or numbness. It may damage the nerves. And headaches may occur to inform you of the brain disorders.

Tips to Reduce The Inflammation

1. Choose healthy and fresh vegetables and fruits.

Fruits and vegetables are among the most effective anti-inflammatory foods with their essential nutrients. Numerous macro- and micronutrients support health, including fibers, antioxidants, minerals, amino acids, vitamins, and phytonutrients that encourage anti-inflammatory and anti-cancer properties. While buying vegetables and fruit, choose fresh and healthy. It is good for your good health.

2.Consume healthy fats.

Many ingredients contain healthy fats such as salmon, sardines, walnuts, chia seeds, flaxseeds, hemp seeds, and dark leafy vegetables such as lettuce and kale, especially for anti-inflammatory diet. It boosts the mood, improves cardiovascular health, enhances the immune system, balances blood sugar, and keeps skin healthy and hydrated.

3.Eat enough protein.

Protein is important for healing, repair of tissues, and healing. It is essential for managing an anti-inflammatory condition. You should use fewer animal products and aim for vegetable sources such as seeds, nuts, vegetables, legumes, and beans. These ingredients are a good source of protein.

4.Drink plenty of water.

Stay hydrated. Water is an essential beverage. It reduces pains digestive tract; minimizes allergy and asthma symptoms. Aim for at least eight glasses per day. You can drink more than eight glasses if you live in a warm area.

5.Get enough sleep.

Sleep is very important for us. It is a time when we recharge, repair, and regenerate. If you don't get enough sleep, it may cause chronic inflammation. It also causes heart disease, food craving, weight gain, and moodiness. Get enough sleep at least eight hours per night.

6.Take your stress under control.

Stress is directly related to chronic inflammation. Chronic stress impacts the body as well as the mind. It may lead to many diseases. So, enjoy your life, go for a walk, play games, and feel relaxed and balanced.

4-Week Diet Plan

Week 1

Day 1:
Breakfast: Mackerel Scrambled Eggs
Lunch: Quinoa Burrito Bowls
Snack: Butternut Squash Mash
Dinner: Garlicky Lamb Stew
Dessert: Banana Pudding Cake

Day 2:
Breakfast: Coconut Milk Smoothie
Lunch: Ramen with Kale and Mushrooms
Snack: Kale Chips
Dinner: Satay Chicken Breast
Dessert: Cinnamon Coconut Cake

Day 3:
Breakfast: Tofu Veggie Eggs
Lunch: Garden Veggies
Snack: Cabbage Slaw
Dinner: Beef and Bell Pepper Fajitas
Dessert: Vanilla Apple Wedges

Day 4:
Breakfast: Blueberry Smoothie
Lunch: Chickpea-Stuffed Squash
Snack: Green Beans with Shallots
Dinner: Shrimp with Spicy Spinach
Dessert: Delicious Blueberry Crisp

Day 5:
Breakfast: Breakfast Sausage
Lunch: Whole-Wheat Penne with White Beans
Snack: Cauliflower with Almond Sauce
Dinner: White Miso Salmon
Dessert: Vanilla Pumpkin Pudding

Day 6:
Breakfast: Cauliflower Rolls
Lunch: Bean Burrito Bowls
Snack: Sautéed Spinach
Dinner: Pan-Fried Pork Chops with Apple Salsa
Dessert: Pecan Pears

Day 7:
Breakfast: Green Apple Smoothie
Lunch: Vegetable Cabbage Cups
Snack: Buffalo Cauliflower Bites
Dinner: Garlic Turkey Breast
Dessert: Apple Bundt Cake

Week 2

Day 1:
Breakfast: Overnight Berries Oats
Lunch: Hummus Burgers
Snack: Black Beans Lentil Balls
Dinner: Lemony Roasted Chicken
Dessert: Coconut Pancakes

Day 2:
Breakfast: Smoked Salmon Stuffed Deviled Eggs
Lunch: Baby Bok Choy Stir-Fry
Snack: Soy Edamame
Dinner: Pork Chops with Kale
Dessert: Vanilla Zucchini Cake

Day 3:
Breakfast: Berry Chia Breakfast
Lunch: Tomato Basil Pasta
Snack: Cinnamon Almonds
Dinner: Beef Tenderloin
Dessert: Strawberry Mason Jar Cakes

Day 4:
Breakfast: Pumpkin Porridge
Lunch: Roasted Broccoli and Cashews
Snack: Broccoli Bites
Dinner: Fennel Baked Salmon Fillets
Dessert: Chia Pudding with Oats

Day 5:
Breakfast: Raspberry Pineapple Smoothie
Lunch: White Beans and Collard Greens
Snack: Baked Sweet Potatoes
Dinner: Shrimp Balls over Garlicky Greens
Dessert: Gluten-Free Apple Cobbler

Day 6:
Breakfast: Sweet Potato Casserole
Lunch: Buddha Bowl
Snack: Garlic Red Chard
Dinner: Broccoli Chicken Meat
Dessert: Creamy Strawberry-Blueberry Ice Pops

Day 7:
Breakfast: Banana Oatmeal
Lunch: Quinoa Penne with Artichoke Hearts
Snack: Ginger Broccoli and Carrots
Dinner: Cod with Black Beans
Dessert: Strawberry-Lime Granita

Week 3

Day 1:
Breakfast: Coconut Strawberry Porridge
Lunch: Zucchini Patties
Snack: Curried Mustard Greens
Dinner: Lime Chicken and Rice
Dessert: Blueberry Parfait with Coconut Cream

Day 2:
Breakfast: Tomatoes Egg Scramble
Lunch: Quinoa and Vegetable Curry
Snack: Cabbage Salad with Quinoa
Dinner: Fried Beef and Broccoli
Dessert: Seasonal Fruit Crisps

Day 3:
Breakfast: Protein Grapes Smoothie
Lunch: Roasted Tri-Color Cauliflower
Snack: Butternut Squash Fries
Dinner: Stewed Lamb Leg with Greens
Dessert: Banana Cream

Day 4:
Breakfast: Mushroom Frittata
Lunch: Mushroom Risotto
Snack: Tilapia Ceviche
Dinner: Thai Seafood Chowder
Dessert: Blueberry Coconut Muffins

Day 5:
Breakfast: Turkey Sausage
Lunch: Vegetable Sticks with Black Bean Dip
Snack: Chickpea and Garlic Hummus
Dinner: Green Tea Poached Salmon
Dessert: Peach-Raspberry Crumble

Day 6:
Breakfast: Kale Egg Casserole
Lunch: Vegan Frittata
Snack: Rosemary and Garlic Sweet Potatoes
Dinner: Herbed Meatballs
Dessert: Chocolate-Avocado Mousse

Day 7:
Breakfast: Coconut Chocolate Oatmeal
Lunch: Mushroom Pasta
Snack: Carrot and Pumpkin Seed Crackers
Dinner: Chicken and Cauliflower Bake
Dessert: Cherry Ice Cream

Week 4

Day 1:
Breakfast: Acai Berry Smoothie
Lunch: Harvest Quinoa suitable bowl
Snack: Zucchini Chips
Dinner: Shrimp Paella
Dessert: Apple Cinnamon Muesli

Day 2:
Breakfast: Artichoke Egg Casserole
Lunch: Kale Bowls
Snack: Roasted Chickpeas
Dinner: Pork Tenderloin with Blueberry Sauce
Dessert: Mango-Peach Yogurt

Day 3:
Breakfast: Blueberry Quinoa Porridge
Lunch: Loaded Sweet Potatoes
Snack: Grilled Flatbread
Dinner: Baked Beef Meatloaf
Dessert: Chocolate Tofu Pudding

Day 4:
Breakfast: Apple Cinnamon Oats
Lunch: Artichoke Chickpea Casserole
Snack: Cucumber and Bulgur Salad
Dinner: Fish Curry with Quinoa
Dessert: Glazed Pears with Hazelnuts

Day 5:
Breakfast: Artichoke Egg Casserole
Lunch: Vegetable Lentil Bowls
Snack: Sweet Potato Mash
Dinner: Creamy Chicken Pesto Pasta
Dessert: Banana Cacao Brownies

Day 6:
Breakfast: Buckwheat Granola
Lunch: Lentil-Stuffed Squash
Snack: Fennel Cabbage Slaw
Dinner: Swordfish with Pineapple
Dessert: Oat and Fruit Bars

Day 7:
Breakfast: Almond Smoothie
Lunch: Broccoli Casserole
Snack: Massaged Kale Chips
Dinner: Grilled Chipotle Shrimp Skewers
Dessert: Apple Bundt Cake

Chapter 1 Breakfast and Smoothies

Mackerel Scrambled Eggs

Prep time: 5 minutes | Cook time: 10 minutes | Serves: 4

6 large eggs
2 ounces goat cheese
7 tablespoons extra-virgin olive oil
1 teaspoon garlic powder
½ teaspoon black pepper
2 Roma tomatoes, chopped

2 tablespoons minced onion
1 (4-ounce) can olive oil-packed mackerel, chopped and oil reserved
¼ cup chopped pitted Kalamata olives
2 tablespoons chopped fresh parsley

1. Mix the eggs, goat cheese, 2 tablespoons of olive oil, garlic powder, and pepper in a suitable bowl. 2. Add 1 tablespoon of oil in a suitable pan and heat over medium-low heat. 3. Add the tomatoes and onion and sauté for almost 2 to 3 minutes, until they are soft and the water from the tomato has evaporated. 4. Add the prepared egg mixture to the skillet and scramble, while stirring constantly with a spatula, for almost 3 to 4 minutes, until the eggs are set and creamy. 5. Remove this skillet from the heat and stir in the mackerel and reserved oil, olives, and parsley. 6. Serve warm with each serving drizzled with an additional 1 tablespoon of olive oil.
Per Serving: Calories 482; Total Fat 43.1g; Sodium 255mg; Total Carbs 5.1g; Fiber 1.3g; Sugars 2.9g; Protein 21.4g

Coconut Milk Smoothie

Prep time: 5 minutes | Cook time: 0 minutes | Serves: 2

1 cup full-fat canned coconut milk
½ cup frozen mixed berries
2 scoops unflavored collagen protein powder
2 tablespoons shredded

unsweetened coconut
2 tablespoons chia or hemp seeds
2 tablespoons chopped macadamia nuts
Grated lime zest

1. Add berries, coconut milk, and protein powder to a suitable blender and process until smooth and lump-free. 2. Divide the smoothie mixture between the serving bowls. 3. Top each with 1 tablespoon of shredded coconut, 1 tablespoon of seeds, and 1 tablespoon of nuts. 4. Garnish with lime zest and serve.
Per Serving: Calories 356; Total Fat 35.1g; Sodium 18mg; Total Carbs 12.1g; Fiber 4.6g; Sugars 6.9g; Protein 3.7g

Pumpkin Pie Yogurt Meal

Prep time: 10 minutes | Cook time: 0 minutes | Serves: 1

1 tablespoon heavy whipping cream
½ cup plain whole-milk Greek yogurt
1 tablespoon unsweetened pumpkin puree

1 teaspoon pumpkin pie spice, no sugar added
2 teaspoons monk fruit extract
½ teaspoon vanilla extract
2 tablespoons coarsely chopped pecans

1. Whisk the cream in a bowl with an electric blender for almost 2 to 3 minutes, until thick and doubled in volume. Set aside. 2. Mix pumpkin puree, yogurt, pumpkin pie spice, monk fruit extract, and vanilla in a suitable bowl. 3. Top the prepared yogurt mixture with the pecans and whipped cream and serve.
Per Serving: Calories 180; Total Fat 6.5g; Sodium 92mg; Total Carbs 22g; Fiber 0.8g; Sugars 14.7g; Protein 5.6g

Matcha Smoothie

Prep time: 5 minutes | Cook time: 0 minutes | Serves: 1

¼ cup full-fat canned coconut milk
1½ teaspoons matcha green tea powder
1 very ripe avocado, pitted and peeled

1 cup unsweetened almond milk
1 scoop unflavored collagen protein powder
½ teaspoon vanilla extract
2 teaspoons monk fruit extract

1. Preheat 2 tablespoons of coconut milk in a suitable container in the microwave for almost 30 seconds. 2. Whisk the matcha into the hot milk until it's smooth. 3. Mix the matcha mixture, avocado, the almond milk, the remaining 2 tablespoons of coconut milk, collagen powder, vanilla, and monk fruit extract in a blender until smooth and creamy. 4. Serve.
Per Serving: Calories 487; Total Fat 45.7g; Sodium 199mg; Total Carbs 20.3g; Fiber 14.5g; Sugars 1.3g; Protein 5.2g

Tofu Veggie Eggs

Prep time: 10 minutes | Cook time: 10 minutes | Serves: 2

8 ounces firm tofu, cut lengthwise into 4 pieces and drain
¼ cup coconut oil
2 tablespoons minced red onion
¼ red bell pepper, chopped
½ teaspoon ground turmeric

½ teaspoon salt
¼ teaspoon freshly ground black pepper
¼ teaspoon garlic powder
¼ cup chopped fresh cilantro or mint

1. Cut the drained tofu into chunks and transfer to a large bowl. Then crumble the chunks into bite-size pieces. 2. reheat 2 tablespoons of coconut oil in a suitable pan over medium heat. 3. Add the onion and chopped bell pepper and sauté for almost 2 to 3 minutes. 4. Stir in the salt, turmeric, black pepper, and garlic powder and sauté for almost 1 minute, or until fragrant. 5. Add the rest of the 2 tablespoons of coconut oil and stir to form a paste. 6. Add the crumbled tofu, increase the heat to medium high, and sauté for almost 3 to 4 minutes, until the tofu is slightly crispy. 7. Remove tofu from the heat and stir in the cilantro. 8. Serve warm.
Per Serving: Calories 213; Total Fat 13.1g; Sodium 1194mg; Total Carbs 9.3g; Fiber 3.3g; Sugars 4g; Protein 19.4g

Cherry Pancakes

Prep time: 5 minutes | Cook time: 25 minutes | Serves: 3

1 cup fresh or frozen dark cherries, thawed and chopped
1 tablespoon water or lemon juice
1 teaspoon vanilla extract
2 to 4 teaspoons monk fruit extract
½ cup almond meal

½ cup coconut flour
¼ cup ground flaxseed
1 teaspoon baking powder
½ teaspoon ground cinnamon
½ cup heavy whipping cream
1 large egg
2 tablespoons coconut oil

1. Cook the cherries, water, and ½ teaspoon of vanilla in a suitable saucepan, over medium-high heat for almost 5 to 6 minutes, until bubbly, adding more water if the mixture is too thick. 2. Stir in the monk fruit extract, as needed. Using a fork, mash the cherries and whisk until the mixture is smooth. 3. Remove from the heat and set aside. 4. Mix the coconut flour, almond meal, flaxseed, baking powder, and cinnamon in a suitable bowl, and whisk to combine. 5. Stir in the egg, cream, the remaining ½ teaspoon of vanilla, 1 tablespoon of coconut oil, and a quarter of the cherry syrup mixture, whisking to combine well. 6. In large nonstick skillet, heat the remaining 1 tablespoon of coconut oil over medium-low heat. 7. Using almost 2 tablespoons of batter for each, form 3 pancakes. 8. Cook for almost 4 to 5 minutes, until bubbles begin to form, then flip. 9. Cook for almost 2 to 3 minutes on the second side, until the pancakes are golden brown. 10. Repeat this process with the remaining batter. 11. Serve warm drizzled with the remaining cherry syrup.
Per Serving: Calories 448; Total Fat 31.1g; Sodium 35mg; Total Carbs 32.9g; Fiber 12.8g; Sugars 8.5g; Protein 9g

Blueberry Smoothie

Prep time: 5 minutes | Cook time: 0 minutes | Serves: 1

1 cup unsweetened almond milk
¼ cup frozen blueberries
2 tablespoons coconut oil
2 teaspoons monk fruit extract,

optional
½ teaspoon vanilla extract
½ teaspoon ground ginger
Grated zest of 1 lemon

1. Blend the almond milk, blueberries, coconut oil, monk fruit extract, vanilla, ginger, and lemon zest in a high speed blender until creamy. More almond milk can be added to reach your desired consistency. 2. Serve.
Per Serving: Calories 304; Total Fat 30.9g; Sodium 181mg; Total Carbs 8.2g; Fiber 2g; Sugars 3.9g; Protein 1.4g

Green Smoothie

Prep time: 5 minutes | Cook time: 0 minutes | Serves: 1

1 cup packed baby spinach
½ green apple
1 tablespoon maple syrup

¼ teaspoon ground cinnamon
1 cup unsweetened almond milk
½ cup ice

1. Blend all the recipe ingredients in a suitable blender until smooth. 2. Serve.
Per Serving: Calories 222; Total Fat 3.8g; Sodium 193mg; Total Carbs 48.2g; Fiber 7.1g; Sugars 35.5g; Protein 2.3g

Cacao Nib Smoothie

Prep time: 5 minutes | Cook time: 0 minutes | Serves: 1

1 cup unsweetened almond milk
¼ cup heavy whipping cream
2 tablespoons unsweetened almond butter
1 tablespoon unsweetened cocoa powder

1 tablespoon cacao nibs, plus more for serving
2 teaspoons monk fruit extract
½ teaspoon almond extract
½ teaspoon cinnamon

1. Blend the almond milk, cream, almond butter, cocoa powder, cacao nibs, monk fruit extract, almond extract, and cinnamon in a blender until smooth and creamy. 2. Serve.
Per Serving: Calories 365; Total Fat 33.6g; Sodium 195mg; Total Carbs 13.6g; Fiber 7g; Sugars 1.8g; Protein 9.7g

Chaffles

Prep time: 5 minutes | Cook time: 10 minutes | Serves: 4

2 large eggs
1 cup freshly shredded mozzarella cheese
¼ cup almond flour
1 teaspoon everything bagel seasoning
½ teaspoon baking powder

5 tablespoons extra-virgin olive oil
4 ounces goat cheese
4 ounces smoked salmon
4 thin slices red onion
8 thin slices cucumber
1 tablespoon chopped capers

1. Preheat a waffle maker on medium heat. 2. Beat the eggs, cheese, baking powder, almond flour, everything seasoning, and 1 tablespoon of olive oil in a suitable bowl, until smooth. 3. Pour in half the prepared batter in to the waffle maker and cook for almost 3 to 4 minutes. 4. Repeat with the remaining half of the prepared batter. 5. Spread 1 ounce of goat cheese over each waffle half and top with 1 ounce of smoked salmon, 1 slice of red onion, 2 slices of cucumber, and chopped capers. 6. Drizzle each with 1 tablespoon of olive oil and serve.
Per Serving: Calories 523; Total Fat 35.5g; Sodium 260mg; Total Carbs 37.9g; Fiber 6.6g; Sugars 16.8g; Protein 20.7g

Almond Smoothie

Prep time: 10 minutes | Cook time: 0 minutes | Serves: 2

1 pear, cored and quartered
2 cups baby spinach
¼ avocado
1 cup silken tofu
1 teaspoon ground turmeric or 1

thin slice peeled turmeric root
½ cup unsweetened almond milk
2 tablespoons honey
1 cup ice

1. Blend all the recipe ingredients in a suitable blender until smooth. 2. Divide between two glasses. 3. Serve.
Per Serving: Calories 202; Total Fat 7.2g; Sodium 87mg; Total Carbs 33.4g; Fiber 5.1g; Sugars 24.9g; Protein 4.9g

Cranberry Breakfast Bars

Prep time: 10 minutes | Cook time: 40 minutes | Serves: 4

1 ½ cups sweet potato purée
1 cup fresh cranberries
¼ cup water
1 ½ tablespoon baking soda
2 tablespoons coconut oil, melted

⅓ cup coconut flour
2 tablespoons maple syrup
2 eggs
1 cup almond meal

1. Preheat the oven to 350 degrees F. 2. Mix the sweet potato purée, water, melted coconut oil, maple syrup, and eggs in a suitable mixing bowl. Stir until everything is well combined. 3. Sift together the almond meal, coconut flour, and baking soda in a separate bowl. 4. Mix in the dry ingredients. Combine all the recipe ingredients in a suitable mixing bowl and stir thoroughly. 5. Line the bottom of a 9" square baking sheet with parchment paper and grease it with coconut oil. 6. Use a moist spatula to level down the top and fill in the corners of the prepared batter in the prepared baking pan. Place the cranberries on top and press them down. 7. Bake for 30–40 minutes in the oven, or until a probe inserted in the center comes out clean. 8. Dice it into squares once it has cooled fully.
Per Serving: Calories 322; Total Fat 21.1g; Sodium 1469mg; Total Carbs 27.5g; Fiber 5.9g; Sugars 10.8g; Protein 8.7g

Pancakes with Strawberries

Prep time: 25 minutes | Cook time: 15 minutes | Serves: 6

Nonstick cooking spray
1½ cups sliced strawberries
2 ½ cups all-purpose flour
2 peaches, pitted and sliced
3 tablespoons granulated sugar
½ teaspoon pure vanilla extract
1 tablespoon baking powder

2 large eggs
¼ teaspoon salt
¼ teaspoon ground cinnamon
2 cups buttermilk
Maple syrup and Confectioners' sugar, for serving

1. At 425 degrees F, preheat your oven. 2. Layer a suitable baking sheet with parchment paper and coat the paper and the sides of the pan with nonstick cooking spray. 3. Mix the sugar, flour, salt, baking powder, and cinnamon in a big mixing bowl. 4. Take a separate bowl, mix the buttermilk, eggs, and vanilla extract. 5. Pour the prepared batter onto the prepared baking sheet and spread evenly. 6. Arrange the strawberries and peaches over the top. 7. Bake for almost 12 to 15 minutes. 8. To serve, top the pancake with confectioners' sugar, cut it into squares, and drizzle with maple syrup.
Per Serving: Calories 334; Total Fat 3.4g; Sodium 211mg; Total Carbs 65.9g; Fiber 4.9g; Sugars 21.4g; Protein 11.5g

Banana-Oat Muffins

Prep time: 15 minutes | Cook time: 25 minutes | Serves: 12

1½ cups oat flour (certified gluten-free, if necessary)
1 cup quick-cooking oats (certified gluten-free, if necessary)
1 tablespoon baking powder

½ teaspoon baking soda
½ teaspoon salt
3 large bananas, mashed
2 large eggs, slightly beaten
⅓ cup extra-virgin olive oil (or almond oil)

1. At 375 degrees F, preheat your oven. 2. Layer a muffin pan with paper baking cups. 3. In a suitable bowl, mix the oat flour, oats, baking powder, baking soda, and salt. 4. Add the mashed bananas, eggs, and oil and mix well. 5. Spoon the prepared batter into the prepared muffin cups. 6. Bake for 20 to 25 minutes. 7. Serve warm.
Per Serving: Calories 282; Total Fat 9.8g; Sodium 162mg; Total Carbs 41.9g; Fiber 5.7g; Sugars 4.3g; Protein 7.8g

Sweet Potato Frittata

Prep time: 15 minutes | Cook time: 30 minutes | Serves: 4

1 tablespoon extra-virgin olive oil
1 large sweet potato, peeled and diced
1 small red onion, chopped
1 teaspoon salt

¼ teaspoon black pepper, freshly ground
1 teaspoon chopped fresh thyme leaves
8 large eggs, well beaten

1. At 375 degrees F, preheat your oven. 2. Grease a cast-iron skillet with a little olive oil. 3. Mix sweet potato and onion in this skillet. 4. Add 1 tablespoon olive oil, salt, and black pepper on top. 5. Bake for almost 10 to 15 minutes until the sweet potato is tender. 6. Remove the sweet potato skillet from the oven and drizzle the thyme on top. 7. Add the beaten eggs over the vegetables and return this skillet to the oven. 8. Bake the eggs for almost 15 minutes. 9. Serve.
Per Serving: Calories 222; Total Fat 13.6g; Sodium 738mg; Total Carbs 12g; Fiber 2g; Sugars 4.4g; Protein 13.7g

Overnight Berries Oats

Prep time: 10 minutes | Cook time: 0 minutes | Serves: 2

1 cup oats (certified gluten-free if necessary)
1¾ cups unsweetened almond milk
Optional Toppings:
¼ cup almond butter
1 cup mixed berries
½ cup Greek yogurt

2 tablespoons maple syrup
1 tablespoon chia seeds
¼ teaspoon vanilla extract

1 tablespoon toasted almonds
1 tablespoon toasted coconut

1. Mix the oats, milk, maple syrup, chia seeds, and vanilla in a jar with a tight-fitting lid and stir well. 2. Refrigerate overnight. 3. Divide the oats mixture between the two serving bowls and add toppings. 4. Serve.
Per Serving: Calories 458; Total Fat 17.5g; Sodium 316mg; Total Carbs 62.3g; Fiber 13.9g; Sugars 19.8g; Protein 16g

Smoked Salmon Stuffed Deviled Eggs

Prep time: 20 minutes | Cook time: 10 minutes | Serves: 4 to 6

6 hardboiled eggs, peeled	⅛ teaspoon black pepper
4 ounces goat cheese	4 ounces smoked salmon, sliced
1 teaspoon Dijon mustard	1 tablespoon chopped fresh chives
½ teaspoon salt	

1. Cut the hardboiled eggs in half lengthwise; then remove the egg yolks and place in a suitable bowl. 2. Mash the egg yolks with the goat cheese, mustard, salt, and pepper. Spoon the prepared egg mixture back into the egg white halves. 3. Top with the smoked salmon and chives and serve.
Per Serving: Calories 257; Total Fat 17.9g; Sodium 1062mg; Total Carbs 1.2g; Fiber 0.1g; Sugars 1.2g; Protein 22.2g

Breakfast Sausages

Prep time: 15 minutes | Cook time: 15 minutes | Serves: 8

Extra-virgin olive oil, for brushing	1 teaspoon salt
1½ pounds ground chicken	¼ teaspoon black pepper, freshly ground
2 scallions, sliced	½ teaspoon ground nutmeg
1 tablespoon chopped fresh sage	1 tablespoon Dijon mustard

1. At 400 degrees F, preheat your oven. 2. Brush a suitable rimmed baking sheet with olive oil. 3. In a suitable bowl, mix the chicken, scallions, sage, salt, pepper, nutmeg, and mustard. 4. Using a 1-ounce ice cream scoop or spoon, scoop the mixture into 24 small mounds onto the prepared baking sheet. 5. With your fingers, gently flatten each mound into a patty shape. 6. Bake for 10 to 15 minutes. 7. Serve warm.
Per Serving: Calories 194; Total Fat 10.4g; Sodium 2576mg; Total Carbs 5.2g; Fiber 2.5g; Sugars 1.2g; Protein 21.1g

Chives Omelet

Prep time: 5 minutes | Cook time: 10 minutes | Serves: 2

3 large eggs	¼ teaspoon ground cumin
1 tablespoon chopped fresh chives	½ teaspoon salt
1 tablespoon chopped fresh parsley	2 tablespoons extra-virgin olive oil
1 teaspoon ground turmeric	

1. Beat the eggs, chives, parsley, turmeric, cumin, and salt in a suitable bowl. 2. In an omelet pan, heat 1 tablespoon of oil over medium-high heat. 3. Pour half of the prepared egg mixture into the hot pan. 4. Lower its heat to medium and let the eggs cook until the bottom starts to set. 5. Using a heat-proof spatula, gently move the eggs around the edges so the uncooked egg can spill over the sides and set. 6. Continue to cook the omelet until just set, but still soft. 7. Use any spatula to fold the omelet in half, then slide it out of the pan and onto a serving dish. 8. Repeat with the remaining egg mixture and 1 tablespoon of oil. Serve.
Per Serving: Calories 123; Total Fat 8.6g; Sodium 762mg; Total Carbs 2.1g; Fiber 0.6g; Sugars 0.7g; Protein 9.8g

Eggs Benedict

Prep time: 15 minutes | Cook time: 0 minutes | Serves: 4

Hollandaise Sauce

6 tablespoon butter, melted and still warm	2 teaspoons lemon juice
2 egg yolks	¾ teaspoon salt
Pinch of cayenne pepper	¼ teaspoon black pepper, freshly ground

Eggs Benedict

8 poached eggs	8 slices thickly-cut cooked ham
4 English muffins, halved and toasted until golden	8 teaspoon butter, softened

1. Toss the egg yolks with the lemon juice in a suitable blender to mix. 2. Pour the melted butter into the blender in a slow, steady stream while it's running. Blend for almost 30 seconds to 1 minute, or until you have a thick sauce. 3. Pulse in the salt, pepper, and cayenne to mix. Remove from the equation. 4. 1 teaspoon soft butter, spread over every English muffin half. Top each dish with two muffin halves, two ham slices, and 1 or 2 poached egg. 5. Top each egg benedict with 2 tablespoons of the hollandaise sauce that has been warmed. Serve right away.
Per Serving: Calories 384; Total Fat 24.7g; Sodium 1130mg; Total Carbs 21.9g; Fiber 2g; Sugars 3.4g; Protein 19.3g

Apple Smoothie Bowl

Prep time: 15 minutes | Cook time: 0 minutes | Serves: 2

3 cups packed baby spinach	1 tablespoon maple syrup
1 green apple, cored	½ cup mixed berries
1 small ripe banana	¼ cup toasted slivered almonds
½ ripe avocado	1 teaspoon sesame seeds

1. Mix the spinach, apple, banana, avocado, and maple syrup in a suitable blender until smooth. 2. Divide the mixture between two bowls. 3. Top with the berries, almonds, and sesame seeds. 4. Serve.
Per Serving: Calories 344; Total Fat 17g; Sodium 66mg; Total Carbs 48.9g; Fiber 12.2g; Sugars 27g; Protein 5.6g

Nutella Butter Pancakes

Prep time: 1 hour 15 minutes | Cook time: 10 minutes | Serves: 3

1½ teaspoon baking powder	2 tablespoons sugar
¾ teaspoon baking soda	4 tablespoons butter, melted
6 pancakes	6 tablespoons Nutella
Maple syrup, for serving	Nonstick cooking spray, as needed
2 cups all-purpose flour	A pinch of salt
1 cup buttermilk	

1. Using parchment paper, layer a suitable baking sheet. 2. Place 6 dollops (1 tablespoon each) of Nutella on the baking sheet, allowing space between them. 3. Spread every dollop into a thin circle using a knife. 4. Place the prepared baking sheet in the freezer and freeze the Nutella for at least an hour until it is firm. 5. Make the pancakes after the Nutella pieces are frozen. 6. Mix together the sugar, flour, baking soda, baking powder, and salt in a suitable mixing bowl. 7. Make a small well at the center of the dry recipe ingredients. 8. Add the butter and buttermilk to the ingredients. To blend, stir everything together. 9. Over medium heat, heat a big skillet or griddle. Using a nonstick spray, coat the heated pan. 10. 13 cups pancake batter, ladled or scooped onto the heated skillet. Put a Nutella round in the middle and top with a little amount of pancake batter. 11. Cook for almost 3 to 4 minutes until golden, then turn and cook for almost 2 to 3 minutes longer until golden on the other side. 12. Remove the rounds from the pan and put them aside while you finish the rest of the prepared batter and Nutella rounds. 13. Stack 3 pancakes on each dish to serve. 14. Serve with maple syrup.
Per Serving: Calories 378; Total Fat 16.2g; Sodium 369mg; Total Carbs 50.8g; Fiber 1.9g; Sugars 15.6g; Protein 7.6g

Creamy Danish

Prep time: 30 minutes | Cook time: 20 minutes | Serves: 12

Streusel Topping

⅓ cup all-purpose flour	¼ cup (4 tablespoons) unsalted butter
2 teaspoons ground cinnamon	
⅓ cup brown sugar	⅓ cup sugar

Cream-Cheese Filling

2 tablespoons all-purpose flour	½ cup confectioners' sugar
1 8-ounce package of cream cheese	1 egg

Danish

¾ cup sugar	¼ cup (4 tablespoons) unsalted butter, melted
1 (16-ounce) package puff pastry, diced and thawed	1 tablespoon ground cinnamon

1. Preheat oven to 350 degrees F. Line two baking pans with parchment paper. 2. Mix the sugar, brown sugar, flour, and cinnamon in a suitable mixing bowl. 3. Mix in the butter until the sugar mixture is crumbly and moist. 4. At 350 degrees F, preheat your oven. 5. Beat the cream cheese, confectioners' sugar, flour, and egg in a suitable mixing bowl. 6. Toss the chopped puff pastry in the melted butter in a suitable mixing dish to moisten and coat. 7. Mix the sugar and cinnamon in a suitable bowl. Toss the greased puff pastry with the cinnamon sugar and toss lightly to coat. 8. Fill the baking sheets with 14 cups puff pastry, allowing at least 1 ½ inches between every mound. 9. Slightly flatten the pieces, but make sure they're all touching. 10. Create a suitable depression in the middle of each mound with your fingertips or the back of a spoon to make a place for the filling. 11. Fill each mound with 2 tablespoons cream cheese filling. Add 2 tablespoons streusel topping to the top. 12. Bake, the Danish for almost 15 to 20 minutes, or until the puff pastry is light brown and the filling is bubbly. 13. Allow cooling before serving.
Per Serving: Calories 383; Total Fat 25.2g; Sodium 184mg; Total Carbs 35g; Fiber 0.9g; Sugars 14.7g; Protein 5.1g

Healthy Scramble

Prep time: 10 minutes | Cook time: 0 minutes | Serves: 2

1 tablespoon turmeric
2 tablespoons coconut oil
2 shredded kale leaves
Radish and clover sprouts to top

1 small clove garlic, minced
2 radishes, grated
2 pastured eggs
1 pinch cayenne pepper

1. Preheat the coconut oil in a pan and softly sauté the garlic. 2. Scramble the eggs in a pan. 3. Add the turmeric, shredded kale, and cayenne then cook until the eggs are done. 4. Enjoy the radish and sprouts on top!
Per Serving: Calories 233; Total Fat 18.5g; Sodium 97mg; Total Carbs 10.4g; Fiber 1.8g; Sugars 0.2g; Protein 8.3g

Turmeric Orange Juice

Prep time: 5 minutes | Cook time: 0 minutes | Serves: 2

3 oranges, peeled and quartered
Pinch of pepper
1 cup unsweetened almond milk

1 teaspoon vanilla extract
½ teaspoon cinnamon
¼ teaspoon turmeric

1. Blend all the recipe ingredients in a suitable blender until smooth. 2. Blend until completely smooth, then serve in a glass.
Per Serving: Calories 158; Total Fat 2.1g; Sodium 90mg; Total Carbs 34.4g; Fiber 7.5g; Sugars 26.1g; Protein 3.1g

Chia Seed Pudding

Prep time: 10 minutes | Cook time: 0 minutes | Serves: 4

4 cups full-fat coconut milk
¼ cup toasted coconut chips for garnishing
3 teaspoons honey
1 cup fresh mixed berries for garnishing

1 teaspoon vanilla extract
¾ cup coconut yogurt for topping
1 teaspoon ground turmeric
½ cup chia seeds
½ teaspoon ground cinnamon
½ teaspoon ground ginger

1. In a suitable mixing bowl, Mix the honey, coconut milk, turmeric, vanilla extract, ground ginger, and cinnamon. 2. To blend, whisk everything together well, resulting in a bright yellow liquid. 3. Stir in the chia seeds, then put them aside for almost 5 minutes to allow them to absorb the liquid. When you're ready, give it another stir. 4. Cover this bowl with plastic sheet and refrigerate for almost 6 hours or overnight. 5. Top each serving glass with a dollop of coconut yogurt and a spoonful of chia seed pudding. 6. Garnish with toasted coconut chips and mixed berries.
Per Serving: Calories 125; Total Fat 3.2g; Sodium 16mg; Total Carbs 20.4g; Fiber 6.9g; Sugars 11.1g; Protein 5.1g

Berry Chia Breakfast

Prep time: 10 minutes | Cook time: 0 minutes | Serves: 1

1 cup fresh or thawed frozen raspberries
1 cup plant milk
1 pinch ground vanilla
Topping
kiwi
nut butter

3 tablespoons desiccated coconut, unsweetened
3 tablespoons chia seeds

hemp seeds
fresh mint

1. In a suitable bowl, use a fork to mash the berries. In a separate bowl, add the vanilla, coconut, and chia seeds. 2. Add the milk and stir to combine. 3. Leave the mashed berries to soak in the fridge for at least 30 minutes or overnight. 4. Top with fruit, hemp seeds, nut butter, and mint, and serve in a suitable bowl or jar.
Per Serving: Calories 353; Total Fat 21.4g; Sodium 119mg; Total Carbs 33.6g; Fiber 12.6g; Sugars 20.2g; Protein 11.7g

Blueberry Spinach Smoothie

Prep time: 10 minutes | Cook time: 0 | Serve: 1

1 cup spinach
½ cup fresh blueberries
½ banana

1 cup coconut milk
½ teaspoon vanilla extract

1. In a blender, combine the spinach, blueberries, banana, coconut milk, and vanilla. Blend until smooth.
Per serving: Calories: 190; Total fat 5.3g; Sodium 768mg; Total carbs 34.1g; Fiber 7g; Sugars 14.7g; Protein 7.1g

Protein Donuts

Prep time: 5 minutes | Cook time: 0 minutes | Serves: 4

1½ cups raw cashews
¼ cup dark chocolate (for topping)
½ cup (7 pieces) Medjool dates, pitted

1 teaspoon turmeric powder
1 teaspoon vanilla protein powder
¼ cup shredded coconut
2 teaspoons maple syrup
¼ teaspoon vanilla essence

1. Mix all ingredients (except the chocolate) and process on high until a thick and sticky cookie dough forms. 2. Form the prepared batter into 8 balls and press them firmly into the silicone donut form. 3. Wrap the ball's molds in plastic wrap and freeze for almost 30 minutes to set. 4. Fill a suitable cooking pan with water and cook to a boil for the chocolate topping. 5. Then, on top of the pan, set a suitable saucepan and pour the chocolate into it. 6. Stir until the chocolate has melted completely. 7. Remove the donuts from the molds after they have set, sprinkle with dark chocolate, and store in a container in the fridge.
Per Serving: Calories 391; Total Fat 21.2g; Sodium 58mg; Total Carbs 40.6g; Fiber 3.5g; Sugars 24.5g; Protein 13.2g

Cauliflower Rolls

Prep time: 10 minutes | Cook time: 40 minutes | Serves: 4

1 medium head cauliflower, riced
3 tablespoons "everything bagel" spice
⅓ cup almond flour

1 teaspoon garlic powder
½ teaspoon kosher salt
3 large eggs, lightly whisked

1. Preheat the oven to 400 degrees F. Spray a baking sheet with nonstick spray before lining it with parchment paper. 2. Mix the cauliflower rice, almond flour, garlic powder, and salt in a suitable mixing bowl. 3. Toss in the whisked eggs and mix well. 4. Make 8 equal portions of the mixture and roll them into balls. 5. Set the prepared balls on the baking sheet and sprinkle 1 heaping teaspoon of "everything bagel" spice on top of each one. 6. Bake for almost 35 to 40 minutes, or until the rolls are lightly browned around the edges and dry to the touch. 7. Allow the rolls to rest on the baking sheet for almost 10 minutes before gently transferring to a cooling rack to cool entirely.
Per Serving: Calories 117; Total Fat 8.2g; Sodium 354mg; Total Carbs 4.1g; Fiber 1.7g; Sugars 1.1g; Protein 7.3g

Nutty Pancakes

Prep time: 5 minutes | Cook time: 1 hour | Serves: 5

For the Chocolate Sauce:
4 teaspoons raw cacao powder
For the Pancakes:
2 tablespoons creamy almond butter
1 tablespoon pure vanilla extract
2 large eggs

¼ coconut oil, melted

2 ripe bananas
Coconut oil, for greasing
2 tablespoons raw cacao powder
⅛ teaspoon salt

1. First, melt the coconut oil and add the cacao powder. Set aside after mixing until thoroughly incorporated. 2. Preheat a suitable pan over medium heat and grease it with a tablespoon of coconut oil. 3. In a suitable food processor, combine all pancake ingredients and pulse until smooth. 4. Scoop the prepared batter into a ¼ measuring cup and add onto the skillet to make one pancake. 5. Cook for almost 5 minutes before gently flipping over and cooking for two more minutes. 6. Repeat until you've made 10 pancakes and all of the prepared batters is disappeared. 7. Before serving, set the pancakes on a baking rack to cool for almost 5 minutes. 8. Pancakes may be stored in the refrigerator for up to 5 days or frozen for up to 30 days.
Per Serving: Calories 316; Total Fat 18.4g; Sodium 235mg; Total Carbs 27.1g; Fiber 10.6g; Sugars 6.9g; Protein 8.2g

Spinach Cucumber Smoothie

Prep time: 10 minutes | Cook time: 0 | Serve: 1

1 pear, cored and quartered
½ fennel bulb
1 thin slice of fresh ginger
1 cup spinach

½ cucumber, peeled
½ cup water
Ice

1. In a blender, combine the fennel, pear, spinach, ginger, cucumber, water, and ice. Blend until smooth.
Per serving: Calories: 185; Total fat 1.5g; Sodium 812mg; Total carbs 42.2g; Fiber 12.5g; Sugars 16.1g; Protein 7.9g

Beets Smoothie

Prep time: 10 minutes | Cook time: 0 | Serve: 1

1 carrot, trimmed
1 small beet, scrubbed and quartered
1 celery stalk
½ cup fresh raspberries
1 cup coconut water
1 teaspoon balsamic vinegar
Ice

1. In a blender, combine the carrot, beet, celery, raspberries, coconut water, balsamic vinegar, and ice. Blend until smooth.
Per serving: Calories: 144; Total fat 1.1g; Sodium 374mg; Total carbs 31.3g; Fiber 10.1g; Sugars 19g; Protein 4.5g

Cherry Smoothie

Prep time: 10 minutes | Cook time: 0 | Serves: 1

1 cup frozen sugar-free pitted cherries
¼ cup fresh, or frozen, raspberries
¾ cup coconut water
1 tablespoon raw honey or maple
syrup
1 teaspoon chia seeds
1 teaspoon hemp seeds
Drop vanilla extract
Ice

1. In a blender, combine the raspberries, cherries, coconut water, honey, chia seeds, hemp seeds, vanilla, and ice. Blend until smooth.
Per serving: Calories: 206; Total fat 8.3g; Sodium 97mg; Total carbs 29.8g; Fiber 8.4g; Sugars 18.2g; Protein 6.5g

Green Apple Smoothie

Prep time: 10 minutes | Cook time: 0 | Serve: 1

½ cup coconut water
1 green apple, cored, seeded, and quartered
1 cup spinach
¼ lemon, seeded
½ cucumber, peeled and seeded
2 teaspoons raw honey or maple syrup
Ice

1. In a blender, combine the coconut water, apple, spinach, lemon, cucumber, honey, and ice. Blend until smooth.
Per serving: Calories: 211; Total fat 0.9g; Sodium 155mg; Total carbs 53.3g; Fiber 8.2g; Sugars 40.5g; Protein 3.3g

Coconut Rice with Berries

Prep time: 10 minutes | Cook time: 30 minutes | Serves: 4

1 cup brown basmati rice
1 cup water
1 cup coconut milk
1 teaspoon salt
2 dates, pitted and chopped
1 cup fresh blueberries or raspberries
¼ cup toasted slivered almonds
½ cup shaved coconut

1. In a suitable saucepan over high heat, combine the basmati rice, water, coconut milk, salt, and date pieces. Stir until the mixture comes to a boil. 2. Reduce its heat to simmer and cook for 20 to 30 minutes, without stirring, or until the rice is tender. 3. Divide the rice among four bowls and top each serving with ¼ cup of blueberries, 1 tablespoon of almonds, and 2 tablespoons of coconut.
Per serving: Calories: 393; Total fat 20.1g; Sodium 596mg; Total carbs 49.2g; Fiber 5.6g; Sugars 6.6g; Protein 6.7g

Spicy Quinoa

Prep time: 10 minutes | Cook time: 20 minutes | Serves: 4

1 cup quinoa, rinsed
2 cups water
½ cup shredded coconut
¼ cup hemp seeds
2 tablespoons flaxseed
1 teaspoon ground cinnamon
1 teaspoon vanilla extract
1 pinch salt
1 cup fresh berries of your choice
¼ cup chopped hazelnuts

1. In a suitable saucepan over high heat, combine the quinoa and water. 2. Bring to a boil, reduce its heat to a simmer, and cook for 15 to 20 minutes, or until the quinoa is cooked through. 3. Stir in the coconut, hemp seeds, flaxseed, cinnamon, vanilla, and salt. 4. Divide the cooked quinoa among four bowls and top each serving with ¼ cup of berries and 1 tablespoon of hazelnuts.
Per serving: Calories: 264; Total fat 10g; Sodium 9mg; Total carbs 35.4g; Fiber 6.8g; Sugars 3.5g; Protein 8g

Mango-Thyme Smoothie

Prep time: 10 minutes | Cook time: 0 | Serve: 1

1 cup fresh or frozen mango chunks
½ cup fresh seedless green grapes
¼ fennel bulb
½ cup unsweetened almond milk
½ teaspoon fresh thyme leaves
Pinch sea salt
Pinch black pepper
Ice

1. In a blender, combine the mango, grapes, fennel, almond milk, thyme leaves, sea salt, pepper, and ice. Blend until smooth.
Per serving: Calories: 182; Total fat 2.5g; Sodium 358mg; Total carbs 41.6g; Fiber 5.6g; Sugars 32.2g; Protein 2.6g

Protein Grapes Smoothie

Prep time: 10 minutes | Cook time: 0 | Serve: 1

1 cup kale leaves, washed
¼ avocado
1 cup fresh grapes
¼ cup cashews
1 tablespoon hemp seed
1 or 2 mint leaves
1 cup coconut milk
Ice

1. In a blender, combine the kale, avocado, grapes, cashews, hemp seed, mint leaves, coconut milk, and ice. Blend until smooth.
Per serving: Calories: 523; Total fat 36.8g; Sodium 59mg; Total carbs 42.3g; Fiber 6.7g; Sugars 16.9g; Protein 14.8g

Overnight Muesli

Prep time: 10 minutes | Cook time: 0 minutes | Serves: 4 to 6

2 cups gluten-free rolled oats
1¾ cups coconut milk
¼ cup sugar-free apple juice
1 tablespoon apple cider vinegar
1 apple, cored and chopped
Dash ground cinnamon

1. In a suitable bowl, stir together the oats, coconut milk, apple juice, and vinegar. Cover and refrigerate overnight. 2. The next morning, stir in the chopped apple and season the muesli with the cinnamon.
Per serving: Calories: 384; Total fat 32.2g; Sodium 20mg; Total carbs 24.2g; Fiber 5.5g; Sugars 9.2g; Protein 5.4g

Mushroom Frittata

Prep time: 15 minutes | Cook time: 20 minutes | Serves: 6

1½ cups chickpea flour
1½ cups water
1 teaspoon salt
2 tablespoons extra-virgin olive oil
1 small red onion, diced
2 pints sliced mushrooms
1 teaspoon ground turmeric
½ teaspoon ground cumin
1 teaspoon salt
½ teaspoon black pepper
2 tablespoons fresh parsley, chopped

1. At 350 degrees F, preheat your oven. 2. In a suitable bowl, slowly whisk the water into the chickpea flour; add the salt and set aside. 3. In a suitable cast-iron or oven-safe skillet over high heat, add the olive oil. When the oil is hot, add the onion. Sauté the onion for 3 to 5 minutes or until onion is softened and slightly translucent. 4. Add the mushrooms and sauté for 5 minutes more. Add the turmeric, cumin, salt, pepper, and sauté for 1 minute. 5. Pour the batter over the vegetables and sprinkle with the parsley. Place the prepared skillet in the preheated oven and bake for 20 to 25 minutes. 6. Serve warm or at room temperature.
Per serving: Calories: 240; Total fat 7.9g; Sodium 410mg; Total carbs 33.5g; Fiber 9.6g; Sugars 6.7g; Protein 11.4g

Chai Spiced Smoothie

Prep time: 10 minutes | Cook time: 0 | Serve: 1

1 cup unsweetened almond milk
1 date, pitted and chopped
¼ teaspoon vanilla extract
½ teaspoon chai spice blend
Pinch salt
1 banana, sliced into ¼-inch rounds
Ice cubes

1. In a blender, combine the almond milk, date, vanilla, chai spice blend, salt, banana, and ice. Blend until smooth.
Per serving: Calories: 171; Total fat 3.9g; Sodium 336mg; Total carbs 35.3g; Fiber 4.7g; Sugars 19.8g; Protein 2.5g

Peach Punch

Prep time: 15 minutes | Cook time: 0 | Serves: 4

1 (10-ounce) bag frozen sugar-free peach slices, thawed
3 tablespoons lemon juice
3 tablespoons raw honey or maple syrup
1 tablespoon lemon zest
2 cups coconut water
2 cups sparkling water
4 fresh mint sprigs
Ice

1. In a suitable food processor, combine the peaches, lemon juice, honey, and lemon zest. Process until smooth. 2. In a suitable pitcher, stir together the peach purée and coconut water. Chill the mixture in the refrigerator. 3. When ready to serve, fill four large (16-ounce) glasses with ice. Add 1 mint sprig to each glass. Add about ¾ cup peach mixture to each glass and top each with sparkling water.
Per serving: Calories: 129; Total fat 0.4g; Sodium 139mg; Total carbs 30.9g; Fiber 2.8g; Sugars 27.9g; Protein 1.4g

Coconut-Ginger Smoothie

Prep time: 10 minutes | Cook time: 0 | Serve: 1

½ cup coconut milk
½ cup coconut water
¼ avocado
¼ cup unsweetened coconut shreds or flakes
1 teaspoon raw honey or maple syrup
1 thin slice of fresh ginger
Pinch ground cardamom
Ice

1. In a blender, combine coconut water, avocado, coconut milk, coconut, honey, ginger, cardamom, and ice. Blend until smooth.
Per serving: Calories: 240; Total fat 18.6g; Sodium 152mg; Total carbs 19.5g; Fiber 6g; Sugars 9.6g; Protein 3.4g

Pear Green Smoothie

Prep time: 10 minutes | Cook time: 0 | Serve: 1

1 cup spinach
½ cucumber, peeled
½ pear
¼ avocado
1 teaspoon raw honey or maple syrup
1 cup unsweetened almond milk
2 mint leaves
Pinch salt
½ lemon
Ice

1. In a blender, combine the spinach, cucumber, pear, avocado, honey, almond milk, mint leaves, salt, 1 or 2 squeezes of lemon juice, and the ice. Blend until smooth.
Per serving: Calories: 271; Total fat 14.4g; Sodium 934mg; Total carbs 35g; Fiber 11g; Sugars 15.3g; Protein 8.1g

Banana Fig Smoothie

Prep time: 5 minutes | Cook time: 0 | Serves: 2

7 whole figs, fresh or frozen, halved
1 banana
1 cup plain whole-milk yogurt
1 cup almond milk
1 tablespoon almond butter
1 teaspoon ground flaxseed
1 teaspoon raw honey
Ice

1. In a blender, combine the figs, banana, yogurt, almond milk, almond butter, flaxseed, and honey. Blend until smooth. Add ice and blend again to thicken. 2. Pour into two tall glasses and serve immediately.
Per serving: Calories: 506; Total fat 37.8g; Sodium 76mg; Total carbs 40.1g; Fiber 6.8g; Sugars 28.3g; Protein 10g

Matcha Blueberry Smoothie

Prep time: 5 minutes | Cook time: 0 | Serves: 2

2 cups almond milk
2 cups frozen blueberries
1 banana
2 tablespoons protein powder, neutral-flavored
1 tablespoon matcha powder
1 tablespoon chia seeds
¼ teaspoon ground cinnamon
¼ teaspoon ground ginger
Pinch salt

1. In a blender, blend the blueberries, nut milk, banana, protein powder, matcha, chia seeds, cinnamon, ginger, and salt until smooth. 2. Pour into two glasses and serve immediately.
Per serving: Calories: 296; Total fat 7.6g; Sodium 228mg; Total carbs 51.3g; Fiber 11.1g; Sugars 28.1g; Protein 10.1g

Pumpkin Pie Smoothie

Prep time: 5 minutes | Cook time: 0 | Serves: 2

1 banana
½ cup unsweetened canned pumpkin
1 cup almond milk
2 or 3 ice cubes
2 heaping tablespoons almond
butter
1 teaspoon ground cinnamon
1 teaspoon ground nutmeg
1 teaspoon pure maple syrup
1 teaspoon vanilla extract

1. In a blender, combine the banana, pumpkin, nut milk, ice, almond butter, cinnamon, nutmeg, maple syrup, and vanilla until smooth. 2. Pour into two tall glasses and serve immediately.
Per serving: Calories: 225; Total fat 11g; Sodium 75mg; Total carbs 29.4g; Fiber 5.8g; Sugars 15.5g; Protein 5.3g

Cranberry-Orange Granola

Prep time: 10 minutes | Cook time: 30-40 minutes | Serves: 8

3 cups gluten-free rolled oats
2 tablespoons flaxseed meal
⅓ cup maple syrup
¼ cup fresh-pressed coconut oil
1 orange, washed
¾ cup chopped pecans, toasted
½ cup dried cranberries

1. At 300 degrees F, preheat your oven. 2. Place the oats and flaxseed meal in a suitable bowl. In a suitable saucepan over low heat, combine the maple syrup and coconut oil. 3. Zest the orange peel directly into the syrup, then cut the orange in half and squeeze 2 tablespoons juice into the pan. Stir just until the coconut oil has melted, about 3 minutes, then remove from the heat. Pour the maple syrup over the oats and stir to coat. 4. Spread the oats evenly onto a baking sheet. Bake for 15 minutes, then stir. Bake for another 10 minutes, then stir in the pecans and cranberries. 5. Bake until the oats are golden and the berries are plumped, another 5 to 10 minutes. Set aside to cool completely. Serve or store in an airtight container at room temperature for up to 5 days.
Per serving: Calories: 275; Total fat 6.1g; Sodium 2mg; Total carbs 49.1g; Fiber 6.9g; Sugars 13.7g; Protein 7.9g

Buckwheat Crêpes with Berries

Prep time: 15 minutes | Cook time: 20 minutes | Serves: 4 to 6

1 cup buckwheat flour
½ teaspoon salt
2 tablespoons coconut oil
1½ cups almond milk
1 egg
1 teaspoon vanilla extract
3 cups fresh berries
6 tablespoons chia jam

1. In a suitable bowl, whisk together the buckwheat flour, salt, 1 tablespoon of melted coconut oil, the almond milk, egg, and vanilla until smooth. 2. In a suitable (12-inch) nonstick skillet over medium-high heat, melt the remaining 1 tablespoon of coconut oil. Tilt the pan, coating it evenly with the melted oil. 3. Ladle ¼ cup of batter into the skillet. Tilt the skillet to coat it evenly with the batter. Cook for 2 minutes or until the edges begin to curl up. 4. Using a spatula, flip the crêpe and cook for 1 minute on the second side. Transfer the crêpe to a plate. 5. Continue making crêpes with the remaining batter. You should have 4 to 6 crêpes. Place 1 crêpe on a plate, top with ½ cup of berries and 1 tablespoon of chia jam. Fold the crêpe over the filling. 6. Repeat with the remaining crêpes and serve.
Per serving: Calories: 338; Total fat 3.6g; Sodium 155mg; Total carbs 74.7g; Fiber 2.3g; Sugars 47g; Protein 2.4g

Chia Morning Pudding

Prep time: 20 minutes | Cook time: 0 minutes | Serves: 4

2 cups almond milk
½ cup chia seeds
¼ cup maple syrup or raw honey
1 teaspoon vanilla extract
1 cup frozen sugar-free pitted cherries, thawed, juice reserved
½ cup chopped cashews

1. In a quart jar, combine the almond milk, chia seeds, maple syrup, and vanilla. Mix well and keep it sit aside for at least 15 minutes. 2. Divide the pudding among four bowls, and top each with ¼ cup of cherries and 2 tablespoons of cashews.
Per serving: Calories: 221; Total fat 10.3g; Sodium 78mg; Total carbs 27.2g; Fiber 2g; Sugars 18g; Protein 4g

Tofu Scramble

Prep time: 10 minutes | Cook time: 8 minutes | Serves: 4

3 tablespoons extra-virgin olive oil
3 green onions, sliced
3 garlic cloves, peeled and sliced
1 (15-oz) package firm tofu, drained and diced
Kosher salt, to taste

1 cup mung bean sprouts
2 tablespoons mint, chopped
2 tablespoons parsley, chopped
1 tablespoon lime juice
Fish sauce for serving
Cooked brown rice for serving

1. Mix olive oil, white parts of the green onions, and garlic in a cold sauté pan. Turn the heat to low. As the aromatics warm, stirring occasionally for 4 minutes almost. 2. Add the tofu and salt and reduce its heat to medium. Cook, occasionally stirring, until the tofu is well coated with the oil and warmed for 3 minutes almost. Add mung bean sprouts and cook for 1 minute. 3. Stir in the green parts of the green onions and the mint, parsley, and lime juice. Stir to combine. 4. Taste, adding fish sauce or additional lime juice, if desired. 5. Serve the scramble on its own or over brown rice with poached eggs on top.
Per serving: Calories: 185; Total fat 14.9g; Sodium 58mg; Total carbs 5.6g; Fiber 1.6g; Sugars 0.9g; Protein 11.1g

Spinach Muffins

Prep time: 15 minutes | Cook time: 15 minutes | Serves: 4

Cooking spray
2 cups spinach
2 eggs
¼ cup raw honey
3 tablespoons extra-virgin olive oil
1 teaspoon vanilla extract

1 cup oat flour
1 cup almond flour
2 teaspoons baking powder
1 teaspoon baking soda
½ teaspoon salt
Pinch black pepper

1. At 350 degrees F, preheat your oven. Line or grease 12 muffin cups with cooking spray. 2. In a suitable food processor, combine spinach, eggs, honey, olive oil, and vanilla. Process until smooth. 3. In a suitable bowl, whisk together the oat flour, almond flour, baking powder, baking soda, salt, and pepper. Transfer the spinach mixture to the bowl and mix well. 4. Fill each muffin cup two-thirds full. Place the prepared muffins in the preheated oven and bake for almost 15 minutes, or until lightly browned and the centers feel firm to the touch. 5. Transfer the pan to a cooling rack, and let cool for 10 minutes before removing the muffins from the tin.
Per serving: Calories: 327; Total fat 17.6g; Sodium 654mg; Total carbs 36.7g; Fiber 3.4g; Sugars 17.8g; Protein 7.8g

Black Bean Breakfast

Prep time: 35 minutes | Cook time: 5-10 minutes | Serves: 4

Pico de Gallo:
2 cups cherry tomatoes, halved
1 jalapeño, minced
2 tablespoons chopped cilantro
Avocado Mash:
2 avocados
Kosher salt
1 tablespoon diced white onion
1 tablespoon lime juice
1 to 2 dashes of hot sauce
1 (15-oz) can black beans, rinsed

2 tablespoons diced white onion
1 tablespoon lime juice
Kosher salt

and drained
1 tablespoon lime juice
Kosher salt
4 eggs, poached or scrambled
Hot sauce for serving

1. For the Pico de Gallo: Combine the jalapeño, tomatoes, cilantro, onion, and lime juice in a suitable bowl. Taste, add salt if desired, and stir to mix. 2. To make the avocado mash: place the avocados in a suitable bowl or molcajete with a generous sprinkling of salt. 3. Using a fork or pastry blender, mash until the avocados are a bit chunky or completely smooth, depending on your preference. 4. Stir in the onion, lime juice, and hot sauce. Taste, adding more salt or more hot sauce if needed. 5. In a suitable saucepan, warm the black beans and lime juice, mash gently with a fork, and season with salt. 6. Place one-fourth of the black beans in each bowl, then one-fourth of the avocado mash. Top with an egg, then the Pico de Gallo and a dash of hot sauce. Serve immediately.
Per serving: Calories: 455; Total fat 24.9g; Sodium 118mg; Total carbs 44.3g; Fiber 15.5g; Sugars 4.8g; Protein 18.9g

Turkey Sausage

Prep time: 20 minutes | Cook time: 15-20 minutes | Serves: 6

2 teaspoons organic canola oil, plus 2 tablespoons
½ cup chopped yellow onion
1½ lb. ground turkey
¾ cup dried cranberries
¼ cup parsley leaves, chopped
1 egg, beaten

1 tablespoon fresh sage, minced
1 tablespoon thyme leaves
1 teaspoon grated lemon zest
1 teaspoon kosher salt
½ teaspoon black pepper
½ teaspoon ground allspice

1. In a suitable skillet over medium heat, warm the 2 teaspoons canola oil. Add the onion and cook, frequently stirring, until soft, 6 to 8 minutes. Let cool. 2. In a suitable bowl, combine cooked onion, ground turkey, dried berries, parsley, egg, sage, thyme, lemon zest, salt, pepper, and allspice. Stir gently to combine well. 3. Cover and refrigerate this turkey mixture for at least 1 hour or up to overnight. 4. Shape the prepared mixture into 12 patties, each about 2½-in [6 cm] wide and ½-in [12 mm] thick. 5. In a suitable nonstick skillet over medium-low heat, warm the 2 tablespoons of canola oil. 6. Set the patties in the pan so they are not touching (you will probably have to do two batches) and cook until they are browned and no longer pink in the center, 3 to 4 minutes per side. 7. Serve.
Per serving: Calories: 261; Total fat 14.9g; Sodium 521mg; Total carbs 3.2g; Fiber 1.2g; Sugars 1g; Protein 32.3g

Breakfast Bibimbap

Prep time: 30 minutes | Cook time: 15 minutes | Serves: 4

4 teaspoons toasted sesame oil
1 carrot, peeled and julienned
1 zucchini, julienned
3 green onions, chopped
Kosher salt, to taste
2 cups sliced mushrooms
1 garlic clove, minced

2 cups cooked brown rice
1 tablespoon chopped basil
1 tablespoon chopped mint
1 teaspoon toasted sesame seeds
4 poached eggs
Hot sauce, such as sriracha, for serving

1. In a suitable nonstick skillet over medium-high heat, warm 1 teaspoon of the sesame oil. 2. Toss in the carrot, zucchini, and green onions, along with a pinch of salt. Cook, frequently stirring, until crisp-tender, for 3 minutes almost. 3. Remove the vegetables from the pan. Place the pan back over medium-high heat, add another 1 teaspoon sesame oil. 4. Stir in the mushrooms and cook for almost 3 minutes, then add the garlic. Cook, frequently stirring, until the mushrooms have released their liquid and are well browned, about 2 minutes more. 5. Remove the mushrooms from the pan. Place the pan back over medium-high heat and add the remaining 2 teaspoon sesame oil. 6. Let the pan to get very hot, then add the brown rice and spread it over the bottom of the pan. 7. Let it crisp before breaking it up and stirring for about 2 minutes. Stir, then spread the rice over the bottom of the pan again and allow to crisp for 2 minutes more. 7. Divide the rice between four bowls and top each serving with vegetables, fresh herbs, sesame seeds, and a poached egg. Add as much hot sauce as desired. 8. Serve immediately!
Per serving: Calories: 478; Total fat 12g; Sodium 85mg; Total carbs 78.4g; Fiber 5g; Sugars 2.8g; Protein 15g

Broccoli Spinach Frittatas

Prep time: 10 minutes | Cook time: 20 minutes | Serves: 4

Olive oil, for greasing the muffin cups
8 eggs
¼ cup almond milk
½ teaspoon chopped fresh basil
½ cup chopped broccoli

½ cup shredded fresh spinach
1 scallion, white and green parts, chopped
Pinch sea salt
Pinch black pepper

1. At 350 degrees F, preheat your oven. Lightly oil a 6-cup muffin tin and keep it aside. 2. In a suitable bowl, whisk the eggs, almond milk, and basil until frothy. Stir in the broccoli, spinach, and scallion. Spoon the prepared egg mixture into the muffin cups. 3. Bake for almost 20 minutes until the frittatas are puffed, golden, and cooked through. 4. Season with sea salt and black pepper and serve.
Per serving: Calories 134; Fat 9g; Sodium 142mg; Carbs 2g; Fiber 0.5g; Sugars 1g; Protein 11.6g

Acai Berry Smoothie

Prep time: 10 minutes | Cook time: 5 minutes | Serves: 840ml

1 (3.5-oz) pack frozen acai puree
1 cup frozen mango chunks
1 cup frozen berries
2 cups cashew milk
2 teaspoon maple syrup

1. Defrost the acai pack to soften with hot water. 2. Blend all the recipe ingredients except maple syrup together. Start the blender on a low setting, puree the mixture until it begins to break up, stop and scrap down the sides if necessary. 3. Slowly turn the blender speed to high and puree until no lumps, for 1 to 2 minutes. 4. Then taste and add the maple syrup as you like and serve.
Per serving (210ml): Calories: 324; Total fat 11.2g; Sodium 213mg; Total carbs 55.7g; Fiber 10.6g; Sugars 40.5g; Protein 2.4g

Chia-Berry Yogurt

Prep time: 10 minutes | Cook time: 5 minutes | Serves: 4

1 (10-ounce) package frozen mixed berries, thawed
2 tablespoons maple syrup
2 tablespoons lemon juice
½ vanilla bean halved lengthwise
1 tablespoon chia seeds
4 cups unsweetened almond yogurt or coconut yogurt

1. In a suitable saucepan over medium-high heat, combine the berries, maple syrup, lemon juice, and vanilla bean. 2. Bring the mixture to a boil, stirring constantly. Reduce its heat to simmer and cook for 3 minutes. 3. Remove this pan from the heat. Remove and discard the vanilla bean from the mixture. Stir in the chia seeds. 4. Let stand for almost 10 minutes to let the seeds thicken. 5. Divide the fruit mixture among four bowls and top each with 1 cup of yoghurt.
Per serving: Calories: 366; Total fat 15g; Sodium 67mg; Total carbs 58.9g; Fiber 14g; Sugars 24.4g; Protein 7.5g

Coconut Pancakes

Prep time: 10 minutes | Cook time: 20 minutes | Serves: 4

4 eggs
1 cup coconut milk
1 tablespoon melted coconut oil
1 tablespoon maple syrup
1 teaspoon vanilla extract
½ cup coconut flour
1 teaspoon baking soda
½ teaspoon salt

1. In a suitable bowl, mix together the eggs, coconut milk, coconut oil, maple syrup, and vanilla with an electric mixer. 2. In a suitable bowl, stir together the coconut flour, baking soda, and salt. Add these dry ingredients to the wet ingredients and beat well until smooth and lump-free. 3. Lightly grease a suitable skillet with coconut oil. Place it over medium-high heat. Add the batter in ½-cup scoops and cook for almost 3 minutes, or until golden brown on the bottom. 4. Flip and cook for almost 2 minutes more. Stack the pancakes on a plate while continuing to cook the remaining batter. This makes about 8 pancakes.
Per serving: Calories: 180; Total fat 10.3g; Sodium 672mg; Total carbs 14.6g; Fiber 6g; Sugars 3.5g; Protein 7.8g

Banana Coconut Pancakes

Prep time: 10 minutes | Cook time: 10 minutes | Serves: 4

½ cup almond flour
¼ cup coconut flour
1 teaspoon baking soda
3 eggs, beaten
2 bananas, mashed
1 teaspoon pure vanilla extract
1 tablespoon coconut oil
Pure maple syrup, for serving
Fresh fruit, for serving

1. In a suitable bowl, stir together the almond flour, coconut flour, and baking soda until well mixed. 2. Make a small well at the center of it and add the eggs, bananas, and vanilla. Beat together until well blended. 3. Place a suitable skillet over medium-high heat and add the coconut oil. 4. For each pancake, pour ¼ cup of batter into this skillet, four per batch. Cook for almost 3 minutes until the bottom is golden and the bubbles on the surface burst. 5. Flip and cook for almost 2 minutes more until golden and cooked through. 6. Transfer to a plate and repeat with any remaining batter. Serve.
Per serving: Calories 213; Fat 10g; Sodium 363mg; Carbs 24.6g; Fiber 7.9g; Sugars 7.6g; Protein 7.5g

Tomatoes Egg Scramble

Prep time: 5 minutes | Cook time: 10 minutes | Serves: 2

4 eggs
2 teaspoons chopped fresh oregano
1 tablespoon extra-virgin olive oil
1 cup cherry tomatoes, halved
½ garlic clove, sliced
½ avocado, sliced

1. In a suitable bowl, beat the eggs until well combined; whisk in the oregano. 2. Place a suitable skillet over medium heat. Once the pan is hot, add the olive oil. 3. Pour the eggs into the skillet and use either a heat-resistant spatula or wooden spoon to scramble the eggs. Transfer the eggs to a serving dish. 4. Add the cherry tomatoes and garlic to the pan and sauté for almost 2 minutes. Spoon the tomatoes over the eggs and top the dish with the avocado slices.
Per serving: Calories: 310; Total fat 25.9g; Sodium 131mg; Total carbs 9.7g; Fiber 5.1g; Sugars 3.4g; Protein 13g

Cucumber Smoked-Salmon Lettuce Wraps

Prep time: 10 minutes | Cook time: 0 minutes | Serves: 4

8 large butter lettuce leaves
½ English cucumber, sliced thin
8 ounces smoked salmon
1 tablespoon chopped fresh chives
4 tablespoons Caesar salad dressing

1. On a serving dish, arrange the lettuce leaves in a single layer. 2. Evenly divide the cucumber slices among the lettuce leaves. Top each leaf with 2 ounces of smoked salmon. 3. Garnish with the chives and drizzle each wrap with 1 tablespoon of Caesar salad dressing.
Per serving: Calories: 145; Total fat 7.6g; Sodium 1245mg; Total carbs 8.2g; Fiber 0.9g; Sugars 2.7g; Protein 11.3g

Sweet Potato Hash

Prep time: 15 minutes | Cook time: 15 minutes | Serves: 4

2 tablespoons coconut oil
½ onion, sliced thin
1 cup sliced mushrooms
1 garlic clove, sliced thin
2 large sweet potatoes, cooked and cut into ½-inch cubes
1 cup chopped Swiss chard
½ cup vegetable broth
1 teaspoon salt
¼ teaspoon freshly ground pepper
1 tablespoon chopped fresh thyme
1 tablespoon chopped fresh sage

1. In a suitable skillet over high heat, melt the coconut oil. 2. Add the onion, mushrooms, and garlic. Sauté for almost 8 minutes, or until the onions and mushrooms are tender. 3. Add the sweet potatoes, Swiss chard, and vegetable broth. Cook for 5 minutes. Stir in the salt, pepper, thyme, and sage.
Per serving: Calories: 336; Total fat 14.6g; Sodium 1410mg; Total carbs 48.6g; Fiber 8.4g; Sugars 3g; Protein 5.6g

Pancake Bites

Prep time:10 minutes | Cook time: 6 minutes approximately | Serves: 3

1¾ cups old fashioned rolled oats
3 small ripe bananas
3 large eggs
2 tablespoons erythritol
1 teaspoon ground cinnamon
1 teaspoon pure vanilla extract
1 teaspoon baking powder

1. Set the oats, bananas, eggs, erythritol, cinnamon, vanilla, and baking powder in a large, powerful blender and blend until very smooth, about 1 minute. 2. Pour the prepared mixture into a silicone mold with seven wells. Place a paper towel on top and then top with aluminum foil. 3. Tighten the edges to prevent extra moisture getting inside. Set the mold on top of your steam rack with handles. 4. Pour 1 cup water into the inner pot. Set the steam rack and mold inside. Close the lid and secure it well. Pressure cook for 6 minutes approximately. 5.When cooked, release the pressure quickly until the float valve drops and then unlock lid. 6. Pull the steam rack and mold out of the instant pot and remove the aluminum foil and paper towel. 7. Allow this pancake bites to cool completely, and then use a knife to pull the edges of the bites away from the mold. 8. Press on the bottom of the mold and this pancake bites will pop right out.
Per serving: Calories 331; Fat 8.2g; Sodium 75mg; Carbs 54.3g; Fiber 7.4g; Sugars 13.4g; Protein 13.1g

Quinoa Cakes

Prep time: 20 minutes | Cook time: 30 minutes | Serves: 4

1 cup tri-colour quinoa
2 teaspoons extra-virgin olive oil, plus 4 tablespoons
1 teaspoon minced garlic
1 teaspoon dried minced onion
2 eggs
½ cup chickpea flour
½ teaspoon ground dry mustard
1 teaspoon kosher salt
⅛ teaspoon black pepper
⅛ teaspoon cayenne pepper
2 tablespoons fresh parsley, chopped
1 tablespoon chopped fresh chives

1. In a fine-mesh strainer, rinse the quinoa well under cold running water and drain. 2. In a suitable saucepan over high heat, bring 1 ¾ cups of water to a boil. Stir in the quinoa, cover, and turn the heat to medium-low. 3. Simmer until the quinoa is tender and white quinoa tails are visible, about 18 minutes. Transfer to a shallow bowl or baking sheet and set aside to cool to room temperature. 4. In a suitable sauté pan over medium heat, warm the 2 teaspoons olive oil. Add the minced garlic and diced shallot (if using dried, whisk into the egg mixture with the other seasonings) and cook, frequently stirring, until fragrant and softened 2 to 3 minutes. 5. In a suitable bowl, whisk together the eggs, chickpea flour, dry mustard, salt, black pepper, cayenne, parsley, chives, and softened garlic and shallot. 6. Fold in cooled quinoa and mix until incorporated. Divide the mixture into eight portions. 7. Using your hands, form the portions into patties. Place the patties on a parchment paper-lined baking sheet, and pat to ½ in [12 mm] thick. 8. In a suitable nonstick sauté pan over medium heat, warm 2 tablespoons of olive oil. Cook half of the patties until golden brown and crispy, 3 to 4 minutes per side. 9. Add the rest of the 2 tablespoons of oil and cook the rest of the patties. Serve immediately.
Per serving: Calories: 302; Total fat 8.7g; Sodium 622mg; Total carbs 43.1g; Fiber 7.5g; Sugars 2.9g; Protein 13.8g

Pumpkin Smoothie

Prep time: 5 minutes | Cook time: 0 minutes | Serves: 2

1 cup almond milk, unsweetened
1 cup pure pumpkin purée
1 tablespoon pure maple syrup
1 teaspoon grated fresh peeled ginger
¼ teaspoon ground cinnamon
⅛ teaspoon ground nutmeg
Pinch ground cloves
Pinch ground cardamom
4 ice cubes

1. In a suitable blender, combine the almond milk, pumpkin, maple syrup, ginger, cinnamon, nutmeg, cloves, and cardamom. Blend until smooth. 2. Add the ice and blend until thick.
Per serving: Calories 89; Fat 2.2g; Sodium 97mg; Carbs 18g; Fiber 4.3g; Sugars 10g; Protein 1.9g

Kale Egg Casserole

Prep time: 5 minutes | Cook time: 0 minutes | Serves: 6

1 tablespoon avocado oil
1 small yellow onion, peeled and chopped
5 large kale leaves, tough stems removed and chopped
1 garlic clove, diced
2 tablespoons lemon juice
½ teaspoon salt
9 large eggs
2 tablespoons water
1½ teaspoons dried rosemary
1 teaspoon dried oregano
¼ teaspoon black pepper
½ cup nutritional yeast

1. Add the oil to a pot, then heat the oil for almost 1 minute. Add the onion and sauté 2 minutes until just softened. 2. Add the kale, garlic, lemon juice, and ¼ teaspoon salt. Stir and allow to cook 2 minutes more. Press the cancel button. 3. Meanwhile, in a suitable bowl, whisk together the eggs, water, rosemary, oregano, ¼ teaspoon salt, pepper, and nutritional yeast. 4. Add the onion and kale mixture to the prepared egg mixture and stir to combine. Rinse the inner pot, add 2 cups water, and place a steam rack inside. 5. Layer a 7" springform pan with cooking spray. Transfer the prepared egg mixture to the springform pan. 6. Place this pan on the steam rack and close the lid and secure it well. Pressure cook for 12 minutes. 7. When done, then release the pressure quickly until the float valve drops and then unlock lid. 8. Remove this pan from pot and allow to cool 5 minutes before slicing and serving.
Per serving: Calories 174; Fat 8.8g; Sodium 314mg; Carbs 10.3g; Fiber 4.5g; Sugars 1.2g; Protein 16.2g

Carob-Avocado Smoothie

Prep time: 5 minutes | Cook time: 0 minutes | Serves: 2

1 cup almond milk, unsweetened
1 cup shredded kale
½ avocado
½ banana
2 tablespoons carob powder
1 tablespoon coconut oil
1 tablespoon raw honey
1 teaspoon pure vanilla extract
4 ice cubes

1. In a suitable blender, combine the almond milk, kale, avocado, banana, carob powder, coconut oil, honey, and vanilla. Blend until smooth. 2. Add the ice and blend until thick.
Per serving: Calories 262; Fat 18.5g; Sodium 108mg; Carbs 24.5g; Fiber 5.2g; Sugars 12.8g; Protein 2.8g

Green Spinach Smoothie

Prep time: 5 minutes | Cook time: 0 minutes | Serves: 2

1 cup canned lite coconut milk
1 cup fresh spinach
1 banana, cut into chunks
½ avocado
½ English cucumber, cut into chunks
2 tablespoons chopped fresh mint
1 tablespoon lemon juice, freshly squeezed
1 tablespoon raw honey
3 ice cubes

1. In a suitable blender, combine the coconut milk, spinach, banana, avocado, cucumber, mint, lemon juice, and honey. Blend until smooth. 2. Add the ice and blend until thick.
Per serving: Calories 274; Fat 16.2g; Sodium 51mg; Carbs 34.9g; Fiber 6.1g; Sugars 17.6g; Protein 4.3g

Artichoke Egg Casserole

Prep time:10 minutes | Cook time: 18 minutes | Serves: 8

12 large eggs
¼ cup water
4 cups baby spinach, chopped
1 (14-ounce) can baby artichoke hearts, drained and chopped
1 tablespoon chopped fresh chives
1 tablespoon fresh lemon juice
¾ teaspoon table salt
½ teaspoon black pepper
¼ teaspoon garlic salt

1. Layer a 6" round pan or 7-cup round glass bowl with cooking spray. 2. In a suitable bowl, whisk together the eggs and water. Stir in the spinach, artichokes, chives, lemon juice, table salt, pepper, and garlic salt. 3. Transfer the prepared mixture to the prepared pan. Place 2 cups water in the insert of the Instant pot and set the steam rack inside. 4. Place this pan on top of the steam rack. Close the lid and secure it well. Pressure cook for 18 minutes. 5. When done, release the pressure quickly until the float valve drops and then unlock lid. 6. Remove egg casserole from pot and allow to cool 5 minutes before slicing and serving.
Per serving: Calories 112; Fat 7.5g; Sodium 335mg; Carbs 1.3g; Fiber 0.4g; Sugars 0.7g; Protein 9.9g

Sweet Potato Casserole

Prep time: 15 minutes | Cook time: 30 minutes | Serves: 4

Olive oil, for greasing the baking dish
1 cup diced cooked sweet potato
1 cup chopped blanched cauliflower
1 cup shredded kale
1 scallion, white and green parts, chopped
1 teaspoon chopped fresh basil
8 eggs
¼ cup almond milk, unsweetened
1 teaspoon ground cumin
1 teaspoon ground coriander
Pinch sea salt
Pinch black pepper, freshly ground

1. At 375 degrees F, preheat your oven. Lightly layer a 9-by-13-inch baking dish with olive oil. 2. Evenly spread the sweet potato, cauliflower, kale, scallion, and basil in the prepared dish. 3. In a suitable bowl, whisk the eggs, almond milk, cumin, coriander, sea salt, and pepper. 4. Pour the prepared egg mixture into the baking dish, lightly tapping the dish on the counter to distribute the eggs among the vegetables. 5. Bake for almost 30 minutes until the eggs are set and the top is lightly golden.
Per serving: Calories 191; Fat 9.2g; Sodium 169mg; Carbs 14.8g; Fiber 2.8g; Sugars 4.6g; Protein 13.3g

Raspberry Oatmeal Bars

Prep time:5 minutes | Cook time: 15 minutes | Serves: 6

3 cups steel cut oats	⅓ cup erythritol
3 large eggs	1 teaspoon pure vanilla extract
2 cups vanilla almond milk, unsweetened	¼ teaspoon salt
	1 cup frozen raspberries

1. In a suitable bowl, mix together all the recipe ingredients except the berries. Fold in berries. Layer a 6" cake pan with cooking oil. 2. Transfer the prepared berry oat mixture to this pan and cover this pan with aluminum foil. 3. Pour 1 cup water into the instant pot and set the steam rack inside. Place this pan with the oat mixture on top of the rack. 4. Close the lid and secure it well. Pressure cook for 15 minutes. 5. When done, release the pressure quickly until the float valve drops and then unlock lid. 6. Carefully remove this pan from the insert of the Instant pot and remove the foil. Let it cool down before cutting into bars and serving.
Per serving: Calories 236; Fat 5.2g; Sodium 135mg; Carbs 38.9g; Fiber 6g; Sugars 9.8g; Protein 8.8g

Blueberry Quinoa Porridge

Prep time:2 minutes | Cook time: 1 minute| Serves: 6

1½ cups dry quinoa	½ teaspoon pure stevia powder
3 cups water	1 teaspoon pure vanilla extract
1 cup frozen wild blueberries	

1. Using a fine-mesh strainer, rinse the quinoa very well until the water runs clear. 2. Add the quinoa, water, blueberries, stevia, and vanilla to the inner pot. Stir to combine. 3. Close the lid and secure it well. Pressure cook for 1 minute. When cooked, release the pressure quickly until the float valve drops and then unlock lid. 4. Allow the quinoa to cool slightly before spooning into bowls to serve.
Per serving: Calories 311; Fat 2.7g; Sodium 673mg; Carbs 64.7g; Fiber 4.5g; Sugars 37.4g; Protein 6.3g

Buckwheat Granola

Prep time:10 minutes | Cook time: 10 minutes | Serves: 8

1½ cups raw buckwheat groats	1" piece fresh ginger, peeled and grated
1½ cups old fashioned rolled oats	3 tablespoons date syrup
⅓ cup walnuts, chopped	1 teaspoon ground cinnamon
⅓ cup shredded coconut, unsweetened	¼ teaspoon salt
¼ cup coconut oil, melted	

1. In a suitable bowl, mix together the buckwheat groats, oats, walnuts, and shredded coconut until well combined. Add the coconut oil, ginger, date syrup, cinnamon, and salt and stir to combine. 2. Transfer this mixture to a 6" cake pan. Pour 1 cup water into the insert of the Instant Pot and place a steam rack inside. 3. Place this pan on the rack. Close the lid and secure it well. Pressure cook for 10 minutes. 4. When cooked, release the pressure quickly until the float valve drops and then unlock lid. 5. Spread the granola onto a large sheet pan and let it cool down, undisturbed, for almost 1 hour. It will crisp as it cools.
Per serving: Calories 229; Fat 14.1g; Sodium 79mg; Carbs 22.8g; Fiber 4.3g; Sugars 1.1g; Protein 5.5g

Coconut Strawberry Porridge

Prep time: 5 minutes | Cook time: 0 minutes | Serves: 4

¾ cup water	¼ cup shredded coconut, unsweetened
¾ cup almond milk, unsweetened	
1 teaspoon pure vanilla extract	2 tablespoons raw honey
¼ cup chia seeds	½ cup sliced fresh strawberries

1. In a suitable bowl, whisk the water, almond milk, and vanilla until well blended. 2. Stir in the chia seeds, cover the bowl, and refrigerate it for a minimum of 30 minutes and up to overnight. 3. Stir the coconut and honey into the chilled porridge. Spoon the porridge into four bowls. Serve topped with the strawberries.
Per serving: Calories 173; Fat 11g; Sodium 41mg; Carbs 17g; Fiber 5.6g; Sugars 10.6g; Protein 2.8g

Orange Oatmeal Muffins

Prep time:7 minutes | Cook time: 15 minutes | Serves: 6

3 cups old fashioned rolled oats	unsweetened
1 teaspoon baking powder	¼ cup fresh orange juice
¼ teaspoon salt	3⅓ cups mashed bananas
1 teaspoon ground cinnamon	1 large egg
¼ cup vanilla almond milk,	¼ cup erythritol

1. In a suitable bowl, mix all of the ingredients together, while stirring until well combined. 2. Place six silicone muffin cups inside of a 6" cake pan. Spoon the oatmeal mixture into the muffin cups. Cover this pan with aluminum foil. 3. Pour 1 cup water into the insert of the Instant Pot and set the steam rack inside. Set the cake pan with the muffins on the rack. 4. Close the lid and secure it well. Pressure cook for 15 minutes. 5. When cooked, release the pressure quickly until the float valve drops and then unlock lid. 6. Carefully remove this pan from the insert of the Instant pot and remove the foil from the top. 7. Let the muffins cool 15 minutes before eating. They will become firmer as they cool.
Per serving: Calories 148; Fat 2.5g; Sodium 117mg; Carbs 29g; Fiber 3.8g; Sugars 8.5g; Protein 4.5g

Turkey Hash

Prep time: 10 minutes | Cook time: 26 minutes | Serves: 4

1½ pounds extra-lean ground turkey	cooked, and diced
	Pinch sea salt
1 sweet onion, chopped, or about	Pinch black pepper, freshly
1 cup precut packaged onion	ground
2 teaspoons bottled minced garlic	Pinch ground cloves
1 teaspoon ground ginger	1 cup chopped kale
2 pounds sweet potatoes, peeled,	

1. In a suitable skillet over medium-high heat, sauté the turkey for almost 10 minutes until it is cooked through. 2. Add the onion, garlic, and ginger. Sauté for almost 3 minutes. Add the sweet potatoes, sea salt, pepper, and cloves. 3. Reduce its heat to medium. Sauté for almost 10 minutes, while stirring until the sweet potato is heated through. 4. Stir in the kale. Cook for almost 3 minutes, while stirring until it has wilted. 5. Divide the hash among four bowls and serve.
Per serving: Calories 356; Fat 8.4g; Sodium 145mg; Carbs 45.6g; Fiber 6.8g; Sugars 1.6g; Protein 25.2g

Banana Oatmeal

Prep time:5 minutes | Cook time: 7 minutes | Serves: 6

3 cups old fashioned rolled oats	heaping cup)
¼ teaspoon salt	2 large eggs, lightly beaten
2 large bananas, mashed (1	⅓ cup xylitol

1. In a suitable bowl, set the oats, salt, bananas, eggs, and xylitol and stir to combine well. Lightly Layer a 6" cake pan with cooking spray. 2. Transfer the oat mixture to this pan. Pour 1½ cups water into the inner pot. Place a steam rack in the insert of the Instant pot and place this pan on the steam rack. 3. Close the lid and secure it well. Pressure cook for 7 minutes. 4. When done, release the pressure quickly until the float valve drops and then unlock lid. 5. Allow the oatmeal to cool 5 minutes before serving.
Per serving: Calories 139; Fat 3.1g; Sodium 122mg; Carbs 24g; Fiber 3.2g; Sugars 5.9g; Protein 5.2g

Raspberry Pineapple Smoothie

Prep time: 5 minutes | Cook time: 0 minutes | Serves: 2

1 cup coconut water	½ cup fresh raspberries
½ cup pineapple juice, unsweetened	½ cup shredded coconut
1 banana	3 ice cubes

1. In a suitable blender, combine the pineapple juice, coconut water, banana, raspberries, and coconut. Blend until smooth. 2. Add the ice and blend until thick.
Per serving: Calories 263; Fat 16.5g; Sodium 95mg; Carbs 25.8g; Fiber 7.3g; Sugars 14g; Protein 3.4g

Coconut Chocolate Oatmeal

Prep time:5 minutes | Cook time: 6 minutes approximately | Serves: 4

1 cup steel cut oats
1 (13.25-ounce) can full-fat coconut milk, unsweetened
2 cups water
½ cup cacao powder
½ cup erythritol
⅛ teaspoon sea salt

1. Set the oats, coconut milk, water, cacao powder, erythritol, and salt in the insert of the Instant pot and stir to combine. 2. Close the lid and secure it well. Pressure cook for 6 minutes approximately. 3. When cooked, release the pressure quickly until the float valve drops and then unlock lid. 4. Allow the oatmeal to cool slightly before spooning into bowls to serve.
Per serving: Calories 280; Fat 14.7g; Sodium 38mg; Carbs 30.6g; Fiber 4.1g; Sugars 0.4g; Protein 6.8g

Banana Date Porridge

Prep time:5 minutes | Cook time: 4 minutes | Serves: 4

1 cup buckwheat groats
1½ cups vanilla almond milk, unsweetened
1 cup water
1 large banana, mashed
5 pitted dates, chopped
¾ teaspoon ground cinnamon
¾ teaspoon pure vanilla extract

1. Set the buckwheat groats, almond milk, water, banana, dates, cinnamon, and vanilla in the insert of the Instant pot and stir. 2. Close the lid and secure it well. Pressure cook for 4 minutes. 3. When done, release the pressure quickly until the float valve drops and then unlock lid. 4. Allow the porridge to cool slightly before spooning into bowls to serve.
Per serving: Calories 178; Fat 2.2g; Sodium 73mg; Carbs 37.9g; Fiber 5.3g; Sugars 12g; Protein 4.8g

Poppy Oatmeal Cups

Prep time:5 minutes | Cook time: 5 minutes | Serves: 4

2 cups old fashioned rolled oats
1 teaspoon baking powder
2 tablespoons erythritol
1 tablespoon poppy seeds
¼ teaspoon salt
1 large egg
Juice and zest from 1 Meyer lemon
1 cup vanilla almond milk, unsweetened

1. Lightly grease four (8-ounce) ramekin dishes. Set aside. 2. In a suitable bowl, mix together the oats, baking powder, erythritol, poppy seeds, and salt. 3. Add the egg, juice and zest from the lemon, and almond milk and stir to combine. Divide the oatmeal mixture into the four dishes. 4. Pour ½ cup water into the insert of your Instant Pot. Set the steam rack inside the insert of the Instant pot and set the ramekins on top of the rack. 5. Close the lid and secure it well. Pressure cook for 5 minutes. 6. When cooked, release the pressure quickly until the float valve drops and then unlock lid. 7. The ramekins will be hot when you open the lid, so be sure to use your mini oven mitts to lift them out of the instant pot and let them cool before serving.
Per serving: Calories 212; Fat 7.1g; Sodium 331mg; Carbs 29.4g; Fiber 4.5g; Sugars 1.2g; Protein 9.2g

Banana Walnut Oats

Prep time:2 minutes | Cook time: 4 minutes | Serves: 4

2 cups steel cut oats
2½ cups water
2½ cups vanilla almond milk, unsweetened
3 medium bananas, sliced
1½ teaspoons ground cinnamon
1 teaspoon pure vanilla extract
¼ teaspoon salt
4 tablespoons walnut pieces

1. Add the steel cut oats, water, almond milk, banana slices, cinnamon, vanilla, and salt to the instant pot and stir to combine. 2. Close the lid and secure it well. Pressure cook for 4 minutes. 3. When cooked, let pressure release naturally for almost 15 minutes, then quick-release any remaining pressure until float valve drops, then unlock lid. 4. Serve the oatmeal in a suitable bowl topped with 1 tablespoon walnut pieces for each serving.
Per serving: Calories 318; Fat 9.5g; Sodium 282mg; Carbs 52.6g; Fiber 9.3g; Sugars 12.2g; Protein 9g

Almond Granola

Prep time:5 minutes | Cook time: 7 minutes | Serves: 8

1½ cups old fashioned rolled oats
½ cup shredded coconut, unsweetened
¼ cup monk fruit sweetener
⅛ teaspoon salt
¾ cup almond butter
¼ cup coconut oil

1. In a suitable bowl, mix together the oats, coconut, sweetener, and salt. Add the almond butter and oil and mix until well combined. 2. Layer a 6" cake pan with nonstick cooking oil. Transfer the oat mixture to this pan. 3. Add 1 cup water to the insert of the Instant pot. Set the steam rack inside, and place this pan on top of the steam rack. 4. Close the lid and secure it well. Pressure cook for 7 minutes. 5. When cooked, release the pressure quickly until the float valve drops and then unlock lid. 6. Remove this pan from the insert of the Instant pot and transfer the granola to a baking sheet to cool completely (at least 30 minutes) before serving.
Per serving: Calories 192; Fat 16.3g; Sodium 1mg; Carbs 10.7g; Fiber 1.8g; Sugars 0.3g; Protein 2.6g

Pumpkin Porridge

Prep time:2 minutes | Cook time: 1 minute| Serves: 4

¾ cup dry quinoa
2 cups water
¾ cup pumpkin purée
¼ cup monk fruit sweetener
1½ teaspoons pumpkin pie spice
1 teaspoon pure vanilla extract
¼ teaspoon salt

1. Using a fine-mesh strainer, rinse the quinoa very well until the water runs clear. 2. Add the quinoa, water, pumpkin purée, sweetener, pumpkin pie spice, vanilla, and salt to the inner pot. Stir to combine. 3. Close the lid and secure it well. Pressure cook for 1 minute. 4. When cooked, release the pressure quickly until the float valve drops and then unlock lid. 5. Allow the quinoa to cool slightly before spooning into bowls to serve.
Per serving: Calories 144; Fat 2.4g; Sodium 156mg; Carbs 25.9g; Fiber 3.9g; Sugars 1.8g; Protein 5.1g

Apple Cinnamon Oats

Prep time:10 minutes | Cook time: 4 minutes | Serves: 6

2 cups steel cut oats
3 cups vanilla almond milk, unsweetened
3 cups water
3 small apples, peeled, cored, and
cut into 1"-thick chunks
2 teaspoons ground cinnamon
¼ cup date syrup
¼ teaspoon salt

1. Add the steel cut oats, almond milk, water, apple chunks, cinnamon, date syrup, and salt to the instant pot and stir to combine. 2. Close the lid and secure it well. Pressure cook for 4 minutes. 3. When cooked, let pressure release naturally for almost 15 minutes, then quick-release any remaining pressure until float valve drops, then unlock lid. 4. Serve warm.
Per serving: Calories 195; Fat 3.5g; Sodium 193mg; Carbs 38.5g; Fiber 6.4g; Sugars 15.1g; Protein 4.5g

Beef Breakfast

Prep time: 20 minutes | Cook time: 20 minutes | Serves: 4

1 tablespoon olive oil
1 pound lean ground beef
2 teaspoons bottled minced garlic
2 cups chopped cauliflower
1 cup diced carrots
1 zucchini, diced
2 scallions, white and green parts, chopped
Sea salt
Black pepper
2 tablespoons chopped fresh parsley

1. Place a suitable skillet over medium-high heat and add the olive oil. 2. Add the ground beef and garlic. Sauté for almost 8 minutes until cooked through. 3. Stir in the cauliflower, carrots, and zucchini. Sauté for almost 10 minutes until tender. Stir in the scallions and sauté for almost 1 minute more. 4. Season the prepared mixture with black pepper and sea salt. Serve topped with the parsley.
Per serving: Calories 277; Fat 10.7g; Sodium 115mg; Carbs 8g; Fiber 2.7g; Sugars 3.6g; Protein 36.4g

Pistachio Smoothie

Prep time: 5 minutes | Cook time: 0 minutes | Serves: 2

1 cup almond milk	½ cup shelled pistachios
1 cup shredded kale	2 tablespoons pure maple syrup
2 frozen bananas	1 teaspoon pure vanilla extract

1. In a suitable blender, combine the milk, kale, bananas, pistachios, maple syrup, and vanilla. Blend until smooth and thick.
Per serving: Calories 190; Fat 6.3g; Sodium 177mg; Carbs 30.2g; Fiber 1.8g; Sugars 20.2g; Protein 4.5g

Apple-Cinnamon Smoothie

Prep time: 5 minutes | Cook time: 0 minutes | Serves: 2

1 cup canned lite coconut milk	1 tablespoon raw honey
1 apple, cored and cut into chunks	½ teaspoon ground cinnamon
1 banana	4 ice cubes
¼ cup almond butter	

1. In a suitable blender, combine the coconut milk, apple, banana, almond butter, honey, and cinnamon. Blend until smooth. 2. Add the ice and blend until thick.
Per serving: Calories 224; Fat 7.5g; Sodium 32mg; Carbs 42.9g; Fiber 4.8g; Sugars 27.5g; Protein 2.9g

Triple Berry Oats

Prep time: 5 minutes | Cook time: 4 minutes | Serves: 6

2 cups steel cut oats	¼ teaspoon salt
3 cups almond milk, unsweetened	1½ cups frozen berry blend with
3 cups water	strawberries, blackberries, and
1 teaspoon pure vanilla extract	raspberries
⅓ cup monk fruit sweetener	

1. Add the steel cut oats, almond milk, water, vanilla, sweetener, and salt to the instant pot and stir to combine. 2. Set the frozen berries on top. Close the lid and secure it well. Pressure cook for 4 minutes. 3. When done, let pressure release naturally for almost 15 minutes, then quick-release any remaining pressure until float valve drops, then unlock lid. 4. Serve warm.
Per serving: Calories 125; Fat 3.5g; Sodium 192mg; Carbs 19.6g; Fiber 3.3g; Sugars 0.4g; Protein 4.1g

Sweet Potato Orange Smoothie

Prep time: 5 minutes | Cook time: 0 minutes | Serves: 2

½ cup almond milk, unsweetened	2 tablespoons pumpkin seeds
½ cup orange juice, freshly squeezed	1 tablespoon pure maple syrup
1 cup cooked sweet potato	½ teaspoon pure vanilla extract
1 banana	½ teaspoon ground cinnamon
	3 ice cubes

1. In a suitable blender, combine the almond milk, orange juice, sweet potato, banana, pumpkin seeds, maple syrup, vanilla, and cinnamon. Blend until smooth. 2. Add the ice and blend until thick.
Per serving: Calories 258; Fat 5.4g; Sodium 85mg; Carbs 50g; Fiber 5.9g; Sugars 25.1g; Protein 5.5g

Fruity Breakfast Bars

Prep time: 15 minutes | Cook time: 30 minutes | Serves: 6

½ cup pitted dates	½ cup dried blueberries
¾ cup toasted sunflower seeds	½ cup dried cherries
¾ cup toasted pumpkin seeds	¼ cup flaxseed
¾ cup white sesame seeds	½ cup almond butter

1. At 325 degrees F, preheat your oven. Layer an 8-by-8-inch baking dish with parchment paper. 2. In a suitable food processor, blend the dates until chopped into a paste. 3. Add the sunflower seeds, pumpkin seeds, sesame seeds, blueberries, cherries, and flaxseed, and pulse to combine. 4. Scoop the prepared mixture into a suitable bowl. Stir in the almond butter. Transfer the prepared mixture to the prepared dish and press it down firmly. 5. Bake for almost 30 minutes until firm and golden brown. Cool for almost 1 hour, until it is at room temperature. 6. Remove from the baking dish and cut into 12 squares. Refrigerate in any sealed container for up to 1 week.
Per serving: Calories 242; Fat 13.2g; Sodium 5mg; Carbs 26.7g; Fiber 4.4g; Sugars 17.4g; Protein 7g

Asian Noodles

Prep time: 10 minutes | Cook time: 3 minutes | Serves: 4

½ cup reduced sodium tamari	2 large carrots, peeled and thickly
2 tablespoons rice vinegar	sliced (½") on the diagonal
2 tablespoons almond butter	8 ounces uncooked brown rice
2 tablespoons erythritol	noodles
2 cups chicken broth	¼ cup sliced scallions
1 pound boneless, chicken breast,	4 tablespoons chopped almonds
cut into bite-sized pieces	

1. Set the tamari, vinegar, almond butter, erythritol, broth, chicken pieces, and carrots in the insert of the Instant pot and then top with noodles. 2. Close the lid and secure it well. Pressure cook for 3 minutes. 3. When cooked, release the pressure quickly until the float valve drops and then unlock lid. 4. Carefully stir the ingredients. Portion into four bowls and top with scallions and a sprinkle of almonds.
Per serving: Calories 384; Fat 12.5g; Sodium 621mg; Carbs 58.3g; Fiber 4.1g; Sugars 7.2g; Protein 10.1g

Chapter 2 Soups and Salads

White Bean Soup

Prep time: 15 minutes | Cook time: 6-7 hours | Servings: 4

1 pound pre-cooked pork sausage, sliced into coins	2 bay leaves
2 (15-ounce) cans cannellini beans, rinsed and drained well	1 teaspoon garlic powder
	½ teaspoon dried oregano
5 carrots, diced	½ teaspoon dried basil leaves
1 medium onion, diced	6 cups broth
1 celery stalk, minced	4 cups shredded, de-ribbed kale

1. In your slow cooker, add the sausage, beans, carrots, onion, celery, bay leaves, garlic powder, oregano, basil, broth, and kale, combine well. 2. Cover the cooker and set to low. Cook for almost 6 to 7 hours. 3. Remove and discard the bay leaves before serving.
Per serving: Calories 201; Fat 4.1g; Sodium 874mg; Carbs 26.5g; Fiber 9.4g; Sugars 4.8g; Protein 14.5g

Miso Mushrooms Soup

Prep time: 10 minutes | Cook time: 26 minutes | Serves: 6

1 tablespoon avocado oil	1 teaspoon dried thyme
1 yellow onion, chopped	½ teaspoon sea salt
1 carrot, diced	⅛ teaspoon black pepper
3 garlic cloves, minced	4 cups vegetable broth
8 ounces cremini mushrooms, sliced	3 cups water
	½ cup barley or brown rice
8 ounces shiitake mushrooms, sliced	1 tablespoon brown rice miso paste

1. Select Sauté on the Instant Pot, pour in the oil, and let the pot preheat. 2. Stir in the onion and carrot and sauté for almost 4 minutes. Add the garlic and cook for almost 1 minute. Add the cremini and shiitake mushrooms, the thyme, salt, and pepper and cook for almost 4 minutes with occasional stirring. 3. Stir in the broth, water, barley, and miso. Select Cancel. Lock the lid. 4. Set the Pressure Cook mode and cook at high pressure for almost 18 minutes. 5. When cooking is complete, use a natural release for almost 10 minutes, then quick release any remaining pressure. 6. Remove the cooker's lid and serve hot.
Per Serving: Calories 128; Total Fat 1.7g; Sodium 771mg; Total Carbs 22.1g; Fiber 4.5g; Sugars 3.9g; Protein 7.1g

Wild Rice Harvest Soup

Prep time: 10 minutes | Cook time: 30 minutes | Serves: 6

1 cup wild rice	1 small yellow onion, diced
4 cups vegetable broth	4 garlic cloves, minced
5 carrots, chopped into disks	1 teaspoon sea salt
5 celery stalks, chopped	1 teaspoon dried thyme
8 ounces cremini mushrooms, sliced	½ teaspoon dried rosemary
	1½ cups coconut milk

1. In the Instant Pot, mix the wild rice, broth, carrots, celery, mushrooms, onion, garlic, salt, thyme, and rosemary. Lock the lid. 2. Set the pressure cook mode and cook at high pressure for almost 30 minutes. 3. When cooking is complete, use a quick release. Remove the cooker's lid and add the coconut milk. Serve warm.
Per Serving: Calories 669; Total Fat 53.8g; Sodium 905mg; Total Carbs 41.7g; Fiber 8.6g; Sugars 12.3g; Protein 14g

Avocado-Cilantro Soup

Prep time: 15 minutes | Cook time: 0 minutes | Serves: 4

2 ripe avocados, pitted and peeled	1 teaspoon salt
½ cup plain whole-milk Greek yogurt	1 teaspoon onion powder
	½ teaspoon black pepper
½ cup chopped fresh cilantro	½ teaspoon garlic powder
¼ cup olive oil	½ teaspoon ground turmeric
¼ cup freshly squeezed lime juice (almost 4 limes)	¼ cup roasted pumpkin seeds, for garnish

1. Place the avocados, yogurt, cilantro, olive oil, lime juice, salt, onion powder, pepper, garlic powder, and turmeric in a suitable blender or a wide cylindrical container. 2. Blend until smooth and creamy. 3. Serve chilled, topped with the pumpkin seeds.
Per Serving: Calories 397; Total Fat 37.7g; Sodium 595mg; Total Carbs 15.1g; Fiber 7.3g; Sugars 4.5g; Protein 5.3g

Potato Broccoli Soup

Prep time: 10 minutes | Cook time: 12 minutes | Serves: 4

2 tablespoons avocado oil	4 cups vegetable broth
1 small yellow onion, diced	1 tablespoon raw apple cider vinegar
2 garlic cloves, minced	
4 pounds Yukon Gold potatoes, diced	1 teaspoon sea salt
	⅛ teaspoon black pepper, freshly ground
1 large head broccoli, cut into florets	

1. Select Sauté on the Instant Pot and let the pot preheat. 2. Pour in the oil and add the onion and garlic. Cook for almost 4 minutes. 3. Add the potatoes, broccoli, broth, vinegar, salt, and pepper to the pot. Select Cancel. Lock the lid. 4. Set the pressure cook mode and cook at high pressure for almost 8 minutes. 5. When cooking is complete, use a quick release. 6. Remove the cooker's lid and serve warm.
Per Serving: Calories 194; Total Fat 2.6g; Sodium 1257mg; Total Carbs 35.4g; Fiber 3.7g; Sugars 3.1g; Protein 9.4g

Root Vegetable Soup

Prep time: 10 minutes | Cook time: 19 minutes | Serves: 4

1 tablespoon avocado oil	1 large parsnip, peeled and chopped
1 medium yellow onion, chopped	
2 garlic cloves, minced	4 cups vegetable broth
1 (1-inch) piece fresh ginger, chopped	1 cup water
	1 teaspoon sea salt
2 pounds carrots, coarsely chopped	¼ teaspoon ground turmeric
	¼ teaspoon black pepper, freshly ground
2 medium red potatoes, chopped	
2 medium yellow beets, peeled and chopped	½ cup coconut milk

1. Select Sauté on the Instant Pot, pour in the oil, and let the pot preheat. 2. Stir in the garlic, onion, and ginger and cook for almost 4 minutes. 3. Add the carrots, potatoes, beets, parsnip, broth, water, salt, turmeric, and pepper. Select Cancel. Lock the lid. 4. Set the pressure cook mode and cook at high pressure for almost 15 minutes. 5. When cooking is complete, use a quick release. 6. Remove the cooker's lid and stir in the coconut milk. Serve.
Per Serving: Calories 244; Total Fat 9.1g; Sodium 1399mg; Total Carbs 34.3g; Fiber 8.7g; Sugars 15.7g; Protein 8.3g

Minestrone Soup

Prep time: 15 minutes | Cook time: 8 hours | Serves: 4

1 (14-ounce) can diced tomatoes with their juice	1 teaspoon sea salt
	½ teaspoon garlic powder
1 (14-ounce) can kidney beans, drained and rinsed well	½ teaspoon dried oregano
	½ teaspoon dried basil leaves
2 celery stalks, diced	½ teaspoon dried rosemary
2 carrots, diced	2 bay leaves
1 zucchini, diced	6 cups vegetable broth
1 small onion, diced	1 cup packed fresh spinach
1 tablespoon lemon juice	

1. In your slow cooker, combine the tomatoes, kidney beans, celery, carrots, zucchini, onion, lemon juice, salt, garlic powder, oregano, basil, rosemary, bay leaves, and broth. 2. Cover the cooker and set to low. Cook for almost 6 to 8 hours. 3. Remove and discard the bay leaves. Stir in the spinach and let wilt (about 5 minutes) before serving.
Per serving: Calories 298; Fat 2.2g; Sodium 1251mg; Carbs 49.9g; Fiber 12.7g; Sugars 6.6g; Protein 21.3g

Summer Gazpacho

Prep time: 10 minutes | Cook time: 0 minutes | Serves: 4

6 large heirloom tomatoes, chopped	2 garlic cloves, minced
	juice of 1 lemon
¼ cup olive oil, extra-virgin	zest of 1 lemon
¼ cup fresh basil leaves	½ to 1 teaspoon hot sauce

1. Blend the tomatoes, olive oil, basil, garlic, lemon juice and zest, and hot sauce. 2. Pulse 20 times, in 1-second bursts, for a chunkier soup, or continue blending until smooth for a smoother texture.
Per Serving: Calories 330; Total Fat 29.1g; Sodium 348mg; Total Carbs 12.6g; Fiber 1.6g; Sugars 0g; Protein 7.7g

Veggie Chicken Soup

Prep time: 15 minutes | Cook time: 15 minutes | Servings: 6

2 tablespoons avocado oil
3 carrots, chopped
3 celery stalks, chopped
1 yellow onion, diced
2 pounds' boneless and skinless chicken breasts or thighs, cubed
3 garlic cloves, minced
1 pound red potatoes, cubed
3 cups vegetable broth
2½ teaspoons Herbes de Provence
1 teaspoon sea salt
¼ teaspoon freshly ground black pepper
1½ cups coconut milk
1 cup frozen peas

1. Select Sauté function and let the Instant pot preheat. 2. Pour in 1 tablespoon of oil and add the chicken. Cook for almost 4 minutes, or until the chicken begins to brown. Transfer to a plate and set aside. 3. Mix the remaining 1 tablespoon of oil, carrots, celery, onion and garlic in the inner pot and cook them for 2 minutes. Stir in the chicken, potatoes, broth, Herbes de Provence, salt and pepper. Press the Cancel button. 4. Lock the lid and select the pressure cook mode, cook the food at high pressure for 7 minutes. 5. When cooking is complete, use a quick release. Press Cancel button. 6. Transfer 1½ cups of the potatoes to a blender. 7. Add the coconut milk and blend until smooth. Return the potato puree to the pot. 8. Add the frozen peas and cook in the residual heat of the pot for 3 minutes, stirring occasionally.
Per Serving: Calories 474; Total Fat 24.82g; Sodium 985mg; Total Carbs 29.83g; Fiber 6.1g; Sugars 7.08g; Protein 36.98g

Grass-Fed Ground Beef with Cabbage Soup

Prep time: 15 minutes | Cook time: 20 minutes | Servings: 4

2 tablespoons avocado oil
1 yellow onion, chopped
3 garlic cloves, minced
pound grass-fed ground beef
1 teaspoon sea salt
1 teaspoon freshly ground black pepper
1 teaspoon dried oregano
3 carrots, chopped
3 celery stalks, chopped
1 head green cabbage, chopped
4 cups bone broth or vegetable broth
1 (14.5-ounce) can diced tomatoes

1. Select Sauté function and let the Instant Pot preheat. 2. Pour in the oil, add the onion, garlic and sauté them for 3 minutes. 3. Add the ground beef, salt, pepper and oregano and sauté for 3 minutes. 4. Add the carrots and celery and sauté for 3 minutes. 5. Stir in the cabbage, broth, the tomatoes and their juices. Select Cancel. 6. Lock the lid. Select the pressure cook mode and cook the food at high pressure for 10 minutes. 7. When cooking is complete, use a natural release for almost 10 minutes, then quick release any remaining pressure. 8. Remove the cooker's lid, stir well and serve.
Per Serving: Calories 366; Total Fat 24.34g; Sodium 1394mg; Total Carbs 14.93g; Fiber 4.4g; Sugars 8.25g; Protein 23.91g

Chicken Meatballs with Spinach Soup

Prep time: 20 minutes | Cook time: 15 minutes | Servings: 4

Meatballs
1½ pounds ground chicken
¾ cup almond meal
2 scallions, minced
For the Soup
1 tablespoon avocado oil
1½ cups chopped carrots
1 cup chopped celery
½ cup diced red onion
½ teaspoon sea salt
2 garlic cloves, minced
½ teaspoon sea salt
2 tablespoons ghee

¼ teaspoon dried basil
¼ teaspoon black pepper
6 cups low-sodium chicken broth
6 ounces' fresh baby spinach

To make the meatballs: 1. Mix the ground chicken, almond meal, scallions, garlic and salt in the bowl until well combined. 2. Shape the mixture into 1-inch meatballs. This should yield 10 meatballs. 3. Select Sauté function and let the Instant Pot preheat. Line a plate with paper towels. 4. Place the ghee in the pot to melt. Place the meatballs in the pot and cook for 2 minutes per side, turning to brown on all sides. Transfer to the prepared plate to rest.
To make the soup: 1. In Sauté mode, pour the oil into the pot and add the carrots, celery, and onion, cook them for 4 minutes or until the onion is translucent. 2. Stir in the salt, basil, and pepper. Add the broth and the browned meatballs. Select Cancel. 3. Lock the lid, select Soup function and set the time to 3 minutes. 4. When cooking is complete, use a quick release. 5. Remove the cooker's lid, add spinach and serve hot.
Per Serving: Calories 426; Total Fat 25.66g; Sodium 877mg; Total Carbs 13.21g; Fiber 3.1g; Sugars 3.76g; Protein 39.17g

Spiced Sweet Potato Soup

Prep time: 15 minutes | Cook time: 8 hours | Serves: 4

4 cups vegetable broth, more if needed
1 (15-ounce) can diced tomatoes
2 medium sweet potatoes, peeled and diced
1 medium onion, diced
1 jalapeño pepper, seeded and diced
½ cup unsalted almond butter
½ teaspoon sea salt
½ teaspoon garlic powder
½ teaspoon ground turmeric
½ teaspoon ground ginger
¼ teaspoon ground cinnamon
Pinch ground nutmeg
½ cup full-fat coconut milk

1. In your slow cooker, combine the broth, tomatoes, sweet potatoes, onion, jalapeño, almond butter, salt, garlic powder, turmeric, ginger, cinnamon, and nutmeg. 2. Cover the cooker and set to low. Cook for almost 6 to 8 hours. Stir in the coconut milk after cooking. 3. Using an immersion blender, purée the soup until smooth and serve.
Per serving: Calories 272; Fat 17.3g; Sodium 676mg; Carbs 24.3g; Fiber 5.2g; Sugars 3.9g; Protein 8.6g

Creamy Asparagus Soup

Prep time: 5 minutes | Cook time: 20 minutes | Serves: 4

6 tablespoons extra-virgin olive oil
1 pound asparagus, cut into 2-inch pieces
½ cup chopped scallions, green parts only
4 garlic cloves, minced
1 teaspoon salt
½ teaspoon red pepper flakes
2 cups vegetable or chicken stock
1 cup water
¼ cup tahini
Grated zest and juice of 1 lemon
2 tablespoons roasted pumpkin seeds

1. In a suitable saucepan, heat 2 tablespoons of olive oil over medium heat. 2. Add the asparagus and sauté for almost 3 minutes, until it is just tender. 3. Add the scallions, garlic, salt, and red pepper flakes and sauté for almost 3 minutes, until fragrant. 4. Pour in stock and water, increase the heat to high, and cook to a boil. Lower its heat to low, cover, and simmer for almost 8 to 10 minutes, or until the vegetables are tender. 5. Add the tahini, the remaining 4 tablespoons of olive oil, and the lemon zest and juice. 6. Using a suitable blender, puree the mixture until smooth and creamy. 7. Serve warm garnished with the pumpkin seeds.
Per Serving: Calories 306; Total Fat 29.6g; Sodium 987mg; Total Carbs 10g; Fiber 4.2g; Sugars 2.9g; Protein 5.8g

Guacamole Salad

Prep time: 15 minutes | Cook time: 0 minutes | Serves: 4

2 avocados, diced
4 Roma tomatoes, quartered
1 green bell pepper, diced
¼ red onion, sliced
½ cup packed whole fresh cilantro
leaves
¼ cup extra-virgin olive oil
Juice of 2 limes
1 teaspoon salt
½ teaspoon black pepper

1. In a suitable bowl, mix the avocados, tomatoes, bell pepper, onion, and cilantro. 2. In a suitable bowl, mix the olive oil, lime juice, salt, and pepper and drizzle over the salad. 3. Toss to coat well and serve.
Per Serving: Calories 348; Total Fat 32.6g; Sodium 595mg; Total Carbs 16.5g; Fiber 8.8g; Sugars 5.5g; Protein 3.4g

Tuna Salad with Pepitas

Prep time: 15 minutes | Cook time: 0 minutes | Serves: 2

1 ripe avocado, halved and pitted
Juice of 1 lime
1 tablespoon avocado or olive oil
1 teaspoon curry powder
½ teaspoon salt
1 (4-ounce) can olive oil–packed
tuna
2 tablespoons chopped fresh cilantro
2 tablespoons roasted pumpkin seeds

1. Using a suitable spoon, scoop out the avocado flesh into a suitable bowl and mash well with a fork. 2. Add the lime juice, avocado oil, curry powder, and salt and mix well. 3. Add the tuna and its oil, cilantro, and pumpkin seeds and mix well with a fork. 4. Serve.
Per Serving: Calories 343; Total Fat 26.6g; Sodium 924mg; Total Carbs 10.2g; Fiber 7.1g; Sugars 0.6g; Protein 20.3g

Red Pepper Soup with Goat Cheese

Prep time: 15 minutes | Cook time: 15 minutes | Serves: 4

tablespoons extra-virgin olive oil	½ teaspoon black pepper
½ small onion, coarsely chopped	3 cups vegetable or chicken stock
(16-ounce) jar roasted red peppers, chopped	1 cup water
	4 ounces goat cheese
garlic cloves, minced	½ cup chopped fresh basil
teaspoon salt	2 tablespoons red wine vinegar

1. In a suitable saucepan, heat 2 tablespoons of olive oil over medium heat. 2. Add the onion and sauté for almost 4 minutes, or until the onion has softened. 3. Add the red peppers, garlic, salt, and pepper and sauté for almost 3 minutes, or until fragrant. 4. Pour in the stock and water, increase the heat to high, and cook to a boil. 5. Lower its heat to low, cover, and simmer for almost 5 minutes to allow flavors to blend. 6. Mix in the goat cheese, basil, the remaining 4 tablespoons of olive oil, and the vinegar. 7. Using a suitable blender to puree the mixture until smooth and creamy. 8. Serve warm, garnished with additional basil.
Per Serving: Calories 354; Total Fat 31.8g; Sodium 1525mg; Total Carbs 9.7g; Fiber 1.7g; Sugars 6.6g; Protein 10.5g

Cream of Mushroom Soup

Prep time: 10 minutes | Cook time: 25 minutes | Serves: 4

tablespoons unsalted butter	1 teaspoon salt
cup sliced fennel bulb	½ teaspoon black pepper
ounces mushrooms, sliced and divided	2 cups vegetable or beef stock
	½ cup heavy whipping cream
garlic cloves, minced	2 tablespoons extra-virgin olive oil
tablespoons chopped fresh thyme or rosemary	

1. In a suitable saucepan, heat the butter over medium heat. 2. Add the fennel and sauté for almost 5 to 6 minutes, or until the fennel is tender and slightly browned. 3. Add 6 ounces of mushrooms, garlic, thyme, salt, and pepper and sauté for almost 4 minutes, until the mushrooms are just soft. 4. Pour in the stock, increase the heat to high, and cook to a boil. 5. Lower its heat to low, cover and simmer for almost 5 minutes, until the vegetables are very tender. 6. Add the cream and olive oil and using an immersion blender, puree the mixture until smooth and creamy. 7. Coarsely chop the remaining 2 ounces of mushrooms. 8. If using a blender, return the creamed soup to the saucepan and heat over low. 9. Stir in the mushrooms and cook, stirring constantly, for almost 4 minutes, or until the mushrooms are tender. 10. Serve warm.
Per Serving: Calories 198; Total Fat 19g; Sodium 1035mg; Total Carbs 5.7g; Fiber 2g; Sugars 1g; Protein 4g

Moroccan-Cauliflower Salad

Prep time: 5 minutes | Cook time: 25 minutes | Serves: 4

cups fresh or frozen cauliflower florets	1 teaspoon garlic powder
tablespoons coconut oil, melted	½ teaspoon ground turmeric
teaspoon salt	½ teaspoon ground ginger
cup extra-virgin olive oil	2 celery stalks, sliced
grated zest and juice of 1 lemon	½ cup sliced fresh mint
teaspoon chili powder	¼ cup sliced red onion
teaspoon ground cinnamon	¼ cup shelled pistachios

1. If using frozen cauliflower, thaw to room temperature in a colander, draining off any excess water. Cut larger florets into bite-size pieces. 2. At 450 degrees F, preheat your oven and layer a suitable baking sheet with aluminum foil. 3. In a suitable bowl, toss the cauliflower with coconut oil and ½ teaspoon of salt. 4. Spread the cauliflower in a single layer on the prepared baking sheet, reserving the seasoned bowl. 5. Roast the cauliflower for almost 20 to 25 minutes, until it is lightly browned and crispy. 6. While the cauliflower roasts, in the reserved bowl, mix the olive oil, lemon zest and juice, the remaining ½ teaspoon of salt, the chili powder, cinnamon, garlic powder, turmeric, and ginger. Stir in the celery, mint, and onion. 7. Toss the warm (but not too hot) cauliflower with the prepared dressing until well combined. 8. Add the pistachios and toss to incorporate. Serve warm or chilled.
Per Serving: Calories 216; Total Fat 20.6g; Sodium 639mg; Total Carbs 8.7g; Fiber 4.3g; Sugars 2.9g; Protein 3.1g

Miso Soup with Tofu

Prep time: 10 minutes | Cook time: 20 minutes | Serves: 4

3 cups water	diced
3 cups vegetable broth	2 cups spiralized or sliced zucchini
3 tablespoons white miso paste	
1 (2-inch) fresh ginger piece, peeled and minced	2 large hard-boiled eggs, peeled and quartered
4 baby bok choy, trimmed and quartered	2 nori seaweed sheets, cut into very thin 2-inch strips
2 cups sliced shiitake mushrooms	¼ cup avocado or olive oil, extra-virgin
2 garlic cloves, very sliced	
1 (14-ounce) package firm tofu,	2 teaspoons toasted sesame oil

1. In a suitable saucepan, bring the water and vegetable broth to a boil over high heat. Lower its heat to low, whisk in the miso paste and ginger, cover and simmer for almost 2 minutes. 2. Add the bok choy, mushrooms, and garlic. Simmer, covered, for almost 5 minutes, or until the vegetables are tender. Stir in the tofu and zucchini. 3. Divide the mixture between bowls. Add 2 egg quarters and the seaweed strips to each bowl. Drizzle 1 tablespoon of avocado oil and ½ teaspoon of sesame oil over each bowl. Serve warm.
Per Serving: Calories 223; Total Fat 12g; Sodium 845mg; Total Carbs 15.4g; Fiber 3.8g; Sugars 4.8g; Protein 17.4g

Omega-3 Salad

Prep time: 15 minutes | Cook time: 0 minutes | Serves: 4

6 cups baby arugula	white and green parts, or red onion
1 (4-ounce) can olive oil–packed tuna, mackerel, or salmon	1 avocado, sliced
¼ cup minced fresh parsley	¼ cup roasted pumpkin or sunflower seeds
10 green or black olives, pitted and halved	
2 tablespoons minced scallions,	6 tablespoons basic vinaigrette or Caesar dressing

1. Divide the greens between bowls. 2. In a suitable bowl, mix the tuna and its oil with the parsley, olives, and scallions. 3. Divide the fish mixture evenly on top of the greens. 4. Divide the avocado slices and pumpkin seeds between the bowls. 5. Drizzle each with the prepared dressing and toss to coat.
Per Serving: Calories 335; Total Fat 26.5g; Sodium 52mg; Total Carbs 13.4g; Fiber 8.6g; Sugars 2.4g; Protein 16g

Green Bean Salad

Prep time: 15 minutes | Cook time: 5 minutes | Serves: 4

¼ cup olive oil, extra-virgin	2 garlic cloves, sliced
1 pound green beans, trimmed	½ cup slivered almonds
2 tablespoons red wine vinegar	¼ cup sliced fresh basil
1 teaspoon salt	2 tablespoons chopped fresh mint
1 teaspoon red pepper flakes	

1. In a suitable skillet, heat 2 tablespoons of olive oil over medium-high heat. 2. Add the green beans and sauté for almost 5 minutes, until they are just tender. 3. Remove the green beans from the heat and transfer to a suitable serving bowl. 4. In a suitable bowl, mix the remaining 2 tablespoons of olive oil, the vinegar, salt, red pepper flakes, and garlic. 5. Pour the prepared dressing over the green beans and toss to coat well. 6. Add the almonds, basil, and mint and toss well. 7. Serve.
Per Serving: Calories 219; Total Fat 18.8g; Sodium 590mg; Total Carbs 11.7g; Fiber 5.7g; Sugars 2.2g; Protein 4.9g

Lentil-Beet Salad

Prep time: 15 minutes | Cook time: 0 minutes | Serves: 4

4 cups baby spinach	1 tablespoon apple cider vinegar
1 (15-ounce) can lentils, drained	1 teaspoon salt
4 cooked peeled beets, cut into 8 pieces	¼ teaspoon black pepper
1 small red onion, sliced	1 teaspoon chopped fresh tarragon leaves
⅓ cup olive oil, extra-virgin	

1. Arrange all the spinach leaves on a serving platter or in a suitable bowl. 2. Top with the lentils, beets, and red onion. 3. In a suitable bowl, mix the olive oil, cider vinegar, salt, and pepper. 4. Drizzle the salad with the prepared dressing, top with the tarragon, and serve.
Per Serving: Calories 579; Total Fat 18.3g; Sodium 689mg; Total Carbs 76.7g; Fiber 35.5g; Sugars 11g; Protein 30.2g

Lettuce Greek Salad

Prep time: 15 minutes | Cook time: 0 minutes | Serves: 4

8 cups coarsely chopped romaine lettuce
4 ounces crumbled sheep's milk feta cheese
½ cup store-bought marinated artichoke hearts

20 Kalamata olives, pitted
2 tablespoons fresh oregano
¼ cup olive oil, extra-virgin
Juice of 1 lemon
½ teaspoon black pepper, freshly ground

1. In a suitable bowl, mix the lettuce, feta, artichoke hearts, olives, and oregano. 2. Drizzle with the oil, then add the lemon juice and pepper. Toss to coat and serve.
Per Serving: Calories 231; Total Fat 21.3g; Sodium 710mg; Total Carbs 7.7g; Fiber 2.5g; Sugars 2.3g; Protein 5g

Thai Vegetable Soup

Prep time: 5 minutes | Cook time: 0 minutes | Serves: 4 to 6

4 cups vegetable broth
½ cup sliced mushrooms
3 carrots, diced
1 bunch baby bok choy
1 sweet potato, peeled and diced
1 small head broccoli, florets chopped
1 small onion, diced
1 lemongrass stalk, chopped into 1-inch segments

1 tablespoon lime juice
1 tablespoon curry paste
2 teaspoons fish sauce
¾ teaspoon sea salt
½ teaspoon ground ginger
½ teaspoon garlic powder
¾ cup full-fat coconut milk
Fresh cilantro leaves, for garnishing

1. In your slow cooker, stir together the broth, mushrooms, carrots, bok choy, sweet potato, broccoli, onion, lemongrass, lime juice, curry paste, fish sauce, salt, ginger, and garlic powder. 2. Cover the cooker and set to low. Cook for almost 6 to 8 hours.
3. Stir in the coconut milk and garnish with the cilantro before serving.
Per serving: Calories 138; Fat 3.8g; Sodium 1408mg; Carbs 18.6g; Fiber 4.1g; Sugars 6.7g; Protein 7.9g

Miso Tofu Soup

Prep time: 10 minutes | Cook time: 15 minutes | Serves: 4

4 cups vegetable broth
2 slices peeled ginger root
2 slices peeled turmeric root
1 garlic clove, lightly crushed

4 tablespoons white miso
½ cup cubed firm tofu
1 scallion, sliced

1. Pour the vegetable broth into a suitable pot and add the ginger root, turmeric root, and garlic. Cook to a boil over medium-high heat. Lower to a simmer and simmer for almost 5 minutes. 2. Use a slotted spoon to remove the turmeric root, ginger root, and garlic. 3. Put the miso in a suitable bowl, add one ladleful of hot broth, and mix until smooth. 4. Return the miso broth mixture back into the pot and mix. 5. Divide the broth among four serving bowls. 6. Divide the tofu and scallion among the bowls, and serve.
Per Serving: Calories 52; Total Fat 2.1g; Sodium 766mg; Total Carbs 1.8g; Fiber 0.3g; Sugars 0.9g; Protein 6.3g

Tomato Soup

Prep time: 10 minutes | Cook time: 15 minutes | Serves: 4

2 tablespoons olive oil, extra-virgin
1 onion, chopped
2 garlic cloves, minced
2 (28-ounce) cans crushed tomatoes, undrained

4 cups no-salt-added vegetable broth
½ teaspoon sea salt
⅛ teaspoon black pepper, freshly ground

1. In a suitable pot over medium-high heat, heat the olive oil until it shimmers. 2. Add the onion. Cook for almost 7 minutes with occasional stirring, until browned. 3. Add the garlic. Cook for almost 30 seconds, stirring constantly. 4. Stir in the tomatoes, vegetable broth, salt, and pepper. Simmer for almost 5 minutes. 5. Transfer the cooked veggie soup to a blender or use an immersion blender. Process until smooth.
Per Serving: Calories 270; Total Fat 8.4g; Sodium 1761mg; Total Carbs 35.7g; Fiber 13.3g; Sugars 24.1g; Protein 14.8g

Salmon Spinach Salad

Prep time: 15 minutes | Cook time: 0 minutes | Serves: 4

3 cups baby spinach
½ cucumber, sliced
1 small fennel bulb, trimmed and sliced
2 baked salmon fillets, flaked
1 small ripe avocado, peeled, pitted, and sliced

¼ cup olive oil, extra-virgin
2 tablespoons fresh lemon juice
1 teaspoon salt
¼ teaspoon black pepper, freshly ground
1 teaspoon chopped fresh dill

1. Arrange all the spinach on a serving platter or in a suitable bowl. 2. Top with the cucumber, fennel, salmon, and avocado. 3. Mix the olive oil, lemon juice, salt, pepper, and dill, or shake in a suitable jar with a lid. 4. Pour the prepared dill dressing over the salad, and serve.
Per Serving: Calories 367; Total Fat 28.6g; Sodium 663mg; Total Carbs 8.5g; Fiber 4.8g; Sugars 1.1g; Protein 22.7g

Chickpea Kale Salad

Prep time: 15 minutes | Cook time: 5 minutes | Serves: 4

¼ cup olive oil, extra-virgin
1 cup canned chickpeas, rinsed and drained
1 garlic clove, sliced
½ teaspoon ground cumin
1 large bunch kale, torn into

pieces
½ cup chopped fennel
¼ cup chopped red onion
1 teaspoon salt
½ teaspoon paprika
¼ cup fresh lemon juice

1. In a suitable skillet, heat the olive oil over high heat. 2. Add the chickpeas, garlic, and cumin and sauté for almost 5 minutes. 3. Put the kale in a suitable bowl. Pour the hot chickpeas over the kale, tossing to slightly wilt the kale. 4. Add the fennel and red onion. Add the salt and paprika, drizzle with the lemon juice, and serve.
Per Serving: Calories 311; Total Fat 15.9g; Sodium 610mg; Total Carbs 34.4g; Fiber 9.7g; Sugars 6g; Protein 10.6g

Turkey Taco Soup

Prep time: 15 minutes | Cook time: 20 minutes | Serves: 4 to 6

1 tablespoon olive oil, extra-virgin
1 pound ground turkey
1 zucchini, sliced
2 garlic cloves, minced
1 teaspoon salt
1 teaspoon chipotle powder
½ teaspoon ground cumin
Optional Toppings
Greek yogurt
Chopped scallions

¼ teaspoon black pepper, freshly ground
1 (15-ounce) can black beans, rinsed and drained
1 (14.5-ounce) can fire-roasted tomatoes with their juice
1 cup frozen corn
4 cups chicken or vegetable broth

Chopped fresh cilantro

1. In a suitable Dutch oven, preheat the oil over high heat. 2. Stir in the minced turkey meat and cook until browned, almost 5 minutes. 3. Add the zucchini, garlic, salt, chipotle powder, cumin, and pepper and sauté until tender, almost 5 minutes. 4. Add the black beans, fire-roasted tomatoes, broth, and corn. 5. Cook to a boil, then lower to a simmer and simmer to heat through and mix the flavors, almost 10 minutes. 6. Ladle into bowls and serve, passing around toppings if desired.
Per Serving: Calories 568; Total Fat 20.8g; Sodium 1493mg; Total Carbs 21.8g; Fiber 3.8g; Sugars 10.2g; Protein 75.8g

Chicken and Vegetable Soup

Prep time: 10 minutes | Cook time: 10 minutes | Serves: 4

2 tablespoons olive oil, extra-virgin
1 onion, chopped
2 red bell peppers, chopped
1 tablespoon grated fresh ginger
3 cups shredded rotisserie

chicken; skin removed
8 cups no-salt-added chicken broth
½ teaspoon sea salt
⅛ teaspoon black pepper, freshly ground

1. In a suitable pot over medium-high heat, heat the olive oil until it shimmers. 2. Add the onion, red bell peppers, and ginger. 3. Sauté for almost 5 minutes with occasional stirring, until the vegetables are soft. 4. Stir in the chicken, chicken broth, salt, and pepper. Bring to a simmer. 5. Lower its heat to medium-low and simmer for almost 5 minutes.
Per Serving: Calories 291; Total Fat 10.8g; Sodium 2153mg; Total Carbs 12.1g; Fiber 1.6g; Sugars 5.6g; Protein 37g

Cream of Kale Soup

Prep time: 10 minutes | Cook time: 20 minutes | Serves: 4

2 tablespoons olive oil, extra-virgin
1 onion, chopped
4 cups kale
1 cup broccoli florets
6 cups no-salt vegetable broth
1 teaspoon garlic powder
½ teaspoon sea salt
¼ teaspoon black pepper, freshly ground
Microgreens, as you like
Coconut milk, as you like

1. In a suitable pot over medium-high heat, heat the olive oil until it shimmers. 2. Add the onion and cook almost 5 minutes with occasional stirring, until it is soft. 3. Add the kale, broccoli, vegetable broth, garlic powder, salt, and pepper. 4. Cook to a boil and Lower its heat to medium-low. Simmer 10 to 15 minutes, until the vegetables are soft. Transfer to a suitable blender and blend until smooth. 5. Serve hot with the additional oil, microgreens, and coconut milk, if using.
Per Serving: Calories 137; Total Fat 7.1g; Sodium 1067mg; Total Carbs 16.2g; Fiber 3.8g; Sugars 4.7g; Protein 3.1g

Sweet Potato Soup

Prep time: 10 minutes | Cook time: 15 minutes | Serves: 4

2 tablespoons olive oil, extra-virgin
1 onion, chopped
4 cups cubed, peeled sweet potato
8 cups no-salt-added vegetable broth
1 teaspoon curry powder
1 teaspoon ground turmeric
½ teaspoon sea salt
⅛ teaspoon black pepper, freshly ground

1. In a suitable pot over medium-high heat, heat the olive oil until it shimmers. 2. Add the onion. Sauté for almost 5 minutes with occasional stirring, until soft. 3. Stir in the sweet potato, vegetable broth, curry powder, turmeric, salt, and pepper. 4. Cook to a boil. Lower its heat to medium and simmer for almost 10 minutes until the sweet potato cubes are soft. 5. Blend until smooth and serve.
Per Serving: Calories 285; Total Fat 7.5g; Sodium 1367mg; Total Carbs 50.6g; Fiber 9.6g; Sugars 18.2g; Protein 4.4g

Lentil and Carrot Soup

Prep time: 15 minutes | Cook time: 10 minutes | Serves: 4 to 6

1 tablespoon coconut oil
2 carrots, sliced thin
1 small white onion, peeled and sliced thin
2 garlic cloves, peeled and sliced thin
1 tablespoon chopped fresh ginger
3 cups water or vegetable broth
1 (15-ounce) can lentils, drained and rinsed
2 tablespoons chopped fresh cilantro or parsley
1 teaspoon salt
¼ teaspoon black pepper

1. In a suitable pot over medium-high heat, melt the coconut oil. Add the carrots, onion, garlic, and ginger. Sauté for 5 minutes. 2. Add the water to the pot and bring to a boil. Reduce its heat to simmer and cook for almost 5 minutes, or until the carrots are tender. 3. Add the lentils, cilantro, salt, and pepper. Stir well, and serve.
Per serving: Calories: 307; Total fat 3.8g; Sodium 789mg; Total carbs 47.2g; Fiber 22.6g; Sugars 3.3g; Protein 21.2g

Dijon Brussels Sprout Slaw

Prep time: 15 minutes | Cook time: 0 minutes | Serves: 4

1 pound Brussels sprouts; stem ends removed and sliced thin
½ red onion, sliced thin
1 apple, cored and sliced thin
1 teaspoon Dijon mustard
1 teaspoon salt
1 tablespoon raw honey or maple syrup
2 teaspoons apple cider vinegar
1 cup plain coconut milk yogurt
½ cup chopped toasted hazelnuts
½ cup pomegranate seeds

1. In a suitable bowl, combine the brussels sprouts, onion, and apple. 2. In a suitable bowl, whisk together the Dijon mustard, salt, honey, cider vinegar, and yogurt. 3. Add the prepared dressing to the brussels sprouts and toss until evenly coated. 4. Garnish the salad with hazelnuts and pomegranate seeds.
Per serving: Calories: 200; Total fat 6.3g; Sodium 647mg; Total carbs 33g; Fiber 7g; Sugars 18.6g; Protein 7g

White Bean and Tuna Salad

Prep time: 15 minutes | Cook time: 0 minutes | Serves: 4

4 cups arugula
2 (5-ounce) cans flaked white tuna, drained
1 (15-ounces) can white beans, drained
½ pint cherry tomatoes halved lengthwise
½ red onion, chopped
½ cup pitted kalamata olives
¼ cup extra-virgin olive oil
2 tablespoons lemon juice
Salt
Black pepper
2 ounces crumbled feta cheese

1. In a suitable bowl, mix together the arugula, tuna, white beans, tomatoes, onion, olives, olive oil, and lemon juice. 2. Season with salt and pepper. Top the salad with the feta cheese.
Per serving: Calories: 400; Total fat 15.2g; Sodium 644mg; Total carbs 23.6g; Fiber 6.3g; Sugars 2.3g; Protein 42.2g

Caesar Salad

Prep time: 15 minutes | Cook time: 0 minutes | Serves: 4

2 romaine lettuce hearts, chopped
1 (14-ounce) can heart of palm, drained and sliced
½ cup sunflower seeds
½ cup Caesar dressing
Salt
Black pepper

1. In a suitable bowl, combine the romaine lettuce, hearts of palm, and sunflower seeds. 2. Add enough Caesar dressing to lightly coat the lettuce leaves. Reserve any remaining dressing for another use. 3. Season the salad with salt and pepper, and serve.
Per serving: Calories: 161; Total fat 8.1g; Sodium 692mg; Total carbs 20.6g; Fiber 5g; Sugars 8.2g; Protein 5.2g

Soba Noodle Soup with Spinach

Prep time: 15 minutes | Cook time: 10 minutes | Serves: 4

2 tablespoons coconut oil
8 ounces shiitake mushrooms, stemmed and sliced thin
4 scallions, sliced thin
1 garlic clove, minced
1 tablespoon minced fresh ginger
1 teaspoon salt
1 bunch spinach, cut into strips
4 cups vegetable broth
3 cups water
4 ounces buckwheat soba noodles
1 tablespoon lemon juice

1. In a suitable pot over medium heat, heat the coconut oil. Stir in the scallions, mushrooms, garlic, ginger, and salt. Sauté for 5 minutes almost. 2. Pour in vegetable broth and water to the pot and bring to a boil. 3. Add the soba noodles and cook for 5 minutes. 4. Remove the pot from the heat. Stir in the spinach and lemon juice. Serve hot.
Per serving: Calories: 361; Total fat 10.3g; Sodium 1557mg; Total carbs 52.2g; Fiber 5.7g; Sugars 3.6g; Protein 16.7g

Jicama Black Bean Salad

Prep time: 10 minutes | Cook time: 50 minutes | Serves: 4

1 cup medium-or long-grain brown rice
5 tablespoons extra-virgin olive oil
2 teaspoons salt
1 (15-ounce) can black beans, drained and rinsed
1 small jicama, peeled and cut into ¼-inch dice
¼ cup chopped fresh cilantro
¼ cup lime juice, freshly squeezed
2 scallions, both white and green parts, sliced
1 small jalapeño pepper, seeded and minced
¼ teaspoon black pepper, freshly ground

1. In a suitable pot, combine the rice, 2 cups of water, 1 tablespoon of oil, and 1 teaspoon of salt. 2. Bring to a boil, reduce its heat to a simmer, cover, and cook until the rice is tender, 40 to 45 minutes. 3. Remove from the heat, let cool to room temperature, and fluff with a fork. 4. Add the beans, jicama, cilantro, lime juice, scallions, jalapeño pepper, remaining 4 tablespoons of oil, remaining 1 teaspoon of salt, and the pepper, and mix well. 5. Serve at room temperature, or chill for several hours to serve cold.
Per serving: Calories: 384; Fat 12.9g; Sodium 782mg; Carbs 53.7g; Fiber 14g; Sugars 2.7g; Protein 16.2g

Roasted Chicken and Kale Salad

Prep time: 10 minutes | Cook time: 0 minutes | Serves: 4

4 cups baby kale
¼ cup extra-virgin olive oil
3 tablespoons red-wine vinegar
1 teaspoon salt
¼ teaspoon black pepper

2 cups shredded rotisserie chicken
1 (15-ounce) can white beans, drained and rinsed
¼ cup chopped red onion
¼ cup chopped walnuts

1. In a suitable bowl, using your hands, mix the kale with the oil, vinegar, salt, and pepper, massaging it into the leaves to soften them. 2. Add the chicken, beans, and onion and mix to combine. 3. Sprinkle with the walnuts and serve.
Per serving: Calories 394; Fat 9.7g; Sodium 596mg; Carbs 50.2g; Fiber 12.2g; Sugars 1.7g; Protein 30.3g

Quinoa and Roasted Asparagus Salad

Prep time: 10 minutes | Cook time: 15 minutes | Serves: 4

1 bunch asparagus, trimmed
3 tablespoons extra-virgin olive oil
1 teaspoon salt, plus additional for seasoning
2 cups cooked quinoa, cold or at

room temperature
¼ red onion, chopped
1 tablespoon apple cider vinegar
¼ cup chopped fresh mint
1 tablespoon flaxseed
Black pepper

1. At 400 degrees F, preheat your oven. 2. In a suitable bowl, toss the asparagus with 1 tablespoon of olive oil and 1 teaspoon of salt. 3. Wrap the asparagus in aluminum foil in a single layer and place the pouch on a baking sheet. 4. Set the asparagus baking sheet in the preheated oven and roast the asparagus for 10 to 15 minutes. 5. While the asparagus is roasting, mix together the quinoa, onion, vinegar, mint, flaxseed, and the remaining 2 tablespoons of olive oil in a suitable bowl. 6. Once the asparagus is cool enough to handle, slice it into ½-inch pieces. Add them to the quinoa and season with salt and pepper.
Per serving: Calories: 223; Total fat 13.1g; Sodium 591mg; Total carbs 22.5g; Fiber 4.2g; Sugars 1g; Protein 5.3g

Chicken Salad with Blueberries

Prep time: 5 minutes | Cook time: 10 minutes | Serves: 4

½ cup anti-inflammatory Mayo
¼ cup extra-virgin olive oil
Grated zest and juice of 1 lemon
1 teaspoon fennel seed, slightly crushed
½ teaspoon salt
¼ teaspoon black pepper, freshly

ground
2 cups shredded cooked chicken
2 celery stalks, chopped
½ cup fresh or frozen blueberries, halved
½ cup slivered almonds

1. In a suitable bowl, mix the mayo, olive oil, lemon zest and juice, fennel, salt, and pepper and whisk well to combine. 2. Add the chicken, celery, blueberries, and almonds and stir to coat. Serve.
Per Serving: Calories 302; Total Fat 21.3g; Sodium 354mg; Total Carbs 6g; Fiber 2.3g; Sugars 2.5g; Protein 23.1g

Vegetable Slaw with Feta Cheese

Prep time: 20 minutes | Cook time: 0 minutes | Serves: 4 to 6

½ cup extra-virgin olive oil
½ cup apple cider vinegar
1 tablespoon raw honey or maple syrup
1 teaspoon Dijon mustard
1 teaspoon salt
¼ teaspoon black pepper
2 large broccoli stems, peeled and shredded

2 carrots, peeled and shredded
½ celery root bulb, peeled and shredded
1 large beet, peeled and shredded
2 zucchinis, shredded
1 small red onion, sliced thin
¼ cup chopped fresh Italian parsley
3 ounces feta cheese, crumbled

1. In a suitable bowl, whisk together the olive oil, cider vinegar, honey, Dijon mustard, salt, and pepper. 2. Add the broccoli, carrots, celery root, beets, zucchini, onion, and Italian parsley. Toss to coat the vegetables with the dressing. 3. Transfer the slaw to a serving bowl and garnish with the feta cheese.
Per serving: Calories: 241; Total fat 20.1g; Sodium 608mg; Total carbs 13.4g; Fiber 2.9g; Sugars 8g; Protein 4.5g

Roasted Vegetable Soup

Prep time: 30 minutes | Cook time: 40 minutes | Serves: 6 to 8

4 carrots, halved lengthwise
½ head cauliflower, broken into florets
2 cups cubed butternut squash
3 shallots, halved lengthwise
3 Roma tomatoes, quartered

4 garlic cloves
½ cup extra-virgin olive oil
1 teaspoon salt
¼ teaspoon black pepper
4 to 6 cups water or vegetable broth

1. At 400 degrees F, preheat your oven. 2. In a suitable bowl, combine the carrots, cauliflower, butternut squash, shallots, tomatoes, and garlic. Add the olive oil, salt, and pepper and toss well. 3. Arrange all the vegetables in a rimmed baking sheet in a single layer. 4. Place this sheet in the preheated oven, and roast all the vegetables for almost 25 minutes, or until they start to brown. 5. Transfer the roasted vegetables to a suitable Dutch oven over high heat. Pour in enough water to cover the vegetables and cook to a boil. 6. Reduce its heat to a simmer and then continue cooking for almost 10 minutes on a simmer. 7. Pour the prepared soup into a blender, working in batches if necessary, and purée until smooth.
Per serving: Calories: 197; Total fat 17g; Sodium 426mg; Total carbs 12.5g; Fiber 3g; Sugars 4.8g; Protein 1.9g

Roasted Sweet Potatoes and Pineapple

Prep time: 10 minutes | Cook time: 25 minutes | Serves: 4

3 tablespoons coconut oil
2 sweet potatoes, peeled and diced
1 cup fresh pineapple, peeled and

diced
2 teaspoons curry powder
1 teaspoon salt
¼ teaspoon black pepper

1. At 400 degrees F, preheat your oven. 2. In a microwave-safe bowl, heat the coconut oil in the microwave on high to melt for almost 1 minute. 3. In a suitable bowl, combine the sweet potatoes and pineapple. Add the melted coconut oil, curry powder, salt, and pepper. 4. Toss to combine. Spoon the mixture onto a rimmed baking sheet. 5. Place the sweet potato baking sheet in the preheated oven and roast for 20 to 25 minutes, or until the sweet potatoes are tender. 6. Serve warm.
Per serving: Calories: 382; Total fat 21g; Sodium 1176mg; Total carbs 49.5g; Fiber 7.2g; Sugars 8.9g; Protein 2.8g

Sweet Potato and Rice Soup

Prep time: 15 minutes | Cook time: 15 minutes | Serves: 4 to 6

4 cups vegetable broth
1 sweet potato, peeled and diced
2 onions, chopped
2 garlic cloves, sliced thin
2 teaspoons minced fresh ginger

1 bunch broccolini, cut into 1-inch pieces
1 cup cooked basmati rice
¼ cup fresh cilantro leaves

1. In a suitable Dutch oven over high heat, add the broth and bring to a boil. 2. Add the sweet potato, onion, garlic, and ginger. Simmer for 5 to 8 minutes, or until the sweet potato is cooked through. 3. Add the broccolini and simmer for an additional 3 minutes. 4. Remove this pan from the heat. Stir in the rice and cilantro.
Per serving: Calories: 186; Total fat 1.3g; Sodium 526mg; Total carbs 36.2g; Fiber 2.5g; Sugars 4.2g; Protein 6.8g

Coconut Curry–Butternut Squash Soup

Prep time: 10 minutes | Cook time: 4 hours | Serves: 4 to 6

2 tablespoons coconut oil
1 pound butternut squash, peeled and cut into 1-inch cubes
1 small head cauliflower, diced
1 onion, sliced
1 tablespoon curry powder

½ cup sugar-free apple juice
4 cups vegetable broth
1 (13.5-ounce) can coconut milk
1 teaspoon salt
¼ teaspoon white pepper
¼ cup chopped fresh cilantro

1. In the slower cooker, combine the coconut oil, butternut squash, cauliflower, onion, curry powder, apple juice, vegetable broth, coconut milk, salt, and white pepper. 2. Set on high for 4 hours. 3. Serve the soup as is or purée it in a blender before serving. Garnish with cilantro.
Per serving: Calories: 277; Total fat 21g; Sodium 925mg; Total carbs 20.1g; Fiber 4.8g; Sugars 8.1g; Protein 6.7g

Fennel Pear Soup

Prep time: 10 minutes | Cook time: 15 minutes | Serves: 4

2 tablespoons extra-virgin olive oil
2 leeks, white part only, sliced
1 fennel bulb, cut into ¼-inch-thick slices
2 pears, peeled, cored, and cut
into ½-inch cubes
1 teaspoon salt
¼ teaspoon black pepper
½ cup cashews
3 cups water or vegetable broth
2 cups spinach or arugula

1. In a suitable Dutch oven over high heat, heat the olive oil. 2. Add the leeks and fennel. Sauté for 5 minutes. 3. Add the pears, salt, and pepper. Sauté for 3 minutes more. 4. Add the cashews and water and bring the soup to a boil. Reduce its heat to simmer and cook for 5 minutes, partially covered. Stir in the spinach. 5. Pour the prepared soup into a blender, working in batches if necessary, and purée until smooth.
Per serving: Calories: 229; Total fat 12.6g; Sodium 875mg; Total carbs 26.2g; Fiber 4.6g; Sugars 8.9g; Protein 5.4g

Mediterranean Chopped Salad

Prep time: 15 minutes | Cook time: 0 minutes | Serves: 4

2 cups spinach
3 large tomatoes, diced
1 bunch radishes, sliced thin
1 English cucumber, peeled and diced
2 scallions, sliced
2 garlic cloves, minced
1 tablespoon chopped fresh mint
1 tablespoon fresh parsley,
chopped
1 cup unsweetened plain almond yogurt
¼ cup extra-virgin olive oil
3 tablespoons lemon juice
1 tablespoon apple cider vinegar
1 teaspoon salt
¼ teaspoon black pepper
1 tablespoon sumac

1. In a suitable bowl, combine the spinach, tomatoes, radishes, cucumber, scallions, garlic, mint, parsley, yogurt, olive oil, lemon juice, cider vinegar, salt, pepper, and sumac. 2. Toss to combine.
Per serving: Calories: 203; Total fat 13.5g; Sodium 990mg; Total carbs 17.9g; Fiber 4.4g; Sugars 8.9g; Protein 5.9g

Sliced Apple and Celery Salad

Prep time: 15 minutes | Cook time: 0 minutes | Serves: 4

2 green apples, cored and quartered
2 small beets, peeled and quartered
4 cups spinach
2 celery stalks, sliced thin
½ red onion, sliced thin
½ cup shredded carrots
1 tablespoon apple cider vinegar
1 tablespoon raw honey or maple syrup
3 tablespoons extra-virgin olive oil
Salt
Black pepper
¼ cup pumpkin seeds

1. Using a slicing disk of a suitable food processor, slice the apples and the beets. 2. Place the spinach on a suitable platter. Arrange the apples and beets over the spinach. 3. Top with celery, red onion, and carrots. 4. In a suitable bowl, whisk together the cider vinegar, honey, and olive oil. Season with salt and pepper. 5. Drizzle the prepared dressing over the salad and garnish with the pumpkin seeds.
Per serving: Calories: 253; Total fat 14.9g; Sodium 121mg; Total carbs 30.3g; Fiber 5.5g; Sugars 21.5g; Protein 4.5g

Mushrooms Broth

Prep time: 15 minutes | Cook time: 10 minutes | Serves: 4

1 tablespoon extra-virgin olive oil
1 onion, halved and sliced thin
3 garlic cloves, sliced thin
1 celery stalk, chopped
1 pound mushrooms, sliced thin
1 teaspoon salt
½ teaspoon black pepper
Pinch nutmeg
4 cups vegetable broth
2 tablespoons chopped fresh tarragon

1. In a suitable pot over high heat, heat the olive oil. Add the onion, garlic, and celery. Sauté for 3 minutes. 2. Add the mushrooms, salt, pepper, and nutmeg. Sauté for 5 to 10 minutes more. 3. Add the vegetable broth and bring the soup to a boil. Reduce its heat to simmer. Cook for an additional 5 minutes. 4. Stir in the tarragon and serve.
Per serving: Calories: 111; Total fat 5.4g; Sodium 1357mg; Total carbs 8.7g; Fiber 2g; Sugars 3.9g; Protein 9.1g

White Bean and Basil Salad

Prep time: 5 minutes | Cook time: 0 minutes | Serves: 2

¼ cup extra-virgin olive oil
¼ cup lemon juice, freshly squeezed
¼ cup chopped fresh basil
1 garlic clove, minced
2 large zucchini, shaved with a vegetable peeler
1 (15½-ounce) can white beans, drained and rinsed
¼ cup sliced scallions, both white and green parts
1 teaspoon salt
¼ teaspoon black pepper, freshly ground

1. In a suitable bowl, combine the oil, lemon juice, basil, and garlic. Use a spoon to mash the ingredients together to release the flavor in the basil and garlic. 2. Add the zucchini, beans, scallions, salt, and pepper and gently mix the ingredients, being careful to not mash the beans, and serve.
Per serving: Calories 309; Fat 13.5g; Sodium 610mg; Carbs 36.9g; Fiber 9.7g; Sugars 4.3g; Protein 14.1g

Italian Squash Soup

Prep time: 10 minutes | Cook time: 15 minutes | Serves: 4

3 tablespoons extra-virgin olive oil
1 small red onion, sliced
1 garlic clove, minced
1 cup shredded zucchini
1 cup shredded yellow squash
½ cup shredded carrot
3 cups vegetable broth
1 teaspoon salt
2 tablespoons chopped fresh basil
1 tablespoon chopped fresh chives
2 tablespoons pine nuts

1. In a suitable pot, heat the oil over high heat. Add the onion and garlic and sauté until softened, 5 to 7 minutes. 2. Add the zucchini, yellow squash, and carrot and sauté until softened, 1 to 2 minutes. Add the broth and salt and bring to a boil. 3. Reduce its heat to a simmer and cook until the vegetables are soft, 1 to 2 minutes. 4. Stir in the basil and chives and serve, sprinkled with the pine nuts.
Per serving: Calories 173; Fat 14.6g; Sodium 1167mg; Carbs 7g; Fiber 2g; Sugars 3.1g; Protein 5.5g

Lentil Spinach Salad

Prep time: 15 minutes | Cook time: 20 minutes | Serves: 2

2 cups peeled butternut squash, cut into 1-inch dice
¼ cup olive oil
1 teaspoon salt
1 (15-ounce) can cooked lentils, drained and rinsed
4 cups baby spinach
¼ cup chopped red onion
¼ cup chopped walnuts
2 tablespoons lemon juice, freshly squeezed
1 tablespoon chopped fresh sage
¼ teaspoon black pepper, freshly ground

1. At 400 degrees F, preheat your oven. 2. In a 9-by-13-inch baking dish, toss together the squash, oil, and ½ teaspoon of salt. 3. Transfer the casserole dish to the oven and roast until the squash is tender, for almost 20 minutes. 4. Remove from the oven; if serving cold, let cool before continuing with the recipe. 5. Add the lentils, spinach, onion, walnuts, lemon juice, sage, remaining ½ teaspoon of salt, and the pepper, mix well, and serve.
Per serving: Calories 394; Fat 13.1g; Sodium 642mg; Carbs 53.3g; Fiber 23.6g; Sugars 1.9g; Protein 21g

Smoked Salmon Salad with Cucumber

Prep time: 15 minutes | Cook time: 0 minutes | Serves: 4

1 cup plain coconut milk yogurt
1 tablespoon chopped fresh chives
1 teaspoon Dijon mustard
½ teaspoon salt
¼ teaspoon black pepper
4 cups romaine hearts cut across
into 1-inch ribbons
1 cup sliced English cucumber
¼ cup sliced red onion
1 ripe avocado, pitted, peeled, and sliced
8 ounces smoked salmon, sliced

1. To make the dressing, in a suitable bowl, whisk together the yogurt, chives, mustard, salt, and pepper until smooth. 2. Add the romaine, cucumber, and onion and mix until the salad is well coated with the dressing. 3. Arrange the avocado and smoked salmon on top of the greens and serve.
Per serving: Calories 200; Fat 13.4g; Sodium 1472mg; Carbs 9.7g; Fiber 5.8g; Sugars 1.3g; Protein 12.7g

Pumpkin Soup with Fried Sage

Prep time: 10 minutes | Cook time: 10 minutes | Serves: 4

4 tablespoons extra-virgin olive oil	4 cups vegetable broth
1 onion, chopped	2 teaspoons chipotle powder
2 garlic cloves, cut into ⅛-inch-thick slices	1 teaspoon salt
	½ teaspoon black pepper
1 (15-ounce) can pumpkin purée	½ cup vegetable oil
	12 sage leaves, stemmed

1. In a large, heavy Dutch over high heat, add olive oil, onion, and garlic. Sauté for almost 5 minutes, or until the vegetables turn golden. 2. Stir in vegetable broth, pumpkin, chipotle powder, salt, and pepper. Cook to a boil then reduce its heat to simmer and cook for 5 minutes. 3. While the soup is simmering, place a suitable sauté pan over high heat. Add the vegetable oil and heat until warm. Move each sage leaf into the oil and cook for almost 1 minute. 4. With a slotted spoon transfer the sage to paper towels to drain. Once cool, discard the vegetable oil. 5. Ladle the soup into bowls and garnish each serving with 3 fried sage leaves.
Per serving: Calories: 350; Total fat 34.4g; Sodium 1079mg; Total carbs 7.8g; Fiber 2.3g; Sugars 3.1g; Protein 4.9g

Salmon Soup

Prep time: 10 minutes | Cook time: 20 minutes | Serves: 4

¼ cup olive oil	ground
2 leeks, white parts only, sliced	¼ teaspoon saffron threads
2 medium carrots, sliced	2 cups baby spinach
2 garlic cloves, sliced	½ cup dry white wine
4 cups vegetable broth	2 tablespoons chopped scallions,
1 pound salmon fillets, skinless, cut into 1-inch pieces	both white and green parts
1 teaspoon salt	2 tablespoons chopped fresh flat-leaf parsley
¼ teaspoon black pepper, freshly	

1. In a suitable pot, heat the oil over high heat. 2. Add the leeks, carrots, and garlic and sauté until softened, 5 to 7 minutes. Add the broth and bring to a boil. 3. Reduce its heat to a simmer and add the salmon, salt, pepper, and saffron. Cook until the salmon is cooked through, about 8 minutes. 4. Add the spinach, wine, scallions, and parsley and cook until the spinach has wilted, 1 to 2 minutes, and serve.
Per serving: Calories 217; Fat 14.2g; Sodium 1388mg; Carbs 12.2g; Fiber 1.9g; Sugars 5.8g; Protein 29.3g

Turmeric Chicken Salad

Prep time: 15 minutes | Cook time: 20 minutes | Serves: 4

4 boneless skinless chicken breasts	¼ teaspoon black pepper
1 tablespoon extra-virgin olive oil	½ cup plain unsweetened almond yogurt
1 tablespoon chopped fresh cilantro	1 tablespoon lemon juice
1 garlic clove, minced	1 teaspoon lemon zest
1 teaspoon salt	½ cup chopped almonds
¼ teaspoon ground turmeric	6 cups chopped romaine lettuce

1. In a shallow baking dish, place the chicken breast. 2. In a suitable bowl, whisk together the olive oil, cilantro, garlic, salt, turmeric, and pepper. Rub the mixture all over the chicken. 3. Cover the chicken and marinate, refrigerated, for at least 30 minutes, or overnight. 4. At 375 degrees F, preheat your oven. Set the baking dish in the preheated oven and bake the chicken for 20 minutes. Remove from the oven and set aside. 5. In a suitable bowl, whisk together the yogurt, lemon juice, and lemon zest. Add the almonds and romaine lettuce and toss to coat the lettuce with the dressing. 6. Transfer the salad to a serving platter. Slice the chicken breasts into strips and arrange them over lettuce.
Per serving: Calories: 393; Total fat 20g; Sodium 718mg; Total carbs 8g; Fiber 2.2g; Sugars 3.2g; Protein 44.1g

Lentil and Vegetable Salad

Prep time: 20 minutes | Cook time: 0 minutes | Serves: 4 to 6

1 cup red lentils	1 (15-ounce) can lentils, drained and rinsed
2 cups water	
4 cups cooked brown rice	
Chicken Lettuce Wraps Sauce	
1 head radicchio, cored and torn into pieces	2 red bartlett (or other) ripe pears, cored, quartered, and sliced
1 small jicama, peeled and cut into thin sticks	2 scallions, sliced

1. In a suitable bowl, combine the red lentils and the water. Cover and refrigerate overnight. Drain the lentils when ready to prepare the salad. 2. In a suitable bowl, combine the brown rice and canned lentils. Stir in half of the chicken lettuce wraps sauce. 3. Let the mixture stand for at least 30 minutes or overnight. 4. Divide the lentil-rice mixture among serving bowls. Top each bowl with equal amounts of the soaked and drained red lentils. 5. Garnish each serving with the radicchio, jicama, pears, and scallions. Drizzle each with some of the remaining chicken lettuce wraps sauce.
Per serving: Calories: 562; Total fat 2.9g; Sodium 19mg; Total carbs 114.7g; Fiber 18.4g; Sugars 8.2g; Protein 19.9g

Kale White Bean Soup

Prep time: 15 minutes | Cook time: 25 minutes | Serves: 4

¼ cup olive oil	3 cups stemmed kale leaves, cut into ½-inch pieces
1 large onion, sliced	
2 garlic cloves, sliced	4 cups vegetable broth
1 teaspoon salt	1 (15½-ounce) can white beans, drained and rinsed
¼ teaspoon black pepper, freshly ground	
⅛ teaspoon red pepper flakes	1 teaspoon chopped fresh rosemary

1. In a suitable pot, heat the oil over high heat. 2. Reduce its heat to medium, and add the onion, garlic, salt, pepper, and red pepper flakes. Sauté until the onion is golden, about 10 minutes. 3. Add the kale, and sauté until wilted, 1 to 2 minutes. Add the broth and bring to a boil. 4. Reduce its heat to simmer, and cook until the kale is soft, about 5 minutes. 5. Add the beans and rosemary. Cook until the beans are warmed through, 2 to 3 minutes, and serve. 6. Tips: this soup can also be made with Swiss chard or spinach instead of kale. Store, covered, in the refrigerator for up to a week, or freeze for several months.
Per serving: Calories 237; Fat 14.2g; Sodium 1371mg; Carbs 19g; Fiber 3.9g; Sugars 2.6g; Protein 10.2g

Chickpea Apple Soup

Prep time: 10 minutes | Cook time: 25 minutes | Serves: 4

¼ cup extra-virgin olive oil or coconut oil	3 cups peeled butternut squash, cut into ½-inch dice
1 medium onion, chopped	3 cups vegetable broth
2 garlic cloves, sliced	1 cup full-fat coconut milk, unsweetened
1 large Granny Smith apple, cored, peeled, and cut into ¼-inch dice	1 (15-ounce) can chickpeas, drained and rinsed
2 teaspoons curry powder	2 tablespoons chopped fresh cilantro
1 teaspoon salt	

1. In a suitable pot, heat the oil over high heat. 2. Add the onion and garlic and sauté until the onion begins to brown, 6 to 8 minutes. Add the apple, curry powder, and salt and sauté to toast the curry powder, 1 to 2 minutes. 3. Add the squash and broth and bring to a boil. 4. Reduce its heat to a simmer and cook until the squash is tender, about 10 minutes. Stir in the coconut milk. 5. Using an immersion blender, purée the soup in the pot until smooth. Stir in the chickpeas and cilantro, heat through for almost 1 to 2 minutes, and serve.
Per serving: Calories 447; Fat 16.7g; Sodium 1143mg; Carbs 64.5g; Fiber 15.2g; Sugars 12.6g; Protein 18g

Chickpea Salad

Prep time: 15 minutes | Cook time: 20 minutes | Serves: 4

- 1 small acorn squash, seeded and sliced
- 1 cup sliced carrots
- ½ cup sliced parsnips
- ½ small red onion, sliced
- 3 tablespoons extra-virgin olive oil
- 1 garlic clove, minced
- 1 teaspoon salt
- ¼ teaspoon black pepper, freshly ground
- 1 (15-ounce) can chickpeas, drained and rinsed
- 2 cups baby arugula
- 1 tablespoon apple cider vinegar

1. At 400 degrees F, preheat your oven. 2. In a 9-by-13-inch casserole dish, toss together the squash, carrots, parsnips, onion, oil, garlic, salt, and pepper until well mixed. 3. Transfer the dish to the oven, and roast until the vegetables are golden brown and tender, 15 to 20 minutes. 4. Remove from the oven and let cool to room temperature. 5. Add the chickpeas, arugula, and vinegar, toss to combine, and serve.

Per serving: Calories 349; Fat 11.4g; Sodium 421mg; Carbs 50.2g; Fiber 13.9g; Sugars 9.4g; Protein 14.4g

Shiitake Miso Soup

Prep time: 10 minutes | Cook time: 45 minutes | Serves: 4

- 2 tablespoons sesame oil
- cup sliced shiitake mushroom caps
- garlic clove, minced
- (1½-inch) piece fresh ginger, peeled and sliced
- 1 cup medium-grain brown rice
- ½ teaspoon salt
- 1 tablespoon white miso
- 2 scallions, both white and green parts, sliced
- 2 tablespoons chopped fresh cilantro

1. In a suitable pot, heat the oil over medium-high heat. 2. Add the mushrooms, garlic, and ginger and sauté until the mushrooms begin to soften, about 5 minutes. 3. Add the rice and stir to evenly coat with the oil. Add 2 cups of water and salt and bring to a boil. 4. Reduce its heat to a simmer and cook until the rice is tender, 30 to 40 minutes. 5. Use a little of the soup broth to soften the miso, then stir it into the pot until well blended. 6. Stir in the scallions and cilantro and serve.

Per serving: Calories 130; Fat 7.4g; Sodium 454mg; Carbs 15.2g; Fiber 1.5g; Sugars 1.8g; Protein 2g

Brussels Sprout Slaw

Prep time: 10 minutes | Cook time: 25 minutes | Serves: 4

- cup quinoa
- teaspoon salt
- 2 ounces Brussels sprouts, trimmed and sliced
- ¼ cup chopped red onion
- ¼ cup extra-virgin olive oil
- 1 tablespoon apple cider vinegar
- 1 cup blueberries
- 1 teaspoon chopped fresh sage
- ¼ cup toasted sliced almonds

1. In a suitable pot, combine the quinoa, 2 cups of water, and salt. Bring to a boil. 2. Reduce its heat to a simmer, and cook, partially covered, until all the water has been absorbed, for almost 20 minutes. 3. Remove from the heat. Add the Brussels sprouts and onion to the warm quinoa (this will slightly soften the vegetables). Let cool to room temperature. 4. Add the oil, vinegar, blueberries, sage, and almonds. Toss to combine, and serve at room temperature, or chill for several hours to serve cold.

Per serving: Calories 361; Fat 18.6g; Sodium 606mg; Carbs 42.3g; Fiber 8g; Sugars 6g; Protein 10.5g

Sweet Potato Salad

Prep time: 10 minutes | Cook time: 20 minutes | Serves: 4

- cups peeled sweet potatoes cut into ½-inch dice
- ½ small red onion, chopped
- ¼ cup extra-virgin olive oil
- teaspoon chipotle chile powder
- teaspoon salt
- ¼ teaspoon black pepper, freshly ground
- 2 cups shredded red cabbage
- 1 (15-ounce) can black beans, drained and rinsed
- 2 tablespoons chopped fresh cilantro
- 1 tablespoon apple cider vinegar

1. At 400 degrees F, preheat your oven. 2. In a 9-by-13-inch baking dish, toss together the sweet potatoes, onion, oil, chile powder, salt, and pepper until well mixed. 3. Transfer the dish to the oven and roast until the sweet potatoes are tender and lightly browned, about 20 minutes. 4. Remove from the oven and let cool to room temperature. 5. Add the cabbage, beans, cilantro, and vinegar, toss to combine, and serve.

Per serving: Calories 389; Fat 9.4g; Sodium 443mg; Carbs 61.5g; Fiber 14.2g; Sugars 7.2g; Protein 17g

Cauliflower Soup

Prep time: 10 minutes | Cook time: 15 minutes | Serves: 4

- 2 tablespoons extra-virgin olive oil or coconut oil
- 1 leek, white part only, sliced
- 3 cups cauliflower florets
- 1 garlic clove, peeled
- 1 (1¼-inch) piece fresh ginger, peeled and sliced
- 1½ teaspoons turmeric
- ½ teaspoon salt
- ¼ teaspoon black pepper, freshly ground
- ¼ teaspoon ground cumin
- 3 cups vegetable broth
- 1 cup full-fat coconut milk, unsweetened
- ¼ cup chopped fresh cilantro

1. In a suitable pot, heat the oil over high heat. 2. Add the leek, and sauté until it just begins to brown, 3 to 4 minutes. 3. Add the cauliflower, garlic, ginger, turmeric, salt, pepper, and cumin and sauté to lightly toast the spices, 1 to 2 minutes. 4. Add the broth and bring to a boil. Reduce its heat to a simmer and cook until the cauliflower is tender, about 5 minutes. 5. Using an immersion blender, purée the soup in the pot until smooth. Stir in the coconut milk and cilantro, heat through, and serve.

Per serving: Calories 431; Fat 42.9g; Sodium 236mg; Carbs 13.9g; Fiber 5.1g; Sugars 7.2g; Protein 5g

Greens Soup

Prep time: 10 minutes | Cook time: 20 minutes | Serves: 4

- ¼ cup extra-virgin olive oil
- 2 leeks, white parts only, sliced
- 1 fennel bulb, trimmed and sliced
- 1 garlic clove, peeled
- 1 bunch Swiss chard, chopped
- 4 cups chopped kale
- 4 cups chopped mustard greens
- 3 cups vegetable broth
- 2 tablespoons apple cider vinegar
- 1 teaspoon salt
- ¼ teaspoon black pepper, freshly ground
- ¼ cup chopped cashews

1. In a suitable pot, heat the oil over high heat. Add the leeks, fennel, and garlic and sauté until softened, for almost 5 minutes. 2. Add the Swiss chard, kale, and mustard greens and sauté until the greens wilt, 2 to 3 minutes. Add the broth and bring to a boil. 3. Reduce its heat to a simmer and cook until the vegetables are completely soft and tender, about 5 minutes. 4. Stir in the vinegar, salt, pepper, and cashews. 5. Using an immersion blender, purée the soup in the pot until smooth and serve.

Per serving: Calories 326; Fat 17.9g; Sodium 1274mg; Carbs 20.7g; Fiber 9g; Sugars 8.8g; Protein 9.7g

Lentil Soup

Prep time: 15 minutes | Cook time: 15 minutes | Serves: 4

- 2 tablespoons extra-virgin olive oil
- 2 medium carrots, sliced
- 1 small white onion, cut into ¼-inch dice
- 2 garlic cloves, sliced
- 1 teaspoon ground cinnamon
- 1 teaspoon salt
- ¼ teaspoon black pepper, freshly ground
- 3 cups vegetable broth
- 1 (15-ounce) can lentils, drained and rinsed
- 1 tablespoon minced or grated orange zest
- ¼ cup chopped walnuts
- 2 tablespoons chopped fresh flat-leaf parsley

1. In a suitable pot, heat the oil over high heat. 2. Add the carrots, onion, and garlic and sauté until softened, 5 to 7 minutes. 3. Add the cinnamon, salt, and pepper and stir to evenly layer the vegetables, 1 to 2 minutes. Add the broth and bring to a boil. 4. Reduce its heat to a simmer, add the lentils, and cook until they are heated through, about 1 minute. 5. Stir in the orange zest and serve, sprinkled with the walnuts and parsley.

Per serving: Calories 359; Fat 9.2g; Sodium 789mg; Carbs 47.7g; Fiber 23.1g; Sugars 3.4g; Protein 22.4g

Roasted Cauliflower Chickpea Salad

Prep time: 15 minutes | Cook time: 15 minutes | Serves: 2

2 cups cauliflower florets
¼ cup melted coconut oil or extra-virgin olive oil
1½ teaspoons curry powder
1 teaspoon salt
3 cups romaine lettuce, cut across into 1-inch ribbons
1 (15-ounce) can chickpeas,
drained and rinsed
2 tablespoons lime juice, freshly squeezed
2 tablespoons chopped fresh cilantro
1 tablespoon extra-virgin olive oil
¼ teaspoon black pepper, freshly ground

1. At 400 degrees F, preheat your oven. 2. In a 9-by-13-inch baking dish, toss together the cauliflower, coconut oil, curry powder, and salt until well mixed. 3. Transfer the dish to the oven, and roast until tender, for almost 15 minutes. Remove from the oven and let cool to room temperature. 4. Add the lettuce, chickpeas, lime juice, cilantro, olive oil, and pepper, toss to combine, and serve.
Per serving: Calories 350; Fat 13g; Sodium 416mg; Carbs 46.9g; Fiber 14.3g; Sugars 8.9g; Protein 15.1g

Pear Soup

Prep time: 15 minutes | Cook time: 20 minutes | Serves: 4

2 tablespoons extra-virgin olive oil
4 pears, cored and cut into ½-inch dice
2 fennel bulbs, trimmed and cut into ½-inch dice
2 shallots, halved
4 cups vegetable broth
¼ cup lemon juice, freshly squeezed
¼ cup honey
1 teaspoon salt
¼ teaspoon black pepper, freshly ground
⅛ teaspoon ground nutmeg
1 teaspoon chopped fresh tarragon

1. In a suitable pot, heat the oil over high heat. 2. Add the pears, fennel, and shallots, and sauté until the pears and fennel just begin to brown, about 5 minutes. 3. Add the broth, and bring to a boil. 4. Reduce its heat to a simmer, and cook, while stirring occasionally, until the fennel is tender, 5 to 8 minutes. Stir in the lemon juice, honey, salt, pepper, and nutmeg. 5. Using an immersion blender, purée the soup in the pot until smooth. Sprinkle with the tarragon and serve.
Per serving: Calories 324; Fat 9g; Sodium 1412mg; Carbs 59.2g; Fiber 10.3g; Sugars 38.8g; Protein 7.3g

Sweet Potato Corn Soup

Prep time: 10 minutes | Cook time: 20 minutes | Serves: 4

¼ cup extra-virgin olive oil or coconut oil
1 medium zucchini, cut into ¼-inch dice
1 cup broccoli florets
1 cup sliced mushrooms
1 small onion, cut into ¼-inch dice
4 cups vegetable broth
2 cups peeled sweet potatoes, cut into ¼-inch dice
1 cup frozen corn kernels
1 cup coconut milk or almond milk, unsweetened
2 tablespoons chopped fresh flat-leaf parsley
1 teaspoon salt
¼ teaspoon black pepper

1. In a suitable pot, heat the oil over high heat. 2. Add the zucchini, broccoli, mushrooms, and onion and sauté until softened, 5 to 8 minutes. Add the broth and sweet potatoes and bring to a boil. 3. Reduce its heat to a simmer and cook until the sweet potatoes are tender, 5 to 7 minutes. 4. Add the corn, coconut milk, parsley, salt, and pepper. Cook over low heat until the corn is heated through and serve.
Per serving: Calories 395; Fat 28.8g; Sodium 1404mg; Carbs 29.2g; Fiber 6.1g; Sugars 9.8g; Protein 10.3g

Chicken Noodle Soup

Prep time: 10 minutes | Cook time: 25 minutes | Serves: 4

¼ cup extra-virgin olive oil
3 celery stalks, cut into ¼-inch slices
2 medium carrots, cut into ¼-inch dice
1 small onion, cut into ¼-inch dice
1 fresh rosemary sprig
4 cups chicken broth
8 ounces gluten-free penne
1 teaspoon salt
¼ teaspoon black pepper, freshly ground
2 cups diced rotisserie chicken
¼ cup chopped fresh flat-leaf parsley

1. In a suitable pot, heat the oil over high heat. 2. Add the celery, carrots, onion, and rosemary and sauté until softened, 5 to 7 minutes. Add the broth, penne, salt, and pepper and bring to a boil. 3. Reduce its heat to a simmer and cook until the penne is tender, 8 to 10 minutes. 4. Remove and discard the rosemary sprig, and add the chicken and parsley. 5. Reduce its heat to low. Cook until the chicken is warmed through, about 5 minutes, and serve.
Per serving: Calories 302; Fat 14.7g; Sodium 1642mg; Carbs 19.2g; Fiber 1.7g; Sugars 3.1g; Protein 24g

Chapter 3 Snacks and Sides

Butternut Squash Mash

Prep time: 15 minutes | Cook time: 30 minutes | Serves: 4

3 cups cubed butternut squash
1 cup coarsely chopped carrot
1 large green apple, peeled, cored, and chopped
3 tablespoons olive oil, extra-

virgin
1 teaspoon salt
¼ teaspoon black pepper, freshly ground
½ cup unsweetened almond milk

1. At 375 degrees F, preheat your oven. 2. Mix the squash, carrot, and apple in a suitable bowl. Add the oil, salt, and pepper and toss to mix well. 3. Transfer the vegetables to a suitable rimmed baking sheet and roast until the vegetables are tender and lightly browned, 20 to 30 minutes. 4. Return the vegetables to the bowl. 5. Using a potato masher, mash the cook vegetables, then add the milk and stir until mostly smooth. (The mixture will be slightly lumpy.) Serve.
Per Serving: Calories 195; Total Fat 12.7g; Sodium 1131mg; Total Carbs 27.7g; Fiber 3.5g; Sugars 5.9g; Protein 2.1g

Cabbage Slaw

Prep time: 15 minutes | Cook time: 0 minutes | Serves: 6

Salad:
2 carrots, grated
1 large head green or red cabbage,
Dressing:
1 cup cashews, soaked in water for at least 4 hours, drained
¼ cup freshly squeezed lemon

sliced thin

juice
¾ teaspoon sea salt
½ cup water

1. Mix the carrots and cabbage in a suitable serving bowl. Toss to combine well. 2. Put the ingredients for the prepared dressing in a suitable food processor, then pulse until creamy and smooth. 3. Dress the salad, then refrigerate for at least 1 hour before serving.
Per Serving: Calories 194; Total Fat 10.9g; Sodium 292mg; Total Carbs 21.7g; Fiber 6.4g; Sugars 9g; Protein 6.4g

Green Beans with Shallots

Prep time: 10 minutes | Cook time: 10 minutes | Serves: 4

1 pound green beans, trimmed
1 teaspoon sea salt
2 tablespoons olive oil, extra-virgin

1 large shallot, sliced thin
1 tablespoon chopped fresh tarragon
black pepper, to taste

1. Put the green beans in a pot, then pour in enough water to cover. Sprinkle with 1 teaspoon of salt. Cook to a boil. 2. Lower its heat to low and simmer for almost 5 minutes or until the beans are tender. 3. Pat the beans dry and place them on a plate. Set aside. 4. Heat the olive oil in a suitable nonstick skillet over medium heat until shimmering. 5. Add the shallots and sauté for almost 3 minutes or until lightly browned.
Top the green beans with the cooked shallots, then sprinkle with tarragon, salt, and black pepper. Serve.
Per Serving: Calories 98; Total Fat 7.2g; Sodium 475mg; Total Carbs 8.7g; Fiber 3.9g; Sugars 1.6g; Protein 2.2g

Cabbage Salad with Quinoa

Prep time: 7 minutes | Cook time: 2 minutes | Serves: 8

½ cup dry quinoa
1 (10-ounce) bag frozen shelled edamame
1 cup vegetable broth
¼ cup reduced-sodium tamari
¼ cup natural almond butter

3 tablespoons toasted sesame seed oil
½ teaspoon pure stevia powder
1 head purple cabbage, cored and chopped

1. Place the quinoa, edamame, and broth in the inner pot of your Instant Pot® and seal the cooker's lid. Select the Manual or Pressure mode and adjust the time to 2 minutes. 2. Meanwhile, in a suitable bowl, mix the tamari, almond butter, sesame seed oil, and stevia. Set aside. 3. Once the timer beeps, quick-release the pressure then unlock lid and remove it. 4. Use any fork to fluff the quinoa, and then transfer the mixture to a suitable bowl. Allow the quinoa and edamame to cool, and then add the purple cabbage to the bowl and toss. 5. Stir in the prepared dressing and toss again until everything is evenly coated. Serve.
Per Serving: Calories 176; Total Fat 9.6g; Sodium 122mg; Total Carbs 15.7g; Fiber 4.5g; Sugars 3.8g; Protein 7.8g

Cauliflower with Almond Sauce

Prep time: 10 minutes | Cook time: 20 minutes | Serves: 4

1 head cauliflower, cut into florets
2 tablespoons olive oil, extra-virgin
Almond Sauce:
1 cup plain unsweetened almond yogurt
1 scallion, sliced
1 tablespoon chopped fresh parsley

1½ teaspoons sea salt
½ teaspoon ground turmeric
½ teaspoon black pepper

¼ cup almond butter
1 garlic clove, minced
1 tablespoon freshly squeezed lemon juice
1 tablespoon pure maple syrup

1. At 400 degrees F, preheat your oven. 2. Put the cauliflower in a suitable bowl, then drizzle with olive oil and sprinkle with 1 teaspoon of salt, turmeric, and ¼ teaspoon of ground black pepper. 3. Arrange the well-coated cauliflower in the single layer on a baking sheet. 4. Put the prepared sheet in the preheated oven and roast for almost 20 minutes or until golden brown. 5. Meanwhile, put the yogurt, scallion, parsley, almond butter, garlic, lemon juice, maple syrup, and remaining salt and pepper in a suitable blender. Pulse to purée until smooth. 6. Transfer the roasted cauliflower on a plate, then baste with the almond sauce and serve.
Per Serving: Calories 171; Total Fat 10g; Sodium 2629mg; Total Carbs 18.6g; Fiber 2.6g; Sugars 13.8g; Protein 4.3g

Cinnamon Applesauce with Lemon Juice

Prep time: 10 minutes | Cook time: 5 minutes | Serves: 12

4 pounds apples, cored and cut into pieces
¼ cup water

2 teaspoons lemon juice
2 teaspoons ground cinnamon

1. Place the apples, water, lemon juice, and cinnamon in the Instant Pot®. Stir to combine. Seal the cooker's lid. 2. Select the Manual or Pressure mode and set time to 5 minutes almost. 3. Once the timer beeps, release the pressure naturally, then unlock lid. 4. Transfer the apples to a suitable blender and blend on high until desired consistency is achieved. 5. Serve cool or store in airtight containers in refrigerator for up to 10 days or a freezer for up to two months.
Per Serving: Calories 42; Total Fat 0g; Sodium 1mg; Total Carbs 10.6g; Fiber 2g; Sugars 7.8g; Protein 0.2g

Raisin Granola Bars

Prep time: 10 minutes | Cook time: 10 minutes | Serves: 10

2 cups quick-cooking oats
⅓ cup date syrup
⅓ cup avocado oil
⅓ cup monk fruit sweetener

⅓ cup almond butter
⅓ cup raisins
½ teaspoon ground cinnamon

1. In a suitable bowl, mix the oats, date syrup, oil, sweetener, almond butter, raisins, and cinnamon. 2. Spray a suitable 5" baking dish with cooking spray. Press the oat mixture firmly into the pan. 3. Add 1 cup water to the inner insert and place the steam rack inside. Place the baking dish on top of the steam rack. Seal the cooker's lid. 4. Select the Manual or Pressure mode and adjust the time to 10 minutes. 5. Once the timer beeps, quick-release the pressure and then unlock lid carefully. 6. Remove this pan from the inner pot and place it on a baking rack to cool completely. Once completely cooled, turn the pan upside down onto a cutting board to remove the granola from the pan. Cut into ten bars.
Per Serving: Calories 120; Total Fat 2.3g; Sodium 2mg; Total Carbs 24.1g; Fiber 2.3g; Sugars 10g; Protein 3.6g

Steamed Broccoli

Prep time: 5 minutes | Cook time: 1 minute | Serves: 6

6 cups broccoli florets

1. Pour 1½ cups water into the inner insert of the Instant Pot®. Place a steam rack inside. 2. Place the broccoli florets inside a steamer basket and place the basket on the steam rack. 3. Hit the Steam button and adjust the time to 1 minute. 4. Once the timer beeps, quick-release the pressure then unlock lid and remove it. 5. Remove the steamer basket and serve.
Per Serving: Calories 31; Total Fat 0.3g; Sodium 30mg; Total Carbs 6g; Fiber 2.4g; Sugars 1.6g; Protein 2.6g

Black Beans Lentil Balls

Prep time: 10 minutes | Cook time: 13 minutes | Serves: 4

For the Lentil Balls

⅓ cup cooked black beans, rinsed and drained
½ cup old-fashioned rolled oats
1¼ cups cooked lentils
¼ cup unsweetened almond milk
¼ teaspoon coarse salt

¼ teaspoon ground ginger
⅛ teaspoon garlic powder
⅛ teaspoon black pepper
2 tablespoons avocado oil
2 tablespoons oat flour

For the Sauce

¾ cup tomato sauce
1 tablespoon tomato paste
¼ cup maple syrup
2 tablespoons coconut aminos

1 tablespoon apple cider vinegar
½ teaspoon ground ginger
¼ teaspoon crushed red pepper flakes

1. In a suitable bowl partially mash the black beans. 2. In a suitable food processor, pulse the oats a few times. Add the lentils and pulse again. Add the milk, salt, ginger, garlic powder, and pepper and pulse. Do not over mix. 3. Mix the lentil mixture and black beans, stirring well. Form into tablespoon-sized balls and refrigerate 30 minutes. 4. Mix all of the sauce recipe ingredients together in a suitable bowl. 5. Hit the Sauté button, then adjust button to change setting to More. Add the avocado oil to the inner insert. Allow it to heat 2 minutes. 6. Place the oat flour in a shallow bowl and dredge each lentil ball in the flour to coat it. 7. Add the lentil balls to the oil and move them around to brown, almost 1 minute per side. Press the Cancel button. 8. Remove the balls and place them inside a 6" cake pan. Cover with the sauce and a paper towel, then cover tightly with foil. 9. Add ½ cup water to inner pot and scrape up any brown bits from the bottom. Place the steam rack in the pot and the pan of lentil balls on top of it. Seal the cooker's lid. 10. Select the Manual or Pressure mode and adjust the time to 5 minutes. 11. Once the timer beeps, quick-release the pressure and unlock its lid. 12. Remove the pan and serve.
Per Serving: Calories 666; Total Fat 3.5g; Sodium 198mg; Total Carbs 118.5g; Fiber 44.1g; Sugars 15.4g; Protein 39g

Grilled Flatbread

Prep time: 15 minutes | Cook time: 20 minutes | Serves: 8

2 cups whole-wheat flour
1 cup all-purpose flour plus up to ½ cup for dusting and kneading
1½ teaspoons instant yeast
¾ teaspoon salt

1¼ cups warm water
3 tablespoons extra-virgin olive oil
½ teaspoon sea salt
1 teaspoon dried oregano

1. In a suitable bowl, combine flours, yeast, and salt. 2. Add 1¼ cups water and mix well. If needed add 1 tablespoon water at a time until all flour has been absorbed. 3. Then, with clean, well-floured hands, lightly knead dough to bring it together into a ball. Place dough in a suitable bowl oiled with 1 teaspoon oil. Cover and put in a warm place. Let it rise 1 hour. 4. Transfer risen dough to a cutting board that is well dusted with flour. Knead a couple of times to bring it into a ball. 5. Cut dough in half, then into four pieces, then eight. Roll each piece into a small ball. 6. Sprinkle a baking sheet with flour and transfer dough balls to it. Put in a warm place for almost 15–30 minutes. 7. Working one ball at a time on a well-floured base, roll balls with a rolling pin until dough is stretched to a (rough) circle about 8" in diameter. 8. Heat a medium cast iron pan over medium-high heat. Don't oil it. Once pan is very hot, transfer one flatbread to it. Flip it after 2–3 minutes. 9. Cook on other side 2–3 minutes. Repeat with remaining flatbreads. 10. Once out of this pan, brush flatbreads with remaining oil and sprinkle with sea salt and oregano. Serve hot!
Per serving: Calories 162; Fat 5.6g; Sodium 336mg; Carbs 24.3g; Fiber 1.1g; Sugars 0.1g; Protein 3.5g

Hard-Boiled Eggs

Prep time: 2 minutes | Cook time: 7 minutes | Serves: 6

6 large eggs

1. Pour 1 cup water into the inner insert of your Instant Pot® and place the steam rack inside. 2. Place the eggs directly onto the steam rack. 3. Hit the Steam button and adjust the time to 7 minutes. 4. Once the timer beeps, quick-release the pressure then unlock lid and remove it. 5. Immediately transfer the eggs to a suitable bowl filled with iced water and let them sit 15 minutes. 6. Remove the cooked eggs from the water and peel the shells away from the eggs. Store in the refrigerator.
Per Serving: Calories 72; Total Fat 5g; Sodium 70mg; Total Carbs 0.4g; Fiber 0g; Sugars 0.4g; Protein 6.3g

Almond Butter Chocolate Granola Bars

Prep time: 10 minutes | Cook time: 10 minutes | Serves: 10

2 cups quick-cooking oats
⅔ cup almond butter
⅓ cup avocado oil
⅓ cup monk fruit sweetener

⅓ cup stevia-sweetened dark chocolate chips
¼ teaspoon salt

1. In a suitable bowl, mix the oats, almond butter, oil, sweetener, chocolate chips, and salt. 2. Spray a suitable 5" baking dish with cooking spray. Press the oat mixture firmly into the pan. 3. Add 1 cup water to the inner insert and place the steam rack inside. Place the baking dish on top of the steam rack. Seal the cooker's lid. 4. Select the Manual or Pressure mode and adjust the time to 10 minutes. 5. Once the timer beeps, quick-release the pressure then unlock lid and remove it. 6. Remove this pan from the inner insert and place it on a baking rack to cool completely. Once completely cooled, turn the pan upside down onto a cutting board to remove the granola from the pan. Cut into ten bars.
Per Serving: Calories 315; Total Fat 20g; Sodium 85mg; Total Carbs 27.5g; Fiber 5.2g; Sugars 2.3g; Protein 9g

Cinnamon Almonds

Prep time: 10 minutes | Cook time: 2 minutes | Serves: 8

2 cups raw unsalted almonds
1 teaspoon ground cinnamon
2 tablespoons water

40 drops pure liquid stevia
½ teaspoon pure vanilla extract
¼ teaspoon coarse salt

1. Place all the recipe ingredients into a 7-cup glass bowl and toss to combine. 2. Pour ½ cup hot water into the Instant Pot® and place the steam rack inside. Place the bowl with the almonds on top of the rack. Seal the cooker's lid. 3. Select the Manual or Pressure mode and adjust the time to 2 minutes. 4. Once the timer beeps, quick-release the pressure then unlock lid and remove it. Serve warm.
Per Serving: Calories 139; Total Fat 11.9g; Sodium 60mg; Total Carbs 5.4g; Fiber 3.1g; Sugars 1g; Protein 5g

Quinoa Almond Energy Balls

Prep time: 15 minutes | Cook time: 1 minute | Serves: 20 balls

½ cup quinoa
1 cup water
¼ cup almond butter
2 teaspoons raw honey

½ teaspoon ground cinnamon
½ teaspoon blackstrap molasses
⅛ teaspoon fine sea salt

1. Keep the quinoa in a fine-mesh strainer and rinse under water until the water runs clear. 2. Place the quinoa and water to the inner insert. Seal the cooker's lid. 3. Select the Manual or Pressure mode and adjust the time to 1 minute. 4. Once the timer beeps, quick-release the pressure then unlock lid and remove it. 5. Transfer the cooked quinoa to a suitable bowl and allow it to cool. Once it is cooled, add the rest of the ingredients to the bowl and stir to combine. 6. Form the quinoa mixture into 1" balls and place them onto a tray or plate. Place them in the freezer almost 30 minutes to firm. Keep stored in the refrigerator.
Per Serving (per ball): Calories 22; Total Fat 0.4g; Sodium 1mg; Total Carbs 3.5g; Fiber 0.4g; Sugars 0.7g; Protein 0.6g

Seasoned Spaghetti Squash

Prep time: 10 minutes | Cook time: 25 minutes | Serves: 4

1 medium spaghetti squash
2 tablespoons extra-virgin olive oil

⅛ teaspoon salt
⅛ teaspoon black pepper

1. Place 1½ cups water in the inner pot of your Instant Pot®. Place the steam rack inside. 2. Wash squash with soap and water and dry it. Place the whole uncut squash on top of the steam rack inside the inner pot. Seal the cooker's lid. 3. Select the Manual or Pressure mode and adjust the time to 25 minutes. 4. Once the timer beeps, quick-release the pressure then unlock lid and remove it. 5. Allow the cooked squash to cool, and then remove it from the pot. Use a sharp knife to cut the squash in half lengthwise. Spoon out the seeds and discard. 6. Use any fork to scrape out the squash strands into a suitable bowl. 7. Drizzle with the oil, add the salt and pepper, and serve.
Per Serving: Calories 136; Total Fat 14.3g; Sodium 9mg; Total Carbs 3.5g; Fiber 0g; Sugars 0g; Protein 0.3g

Buffalo Cauliflower Bites

Prep time: 10 minutes | Cook time: 2 minutes | Serves: 4

1 large cauliflower head, cut into large pieces
½ cup buffalo hot sauce

1. Pour almost a cup of water into the insert of the Instant Pot and place the steam rack inside. 2. Set the cauliflower in a glass bowl and stir in the buffalo hot sauce. 3. Mix to evenly coat. Place this bowl on top of the steam rack. Seal the cooker's lid. 4. Select the Manual or Pressure mode and adjust the time to 2 minutes. 5. Once the timer beeps, quick-release the pressure then unlock lid and remove it. 6. Serve.
Per Serving: Calories 84; Total Fat 0.2g; Sodium 453mg; Total Carbs 18.1g; Fiber 5.3g; Sugars 10g; Protein 4.2g

Garlic Green Beans

Prep time: 10 minutes | Cook time: 5 minutes | Serves: 4

12 ounces green beans, ends trimmed
4 cloves garlic, minced
1 tablespoon avocado oil
½ teaspoon salt
1 cup water

1. Place the green beans in a suitable bowl and toss with the garlic, oil, and salt. Transfer this mixture to the steamer basket. 2. Pour about a cup of water into the insert and place the steam rack inside. Place the steamer basket with the green beans on top of the steam rack. Seal the cooker's lid. 3. Select the Manual or Pressure mode and adjust the time to 5 minutes. 4. Once the timer beeps, quick-release the pressure then unlock lid and remove it. 5. Transfer to a suitable bowl for serving.
Per Serving: Calories 35; Total Fat 0.6g; Sodium 296mg; Total Carbs 7.3g; Fiber 3.1g; Sugars 1.2g; Protein 1.8g

Broccoli Bites

Prep time: 7 minutes | Cook time: 1 minute | Serves: 4

1 large crown broccoli, cut into large pieces
2 tablespoons toasted sesame oil
½ teaspoon salt
¼ teaspoon ground ginger
⅛ teaspoon garlic powder
2 tablespoons sesame seeds

1. Place the broccoli pieces into a 6" cake pan. 2. In a suitable bowl, mix the oil, salt, ginger, and garlic powder. Add it to the broccoli and toss to coat. 3. Add a cup of water into the Instant Pot® and place the steam rack inside. Set the pan with broccoli on top of the steam rack. Seal the cooker's lid. 4. Select the Manual or Pressure mode and adjust the time to 1 minute. 5. Once the timer beeps, quick-release the pressure then unlock lid and remove it. 6. Remove this pan from the inner insert. 7. Add the sesame seeds to the broccoli and toss to coat. 8. Transfer to a plate and serve with toothpicks.
Per Serving: Calories 187; Total Fat 18.3g; Sodium 596mg; Total Carbs 4.9g; Fiber 1.1g; Sugars 0g; Protein 3.1g

Avocado Deviled Eggs

Prep time: 15 minutes | Cook time: 7 minutes | Serves: 12

6 large eggs
1 medium avocado, peeled, pitted, and diced
2½ tablespoons mayonnaise
2 teaspoons lime juice
1 clove garlic, crushed
⅛ teaspoon cayenne pepper
⅛ teaspoon salt
1 medium jalapeño pepper, sliced
12 dashes hot sauce

1. Pour 1 cup water into the inner insert of your Instant Pot® and place the steam rack inside. 2. Place the eggs directly onto the steam rack. 3. Hit the Steam button and adjust the time to 7 minutes. 4. Once the timer beeps, quick-release the pressure then unlock lid and remove it. 5. Immediately transfer the eggs to a suitable bowl filled with iced water and let them sit 15 minutes. 6. Remove the cooked eggs from the water and peel the shells away from the eggs. Slice the eggs in half. 7. Scoop egg yolks into a suitable bowl and add the avocado, mayonnaise, lime juice, garlic, cayenne pepper, and salt. 8. Mash the egg yolk mixture until filling is evenly combined. 9. Spoon the filling into a piping bag and pipe filling into each egg white. Top each with a jalapeño slice and a dash of hot sauce.
Per Serving: Calories 122; Total Fat 10.1g; Sodium 143mg; Total Carbs 4.9g; Fiber 1.2g; Sugars 1.1g; Protein 3.6g

Boiled Cabbage

Prep time: 5 minutes | Cook time: 5 minutes | Serves: 6

1 green cabbage head, chopped
3 cups vegetable broth
1 teaspoon salt
½ teaspoon black pepper

1. Place the cabbage, broth, salt, and pepper in the inner pot. Seal the cooker's lid. 2. Select the Manual or Pressure mode and adjust the time to 5 minutes. 3. Once the timer beeps, quick-release the pressure then unlock lid and remove it. 4. Serve the cabbage with a little of the cooking liquid.
Per Serving: Calories 36; Total Fat 1g; Sodium 1159mg; Total Carbs 2.1g; Fiber 0.6g; Sugars 1.3g; Protein 3.9g

Steamed Cauliflower

Prep time: 5 minutes | Cook time: 2 minutes | Serves: 6

1 large head cauliflower, cored
and cut into large florets

1. Pour 2 cups water into the inner insert of the Instant Pot®. Place a steam rack inside. 2. Place the cauliflower florets inside a steamer basket and place the basket on the steam rack. 3. Hit the Steam button and adjust the time to 2 minutes. 4. Once the timer beeps, quick-release the pressure then unlock lid and remove it. 5. Remove the steamer basket and serve.
Per Serving: Calories 54; Total Fat 0.2g; Sodium 63mg; Total Carbs 11.1g; Fiber 5.3g; Sugars 5g; Protein 4.2g

Soy Edamame

Prep time: 10 minutes | Cook time: 1 minutes | Serves: 4

1 (10-ounce) bag frozen edamame in pods
2 tablespoons reduced-sodium
tamari
¼ teaspoon kosher salt

1. Pour almost a cup of water into the insert of Instant Pot and place a steam rack in the pot. 2. Place the edamame in a steamer basket and place basket on top of the steam rack. 3. Hit the "Steam" button and adjust the time to 1 minute. 4. Once the timer beeps, quick-release the pressure then unlock lid and remove it. 5. Transfer the edamame to a suitable bowl and top with the tamari and salt and serve.
Per Serving: Calories 60; Total Fat 2.4g; Sodium 293mg; Total Carbs 5g; Fiber 2.5g; Sugars 0.5g; Protein 6.5g

Baked Sweet Potatoes

Prep time: 10 minutes | Cook time: 18 minutes | Serves: 4

4 medium sweet potatoes
2 tablespoons coconut oil
½ teaspoon ground cinnamon

1. Pour 1½ cups water into the Instant Pot® and place the steam rack inside. 2. Place the sweet potatoes on the rack. It's okay if they overlap. Seal the cooker's lid. 3. Select the Manual or Pressure mode and adjust the time to 18 minutes. 4. Once the timer beeps, quick-release the pressure then unlock lid and remove it. 5. Remove the cooked sweet potatoes from the Instant pot. Use a knife to cut each sweet potato lengthwise and open the potato slightly. Add ½ tablespoon coconut oil and ⅛ teaspoon cinnamon to each potato and serve.
Per Serving: Calories 236; Total Fat 8.1g; Sodium 14mg; Total Carbs 42.1g; Fiber 6.3g; Sugars 0.8g; Protein 2.3g

Steamed Asparagus

Prep time: 10 minutes | Cook time: 0 minutes | Serves: 4

1 pound asparagus, woody ends removed
Juice from ½ large lemon
¼ teaspoon kosher salt

1. Add ½ cup water to the inner insert and add the steam rack. Add the asparagus to the steamer basket and place the basket on top of the rack. 2. Hit the Steam button and adjust the time to 0 minutes. 3. Once the timer beeps, quick-release the pressure then unlock lid and remove it. 4. Transfer the asparagus to a plate and top with lemon juice and salt.
Per Serving: Calories 23; Total Fat 0.1g; Sodium 150mg; Total Carbs 4.4g; Fiber 2.4g; Sugars 2.1g; Protein 2.5g

Garlic Red Chard

Prep time: 10 minutes | Cook time: 7 minutes | Serves: 4

1 tablespoon avocado oil
1 small yellow onion, peeled and diced
1 bunch red chard, leaves and stems chopped and kept separate
(almost 12 ounces)
3 cloves garlic, minced
¾ teaspoon salt
Juice from ½ medium lemon
1 teaspoon lemon zest

1. Add the oil to the inner insert of the Instant Pot® and allow it to heat 1 minute. 2. Add the onion and chard stems and sauté 5 minutes. 3. Stir in the garlic and sauté another 30 seconds. Add the chard leaves, salt, and lemon juice and stir to combine. Press the Cancel button. Seal the cooker's lid. 4. Select the Manual or Pressure mode and adjust the time to 0 minutes. 5. Once the timer beeps, quick-release the pressure then unlock lid and remove it. 6. Spoon the chard mixture into a serving bowl and top with lemon zest.
Per Serving: Calories 59; Total Fat 3.7g; Sodium 618mg; Total Carbs 6g; Fiber 1.7g; Sugars 1.8g; Protein 1.9g

Ginger Broccoli and Carrots

Prep time: 10 minutes | Cook time: 5 minutes | Serves: 6

1 tablespoon avocado oil
1" fresh ginger, peeled and sliced
1 clove garlic, chopped
2 broccoli crowns, destemmed, cut into large florets
2 large peeled carrots, sliced
½ teaspoon kosher salt
Juice from ½ large lemon
¼ cup water

1. Pour the oil to the inner insert. Hit the Sauté button and heat oil 2 minutes. 2. Stir in the minced ginger and chopped garlic then sauté 1 minute. 3. Stir in the carrots, broccoli, and salt. 4. Pour in lemon juice and water and mix. Seal the cooker's lid. 5. Select the Manual or Pressure mode and adjust the time to 2 minutes. 6. Once the timer beeps, quick-release the pressure then unlock lid and remove it. 7. Serve.
Per Serving: Calories 70; Total Fat 1.2g; Sodium 662mg; Total Carbs 13.5g; Fiber 4.5g; Sugars 5.1g; Protein 3.2g

Curried Mustard Greens

Prep time: 15 minutes | Cook time: 10 minutes | Serves: 6

1 tablespoon avocado oil
1 medium white onion, peeled and chopped
1 tablespoon peeled and chopped ginger
3 cloves garlic, minced
2 tablespoons curry powder
½ teaspoon salt
¼ teaspoon black pepper
2 cups vegetable broth
½ cup coconut cream
1 large bunch mustard greens (almost 1 pound), tough stems removed and roughly chopped

1. Add the oil to the inner insert. Hit the Sauté button and heat the oil 2 minutes. 2. Add the onion and sauté until softened, almost 5 minutes. 3. Add the ginger, garlic, curry, salt, and pepper and sauté 1 more minute. 4. Stir in the vegetable broth and coconut cream until combined and then allow it to come to a boil, almost 2–3 minutes more. Press the Cancel button. 5. Stir in the mustard greens until everything is well combined. Seal the cooker's lid. 6. Select the Manual or Pressure mode and adjust the time to 0 minutes. 7. Once the timer beeps, quick-release the pressure then unlock lid and remove it. 8. Transfer to a suitable bowl and serve.
Per Serving: Calories 110; Total Fat 3.4g; Sodium 1446mg; Total Carbs 13.9g; Fiber 5.4g; Sugars 3.8g; Protein 8.2g

Cheesy Brussels Sprouts and Carrots

Prep time: 10 minutes | Cook time: 10 minutes | Serves: 4

1 pound Brussels sprouts, tough ends removed and cut in half
1 pound baby carrots
1 cup chicken stock
2 tablespoons lemon juice
½ cup nutritional yeast
¼ teaspoon salt

1. Add the Brussels sprouts, carrots, stock, lemon juice, nutritional yeast, and salt to the inner insert of your Instant Pot®. Stir well to combine. Seal the cooker's lid. 2. Select the Manual or Pressure mode and adjust the time to 10 minutes. 3. Once the timer beeps, quick-release the pressure then unlock lid and remove it. Transfer the vegetables and sauce to a suitable bowl and serve.
Per Serving: Calories 164; Total Fat 1.8g; Sodium 469mg; Total Carbs 29.2g; Fiber 12.6g; Sugars 8.2g; Protein 14g

Saucy Brussels Sprouts

Prep time: 15 minutes | Cook time: 12 minutes | Serves: 4

1 tablespoon coconut oil
12 ounces Brussels sprouts, tough ends removed and cut in half
12 ounces carrots (almost 4 medium), peeled, ends removed,
and cut into 1" chunks
¼ cup fresh lime juice
¼ cup apple cider vinegar
½ cup coconut aminos
¼ cup almond butter

1. Hit the Sauté button and melt the oil in the inner pot. Add the Brussels sprouts and carrots and sauté until browned, almost 5–7 minutes. 2. While the vegetables are browning, make the sauce. In a suitable bowl, mix the lime juice, vinegar, coconut aminos, and almond butter. 3. Pour the sauce over the vegetables and press the Cancel button. Seal the cooker's lid. 4. Select the Manual or Pressure mode and adjust the time to 6 minutes. 5. Once the timer beeps, quick-release the pressure then unlock lid and remove it.
Per Serving: Calories 110; Total Fat 4.3g; Sodium 81mg; Total Carbs 16.4g; Fiber 5.4g; Sugars 6.1g; Protein 3.8g

Sweet and Spicy Pepitas

Prep time: 10 minutes | Cook time: 30 minutes | Serves: 4

1 tablespoon chili powder
1 teaspoon ground cumin
Pinch of cayenne pepper
½ teaspoon kosher salt
¼ teaspoon black pepper
1 tablespoon canola oil
3 tablespoons maple syrup
1 egg white
2 cups raw pumpkin seeds

1. At 300 degrees F, preheat your oven. Layer a baking sheet with parchment paper. 2. Combine the chili powder, cumin, cayenne, salt, and black pepper in a suitable bowl. 3. Whisk the canola oil, maple syrup, and egg white in a suitable bowl. Add the spices and stir to combine. Add the pumpkin seeds and toss well. 4. Spread the prepared mixture on the prepared baking sheet. Bake, stirring once, for 25 to 30 minutes. Let cool on the baking sheet. 5. Serve or store in an airtight container at room temperature for up to 3 days.
Per serving: Calories: 228; Total fat 17.8g; Sodium 168mg; Total carbs 11.9g; Fiber 1.7g; Sugars 4.9g; Protein 9.1g

Dark Chocolate–Cherry Trail

Prep time: 5 minutes | Cook time: 10 minutes | Serves: 8

1 cup almonds
1 cup pumpkin seeds, toasted
½ cup pistachios
½ cup dried cherries
½ cup dark chocolate chips

1. At 350 degrees F, preheat your oven. 2. Place the almonds on a baking sheet in a single layer. Bake, stirring once until the almonds are fragrant and beginning to brown, about 10 minutes. Let cool, then chop. 3. Place the chopped almonds, pumpkin seeds, pistachios, cherries, and chocolate chips in a suitable bowl and stir to combine. 4. Serve or store in an airtight container at room temperature for up to 5 days.
Per serving: Calories: 235; Total fat 17.6g; Sodium 24mg; Total carbs 15.8g; Fiber 3.8g; Sugars 7.2g; Protein 8.1g

Butternut Squash Fries

Prep time: 20 minutes | Cook time: 40 minutes | Serves: 4

1 large butternut squash
2 tablespoons coconut oil
¾ teaspoon sea salt
3 fresh rosemary sprigs, chopped

1. Peel and slice the butternut squash into fry-size pieces, about 3 inches long and ½ inch thick. 2. At 375 degrees F, preheat your oven. Layer a baking sheet with parchment paper. 3. Put the butternut squash in a suitable bowl, then drizzle with coconut oil and sprinkle with salt. Toss to coat well. 4. Arrange the butternut squash pieces in a single layer on the prepared baking sheet. Bake in the preheated oven for 40 minutes or until golden brown and crunchy. 5. Flip the zucchini fries at least three times during the cooking and top the fries with rosemary sprigs halfway through. 6. Transfer the fries to a cooling rack and allow them to cool for a few minutes. Serve warm.
Per serving: Calories: 149; Total fat 13.7g; Sodium 705mg; Total carbs 8.2g; Fiber 1.4g; Sugars 1.5g; Protein 0.7g

Citrus Spinach

Prep time: 10 minutes | Cook time: 7 minutes | Serves: 4

tablespoons extra-virgin olive oil	Juice of ½ orange
cups fresh baby spinach	Zest of ½ orange
garlic cloves, minced	½ teaspoon sea salt
	⅛ teaspoon black pepper

. In a suitable skillet over medium-high heat, heat the olive oil until it shimmers. 2. Toss in the spinach and cook for 3 minutes, stirring occasionally. 3. Add the garlic. Cook for 30 seconds, stirring constantly. 4. Add the orange juice, orange zest, salt, and pepper. Cook for almost 2 minutes, constantly stirring, until the juice evaporates.
Per serving: Calories: 117; Total fat 7.1g; Sodium 258mg; Total carbs 2.8g; Fiber 0.7g; Sugars 2g

Brown Rice with Bell Peppers

Prep time: 10 minutes | Cook time: 10 minutes | Serves: 4

tablespoons extra-virgin olive oil	1 onion, chopped
red bell pepper, chopped	2 cups cooked brown rice
green bell pepper, chopped	2 tablespoons low-sodium soy sauce

. In a suitable nonstick skillet over medium-high heat, heat the olive oil until it shimmers. 2. Add the red and green bell peppers and onion. Cook for almost 7 minutes, frequently stirring, until the vegetables start to brown. 3. Add the rice and the soy sauce. Cook for almost 3 minutes, constantly stirring, until the rice warms through.
Per serving: Calories: 285; Total fat 6.4g; Sodium 297mg; Total carbs 1.8g; Fiber 2.8g; Sugars 2.1g; Protein 5.5g

Almond–Stuffed Dates

Prep time: 15 minutes | Cook time: 2 minutes | Serves: 4–6

0 Medjool dates	2 teaspoons grated orange zest
0 to 40 Marcona almonds	½ teaspoon fleur de sel
tablespoons olive oil	

. Remove the pits from the dates. Gently stuff each date with 1 or 2 almonds, depending on the size of the date. Seal the almond inside by pressing the date around it. 2. In a suitable sauté pan over medium heat, heat the olive oil. Add the dates and gently sauté until warmed through, about 2 minutes. 3. Remove it from the heat and sprinkle with the orange zest and fleur de sel. 4. Serve or store in an airtight container in the refrigerator up to 2 days.
Per serving: Calories: 197; Total fat 16.8g; Sodium 0mg; Total carbs .1g; Fiber 3.9g; Sugars 3.3g; Protein 6g

Blueberry Trail Mix

Prep time: 5 minutes | Cook time: 5 minutes | Serves: 4

tablespoon extra-virgin olive oil	½ teaspoon Chinese five-spice powder
cup almonds	½ cup dried blueberries
inch salt	

. In a suitable nonstick skillet over medium-high heat, heat the olive oil until it shimmers. 2. Add the almonds, salt, and Chinese five-spice and cook for 2 minutes, stirring constantly. 3. Remove from the heat and cool. Stir in the blueberries.
Per serving: Calories: 178; Total fat 15.4g; Sodium 39mg; Total carbs .7g; Fiber 3.4g; Sugars 2.8g; Protein 5.2g

Chickpea and Garlic Hummus

Prep time: 5 minutes | Cook time: 0 | Serves: 6

garlic cloves, minced	drained
tablespoons extra-virgin olive oil	Juice of 1 lemon
	½ teaspoon sea salt
tablespoons tahini	Paprika, for garnish
(14-ounce) can chickpeas,	

. In a suitable blender, combine the garlic, olive oil, tahini, chickpeas, lemon juice, and salt. Blend until smooth. 2. Garnish as desired.
Per serving: Calories: 134; Total fat 10.8g; Sodium 129mg; Total carbs 8.6g; Fiber 3.1g; Sugars 1.6g; Protein 3.6g

Broccoli-Sesame Stir-Fry

Prep time: 10 minutes | Cook time: 8 minutes | Serves: 4

2 tablespoons extra-virgin olive oil	¼ teaspoon sea salt
1 teaspoon sesame oil	2 garlic cloves, minced
4 cups broccoli florets	2 tablespoons toasted sesame seeds
1 tablespoon grated fresh ginger	

1. In a suitable nonstick skillet over medium-high heat, heat the olive oil and sesame oil until they shimmer. 2. Add the broccoli, ginger, and salt. Cook for 5 to 7 minutes, frequently stirring, until the broccoli begins to brown. 3. Add the garlic. Cook for 30 seconds, stirring constantly. Remove it from the heat and stir in the sesame seeds. 4. Serve.
Per serving: Calories: 134; Total fat 10.8g; Sodium 129mg; Total carbs 8.6g; Fiber 3.1g; Sugars 1.6g; Protein 3.6g

Coconut Rice with Blueberries

Prep time: 10 minutes | Cook time: 30 minutes | Serves: 4

1 cup brown basmati rice	1 cup water
2 dates, pitted and chopped	¼ cup toasted slivered almonds
1 cup coconut milk	½ cup shaved coconut
1 teaspoon sea salt	1 cup fresh blueberries

1. Combine the basmati rice, dates, coconut milk, salt, and water in a saucepan. Stir to mix well. Bring to a boil. 2. Reduce its heat to low, then simmer for 30 minutes or until the rice is soft. 3. Divide them into four bowls and serve with almonds, coconut, and blueberries on top.
Per serving: Calories: 397; Total fat 20g; Sodium 483mg; Total carbs 50.8g; Fiber 4.5g; Sugars 8.8g; Protein 6.6g

Mini Spinach Muffins

Prep time: 15 minutes | Cook time: 15 minutes | Serves: 12 muffins

2 cups spinach	1 cup almond flour
¼ cup raw honey	1 cup oat flour
1 teaspoon vanilla extract	1 teaspoon baking soda
3 tablespoons extra-virgin olive oil	2 teaspoons baking powder
	½ teaspoon salt
2 eggs	Pinch black pepper

1. At 350 degrees F, preheat your oven. Layer a 12-cup muffin pan with paper muffin cups. 2. Put the spinach, honey, vanilla, and olive oil in a suitable food processor, then break the eggs into it. Pulse to mix well until creamy and smooth. 3. Combine the flours, baking soda, baking powder, salt, and black pepper in a suitable bowl. Stir to mix well. 4. Make a well in the center of the flour mixture, then pour the spinach mixture into the well. Stir to mix well. 5. Divide the batter into muffin cups, then arrange the muffin pan in the preheated oven and bake for 15 minutes or until a toothpick inserted in the centre comes out clean. 6. Remove this pan from the oven. Allow it to cool for almost 10 minutes, then serve.
Per serving: Calories: 115; Total fat 6g; Sodium 337mg; Total carbs 13.2g; Fiber 1.7g; Sugars 5.9g; Protein 3.3g

Kale Chips

Prep time: 15 minutes | Cook time: 14 to 16 minutes | Serves: 4

1 bunch lacinato kale, rinsed, dried, and stems removed	1 to 2 tablespoons olive oil
	¼ teaspoon sea salt

1. At 350 degrees F, preheat your oven. 2. Cut or tear the kale leaves into 2-in [5-cm] pieces and then place them in a suitable bowl. 3. Add 1 tablespoon of olive oil and salt. Rub the leaves with your fingers, making sure they are well coated with the oil, adding up to another 1 tablespoon if necessary. 4. Place the kale on two baking sheets, ensuring there is about 1-in [2.5 cm] between the leaves. 5. If they're too close together, the leaves will steam instead of crisping. Bake for almost 8 minutes. 6. Remove from the oven and toss the leaves, then bake another 6 to 8 minutes until the leaves are crisp. Let cool. 7. Serve.
Per serving: Calories: 68; Total fat 7g; Sodium 124mg; Total carbs 1.8g; Fiber 0.3g; Sugars 0g; Protein 0.5g

Hummus with Pine Nuts

Prep time: 20 minutes | Cook time: 0 minutes | Serves: 6

2 (15-oz) cans chickpeas, drained	4 tablespoons extra-virgin olive oil
3 tablespoons lemon juice	3 tablespoons tahini
2 garlic cloves, crushed	1 tablespoon pine nuts, toasted
2 teaspoons za'atar	1 teaspoon chopped parsley
Kosher salt	
1 cup water	

1. Blend the lemon juice, chickpeas, garlic, za'atar, and 1 ½ teaspoons salt in a suitable food processor. 2. Add ½ cup [120 ml] of the water, tahini and 2 tablespoons of olive oil. 3. Blend until this mixture is creamy, while pouring in ½ cup [120 ml] of the remaining water, 2 tablespoons at a time. 4. Add lemon juice and salt to adjust the taste as you like. 5. Drizzle pine nuts, the remaining olive oil and parsley on top to serve or store in an airtight container in the refrigerator for up to 2 weeks.
Per serving: Calories: 490; Total fat 17.2g; Sodium 33mg; Total carbs 66.2g; Fiber 19.1g; Sugars 11.6g; Protein 21.7g

Tilapia Ceviche

Prep time: 40 minutes | Cook time: 30 minutes | Serves: 6–10

1 lb. tilapia, diced	1 mango, peeled, pitted, and diced
½ cup lime juice	¼ cup cucumber, diced
Kosher salt	2 tablespoons cilantro, minced
2 jalapeños, minced	2 avocados, pitted and diced
¼ cup red onion, diced	2 to 3 dashes of hot sauce
2 Roma tomatoes, diced	Black pepper

1. Place the tilapia, lime juice, and 1 teaspoon salt in a shallow, nonreactive dish, such as ceramic or glass. Stir to coat the fish with the lime juice, then add the jalapeños and red onion. 2. Cover and refrigerate for 30 minutes, allowing the citrus to cook the fish through. The fish will be opaque when ready. 3. Add the tomatoes, mango, cucumber, and cilantro to the fish. Stir to combine. Gently fold in the avocado. Season with hot sauce, pepper, and additional salt. 4. Serve immediately.
Per serving: Calories: 245; Total fat 14.1g; Sodium 69mg; Total carbs 17g; Fiber 6.2g; Sugars 9.6g; Protein 16.3g

Rosemary and Garlic Sweet Potatoes

Prep time: 10 minutes | Cook time: 15 minutes | Serves: 4

2 tablespoons extra-virgin olive oil	leaves, chopped
2 sweet potatoes, cut into ½-inch cubes	½ teaspoon sea salt
1 tablespoon fresh rosemary	3 garlic cloves, minced
	¼ teaspoon black pepper

1. In a suitable nonstick skillet over medium-high heat, heat the olive oil until it shimmers. 2. Add the sweet potatoes, rosemary, and salt. Cook for 10 to 15 minutes, occasionally stirring, until the sweet potatoes begin to brown. 3. Add the garlic and pepper. Cook for 30 seconds, stirring constantly.
Per serving: Calories: 155; Total fat 7.3g; Sodium 242mg; Total carbs 22.3g; Fiber 3.5g; Sugars 0.4g; Protein 1.3g

Zucchini Chips

Prep time: 15 minutes | Cook time: 2 hours | Serves: 6

2 zucchinis, sliced thin	1½ teaspoons dried oregano
2 tablespoons extra-virgin olive oil	1½ teaspoons dried basil
1½ teaspoons dried rosemary	½ teaspoon sea salt

1. At 200 degrees F, preheat your oven. Layer a baking sheet with parchment paper. 2. Combine the zucchini slices with olive oil in a suitable bowl, then toss to coat well. 3. Combine the remaining ingredients in a separate bowl. Stir to mix well. 4. Pour the mixture in the bowl of zucchini, then toss to coat well. 5. Arrange the zucchini slices in a single layer on the prepared baking sheet. Bake in the preheated oven for 2 hours or until golden brown and crispy. 6. Transfer the zucchini chips to a cooling rack and allow them to cool for a few minutes. Serve warm.
Per serving: Calories: 59; Total fat 5.1g; Sodium 163mg; Total carbs 3.8g; Fiber 1.8g; Sugars 1.2g; Protein 1g

Sweet Potato and Celery Root Mash

Prep time: 5 minutes | Cook time: 20 to 25 minutes | Serves: 4

2 cups chopped sweet potatoes	1 teaspoon lemon juice
2 cups chopped celery root	½ teaspoon salt
2 tablespoons almond butter	Pinch cayenne pepper

1. Place a steamer basket in a suitable saucepan with 1 to 2 inches of filtered water. Put the sweet potatoes and celery root in the steamer basket. 2. Cover and steam over medium heat for almost 20 to 25 minutes until fork-tender. 3. Transfer them to a suitable blender, along with the almond butter, lemon juice, sea salt, and cayenne pepper. Blend until completely smooth. Serve immediately.
Per serving: Calories: 171; Total fat 4.9g; Sodium 376mg; Total carbs 29.6g; Fiber 5.3g; Sugars 2g; Protein 4g

Buckwheat Waffles

Prep time: 15 minutes | Cook time: 12 minutes | Serves: 4

1½ cups buckwheat flour	1 tablespoon pure maple syrup
½ cup brown rice flour	1½ cups almond milk, unsweetened
1 teaspoon baking soda	1 cup water
2 teaspoons baking powder	Coconut oil for greasing the waffle iron
½ teaspoon sea salt	
1 egg	
2 teaspoons vanilla extract	

1. Combine the flours, baking soda, baking powder, and salt in a bowl. Stir to mix well. 2. Whisk together the egg, vanilla, maple syrup, almond milk, and water in a separate bowl. Pour the egg mixture into the flour mixture and keep stirring until a smooth batter forms. Let the batter stand for 10 minutes. 3. Preheat the waffle iron and grease with coconut oil. Pour the batter in the waffle iron to cover ¾ of the bottom. Cook for 10 to 12 minutes or until golden brown and crispy. 4. Flip the waffle halfway through the cooking time. The cooking time will vary depending on the waffle iron you use. 5. Serve the waffles immediately.
Per serving: Calories: 282; Total fat 4g; Sodium 626mg; Total carbs 54.7g; Fiber 5.5g; Sugars 6.9g; Protein 8.9g

Blueberry Yogurt Bites

Prep time: 10 minutes | Cook time: 0 | Serves: 50 bites

2 cups yogurt	½ cup fresh blueberries
1 banana	1 tablespoon raw honey

1. Layer a baking sheet with a piece of wax paper. 2. Pulse the banana, yogurt, blueberries, and honey in a blender until smooth and creamy. 3. Transfer the smooth mixture to a suitable resealable plastic bag with the corner snipped off. 4. Squeeze the mixture into quarter-sized dots onto the prepared baking sheet. Transfer to the freezer to freeze until solid. 5. Store leftovers in an airtight container in the freezer.
Per serving: Calories: 70; Total fat 0.8g; Sodium 43mg; Total carbs 11.2g; Fiber 0.6g; Sugars 9.2g; Protein 3.7g

Tomatillo Jalapeño Salsa Verde

Prep time: 30 minutes | Cook time: 10 minutes | Serves: 8

1 ¼ lb. tomatillos, skins removed and rinsed	oil
1 white onion, quartered	Kosher salt
2 jalapeños, halved lengthwise	3 tablespoons lime juice, plus more as needed
2 tablespoons extra-virgin olive	2 tablespoons chopped cilantro

1. Prepare your grill over medium-high heat. 2. Add the onion, tomatillos, and jalapeños in a suitable bowl and add the olive oil and ½ teaspoon salt. 3. Toss well, then place in a grilling basket or directly on the grill grates if they are narrowly spaced enough. 4. Grill the vegetables until they begin to lightly char and soften 5 to 10 minutes. 5. Remove the vegetables from the grill as they are ready. 6. Blend the grilled vegetables with remaining ingredients in a blender in a low speed or pulse until the mixture reaches the texture of salsa for 1 minute. 7. Taste and adjust with more salt or lime juice. Serve or store in an airtight container in the refrigerator for up to 5 days.
Per serving: Calories: 59; Total fat 4.3g; Sodium 21mg; Total carbs 5.6g; Fiber 1.8g; Sugars 0.7g; Protein 0.9g

Spiced Nuts

Prep time: 10 minutes | Cook time: 10 to 15 minutes | Serves: 2 cups

1 cup almonds
½ cup walnuts
¼ cup pumpkin seeds
¼ cup sunflower seeds
½ teaspoon ground cumin
1 teaspoon ground turmeric
¼ teaspoon red pepper flakes
¼ teaspoon garlic powder

1. At 350 degrees F, preheat your oven. 2. In a suitable bowl, stir together all the recipe ingredients until well combined. 3. Spread the nuts out onto a rimmed baking sheet and bake for 10 to 15 minutes, stirring once or twice halfway through, or until the nuts are lightly browned and fragrant. 4. Let the nuts cool for 5 to 10 minutes before serving.
Per serving: Calories: 151; Total fat 13.3g; Sodium 2mg; Total carbs 4.7g; Fiber 2.4g; Sugars 0.7g; Protein 5.8g

Lemony Berry Gummies

Prep time: 5 minutes | Cook time: 10 minutes | Serves: about 24 gummies

1 cup fresh blueberries
½ cup lemon juice
3 tablespoons raw honey
¼ cup filtered water
¼ cup gelatin powder

1. Purée the berries, lemon juice, honey, and water in a blender. 2. Transfer the purée to a suitable saucepan and heat over medium heat until it warms. 3. Add the gelatin powder and continue whisking for 5 minutes until well combined. 4. Pour the mixture into a mini muffin tin and freeze until the mixture gels, about 15 minutes. 5. Serve immediately or refrigerate for up to 1 week.
Per serving: Calories: 77; Total fat 0.4g; Sodium 8mg; Total carbs 18.9g; Fiber 1g; Sugars 17.2g; Protein 1g

Carrot and Pumpkin Seed Crackers

Prep time: 10 minutes | Cook time: 15 minutes | Serves: 10

1⅓ cups pumpkin seeds
½ cup carrot, shredded
3 tablespoons fresh dill, chopped
¼ teaspoon salt
2 tablespoons extra-virgin olive oil

1. At 350 degrees F, preheat your oven. Layer a baking sheet with parchment paper. 2. Ground the pumpkin seeds in a suitable food processor, then add the carrot, dill, salt, and olive oil to the food processor and pulse to combine well. 3. Pour them into the prepared baking sheet, then shape the mixture into a rectangle with a spatula. 4. Layer a sheet of parchment paper over the rectangle, then flatten the rectangle to about ⅛ inch thick with a rolling pin. 5. Remove the parchment paper-lined over the rectangle, then score it into 40 small rectangles with a sharp knife. 6. Arrange the baking sheet in the preheated oven and bake for 15 minutes or until golden browned and crispy. 7. Transfer the crackers to a suitable plate and allow them to cool for a few minutes before serving.
Per serving: Calories: 123; Total fat 10.4g; Sodium 111mg; Total carbs 3.7g; Fiber 0.9g; Sugars 0.5g; Protein 4.6g

White Fish Ceviche with Avocado

Prep time: 20 minutes | Cook time: 0 | Serves: 6

Juice of 5 limes
Juice of 8 lemons
1 pound fresh wild white fish, cut into ½-inch cubes
1 teaspoon minced fresh ginger
3 garlic cloves, minced
1 cup minced red onions
½ cup minced fresh cilantro
1 teaspoon Himalayan salt
1 teaspoon ground black pepper
½ medium hass avocado, peeled, pitted, and diced

1. Combine the lime juice and lemon juice in a suitable bowl, then dunk the fish cubes in the mixture press, so the fish is submerged in the juice. 2. Cover the bowl in plastic and refrigerate for at least 40 minutes. 3. Meanwhile, combine the ginger, garlic, onions, cilantro, salt, and ground black pepper in a suitable bowl. Stir to mix well. 4. Remove the fish bowl from the refrigerator, then sprinkle with the powder mixture. Toss to coat well. 5. Spread the diced avocado over the ceviche and serve immediately.
Per serving: Calories: 125; Total fat 6.3g; Sodium 748mg; Total carbs 6.3g; Fiber 2.6g; Sugars 1.4g; Protein 11.2g

Simple Coconut Pancakes

Prep time: 10 minutes | Cook time: about 5 minutes | Serves: 8 pancakes

4 eggs
1 cup coconut milk
1 tablespoon pure maple syrup
1 teaspoon vanilla extract
1 tablespoon coconut oil, melted
½ cup coconut flour
1 teaspoon baking soda
½ teaspoon sea salt

1. Whisk together the eggs, coconut milk, maple syrup, vanilla, and coconut oil in a suitable bowl. Stir to mix well. 2. Combine the coconut flour, baking soda, and salt in a separate bowl. Stir to mix well. 3. Make a well in the middle of the coconut flour mixture, then pour the egg mixture into the well. Stir to mix well until smooth and no lump. 4. Grease a nonstick skillet with coconut oil, then heat over medium-high heat until shimmering. 5. Divide the batter and pour ½ cup of batter in the skillet and cook for 5 minutes or until lightly browned. Flip halfway through the cooking time. Repeat with the remaining batter. 6. Transfer the pancakes to four plates and serve immediately.
Per serving: Calories: 174; Total fat 9.3g; Sodium 611mg; Total carbs 14.8g; Fiber 6.9g; Sugars 3.5g; Protein 7.8g

Roasted Chickpeas

Prep time: 5 minutes | Cook time: 20 minutes | Serves: 4 cups

4 cups cooked chickpeas
2 tablespoons extra-virgin olive oil
1 teaspoon garlic powder
1 teaspoon salt
Black pepper, to taste

1. At 400 degrees F, preheat your oven. 2. Spread the chickpeas out in an even layer on a rimmed baking sheet. Drizzle with the olive oil and toss to coat well. 3. Bake in the preheated oven for 20 minutes, stirring the chickpeas halfway through the cooking time until browned and crunchy. 4. Remove from the oven to a suitable bowl. Season with garlic powder, salt, and pepper, then serve.
Per serving: Calories: 153; Total fat 13g; Sodium 82mg; Total carbs 7.9g; Fiber 0.7g; Sugars 1.2g; Protein 3.6g

Almond Yogurt and Walnut Parfait

Prep time: 10 minutes | Cook time: 0 | Serves: 2

2 cups almond yogurt, unsweetened
2 tablespoons honey
1 cup fresh raspberries
1 cup fresh blueberries

1. Combine the yogurt and honey in a bowl. Stir to mix well, then pour half of the honey-yoghurt in a suitable glass. 2. Top the honey-yogurt with berries, then top the berries with the remaining honey-yogurt. 3. Spread the walnut pieces on top and serve immediately.
Per serving: Calories: 480; Total fat 23.6g; Sodium 88mg; Total carbs 63.2g; Fiber 8.9g; Sugars 44.5g; Protein 11.9g

Guacamole

Prep time: 10 minutes Cook time: 0 | Serves: 4

2 avocados, peeled, pitted, and cubed
½ red onion, minced
2 garlic cloves, minced
Juice of 1 lime
2 tablespoons chopped fresh cilantro leaves
½ teaspoon sea salt

1. In a suitable bowl, combine the avocados, red onion, garlic, lime juice, cilantro, and salt. 2. Lightly mash with a fork to mix.
Per serving: Calories: 213; Total fat 19.6g; Sodium 241mg; Total carbs 10.4g; Fiber 7.1g; Sugars 1.1g; Protein 2.2g

Raisins Trail Mix

Prep time: 5 minutes | Cook time: 0 | Serves: 12

1 cup sunflower seeds
1 cup pumpkin seeds
1 cup large coconut flakes
1 cup dried cranberries
1 cup raisins
½ cup cacao nibs

1. Combine the sunflower seeds, pumpkin seeds, coconut flakes, cranberries, raisins, and cacao nibs in a suitable bowl. 2. Serve immediately or store covered in a cool, dry place.
Per serving: Calories: 154; Total fat 9.1g; Sodium 15mg; Total carbs 15.9g; Fiber 2.4g; Sugars 9.4g; Protein 4.5g

Massaged Kale Chips

Prep time: 5 minutes | Cook time: 20 minutes | Serves: 2 cups

4 cups kale, stemmed	1 teaspoon sea salt
2 tablespoons olive oil	2 tablespoons apple cider vinegar

1. Rinse the stemmed kale, drain, and then torn into 2-inch pieces. 2. At 350 degrees F, preheat your oven. 3. Combine all the recipe ingredients in a suitable bowl. Stir to mix well. 4. Gently massage the kale leaves in the bowl for 5 minutes or until wilted and bright. 5. Place the kale on a baking sheet. Bake in the preheated oven for 20 minutes or until crispy. Toss the kale halfway through. 6. Remove the kale from the oven and serve immediately.
Per serving: Calories: 189; Total fat 14g; Sodium 995mg; Total carbs 14.1g; Fiber 2g; Sugars 0.1g; Protein 4g

Roasted Apricots

Prep time: 10 minutes | Cook time: 25 to 30 minutes | Serves: 4

20 fresh apricots, pitted and quartered	2 tablespoons coconut oil
	⅛ teaspoon cardamom

1. At 350 degrees F, preheat your oven. 2. Toss the apricots with the coconut oil and cardamom in a baking dish until well coated. 3. Roast in the preheated oven for 25 to 30 minutes, stirring once or twice during cooking, or until the apricots are beginning to caramelize. 4. Let the apricots cool for 5 to 10 minutes before serving.
Per serving: Calories: 142; Total fat 7.9g; Sodium 2mg; Total carbs 19.2g; Fiber 3.4g; Sugars 15.8g; Protein 2.3g

Cashew Hummus

Prep time: 20 minutes | Cook time: 0 | Serve: 1 cup

1 cup raw cashews, soaked and drained	1 teaspoon lemon juice
¼ cup filtered water	2 teaspoons coconut aminos
2 garlic cloves	½ teaspoon ground ginger
1 tablespoon extra-virgin olive oil	¼ teaspoon sea salt
	Pinch cayenne pepper

1. Place all the recipe ingredients in a blender and blend until completely mixed. You'll need to stop the blender occasionally to scrape down the sides. 2. Serve immediately or refrigerate to chill for at least 2 hours for the best flavor.
Per serving: Calories: 153; Total fat 13g; Sodium 82mg; Total carbs 7.9g; Fiber 0.7g; Sugars 1.2g; Protein 3.6g

Cauliflower Rice with Beans

Prep time: 15 minutes | Cook time: 20 minutes | Serves: 4

2 tablespoons olive oil	½ teaspoon salt
2 garlic cloves, peeled and minced	½ teaspoon ground black pepper
½ teaspoon ground coriander	1 (15 ½-ounce) can black beans, drained and rinsed
½ teaspoon ground cumin	2 tablespoons chopped cilantro
1 pound (about 4 cups) cauliflower rice	¼ cup lime juice

1. In a large sauté pan over medium-low heat, combine oil, garlic, coriander, and cumin. Sauté 30 seconds, taking care not to brown garlic. 2. Add rice and sauté 10–15 minutes until cauliflower is tender. Season with black pepper and salt. 3. Add beans, cilantro, and lime juice. Cook another 5 minutes until beans are warmed through.
Per serving: Calories 494; Fat 10.4g; Sodium 417mg; Carbs 76g; Fiber 16.8g; Sugars 6.4g; Protein 27.8g

Pico De Gallo

Prep time: 5 minutes | Cook time: 0 minutes | Serves: 4

2 large ripe tomatoes, diced	¼ cup chopped fresh cilantro
¼ cup chopped onion	2 tablespoons lime juice
¼ cup small diced green bell pepper	¾ teaspoon salt
	⅛ teaspoon cayenne pepper

1. In a suitable bowl, combine all the recipe ingredients and mix well. 2. Taste and adjust seasonings if necessary.
Per serving: Calories 21; Fat 0.2g; Sodium 443mg; Carbs 4.6g; Fiber 1.4g; Sugars 2.9g; Protein 1g

Zucchini Fritters

Prep time: 20 minutes | Cook time: 20 minutes | Serves: 4

¼ cup sriracha sauce	1 cup almond meal
1 cup plain, whole milk Greek yogurt	¼ cup chopped fresh parsley
1 cup shredded zucchini	1 teaspoon salt
1 cup chickpeas, mashed well	½ teaspoon ground black pepper
1 cup fresh corn kernels	½ teaspoon turmeric
3 large eggs, whisked	¼ cup avocado oil

1. In a suitable bowl, whisk together sriracha and yogurt. Set aside to serve with fritters. 2. In a suitable bowl, combine zucchini, chickpeas, corn, eggs, almond meal, parsley, salt, pepper, and turmeric. 3. In a medium sauté pan over medium heat, heat 1 tablespoon oil, taking care not to let it smoke. Scoop about 2 tablespoons batter for each fritter onto pan into round disks. 4. Cook on both sides for almost 3 minutes or until golden brown. Repeat with remaining batter, adding oil as necessary. 5. Serve fritters hot or at room temperature with dipping sauce.
Per serving: Calories 470; Fat 22g; Sodium 674mg; Carbs 47.3g; Fiber 13.9g; Sugars 10.5g; Protein 26.3g

Maple Collard Greens

Prep time: 15 minutes | Cook time: 40 minutes | Serves: 4

2 tablespoons extra-virgin olive oil	1 ½ cups water
1 cup small diced yellow onion	3 tablespoons apple cider vinegar
2 garlic cloves, peeled and minced	¼ teaspoon salt
1 bunch collard greens, hard stems removed and cut into 1" strips	¼ teaspoon ground black pepper
	1 teaspoon ground coriander
	1 tablespoon pure maple syrup
	¼ teaspoon red pepper flakes

1. In a large sauté pan over low heat, warm oil. Add onions and cook 7 minutes until they are tender and transparent. 2. Add garlic and sauté 30 seconds, just until fragrant. 3. Add collards and water to pan. After 1 minute, once greens have wilted down a bit, add remaining ingredients to pan. 4. Cover with a lid and cook 30 minutes. Check on greens every 5 minutes. If they look dry, add water, 1 cup at a time. It's important that they are cooking in liquid throughout. 5. Serve hot.
Per serving: Calories 96; Fat 7.2g; Sodium 156mg; Carbs 8.3g; Fiber 1.6g; Sugars 5.3g; Protein 0.9g

Toasted Nut Mix

Prep time: 5 minutes | Cook time: 6 minutes approximately | Serves: 6

1 cup raw cashews	¼ teaspoon curry powder
1 cup raw almonds	¼ teaspoon garlic powder
1 teaspoon ghee	¼ teaspoon sea salt

1. Layer a plate with a paper towel and set aside. Select sauté on the instant pot and let the pot preheat. 2. In the pot, combine the cashews and almonds. Toast for almost 6 minutes, while stirring frequently to keep the nuts from burning, until they begin to brown lightly. 3. Add the ghee, curry powder, garlic powder, and salt, mixing well until the nuts are thoroughly coated. 4. Transfer the seasoned nuts to the prepared plate to cool. The cashews will be slightly chewy when warm. 5. Store in an airtight container in a cool dark cabinet for up to 5 days.
Per serving: Calories 172; Fat 14.4g; Sodium 61mg; Carbs 8.3g; Fiber 2g; Sugars 1.4g; Protein 5.2g

Green Smoothie Bowl

Prep time: 5 minutes | Cook time: 0 minutes | Serves: 2

½ cup water	1 medium pitted date
¼ cup frozen pineapple cubes	1 medium banana, peeled and sliced in half
¼ cup tightly packed spinach	1 tablespoon hemp seeds
¼ cup ice	

1. In a suitable blender, purée water, pineapple, spinach, ice, date, and half of banana until smooth and thick. 2. Divide into two bowls. Arrange remaining banana and hemp seeds on top. 3. Serve.
Per serving: Calories 75; Fat 0.2g; Sodium 6mg; Carbs 19.4g; Fiber 2.2g; Sugars 11.9g; Protein 1g

Sweet Potato Dumplings

Prep time: 25 minutes | Cook time: 60 minutes | Serves: 6

Dipping Sauce

¼ cup tamari
1 tablespoon brown rice vinegar
1 teaspoon honey

1 tablespoon water
1 tablespoon sliced scallions

Dumplings

6 small sweet potatoes
2 tablespoons plus 1 ½ teaspoons sesame oil
1 2" piece fresh ginger, peeled and minced
3 small leeks, white and light green parts only, cut into half-moons

¾ cup sliced shiitake mushrooms
3 cups sliced napa cabbage
2 teaspoons tamari
2 teaspoons rice vinegar
¼ teaspoon salt
1 (12-ounce) package dumpling wrappers

1. At 375 degrees F, preheat your oven. 2. In a suitable bowl, combine all dipping sauce ingredients; set aside. Bake potatoes 30–40 minutes until fork-tender. 3. Slice potatoes lengthwise, scoop out the flesh, and place in a suitable bowl. Discard skin. Mash flesh with a fork until there are no lumps left. 4. While potatoes are baking, in a large sauté pan over medium heat, heat 1 tablespoon oil. 5. Add ginger and leeks and sauté 3–5 minutes until leeks are translucent but not browned. Then add mushrooms, cabbage, tamari, vinegar, and salt. Sauté 10 minutes until cabbage is well wilted. 6. Remove it from the heat. Add leek mixture to the bowl with mashed sweet potatoes and mix well. 7. Fill a suitable bowl with warm water and set nearby. Take a dumpling wrapper and place a spoonful of filling in middle. 8. Using your fingertip, lightly wet outer rim of wrapper. Fold dumpling wrapper in half so it creates a half-moon shape and pinch edges together well. Repeat until all wrappers are used. 9. In a large sauté pan, heat 1 ½ teaspoons oil. Place dumplings in pan in a single layer. 10. When underside is browned and crispy, about 2 minutes, add 2 tablespoons water to pan and cover with a tight-fitting lid. Cook another 1–2 minutes and remove it from the heat. 11. Repeat with rest of dumplings and oil. Arrange dumplings on a platter with dipping sauce and serve.
Per serving: Calories 297; Fat 0.8g; Sodium 744mg; Carbs 64g; Fiber 2.2g; Sugars 1.8g; Protein 9g

Hazelnut Bars

Prep time: 15 minutes | Cook time: 30 minutes | Serves: 8

3 medium bananas, mashed
¼ cup melted coconut oil
1 tablespoon pure maple syrup
1 teaspoon vanilla extract
1 ½ cups rolled oats (not instant)
1 cup shredded coconut,

unsweetened
1 tablespoon ground flax
½ teaspoon salt
¾ cup chopped hazelnuts
½ cup dried blueberries

1. At 350 degrees F, preheat your oven layer a 9" × 9" pan with parchment paper. 2. In a suitable bowl, combine bananas, oil, maple syrup, and vanilla extract and mix until well combined. 3. In a suitable bowl, combine oats, coconut, flax, salt, hazelnuts, and blueberries and mix well until combined. 4. Add the wet ingredients to the dry ingredients and mix well with a spatula until evenly incorporated. 5. Spread mixture out in an even layer in prepared pan. Bake 25–30 minutes or until lightly golden brown on top. 6. Let cool to room temperature. Once cool, cut into sixteen squares.
Per serving: Calories 223; Fat 11.8g; Sodium 151mg; Carbs 27.4g; Fiber 5.4g; Sugars 9.1g; Protein 4.9g

Brussels Sprouts with Walnuts

Prep time: 15 minutes | Cook time: 11 minutes | Serves: 4

1 ½ pounds Brussels sprouts
¼ cup ghee
4 garlic cloves, minced
1 teaspoon sea salt

¼ teaspoon black pepper
1 cup vegetable broth
1 tablespoon Dijon mustard
½ cup raw walnuts, chopped

1. Select sauté on the instant pot and let the pot preheat. 2. Set the Brussels sprouts in the pot and add the ghee, garlic, salt, and pepper. Cook for almost 6 minutes approximately. 3. Stir in the broth and mustard, mixing well to combine. 4. Turn off heat. Lock the lid. Pressure cook at high for almost 5 minutes. 5. When cooking is complete, use a quick release. Remove the lid. 6. Sprinkle the Brussels sprouts with the walnuts and serve.
Per serving: Calories 298; Fat 23.1g; Sodium 513mg; Carbs 18.3g; Fiber 7.7g; Sugars 4.1g; Protein 11.1g

Sweet Potato Mash

Prep time: 10 minutes | Cook time: 25 minutes | Serves: 4

1 cup water
4 large (8- to 12-ounce) sweet potatoes, pierced with a fork multiple time
1 teaspoon ghee
½ teaspoon sea salt, more for garnish

¼ teaspoon ground nutmeg
½ cup chopped walnuts
½ cup nondairy milk (such as coconut milk)
Freshly grated nutmeg, for garnish

1. Place a metal trivet or steam rack in the instant pot and pour in the water. Set the sweet potatoes on the trivet. Lock the lid. 2. Select pressure cook and cook at high pressure for almost 25 minutes. To ensure the sweet potatoes cook evenly, make sure they are all the same size. 3. While the sweet potatoes cook, in a suitable bowl, stir together the ghee, salt, nutmeg, walnuts, and milk. Set aside. 4. When cooking is complete, use a natural release for almost 10 minutes, then quick release any remaining pressure. 5. Remove the lid. Using potholders, remove the trivet and place it in a clean sink or on a cutting board to cool. 6. Gently pull off the skins from the cooked sweet potatoes and discard them. Add the sweet potato flesh to the prepared mixture in the bowl. 7. Using a large spoon or potato masher, mash the ingredients until combined. Garnish with sea salt or nutmeg.
Per serving: Calories 299; Fat 11.2g; Sodium 264mg; Carbs 44.9g; Fiber 7.2g; Sugars 2.3g; Protein 7.1g

Bean Salsa

Prep time: 20 minutes | Cook time: 30 minutes | Serves: 6

1 cup dried pinto beans, rinsed
3 cups vegetable broth
1 teaspoon sea salt
1 red onion, chopped
1 cup fresh cilantro, chopped
1 cup chopped tomatoes
1 avocado, peeled, halved, pitted,

and diced
1 small jalapeño pepper, seeded and minced
1 cup frozen corn
Juice of 1 lime
Organic blue corn chips, for serving

1. In the instant pot, combine the beans, broth, and salt. 2. Lock the lid. Pressure cook at high for almost 30 minutes. 3. While the beans cook, in a suitable bowl, stir together the red onion, cilantro, tomatoes, avocado, and jalapeño. Set aside. 4. When cooking is complete, use a natural release. Remove the lid and stir in the frozen corn. 5. Transfer the bean mixture to the bowl with the tomato and cilantro mixture, add the lime juice, and stir to combine well. 6. Serve with the corn chips.
Per serving: Calories 235; Fat 8g; Sodium 707mg; Carbs 31.3g; Fiber 8.8g; Sugars 3.6g; Protein 11.3g

Chickpea Smash

Prep time: 20 minutes | Cook time: 0 minutes | Serves: 8

1 (14-ounce) can chickpeas, drained and rinsed
¼ cup lemon juice
2 tablespoons chopped fresh parsley

3 tablespoons chopped pitted kalamata olives
½ teaspoon ground black pepper
½ teaspoon salt

1. In a suitable bowl, using a fork or potato masher, mash chickpeas to the consistency of a chunky paste. 2. Add lemon juice, parsley, olives, pepper, and salt. Mix well and serve.
Per serving: Calories 187; Fat 3.4g; Sodium 189mg; Carbs 30.6g; Fiber 8.8g; Sugars 5.5g; Protein 9.7g

Cinnamon Applesauce

Prep time: 15 minutes | Cook time: 8 minutes | Serves: 6

8 honey crisp apples, peeled, cored, and chopped

1 cup water
½ teaspoon ground cinnamon

1. In the instant pot, combine the apples, water, and cinnamon. Lock the lid. Pressure cook at high for 8 minutes. 2. When cooking is complete, use a quick release. Remove the lid. 3. Pour the cooked apples into a high-powered blender and blend until smooth. 4. Refrigerate in mason jars for up to 10 days.
Per serving: Calories 155; Fat 0.5g; Sodium 4mg; Carbs 41.2g; Fiber 7.3g; Sugars 30.9g; Protein 0.8g

Yogurt with Dates

Prep time: 5 minutes | Cook time: 0 minutes | Serves: 4

2 cups coconut yogurt,
unsweetened
¼ cup chopped almonds

¼ cup chopped walnuts
2 pitted dates, chopped
½ teaspoon ground cinnamon

1. In a suitable bowl, stir together the yogurt, almonds, walnuts, dates, and cinnamon. 2. Serve immediately.
Per serving: Calories 161; Fat 10.7g; Sodium 25mg; Carbs 11.8g; Fiber 2g; Sugars 8.9g; Protein 6.3g

Mixed Mushrooms with Herbs

Prep time: 15 minutes | Cook time: 6 minutes approximately | Serves: 4

¼ cup ghee
3 garlic cloves, minced
1 cup cremini mushrooms, chopped
1 cup shiitake mushrooms, chopped

1 cup beech mushrooms, chopped
¼ cup vegetable broth
½ cup fresh parsley, chopped
1 teaspoon Italian seasoning
1 teaspoon sea salt
½ teaspoon black pepper

1. Select sauté on the instant pot and let the pot preheat. 2. Set the ghee and garlic into the pot and cook until lightly browned. 3. Stir in the cremini, shiitake, and beech mushrooms, the broth, parsley, Italian seasoning, salt, and pepper until well coated. 4. Turn off the heat. Lock the lid. Select pressure cook and cook at high pressure for almost 1 minute. 5. When cooking is complete, use a quick release. Remove the lid and serve.
Per serving: Calories 172; Fat 13.9g; Sodium 610mg; Carbs 14.7g; Fiber 5.2g; Sugars 1.8g; Protein 4.8g

Fennel Cabbage Slaw

Prep time: 25 minutes | Cook time: 0 minutes | Serves: 6

2 cups shredded red cabbage
1 teaspoon salt
1 tablespoon orange juice
2 tablespoons lime juice
2 teaspoons rice wine vinegar
3 tablespoons extra-virgin olive oil

1 tablespoon raw honey
1 medium carrot, grated (about ½ cup)
1 medium bulb fennel, sliced (about 1 cup)
¼ cup chopped fresh cilantro
½ cup toasted pumpkin seeds

1. In a suitable bowl, place cabbage and ½ teaspoon salt. Massage with your hands for almost 3–4 minutes. Leave to rest. 2. In a suitable bowl, whisk orange juice, lime juice, vinegar, oil, honey, and remaining salt. 3. To the bowl with cabbage, add carrots, fennel, cilantro, pumpkin seeds, and dressing. Mix well. 4. Serve.
Per serving: Calories 150; Fat 12.3g; Sodium 409mg; Carbs 8.6g; Fiber 1.8g; Sugars 4.5g; Protein 3.4g

Pickled Shiitake

Prep time: 10 minutes | Cook time: 15 minutes | Serves: 8

2 cups dried shiitake mushroom caps
¼ cup tamari
¼ cup brown rice vinegar

2 tablespoons pure maple syrup
1 2" piece fresh ginger, peeled and cut into thin slices

1. Put mushrooms in a small saucepan and cover with boiling water. Let them soak about 30 minutes. 2. Drain mushrooms, reserving 1 cup soaking liquid. Slice rehydrated mushrooms into ¼" slices. 3. Return mushrooms and reserved soaking liquid to saucepan and add tamari, vinegar, maple syrup, and ginger. Simmer 15 minutes over low heat. 4. Remove it from the heat and cool to room temperature. Store in an airtight container (along with liquid). 5. Eat immediately or keep refrigerated up to two weeks.
Per serving: Calories 153; Fat 0.4g; Sodium 8mg; Carbs 34.3g; Fiber 3.1g; Sugars 17.1g; Protein 2.3g

Pickled Vegetables

Prep time: 15 minutes | Cook time: 5 minutes | Serves: 4

½ cup cucumber slices
½ cup onion slices
½ cup carrot slices
½ cup red bell pepper strips

½ cup apple cider vinegar
½ cup water
1 ½ teaspoons salt
2 teaspoons mustard seeds

1. Pack cut vegetables tightly into a mason jar. 2. In a small saucepan over high heat, combine vinegar, water, salt, and mustard seeds. Bring to a boil. 3. Pour hot liquid over vegetables. Cap jar and let steep at least 1 hour at room temperature. If not using the same day, put in refrigerator until ready to serve.
Per serving: Calories 30; Fat 0.5g; Sodium 885mg; Carbs 4.6g; Fiber 1.1g; Sugars 2g; Protein 0.8g

Cucumber and Bulgur Salad

Prep time: 15 minutes | Cook time: 10 minutes | Serves: 4

½ cup bulgur
1 ½ cups water
¾ teaspoon salt
2 tablespoons lemon juice
3 tablespoons extra-virgin olive

oil
1 cup medium diced tomato
1 cup medium diced cucumber
⅓ cup chopped fresh parsley

1. In a small saucepan over medium-high heat, combine bulgur, water, and ¼ teaspoon salt. Bring to a boil. 2. Then cover, reduce heat to simmer, and cook 10 minutes. 3. Turn off heat and let sit, covered, another 5 minutes. 4. Drain off any excess liquid, fluff bulgur with a fork, and place in a serving bowl, letting it come to room temperature while preparing rest of salad. 5. In a suitable bowl, whisk together lemon juice, oil, and remaining ½ teaspoon salt. 6. Add tomato, cucumber, and parsley to the bowl with bulgur. 7. Add dressing, toss well to combine, and serve.
Per serving: Calories 164; Fat 10.9g; Sodium 450mg; Carbs 16g; Fiber 4g; Sugars 1.7g; Protein 2.8g

Flaxseed Power Bites

Prep time: 20 minutes | Cook time: 0 minutes | Serves: 1

1 cup almond butter, unsweetened
½ cup ground flaxseed
¼ cup almond or coconut flour
¼ cup cocoa powder, unsweetened
¼ cup coconut flakes,

unsweetened
¼ cup roasted pumpkin seeds
¼ cup chia seeds
1 teaspoon ground cinnamon
1 to 2 teaspoons monk fruit extract

1. In a suitable bowl, combine the almond butter, flaxseed, almond flour, cocoa powder, coconut flakes, pumpkin seeds, chia seeds, cinnamon, and monk fruit extract. 2. Using your hands, mix everything together and shape the prepared mixture into 12 (1-inch) balls. 3. Place them in a single layer on a baking sheet or in a large container. Cover and refrigerate for at least 1 hour before serving. 4. Store the balls in an airtight container in the refrigerator for up to one week or in the freezer for up to three months.
Per serving: Calories 251; Fat 19.7g; Sodium 9mg; Carbs 11.7g; Fiber 6.2g; Sugars 0.8g; Protein 10.7g

Chapter 4 Vegetarian Mains

Broccoli Casserole

Prep time: 15 minutes | Cook time: 37 minutes | Serves: 6

1 tablespoon avocado oil	3 cups large broccoli florets
1 medium yellow onion, peeled and diced	1 (15-ounce) can cooked chickpeas, drained
2 cloves garlic, minced	½ cup nutritional yeast
1½ cups brown rice	1 teaspoon paprika
4 cups vegetable broth	½ teaspoon salt

1. Add the oil to the inner insert. Hit the Sauté button and heat the oil for 1 minute. Add the onion and sauté for 5 minutes. 2. Stir in the garlic and sauté an additional 30 seconds. Add the rice and stir to coat with the onions, oil, and garlic. Press the Cancel button. 3. Add the broth and seal the cooker's lid. Select the Manual or Pressure mode and then adjust the pressure to low and adjust the time to 25 minutes. 4. Once the timer beeps, quick-release the pressure then unlock lid and remove it. 5. Add broccoli and seal the cooker's lid. Select the Manual or Pressure mode and then adjust the pressure to low and adjust the time to 5 minutes. 6. Once the timer beeps, quick-release the pressure then unlock lid and remove it. 7. Stir in the chickpeas, nutritional yeast, paprika, and salt. Spoon into bowls and serve.

Per Serving: Calories 529; Total Fat 7.7g; Sodium 743mg; Total Carbs 91g; Fiber 19g; Sugars 9.5g; Protein 28g

Lentil-Stuffed Squash

Prep time: 10 minutes | Cook time: 27 minutes | Serves: 2

1 tablespoon avocado oil	2 cups vegetable broth
1 small yellow onion, peeled and diced	1 teaspoon ground cumin
1 teaspoon minced garlic	1 teaspoon turmeric
1½ teaspoons peeled and coarsely chopped fresh ginger	½ teaspoon kosher salt
	¼ teaspoon black pepper
1 cup brown lentils	2 medium cooked spaghetti squash halves

1. Add the oil to the inner insert. Hit the Sauté button and heat the oil for 1 minute. Add the onion and sauté for 5 minutes. 2. Stir in the garlic and ginger and sauté an additional 30 seconds. Press the Cancel button. 3. Add the lentils, broth, cumin, turmeric, salt, and pepper and stir to combine. Seal the cooker's lid. 4. Select the Manual or Pressure mode and adjust the time to 20 minutes. 5. Once the timer beeps, quick-release the pressure then unlock lid and remove it. 6. Meanwhile, scrape the spaghetti squash strands from the cooked spaghetti squash halves into a suitable bowl. Reserve the shells. 7. Mix the lentils with the squash and toss to combine. 8. Divide the mixture between the shells and serve.

Per Serving: Calories 300; Total Fat 4.3g; Sodium 1377mg; Total Carbs 45.2g; Fiber 7.7g; Sugars 6.2g; Protein 21.6g

Harvest Quinoa suitable bowl

Prep time: 10 minutes | Cook time: 5 minutes | Serves: 4

3 tablespoons olive oil, extra-virgin	1¼ cups vegetable stock
2 tablespoons apple cider vinegar	1 (10-ounce) bag frozen butternut squash cubes
½ teaspoon Dijon mustard	1 (15-ounce) can cannellini beans, drained
½ teaspoon minced garlic	
½ teaspoon dried thyme	4 cups baby kale leaves
½ teaspoon dried rosemary	½ cup fruit-juice sweetened dried cranberries
½ teaspoon salt	
¼ teaspoon black pepper	½ cup chopped walnuts
1 cup quinoa	½ cup chopped fresh parsley

1. In a suitable jar or container with a tight lid, place the oil, vinegar, mustard, garlic, thyme, rosemary, salt, and pepper and shake until well combined. Set aside. 2. Place the quinoa, stock, frozen butternut squash cubes, and beans into the inner insert and stir to combine. Seal the cooker's lid. 3. Select the Manual or Pressure mode and adjust the time to 5 minutes. 4. Once the timer beeps, quick-release the pressure then unlock lid and remove it. 5. Stir in the kale leaves until they are wilted. Spoon the quinoa mixture into four bowls and top with the dried cranberries, walnuts, and fresh parsley. Drizzle each bowl with one quarter of the prepared dressing and toss to combine.

Per Serving: Calories 589; Total Fat 22.7g; Sodium 266mg; Total Carbs 76.5g; Fiber 23.9g; Sugars 5.1g; Protein 25.5g

Chickpea-Stuffed Squash

Prep time: 5 minutes | Cook time: 12 minutes | Serves: 2

½ teaspoon salt	drained
1 tablespoon avocado oil	¼ teaspoon black pepper
1 acorn squash, halved and seeded	½ teaspoon allspice
1 (15-ounce) can chickpeas,	½ teaspoon ground ginger

1. Place ½ cup water in the inner pot of your Instant Pot® and place the steam rack inside. 2. Sprinkle the acorn squash halves with ⅛ teaspoon salt each. Place the acorn squash, cut side up, on the steam rack. Seal the cooker's lid. 3. Select the Manual or Pressure mode and adjust the time to 5 minutes. 4. Once the timer beeps, quick-release the pressure then unlock lid and remove it. 5. Remove the squash and place on a plate. Cover with aluminum foil to keep warm. 6. Remove the water and steam rack from the inner pot and dry the pot. 7. Hit the Sauté button and then use the Adjust button to change to the More setting. Add the oil to the inner insert. Allow it to heat 2 minutes. 8. Add the chickpeas, ¼ teaspoon salt, pepper, allspice, and ginger to the inner insert and sauté until the chickpeas are lightly browned, almost 5 minutes. Press the Cancel button. 9. Remove the chickpeas from the inner pot and add half to each of the cooked acorn squash shells. Serve.

Per Serving: Calories 224; Total Fat 6.6g; Sodium 556mg; Total Carbs 35.6g; Fiber 8.6g; Sugars 4.3g; Protein 8.4g

Loaded Sweet Potatoes

Prep time: 10 minutes | Cook time: 26 minutes | Serves: 2

1½ tablespoons avocado oil	½ teaspoon kosher salt
1 small white onion, peeled and diced	½ teaspoon dried oregano
	¼ teaspoon black pepper
3 cloves garlic, minced	¼ pound dry pinto beans
1 teaspoon ground cumin	1½ cups vegetable broth
1 teaspoon ground chili powder	2 medium sweet potatoes

1. Add the oil to the inner insert. Hit the Sauté button and heat the oil for 1 minute. 2. Add the onion and sauté until brown, almost 6–7 minutes. 3. Add the garlic, cumin, chili powder, salt, oregano, and pepper and sauté an additional 1 minute. Press the Cancel button. 4. Add the beans and broth to the inner insert. Place the steam rack inside and place the sweet potatoes on top of the rack. Seal the cooker's lid. 5. Select the Manual or Pressure mode and adjust the time to 18 minutes. 6. Once the timer beeps, quick-release the pressure then unlock lid and remove it. 7. Cut the sweet potatoes in half and top with half of the bean mixture.

Per Serving: Calories 557; Total Fat 10g; Sodium 2706mg; Total Carbs 87.6g; Fiber 17.8g; Sugars 5.6g; Protein 29.2g

Rice and Beans with Turmeric

Prep time: 10 minutes | Cook time: 44 minutes | Serves: 4

1 tablespoon avocado oil	¼ teaspoon salt
1 small yellow onion, peeled and diced	⅛ teaspoon black pepper
	1 cup long grain brown basmati rice
2 medium carrots, peeled, ends removed and chopped	
2 medium stalks celery, ends removed and chopped	1⅓ cups vegetable stock
	1 (15-ounce) can red kidney beans, rinsed
2 teaspoons peeled and chopped fresh turmeric	1 cup chopped fresh parsley

1. Pour the oil into the inner insert and hit the Sauté button. 2. Allow the oil to preheat for 1 minute and then add the onion, carrots, and celery. Cook 5 minutes with occasional stirring. 3. Add the turmeric, salt, pepper, and rice and sauté, stirring frequently, another 5 minutes. 4. Add the stock and use a wooden spoon to scrape up any brown bits from the bottom of the Instant Pot®. Press the Cancel button. Seal the cooker's lid. 5. Select the Manual or Pressure mode and adjust the time to 33 minutes. Release the pressure completely then remove its lid. 6. While the Instant Pot® is still in Keep Warm mode, stir in the beans. 7. Divide the rice and bean mixture among four plates and top each with ¼ cup fresh parsley.

Per Serving: Calories 562; Total Fat 2.1g; Sodium 238mg; Total Carbs 108.8g; Fiber 19g; Sugars 5.3g; Protein 28.6g

Quinoa Burrito Bowls

Prep time: 5 minutes | Cook time: 10 minutes | Serves: 4

2 teaspoons avocado oil
½ medium red onion, diced
½ teaspoon salt
1 teaspoon cumin
1 red bell pepper, diced
1 teaspoon minced garlic
1 cup quinoa
1 cup no-sugar-added, low-sodium salsa

1 cup vegetable stock
1 (15-ounce) can black beans, rinsed
1 medium avocado, peeled pitted and sliced
1 cup chopped fresh cilantro
1 scallion, sliced
1 medium lime, cut into 4 wedges

1. Hit the Sauté button and add the oil to the inner insert. Add the onion, bell pepper, salt, and cumin and cook for 5 minutes. 2. Toss in the garlic and sauté 30 seconds. Press the Cancel button. 3. Add the quinoa, salsa, stock, and beans and stir to combine, scraping up any brown bits. Seal the cooker's lid. 4. Select the Manual or Pressure mode and adjust the time to 5 minutes. 5. Once the timer beeps, let the pressure release naturally and remove it. 6. Spoon the quinoa mixture into four bowls and top with the avocado, cilantro, and scallions. Serve with the lime wedges.
Per Serving: Calories 425; Total Fat 8.8g; Sodium 284mg; Total Carbs 68.6g; Fiber 15.2g; Sugars 3.1g; Protein 20.6g

Vegetable Lentil Bowls

Prep time: 10 minutes | Cook time: 26 minutes | Serves: 4

1 tablespoon avocado oil
1 medium yellow onion, peeled and chopped
6 cloves garlic, minced
1 large carrot, peeled and chopped
1 large parsnip, peeled and chopped
1 small turnip, peeled and chopped

2 medium stalks celery, ends removed and sliced
1 teaspoon salt
1 teaspoon dried thyme
1 teaspoon dried oregano
¼ teaspoon black pepper
1 cup brown lentils
2½ cups vegetable stock

1. Pour the oil into the inner insert. Hit the Sauté button. 2. Toss in the onion and sauté for 5 minutes with occasional stirring. 3. Add the carrot, garlic, turnip, oregano, parsnip, salt, celery, thyme, and black pepper. Stir to combine and cook another 30 seconds. Press the Cancel button. 4. Add the lentils and stir to combine, then add the stock. Seal the cooker's lid. 5. Select the Manual or Pressure mode and adjust the time to 20 minutes. 6. Once the timer beeps, quick-release the pressure then unlock lid and remove it. Spoon into bowls and serve.
Per Serving: Calories 100; Total Fat 1.1g; Sodium 741mg; Total Carbs 19.4g; Fiber 5.2g; Sugars 6.2g; Protein 4.3g

Mexican Salad with Avocado Dressing

Prep time: 15 minutes | Cook time: 15 minutes | Serves: 4

¼ pound dry black beans
1 cup water
1 small ripe avocado, peeled, pitted, and chopped
1 tablespoon olive oil, extra-virgin
¾ cup chopped cilantro
Juice from 2 medium limes
⅛ teaspoon fine sea salt
1 teaspoon minced garlic
¼ teaspoon hot sauce

3–5 tablespoons water
2 hearts romaine lettuce, torn
1 medium red bell pepper, deseeded, chopped
1 cup grape tomatoes, cut into eighths
1 scallion, green part sliced
½ teaspoon coarse salt
¼ teaspoon freshly cracked black pepper

1. Place the black beans in a suitable bowl and cover with 3" water. Soak the beans 4–8 hours. Drain the beans. 2. Place the soaked beans and 1 cup water in the inner pot. Seal the cooker's lid. 3. Select the Manual or Pressure mode and adjust the time to 15 minutes. 4. Meanwhile, prepare the spicy Avocado Dressing. In a suitable blender, place the avocado, olive oil, ¼ cup cilantro, lime juice, fine sea salt, garlic, and hot sauce and blend until smooth. 5. Stir in enough water to create the consistency you desire. Set aside. 6. Release the pressure completely then remove its lid. 7. In a suitable bowl, place the remaining cilantro, romaine lettuce, bell pepper, tomatoes, and scallion. Add the cooked black beans and drizzle with the prepared dressing. Toss to coat. Top with the coarse salt and pepper and serve.
Per Serving: Calories 253; Total Fat 13.9g; Sodium 21mg; Total Carbs 27g; Fiber 9.3g; Sugars 3.8g; Protein 8.3g

Artichoke Chickpea Casserole

Prep time: 7 minutes | Cook time: 6 minutes | Serves: 2

1 tablespoon avocado oil
1 medium yellow onion, peeled and chopped
2 cloves garlic, minced
1 (15.5-ounce) can chickpeas, drained and dried
1 (14-ounce) can baby artichokes,

drained and roughly chopped
½ cup vegetable stock
1 tablespoon fresh lemon juice
1 tablespoon fresh thyme leaves
1 teaspoon lemon zest
2½ ounces baby spinach

1. Hit the Sauté button and pour the oil into the inner insert. After it heats 1 minute, add the onion. Allow it to cook with occasional stirring, 3 minutes. 2. Add the garlic and chickpeas, stir to combine, and cook 1 more minute. Press the Cancel button. 3. Add the artichokes and stock. Seal the cooker's lid. 4. Select the Manual or Pressure mode and adjust the time to 1 minute. 5. Once the timer beeps, quick-release the pressure then unlock lid and remove it. 6. Stir in the lemon juice, thyme leaves, lemon zest, and half of the baby spinach. Stir until well combined and then add the rest of the spinach. 7. Stir until all of the spinach leaves are wilted. Transfer to bowls and serve.
Per Serving: Calories 300; Total Fat 4g; Sodium 429mg; Total Carbs 56.8g; Fiber 22.7g; Sugars 11.3g; Protein 19.7g

Chickpea Hash

Prep time: 10 minutes | Cook time: 12 minutes | Serves: 2

1½ tablespoons avocado oil
1 medium yellow onion, peeled and diced
2 cloves garlic, minced
1 cup vegetable stock
1 medium sweet potato, cut into

cubes (peeling not necessary)
1 (15-ounce) can chickpeas, rinsed and drained
½ teaspoon salt
1 teaspoon Italian seasoning blend
½ cup chopped flat-leaf parsley

1. Hit the Sauté button on Instant Pot and add the oil to preheat. 2. Stir in the onion and cook for 5 minutes until soft. 3. Stir in the garlic and sauté for 30 seconds. Press the Cancel button. 4. Add stock, sweet potato, chickpeas, salt, and Italian seasoning and stir to combine. Seal the cooker's lid. 5. Select the Manual or Pressure mode and adjust the time to 5 minutes. 6. Once the timer beeps, quick-release the pressure then unlock lid and remove it. 7. Spoon the prepared mixture into bowls and top with the parsley.
Per Serving: Calories 460; Total Fat 10.1g; Sodium 332mg; Total Carbs 73.9g; Fiber 20.3g; Sugars 14.5g; Protein 21.7g

Buddha Suitable Bowls with Carrot Dressing

Prep time: 20 minutes | Cook time: 26 minutes | Serves: 4

1 cup short-grain brown rice
1¼ cups vegetable stock
2½ tablespoons olive oil, extra-virgin
2½ tablespoons apple cider vinegar
2 large carrots, peeled and sliced
1 tablespoon peeled and chopped fresh ginger
1 tablespoon fresh lime juice
¼ teaspoon pure stevia powder

¾ teaspoon toasted sesame oil
⅛ teaspoon salt
1½ cups frozen shelled edamame, thawed
1½ cups sliced broccoli florets
4 cups sliced red cabbage
1 medium cucumber, sliced
2 medium avocados, peeled, pitted, and sliced
2 tablespoons sesame seeds
2 scallions, sliced

1. Add the rice and 1 cup stock to the inner pot. Seal the cooker's lid. 2. Select the Manual or Pressure mode and adjust the time to 2... minutes. 3. While the rice is cooking, make the prepared dressing. 4. In a suitable blender, blend the vinegar, olive oil, ginger, lime juice, half of the carrot slices, stevia, sesame oil, and salt until the mixture is super smooth. Set aside. 5. Release the pressure completely then remove its lid. Use a fork to fluff the rice. Press the Cancel button. 6. Hit the Sauté button and add ¼ cup stock with the broccoli and edamame. 7. Stir and cook until warm for 2 minutes. 8. To assemble the vegetable Buddha bowls, spoon ¼ of the rice mixture into each of the four bowls. 9. Add ¼ each of the cabbage, remaining carrot slices, avocado slices, and cucumber, to each bowl, separated. 10. Sprinkle ¼ of the sesame seeds and scallions over each bowl. 11. Drizzle with ¼ of the Carrot Ginger Dressing.
Per Serving: Calories 448; Total Fat 32.9g; Sodium 71mg; Total Carbs 28.1g; Fiber 9.4g; Sugars 6.3g; Protein 14.6g

Vegan Frittata

Prep time: 15 minutes | Cook time: 20 minutes | Serves: 6

½ cups garbanzo bean flour	1½ cups water
teaspoon salt	2 tablespoons olive oil, extra-virgin
teaspoon ground turmeric	
½ teaspoon ground cumin	1 zucchini, sliced
teaspoon chopped fresh sage	2 scallions, sliced

. At 350 degrees F, preheat your oven. 2. In a suitable bowl, mix the garbanzo bean flour, salt, turmeric, cumin, and sage. 3. Slowly add he water, while stirring constantly to prevent the prepared batter from getting lumpy. Set aside. 4. In a suitable oven-safe skillet, preheat the il over high heat. Sauté the zucchini until softened, 3 minutes. Stir n the scallions, then spoon the prepared batter over the vegetables. . Place this zucchini skillet in the oven and cook for almost 20 to 25 minutes. 6. Serve warm or at room temperature.
Per Serving: Calories 241; Total Fat 9.8g; Sodium 605mg; Total Carbs 29.8g; Fiber 8.5g; Sugars 1.1g; Protein 9.8g

Kale Bowls

Prep time: 10 minutes | Cook time: 5 minutes | Serves: 4

¼ cup buckwheat groats	3 tablespoons water
¾ cups vegetable broth	1 teaspoon Dijon mustard
(10-ounce) bag frozen butternut squash cubes	1 medium bunch red kale, stems removed and chopped (almost 6 ounces)
¼ cup fresh lemon juice	
¼ cup tahini	¼ teaspoon salt
clove garlic	¼ teaspoon black pepper
tablespoons nutritional yeast	

. Place the buckwheat groats, broth, and squash in the inner pot. Seal he cooker's lid. 2. Select the Manual or Pressure mode and adjust the me to 5 minutes. 3. Meanwhile, in a suitable blender, place the lemon uice, tahini, garlic, nutritional yeast, water, and mustard and blend ntil smooth. Set aside. 4. Once the timer beeps, quick-release the ressure then unlock lid and remove it. 5. Place the chopped kale in suitable bowl. Top with the butternut squash and buckwheat groats nd toss to combine. Add the lemon-tahini dressing, salt, and pepper, nd toss again to coat. Serve warm.
Per Serving: Calories 276; Total Fat 11.8g; Sodium 888mg; Total Carbs 33.1g; Fiber 6.2g; Sugars 2.6g; Protein 14.4g

Mediterranean Sweet Potatoes

Prep time: 10 minutes | Cook time: 29 minutes | Serves: 4

½ cups water	¼ teaspoon pepper
medium sweet potatoes	3–5 tablespoons water
¼ cup tahini	1 tablespoon avocado oil
uice of 1 medium lemon	1 (15-ounce) can chickpeas, drained
tablespoon apple cider vinegar	
cloves garlic	½ cup sliced black olives
¼ cup fresh basil	½ cup sliced grape tomatoes
teaspoon fresh oregano	½ cup chopped fresh flat-leaf parsley
teaspoon fresh thyme leaves	
teaspoon salt	

. Pour 1½ cups water into your Instant Pot® and place the steam ck inside. 2. Place the sweet potatoes on the rack. It's okay if they verlap. Seal the cooker's lid. 3. Select the Manual or Pressure mode nd adjust the time to 18 minutes. 4. Make the prepared dressing. 5. lend the lemon juice, tahini, vinegar, garlic, basil, oregano, thyme, ¼ aspoon salt, and ⅛ teaspoon pepper and blend until smooth. 6. Pour water, a tablespoon at a time, as needed until desired consistency is ached. Set aside. 7. Once the timer beeps, quick-release the pressure en unlock lid and remove it. 8. Remove sweet potatoes, place on a late, and cover with aluminum foil to keep warm. 9. Remove the rack nd water from the inner pot and dry it. 10. Hit the Sauté button and se the Adjust button to change the setting to More. Add the oil and let heat 1 minute. 11. Add the chickpeas and remaining ¼ teaspoon salt nd ⅛ teaspoon pepper to the inner insert. Sauté, stirring frequently ntil the chickpeas are browned and crisp, almost 10 minutes. Press e Cancel button. 12. Cut the sweet potatoes in half and top with one uarter of the chickpeas, olives, tomatoes, and parsley. Drizzle with e prepared dressing.
Per Serving: Calories 687; Total Fat 17.1g; Sodium 495mg; Total arbs 112.7g; Fiber 27.3g; Sugars 12.9g; Protein 26g

Quinoa and Vegetable Curry

Prep time: 10 minutes | Cook time: 7 minutes | Serves: 4

1 tablespoon avocado oil	2 medium sweet potatoes, diced
1 small red onion, chopped	1 medium red bell pepper, chopped
3 garlic cloves, chopped	
1 cup quinoa, rinsed	1 cup chopped broccoli
1¼ teaspoons curry powder	1½ cups water
¾ teaspoon sea salt	1 tablespoon fresh cilantro, chopped
½ teaspoon ground cumin	

1. Select Sauté on the Instant Pot and let the pot preheat. 2. Pour in the oil and add the red onion and garlic. Cook for almost 3 minutes. 3. Add the quinoa, curry powder, salt, and cumin. Cook for almost 2 minutes, stirring to coat well. 4. Add the sweet potatoes, bell pepper, broccoli, and water. Select Cancel. Lock the lid. 5. Set the Pressure Cook mode and cook at high pressure for almost 1 minute. 6. When cooking is complete, use a natural release for almost 10 minutes, then quick release any remaining pressure. 7. Remove the cooker's lid and top with the cilantro to serve.
Per Serving: Calories 283; Total Fat 3.6g; Sodium 381mg; Total Carbs 55.4g; Fiber 8.1g; Sugars 3.1g; Protein 8.7g

Avocado Egg Salad

Prep time: 10 minutes | Cook time: 7 minutes | Serves: 2

3 large eggs	¼ teaspoon dried dill weed
1 small avocado, peeled, pitted, and mashed	¼ teaspoon salt
	1 tablespoon flat-leaf parsley, chopped
1 teaspoon Dijon mustard	
1 tablespoon apple cider vinegar	2 cups baby arugula leaves
¼ teaspoon garlic powder	

1. Pour 1 cup water into the inner insert of your Instant Pot® and place the steam rack inside. 2. Place eggs directly onto the steam rack. 3. Hit the Steam button and adjust the time to 7 minutes. 4. Once the timer beeps, quick-release the pressure then unlock lid and remove it. 5. Immediately transfer the eggs to a suitable bowl filled with iced water and let them sit for almost 15 minutes. 6. Remove the cooked eggs from the water and peel the shell away from the eggs. 7. Roughly chop the eggs and add them to a suitable bowl. Add the avocado, mustard, vinegar, garlic powder, dill weed, salt, and parsley and stir to combine. 8. Serve on top of arugula leaves.
Per Serving: Calories 353; Total Fat 28.2g; Sodium 472mg; Total Carbs 14.9g; Fiber 9.9g; Sugars 1.2g; Protein 14.6g

Spinach Salad with Avocado Dressing

Prep time: 10 minutes | Cook time: 11 minutes | Serves: 4

½ cup dry quinoa	2 tablespoons lemon juice
1 cup vegetable stock	¼–¾ cup water
1 tablespoon avocado oil	5 ounces baby spinach leaves, torn
1 (15-ounce) can chickpeas, drained	
	1 large tomato, cored, deseeded, diced
¾ teaspoon salt	
1 medium ripe avocado	¼ teaspoon black pepper, freshly ground
5 whole basil leaves	
1 clove garlic, minced	

1. Keep the quinoa in a fine-mesh strainer and rinse under water until the water runs clear. 2. Place the quinoa and stock in the inner pot. Seal the cooker's lid. 3. Select the Manual or Pressure mode and adjust the time to 1 minute. 4. Once the timer beeps, quick-release the pressure then unlock lid and remove it. 5. Transfer the quinoa to a suitable bowl to cool. 6. Wipe the inner pot clean and add the oil. Hit the Sauté button and use the Adjust button to change the setting to More. 7. Add the chickpeas and ¼ teaspoon salt to the inner insert and cook with occasional stirring until the chickpeas are browned and getting crispy, almost 10 minutes. Press the Cancel button. 8. Meanwhile, make the prepared dressing. Put the avocado, basil, garlic, lemon juice, ¼ teaspoon salt, and ¼ cup water in a suitable blender and blend until smooth. 9. In a suitable bowl, place the spinach, tomato, quinoa, and chickpeas and then drizzle with the prepared dressing. 10. Toss well to coat and top with the ¼ teaspoon salt and pepper.
Per Serving: Calories 589; Total Fat 18.2g; Sodium 513mg; Total Carbs 85.6g; Fiber 24.5g; Sugars 13.2g; Protein 26g

Lentil Chickpea suitable bowls

Prep time: 10 minutes | Cook time: 8 minutes | Serves: 4

¾ cup red lentils
1 (15-ounce) can diced tomatoes
1 (13.66-ounce) can coconut milk
1 cup vegetable broth
1 tablespoon curry powder
1 teaspoon peeled and grated fresh ginger
1 teaspoon turmeric

1 teaspoon salt
1 tablespoon lime juice
1 (15-ounce) can chickpeas, drained
4 cups chopped, deveined kale
⅓ cup fresh cilantro leaves, chopped

1. Add all the recipe ingredients, except the lime juice, kale, and cilantro leaves, in the inner pot and stir to combine well. Seal the cooker's lid. 2. Select the Manual or Pressure mode and adjust the time to 8 minutes approximately. 3. Once the timer beeps, let pressure release naturally and remove it. 4. Stir in the kale and lime juice. Serve topped with cilantro.
Per Serving: Calories 390; Total Fat 15.3g; Sodium 1086mg; Total Carbs 50g; Fiber 17.3g; Sugars 6.6g; Protein 18.2g

Vegetable Rice Casserole

Prep time: 15 minutes | Cook time: 8 minutes | Serves: 4

1 cup vegetable broth
¼ cup fresh lime juice
¼ cup apple cider vinegar
½ cup coconut aminos
¼ cup almond butter
1 tablespoon coconut oil

12 ounces Brussels sprouts, tough ends removed and cut in half
12 ounces carrots (almost 4 medium), peeled, ends removed, and cut into 1" chunks
1 cup jasmine rice

1. In a suitable bowl, mix the broth, lime juice, vinegar, coconut aminos, and almond butter until well combined. Set aside. 2. Hit the Sauté button and add the oil to the inner insert. When the oil is melted, add the Brussels sprouts and carrots and sauté with occasional stirring, for about 5 minutes. Press the Cancel button. 3. Add the rice and sauce to the inner insert and stir until well combined. Seal the cooker's lid. 4. Select the Manual or Pressure mode and adjust the time to 3 minutes. 5. Release the pressure completely then remove its lid.
Per Serving: Calories 280; Total Fat 4.6g; Sodium 271mg; Total Carbs 52.7g; Fiber 7.4g; Sugars 6.3g; Protein 8g

Asian Noodle Bowls

Prep time: 10 minutes | Cook time: 3 minutes | Serves: 4

½ cup reduced-sodium tamari
2 tablespoons rice vinegar
2 tablespoons almond butter
2 tablespoons erythritol
2 cups vegetable broth
2 cups sugar snap peas, roughly chopped

2 large peeled carrots, thickly sliced
8 ounces uncooked brown rice noodles
¼ cup sliced scallions
4 tablespoons chopped almonds

1. Place the tamari, vinegar, almond butter, erythritol, broth, peas, and carrots in the inner pot and top with the noodles. Seal the cooker's lid. 2. Select the Manual or Pressure mode and adjust the time to 3 minutes. 3. Once the timer beeps, quick-release the pressure then unlock lid and remove it. 4. stir the ingredients. Portion into four bowls and top with scallions and a sprinkle of almonds.
Per Serving: Calories 254; Total Fat 10.3g; Sodium 514mg; Total Carbs 32.8g; Fiber 3.3g; Sugars 5g; Protein 7.9g

White Beans and Collard Greens

Prep time: 10 minutes | Cook time: 30 minutes | Serves: 4

1 bunch collard greens, chopped
1 cup diced tomatoes
1 small yellow onion, chopped
5 garlic cloves, minced

½ teaspoon sea salt
1 cup dried navy beans
3 cups vegetable broth

1. In the Instant Pot, mix the collard greens, tomatoes, onion, garlic, salt, beans, and broth. Give it a stir. Lock the lid. 2. Set the Pressure Cook mode and cook at high pressure for almost 30 minutes. 3. When cooking is complete, use a natural release for almost 20 minutes, then quick release any remaining pressure. 4. Remove the cooker's lid, stir well, and serve hot.
Per Serving: Calories 231; Total Fat 2.1g; Sodium 816mg; Total Carbs 38.1g; Fiber 14.4g; Sugars 4.5g; Protein 16.6g

Sautéed Spinach

Prep time: 5 minutes | Cook time: 5 minutes | Serves: 4

1 tablespoon olive oil, extra-virgin
1 (10-ounce) package chopped spinach, drained
1 garlic clove, minced

1 teaspoon salt
¼ teaspoon black pepper, freshly ground
1 tablespoon fresh lemon juice

1. In a suitable skillet, heat the oil over high heat. 2. Add the spinach, garlic, salt, and pepper and sauté until the spinach is heated through almost 5 minutes. 3. Stir in the lemon juice and serve.
Per Serving: Calories 49; Total Fat 3.8g; Sodium 638mg; Total Carbs 3g; Fiber 1.6g; Sugars 0.4g; Protein 2.1g

Lentil Muffins

Prep time: 10 minutes | Cook time: 17 minutes | Serves: 3

½ tablespoon avocado oil
¼ cup diced onion
⅛ cup diced celery
⅛ cup diced carrots
1 clove garlic, minced
1 large egg
1½ cups cooked lentils
½ tablespoon Italian seasoning

blend
1 tablespoon tomato paste
½ tablespoon Dijon mustard
½ cup gluten-free panko bread crumbs
¼ teaspoon salt
⅛ teaspoon black pepper

1. Hit the Sauté button and add the oil to the inner insert. 2. Allow the oil to preheat 1 minute, and then add the onion, celery, and carrots then sauté for 5 minutes. 3. Toss in garlic then stir and cook for 30 sec. 4. Beat the egg in a suitable bowl. Add the lentils, Italian seasoning, tomato paste, mustard, bread crumbs, salt, pepper, and the vegetable mixture. Stir until the ingredients are well combined. 5. Place six silicone muffin cups inside a 6" cake pan. Divide the mixture into the six cups. Cover with aluminum foil. 6. Pour 1 cup water into the inner insert, stirring with a wooden spoon to ensure there are no food bit stuck to the pot. Place the steam rack inside and place the cake pan with the lentil muffins on top of the steam rack. Seal the cooker's lid. 7. Select the Manual or Pressure mode and adjust the time to 10 minutes. 8. Once the timer beeps, quick-release the pressure then unlock lid and remove it. 9. Remove this pan from the inner insert and remove the aluminum foil. Let the lentil muffins rest 5–10 minutes before serving.
Per Serving: Calories 483; Total Fat 6g; Sodium 184mg; Total Carbs 77.2g; Fiber 31.2g; Sugars 6g; Protein 30.4g

Egg Salad Cups

Prep time: 10 minutes | Cook time: 0 minutes | Serves: 4

8 hard-boiled eggs, peeled and chopped
½ red bell pepper, chopped
¼ cup mayonnaise, anti-inflammatory

1 teaspoon Dijon mustard
½ teaspoon sea salt
⅛ teaspoon black pepper
4 large lettuce leaves

1. In a suitable bowl, combine the eggs, red bell pepper, mayonnaise, mustard, salt, and pepper. Mix gently to combine. 2. Spoon the mixture into the lettuce leaves.
Per serving: Calories: 196; Total fat 13.9g; Sodium 479mg; Total carbs 7g; Fiber 0.6g; Sugars 2.9g; Protein 11.7g

Vegetable Sticks with Black Bean Dip

Prep time: 15 minutes | Cook time: 0 minutes | Serves: 4 to 6

1 (15-ounces) can black beans, rinsed and drained
2 scallions, chopped
1 tablespoon chopped fresh cilantro
2 tablespoons olive oil, extra-virgin

2 tablespoons fresh lime juice
1 teaspoon chipotle powder
1 teaspoon salt
½ teaspoon ground cumin
1 cup carrot sticks, for serving
1 cup celery sticks, for serving

1. Combine all the recipe ingredients except for the vegetable sticks in a suitable bowl and toss to mix. 2. Using a potato masher, mash all the recipe ingredients until the mixture has a texture that's slightly smooth but still lumpy. 3. Serve with the vegetable sticks for dipping.
Per Serving: Calories 426; Total Fat 8.6g; Sodium 588mg; Total Carbs 67g; Fiber 16.4g; Sugars 2.4g; Protein 23.2g

Mushroom Pasta

Prep time: 15 minutes | Cook time: 20 minutes | Serves: 4 to 6

2 tablespoons olive oil, extra-virgin
2 cups button mushrooms, quartered
1 teaspoon salt
¼ teaspoon pepper, freshly ground

¼ cup dry red wine
1 shallot, minced
1 garlic clove, minced
1 (12-ounce) package rigatoni
4 to 4½ cups water
1 teaspoon chopped fresh rosemary

1. Preheat the olive oil in a Dutch oven over high heat. 2. Once hot, add the mushrooms, salt, pepper, and red wine. Cook with occasional stirring, until the mushrooms are cooked, almost 5 minutes. 3. Add the shallot and garlic and stir to combine. 4. Add the rigatoni and 4 cups of water and cook to a boil. Lower to a simmer, cover, and cook until the pasta is tender and most of the water is absorbed, 12 to 15 minutes. 5. Transfer the cooked rigatoni to a serving bowl, drizzle with olive oil, top with the rosemary, and serve.
Per Serving: Calories 396; Total Fat 8.6g; Sodium 596mg; Total Carbs 65.9g; Fiber 3.4g; Sugars 3.8g; Protein 12.1g

Roasted Sweet Potatoes

Prep time: 10 minutes | Cook time: 20 minutes | Serves: 4 to 6

2 tablespoons olive oil, extra-virgin
3 sweet potatoes, cut into thin wedges
1 teaspoon salt

1 teaspoon ground turmeric
½ teaspoon ground coriander
¼ teaspoon ground ginger
¼ teaspoon chipotle powder
1 lime

1. At 400 degrees F, preheat your oven. 2. Brush two suitable rimmed baking sheets with olive oil. 3. Put the sweet potato wedges in a suitable bowl. 4. Stir in 2 tablespoons oil and toss to coat the potatoes. 5. In a suitable bowl, mix the salt, turmeric, coriander, ginger, and chipotle powder. Sprinkle the spice mix over the potatoes, mixing well to coat evenly. 6. Arrange the sweet potato wedges in a single layer on the prepared baking sheets. 7. Bake until the sweet potatoes are tender in the middle and slightly browned and caramelized on the edges, almost 20 minutes. 8. Remove from the oven, squeeze lime juice over the wedges, and serve.
Per Serving: Calories 195; Total Fat 7.3g; Sodium 592mg; Total Carbs 31.8g; Fiber 4.7g; Sugars 0.6g; Protein 1.8g

Buckwheat Noodles with Peanut Sauce

Prep time: 20 minutes | Cook time: 0 minutes | Serves: 4

1 (8-ounce) package buckwheat noodles, cooked
4 tablespoons peanut sauce
¼ cup fresh cilantro leaves,

chopped
¼ cup peanuts, chopped
6 scallions, sliced

1. In a suitable bowl, toss the buckwheat noodles with the peanut sauce to coat. 2. Garnish with cilantro, peanuts, and scallions.
Per serving: Calories: 319; Total fat 9.8g; Sodium 282mg; Total carbs 50.2g; Fiber 7.8g; Sugars 7.4g; Protein 12g

Lentil Stew

Prep time: 10 minutes | Cook time: 15 minutes | Serves: 4 to 6

1 tablespoon olive oil, extra-virgin
1 onion, chopped
3 carrots, peeled and sliced
8 Brussels sprouts, halved
1 large turnip, peeled, quartered, and sliced
1 garlic clove, sliced

6 cups vegetable broth
1 (15-ounce) can lentils, drained
1 cup frozen corn
1 teaspoon salt
¼ teaspoon black pepper
1 tablespoon chopped fresh parsley

1. In a suitable Dutch oven, heat the oil over high heat. 2. Add the onion and sauté until softened, almost 3 minutes. 3. Add the carrots, Brussels sprouts, turnip, and garlic and sauté for an additional 3 minutes. 4. Pour in broth and continue cooking to a boil. Lower to a simmer and cook until the vegetables are tender, almost 5 minutes. 5. Add the lentils, corn, salt, pepper, and parsley and cook for an additional minute to heat the lentils and corn. Serve hot.
Per Serving: Calories 371; Total Fat 4.9g; Sodium 1207mg; Total Carbs 57.5g; Fiber 25g; Sugars 7g; Protein 25.6g

Roasted Tri-Color Cauliflower

Prep time: 10 minutes | Cook time: 20 minutes | Serves: 4 to 6

1½ cups white cauliflower florets
1½ cups purple cauliflower florets
1½ cups yellow cauliflower florets
3 tablespoons olive oil, extra-

virgin
¼ cup fresh lemon juice
1 teaspoon salt
¼ teaspoon black pepper, freshly ground

1. At 400 degrees F, preheat your oven. 2. In a suitable bowl, mix the cauliflower, olive oil, and lemon juice. Toss to coat well. 3. Spread the prepared cauliflower on a rimmed baking sheet and add the salt and pepper. 4. Cover with aluminum foil and bake for almost 15 minutes. 5. Remove the foil sheet and continue to bake in the preheated oven until the cauliflower starts to brown around the edges, almost 5 minutes more. Serve warm or at room temperature.
Per Serving: Calories 99; Total Fat 7.1g; Sodium 417mg; Total Carbs 6.7g; Fiber 3.7g; Sugars 3g; Protein 2.8g

Quinoa with Vegetables

Prep time: 10 minutes | Cook time: 15 minutes | Serves: 4 to 6

3 tablespoons olive oil, extra-virgin
1½ cups quartered Brussels sprouts
1 large zucchini, chopped
1 onion, chopped
3 garlic cloves, sliced
2½ cups cooked quinoa

1 cup vegetable broth or tomato sauce
1 tablespoon fresh lemon juice
1 teaspoon dried oregano
1 teaspoon salt
¼ teaspoon black pepper, freshly ground

1. In a suitable skillet, heat the oil over high heat. 2. Add the Brussels sprouts, zucchini, onion, and garlic and sauté until the vegetables are tender, 5 to 7 minutes. 3. Add the quinoa and broth, cover, and cook for an additional 5 minutes. 4. Add the lemon juice, oregano, salt, and pepper and stir to fluff the quinoa. 5. Serve warm or at room temperature.
Per Serving: Calories 542; Total Fat 17.8g; Sodium 801mg; Total Carbs 79g; Fiber 10.7g; Sugars 3.9g; Protein 19.2g

Whole-Wheat Penne with White Beans

Prep time: 10 minutes | Cook time: 18 minutes | Serves: 6

1 (12-ounce) package whole-wheat penne
2 tablespoons olive oil, extra-virgin
1 bunch Swiss chard, cut into thin ribbons

1 garlic clove, sliced
1 teaspoon salt
⅛ teaspoon red pepper flakes
1 (15-ounce) can white beans, drained
¼ cup chopped toasted walnuts

1. Cook the penne in a suitable pot of boiling water according to the package directions, then drain. 2. While the pasta is cooking, in a suitable skillet, heat the oil over high heat. 3. Add the chard, garlic, salt, and red pepper flakes and cook until the chard has wilted, almost 3 minutes. Stir in the white beans until warm. 4. In a suitable serving bowl, toss together the penne and chard-bean mixture, mixing well. Sprinkle with the walnuts and serve.
Per Serving: Calories 499; Total Fat 9.4g; Sodium 422mg; Total Carbs 83.4g; Fiber 17.2g; Sugars 1.6g; Protein 26.9g

Red Quinoa Salad

Prep time: 10 minutes | Cook time: 1 minutes | Serves: 4

1 cup red quinoa, rinsed
1 cup water
½ teaspoon sea salt
¼ teaspoon black pepper
1 cup coarsely chopped tomatoes

1 cup fresh basil, chopped
2 tablespoons olive oil
Juice of 1 lemon
¼ cup pumpkin seeds

1. In the Instant Pot, mix the quinoa and water. Lock the lid. 2. Set Pressure Cook mode and cook at high pressure for almost 1 minute. 3. When cooking is complete, use a natural release for almost 10 minutes, then quick release any remaining pressure. 4. Remove the cooker's lid and stir in the salt, pepper, tomatoes, basil, olive oil, and lemon juice to combine well. 5. Top with the pumpkin seeds and serve warm or chilled.
Per Serving: Calories 161; Total Fat 12.4g; Sodium 375mg; Total Carbs 9.8g; Fiber 1.5g; Sugars 2.6g; Protein 3.8g

Mediterranean Millet Salad

Prep time: 10 minutes | Cook time: 10 minutes | Serves: 4

1 cup millet
1¾ cups water
1 red bell pepper, diced
1 English cucumber, seeded and diced
½ cup chopped feta cheese
⅓ cup pitted Kalamata olives,
chopped
½ cup fresh parsley, chopped
¼ cup chopped almonds
Juice of 1 lemon
1 tablespoon olive oil
½ teaspoon sea salt

1. In the Instant Pot, mix the millet and water. Lock the lid. 2. Set the Pressure Cook mode and cook at high pressure for almost 10 minutes. 3. When cooking is complete, use a natural release for almost 10 minutes, then quick release any remaining pressure. 4. Remove the cooker's lid and stir in the bell pepper, cucumber, feta, olives, parsley, almonds, lemon juice, olive oil, and salt. Serve warm or chilled.
Per Serving: Calories 339; Total Fat 14g; Sodium 556mg; Total Carbs 44.6g; Fiber 6.4g; Sugars 3.8g; Protein 10.5g

Red Beans and Brown Rice

Prep time: 10 minutes | Cook time: 30 minutes | Serves: 6

1 tablespoon avocado oil
1 yellow onion, chopped
3 celery stalks, chopped
1 green bell pepper, diced
3 garlic cloves, minced
1 teaspoon dried thyme
½ teaspoon sea salt
1½ cups dried red beans, rinsed
1½ cups brown rice
4 cups vegetable broth
1 bay leaf
1½ cups water

1. Select Sauté on the Instant Pot, pour in the oil, and let the pot preheat. 2. Add the onion, celery, and bell pepper. Cook for almost 6 minutes. 3. Stir in the garlic, thyme, and salt and cook for almost 30 seconds. 4. Add the beans, brown rice, broth, bay leaf, and water. Select Cancel. Lock the lid. 5. Set the Pressure Cook mode and cook at high pressure for almost 30 minutes. 6. When cooking is complete, use a natural release for almost 20 minutes, then quick release any remaining pressure. 7. Remove the cooker's lid, remove the bay leaf, and serve.
Per Serving: Calories 373; Total Fat 3.1g; Sodium 687mg; Total Carbs 69.2g; Fiber 9.6g; Sugars 3.4g; Protein 17.8g

Kale Fried Rice

Prep time: 10 minutes | Cook time: 12 minutes | Serves: 4

2 tablespoons extra-virgin olive oil
8 ounces tofu, chopped
6 scallions, white and green parts, thinly sliced
2 cups kale, stemmed and chopped
3 cups cooked brown rice
¼ cup stir-fry sauce

1. In a suitable skillet over medium-high heat, heat the olive oil until it shimmers. 2. Add the tofu, scallions, and kale. Cook for 5 to 7 minutes, frequently stirring, until the vegetables are soft. 3. Add the brown rice and stir-fry sauce. Cook for 3 to 5 minutes, occasionally stirring until heated through.
Per serving: Calories: 426; Total fat 8.8g; Sodium 20mg; Total carbs 76.4g; Fiber 4.3g; Sugars 0.6g; Protein 11.2g

Grain Bowls

Prep time: 10 minutes | Cook time: 20 minutes | Serves: 4

½ cup quinoa, rinsed
½ cup farro
½ cup spelt
½ cup brown rice
2¾ cups water
2 garlic cloves, minced
1 teaspoon sea salt
½ teaspoon ground turmeric
¼ teaspoon ground ginger
¼ teaspoon black pepper, freshly ground

1. In the Instant Pot, mix the quinoa, farro, spelt, the brown rice, water, garlic, salt, turmeric, ginger, and pepper. Lock the lid. 2. Set the Pressure Cook mode and cook at high pressure for almost 20 minutes. 3. Let sit for almost 10 minutes to allow the grains to become tender and further mix the flavors. 4. Remove the cooker's lid and serve warm.
Per Serving: Calories 254; Total Fat 2.6g; Sodium 482mg; Total Carbs 49.1g; Fiber 4.8g; Sugars 0.2g; Protein 7.8g

Mushroom Risotto

Prep time: 10 minutes | Cook time: 20 to 25 minutes | Serves: to 6

2 tablespoons olive oil, extra-virgin
1 large shallot, sliced
10 large button or cremini mushrooms, sliced
½ cup dry red wine
1 cup Arborio rice
1½ to 2 cups vegetable broth
½ cup grated Parmesan cheese
1 tablespoon chopped fresh parsley
1 teaspoon salt
¼ teaspoon black pepper, freshly ground

1. Heat the olive oil in a suitable skillet over high heat. Add the shallot and sauté until softened, 3 to 5 minutes. 2. Add the mushrooms and red wine and simmer until all the wine has evaporated. 3. Add the rice and sauté for almost 3 minutes to coat the rice with the flavors in the pan. 4. Add ½ cup of broth and cook and stir occasionally until the broth has been absorbed. Add another ½ cup of broth and repeat. Continue until the risotto is tender but not mushy, almost 20 minutes. 5. Remove from the heat. Sprinkle with the Parmesan cheese, parsley, salt, and pepper, and serve.
Per Serving: Calories 336; Total Fat 9.9g; Sodium 1672mg; Total Carbs 42.6g; Fiber 1.7g; Sugars 2.1g; Protein 12.3g

Ramen with Kale and Mushrooms

Prep time: 10 minutes | Cook time: 8 minutes | Serves: 4

1 (12-ounce) bag kelp noodles
4 cups vegetable broth
2 cups kale, ribs removed, chopped into bite-size pieces
5 ounces cremini mushrooms, sliced
1 small yellow onion, diced
3 garlic cloves, minced
1 tablespoon brown rice miso paste
1 cup fresh bean sprouts
½ cup chopped scallions, white and green parts
2 teaspoons toasted sesame seeds

1. Place the kelp noodles in a suitable bowl and cover with cool water. Set aside to soak for almost 10 minutes while you prepare the remaining ingredients. 2. In the Instant Pot, mix the broth, kale, mushrooms, onion, garlic, and miso. Lock the lid. 3. Set the pressure cook mode and cook at high pressure for almost 5 minutes. 4. When cooking is complete, use a quick release. 5. Remove the cooker's lid. Drain the cooked noodles and transfer them to the pot. Select Cancel. 6. Select Sauté on the Instant Pot. Cook for almost 3 minutes. Select Cancel. 7. Transfer the ramen to bowls and top with the sprouts, scallions, and sesame seeds to serve.
Per Serving: Calories 105; Total Fat 2.4g; Sodium 812mg; Total Carbs 12.2g; Fiber 2.4g; Sugars 2.4g; Protein 9.5g

Baked Spiced Tofu

Prep time: 5 minutes | Cook time: 20 minutes | Serves: 4

2 teaspoons ground cumin
2 teaspoons smoked paprika
1 teaspoon ground cinnamon
1 teaspoon garlic powder
1 teaspoon ground turmeric
1 teaspoon red pepper flakes
1 teaspoon salt
1 (14-ounce) package extra-firm tofu, drained
⅓ cup extra-virgin olive oil
2 tablespoons tahini or unsweetened almond butter

1. At 400 degrees F, preheat your oven and layer a baking sheet with parchment paper. 2. In a suitable bowl, combine the cumin, paprika, cinnamon, garlic powder, turmeric, red pepper flakes, and salt. 3. Place half of the spice mixture in a suitable bowl, reserving the other half. 4. Cut the tofu block into four large rectangles and place on several layers of paper towels. Cover with additional paper towels and press down to release the water. 5. Cut the rectangles into 1-inch cubes and transfer to the bowl with the spice mixture. Toss to coat well. 6. Arrange the tofu cubes ½ inch apart in a single layer on the prepared baking sheet, reserving the bowl. Bake the tofu for almost 15 to 20 minutes, until it is crispy and golden. 7. While the tofu bakes, add the olive oil and tahini to the reserved spice mixture and whisk until smooth. 8. In the large reserved bowl, combine the baked tofu with the oil-tahini mixture and toss well to coat. Let it cool down if not serving warm. 9. Transfer to a storage container, cover and allow to marinate 24 hours refrigerated.
Per serving: Calories 293; Fat 27.1g; Sodium 601mg; Carbs 6.2g; Fiber 2.2g; Sugars 0.9g; Protein 11.7g

Buddha Bowl

Prep time: 15 minutes | Cook time: 35 minutes | Serves: 4 to 6

1 cup brown basmati rice
2 cups vegetable broth
3 tablespoons coconut oil
2 teaspoons salt
1 pint sliced mushrooms
2 garlic cloves, sliced thin
4 ounces fresh snow peas, strings removed
2 carrots, sliced thin

½ cup frozen peas, thawed
2 scallions, sliced thin
3 tablespoons chopped fresh cilantro
3 tablespoons lime juice
1 tablespoon toasted sesame oil
1 tablespoon coconut aminos
½ teaspoon red pepper flakes

1. In a suitable saucepan over high heat, stir together the basmati rice, vegetable broth, 1 tablespoon of coconut oil, and 1 teaspoon of salt. 2. Bring to a boil, then reduce its heat to simmer. Cover the pot and cook the rice for 25 to 35 minutes, or until tender. 3. In a suitable pan over high heat, melt the remaining 2 tablespoons of coconut oil. Add the mushrooms. Sauté for almost 5 minutes, or until they are slightly browned. 4. Add the garlic, snow peas, and carrots. Sauté for 3 minutes more. 5. Add the thawed peas and cover the pan to warm them through. 6. Add the sautéed vegetables to the rice and stir to combine. When ready to serve, stir in the scallions, cilantro, lime juice, sesame oil, coconut aminos, red pepper flakes, and the remaining 1 teaspoon of salt.
Per serving: Calories: 239; Total fat 9.9g; Sodium 1058mg; Total carbs 31.8g; Fiber 2.6g; Sugars 3.2g; Protein 6.2g

Crispy Tofu with Mushrooms

Prep time: 10 minutes | Cook time: 25 minutes | Serves: 4

1 (14-ounce) package extra-firm tofu, drained
¼ cup tamari
2 tablespoons almond or cashew butter, unsweetened
1 tablespoon rice vinegar
1 tablespoon sesame oil
1 teaspoon red curry paste or red pepper flakes

¼ cup coconut oil
1 (2-inch) piece fresh ginger, peeled and minced
4 baby bok choy, trimmed and quartered
4 ounces shiitake mushrooms, sliced
4 garlic cloves, sliced

1. At 400 degrees F, preheat your oven and layer a baking sheet with parchment paper. 2. Cut the tofu into ½-inch cubes and arrange them at least ½ inch apart in a single layer on the prepared baking sheet. 3. Bake on the middle rack of the oven for almost 15 to 20 minutes until the tofu is golden and crispy, being careful not to burn it. Remove from the oven. 4. While the tofu bakes, in a suitable bowl, whisk together the tamari, almond butter, rice vinegar, sesame oil, and red curry paste. Set aside. 5. In large skillet, heat the coconut oil over medium-high heat. Add the ginger and sauté for almost 2 to 3 minutes, until fragrant. 6. Add the bok choy and mushrooms and sauté for almost 5 to 6 minutes, until they are just tender and wilted. 7. Add the garlic and sauté for almost 1 minute until fragrant. Pour the reserved tamari mixture over the vegetables, add the baked tofu, and stir to coat well. 8. Reduce its heat to low, cover, and simmer for almost 3 to 4 minutes until the sauce is slightly thickened. 9. Uncover, toss to coat, and serve warm.
Per serving: Calories 432; Fat 35.8g; Sodium 1196mg; Carbs 16.6g; Fiber 2.4g; Sugars 2.7g; Protein 17.8g

Quinoa Penne with Artichoke Hearts

Prep time: 10 minutes | Cook time: 8 minutes | Serves: 4

1 teaspoon avocado oil
4 garlic cloves, minced
1 (24-ounce) jar reduced-sodium marinara sauce
¾ teaspoon sea salt

9 ounces quinoa penne
1 cup water, plus more as needed
1 (14-ounce) can artichoke hearts, drained

1. Select Sauté on the Instant Pot and let the pot preheat. 2. Pour in the oil and add the garlic. Cook for almost 2 minutes. 3. Stir in the marinara sauce and salt to combine. Cook for almost 2 minutes until just beginning to simmer. 4. Add the pasta and water. Select Cancel. Lock the lid. 5. Set the pressure cook mode and cook at high pressure for almost 4 minutes. 6. When cooking is complete, use a quick release. 7. Remove the cooker's lid and stir in the artichoke hearts.
Per Serving: Calories 344; Total Fat 3g; Sodium 603mg; Total Carbs 73.8g; Fiber 11.5g; Sugars 8.6g; Protein 9.4g

Garden Veggies

Prep time: 10 minutes | Cook time: 0 minutes | Serves: 4

1 (1-pound) bag frozen vegetables
1 cup vegetable broth
1 teaspoon ghee

½ teaspoon sea salt
¼ teaspoon garlic powder
⅛ teaspoon black pepper

1. In the Instant Pot, mix the vegetables, broth, ghee, salt, garlic powder, and pepper. Lock the lid. 2. Set the pressure cook mode and cook at high pressure for 0 minutes. 3. When cooking is complete, use a quick release. 4. Remove the cooker's lid and give the vegetables a stir before serving.
Per Serving: Calories 93; Total Fat 1.6g; Sodium 465mg; Total Carbs 15.2g; Fiber 5g; Sugars 3.8g; Protein 4.5g

Bean Burrito Bowls

Prep time: 10 minutes | Cook time: 20 minutes | Serves: 4

1 tablespoon avocado oil
1 small yellow onion, chopped
1 green bell pepper, chopped
1 cup black rice
1 (15.5-ounce) can black beans, rinsed
1 cup water
1 cup diced tomatoes

½ teaspoon sea salt
½ teaspoon paprika
¼ teaspoon ground cumin
¼ teaspoon garlic powder
⅛ teaspoon black pepper
1 tablespoon coconut yogurt
1 avocado, peeled, halved, pitted, and sliced

1. Select Sauté on the Instant Pot and let the pot preheat. 2. Pour in the oil and add the onion and bell pepper. Cook for almost 3 minutes. 3. Stir in the black rice, black beans, water, tomatoes, salt, paprika, cumin, garlic powder, and pepper. Select Cancel. Lock the lid. 4. Set the pressure cook mode and cook at high pressure for almost 17 minutes. 5. When cooking is complete, use a natural release for almost 10 minutes, then quick release any remaining pressure. 6. Remove the cooker's lid and stir the ingredients. 7. Garnish with yogurt and sliced avocado, and serve.
Per Serving: Calories 541; Total Fat 12.4g; Sodium 250mg; Total Carbs 85.4g; Fiber 21.3g; Sugars 6.1g; Protein 26.5g

Fried Wild Rice

Prep time: 10 minutes | Cook time: 34 minutes | Serves: 4

2 cups wild rice, rinsed
1½ cups vegetable broth
1 tablespoon tamari
¼ teaspoon ghee
2 teaspoons avocado oil

1 small yellow onion, diced
3 garlic cloves, minced
3 cups frozen mixed vegetables
½ teaspoon sea salt
3 large eggs whisked

1. In the Instant Pot, mix the wild rice, broth, tamari, and ghee. Lock the lid. 2. Set the pressure cook mode and cook at high pressure for almost 28 minutes. 3. When cooking is complete, use a quick release. Select Cancel. 4. Remove the cooker's lid and transfer the cooked rice to a suitable bowl. 5. Select Sauté on the Instant Pot and let the pot preheat. 6. Pour in the oil and add the onion and garlic. 7. Cook for almost 2 minutes, or until the onion is translucent and the garlic begins to brown lightly. 8. Add the mixed vegetables and cook for almost 2 minutes. Stir the cooked rice into the pot and add the salt. Mix well to combine. 9. Pour in the beaten eggs and sauté for almost 2 minutes, or until the eggs firm up. Select Cancel and serve.
Per Serving: Calories 459; Total Fat 3.6g; Sodium 1614mg; Total Carbs 82g; Fiber 11.5g; Sugars 8.3g; Protein 25.9g

Roasted Broccoli and Cashews

Prep time: 10 minutes | Cook time: 20 minutes | Serves: 4

6 cups broccoli florets
2 tablespoons extra-virgin olive oil

1 teaspoon salt
1 tablespoon coconut aminos
½ cup toasted cashews

1. At 375 degrees F, preheat your oven. 2. In a suitable bowl, toss the broccoli with olive oil and salt. 3. Transfer the prepared broccoli in a baking sheet into a single layer. 4. Place the broccoli sheet in the preheated oven and roast for 15 to 20 minutes, or until the broccoli is tender. 5. In a suitable bowl, toss the roasted broccoli with the coconut aminos and cashews, and serve.
Per serving: Calories: 108; Total fat 7.5g; Sodium 628mg; Total carbs 9.3g; Fiber 3.6g; Sugars 2.3g; Protein 3.8g

Braised Bok Choy with Shiitake Mushrooms

Prep time: 10 minutes | Cook time: 10 minutes | Serves: 4

1 tablespoon coconut oil
8 baby bok choy, halved lengthwise
½ cup water
1 tablespoon coconut aminos
1 cup shiitake mushrooms,
stemmed, sliced thin
Salt
Black pepper
1 scallion, sliced thin
1 tablespoon toasted sesame seeds

1. In a suitable pan over high heat, melt the coconut oil. Spread the bok choy in a single layer. Add the water, coconut aminos, and mushrooms to the pan. 2. Cover and braise the vegetables for 5 to 10 minutes, or until the bok choy is tender. 3. Remove this pan from the heat. Season the vegetables with salt and pepper. 4. Transfer the cooked bok choy and mushrooms to a serving dish and garnish with scallions and sesame seeds.
Per serving: Calories: 165; Total fat 9.8g; Sodium 440mg; Total carbs 18.3g; Fiber 5.1g; Sugars 6.1g; Protein 6.3g

Quinoa-Broccoli Sauté

Prep time: 10 minutes | Cook time: 10 minutes | Serves: 4

1 tablespoon coconut oil
2 leeks, white part only, sliced
2 garlic cloves, chopped
4 cups chopped broccoli
½ cup vegetable broth, or water
1 teaspoon curry powder
2 cups cooked quinoa
1 tablespoon coconut aminos

1. In a suitable skillet over high heat, melt the coconut oil. Add the leeks and garlic. Sauté for 2 minutes. 2. Add the broccoli and vegetable broth. Cover the pan and cook for 5 minutes. 3. Stir in the curry powder, quinoa, and coconut aminos. Cook for 2 to 3 minutes, uncovered, or until the quinoa is warmed through. 4. Serve warm as a side dish or at room temperature as a salad.
Per serving: Calories: 259; Total fat 5.9g; Sodium 20mg; Total carbs 43g; Fiber 5.4g; Sugars 1.7g; Protein 9.4g

Tomato Basil Pasta

Prep time: 5 minutes | Cook time: 10 minutes | Serves: 4

2 tablespoons extra-virgin olive oil
1 onion, sliced thin
2 garlic cloves, sliced thin
1 pound gluten-free penne pasta
1 (15-ounce) can chopped
tomatoes
1½ teaspoons salt
¼ teaspoon black pepper
¼ cup chopped fresh basil, plus 4 whole basil leaves
4½ cups water

1. In a large, heavy-bottomed Dutch oven over medium heat, heat 2 tablespoons of olive oil. 2. Add the onion and garlic. Stir to coat with the oil. Add the pasta, tomatoes, salt, pepper, the 4 whole basil leaves, and water to the pot. 3. Cook the liquid to a boil and cover the pot. Cook for 8 to 10 minutes. Check the pasta to see if it is cooked; add more water if necessary. Continue cooking until the pasta is tender. 4. Transfer the pasta to a serving bowl and garnish with the remaining ¼ cup of chopped basil and a drizzle of olive oil.
Per serving: Calories: 408; Total fat 8.8g; Sodium 3204mg; Total carbs 68.8g; Fiber 3.5g; Sugars 7g; Protein 11.9g

Zucchini Patties

Prep time: 15 minutes | Cook time: 20 minutes | Serves: 2

2 medium zucchinis, shredded
1 teaspoon salt
2 eggs
2 tablespoons chickpea flour
1 scallion, chopped
1 tablespoon chopped fresh mint
½ teaspoon salt
2 tablespoons extra-virgin olive oil

1. Place the shredded zucchini in a fine-mesh strainer and sprinkle it with ½ teaspoon of salt. Set aside to drain while assembling the other ingredients. 2. In a suitable bowl, beat together the eggs, chickpea flour, scallion, mint, and the remaining ½ teaspoon of salt. 3. Gently squeeze the zucchini to drain as much liquid as possible before adding it to the egg mixture. Stir to mix well. 4. Place a suitable skillet over medium-high heat. When the pan is hot, add the olive oil. Drop the zucchini mixture by spoonfuls into the pan. 5. Gently flatten. Cook for 2 to 3 minutes, or until golden brown. Flip and cook for almost 2 minutes more on the other side. 6. Serve warm or at room temperature.
Per serving: Calories: 263; Total fat 19.5g; Sodium 1249mg; Total carbs 15.3g; Fiber 4.7g; Sugars 5.2g; Protein 10.6g

Ginger Sweet Potatoes and Pea Hash

Prep time: 10 minutes | Cook time: 10 minutes | Serves: 4

2 tablespoons coconut oil
4 scallions, sliced
3 garlic cloves, minced
2 teaspoons minced fresh ginger
1 teaspoon curry powder
1 teaspoon salt
½ teaspoon ground turmeric
2 sweet potatoes, roasted, peeled and chopped
1 cup frozen peas
2 cups cooked brown rice
1 tablespoon coconut aminos
¼ cup chopped fresh cilantro
½ cup chopped cashews

1. In a suitable skillet over medium-high heat, melt the coconut oil. Add the scallions, garlic, ginger, curry powder, salt, and turmeric. Sauté for 2 minutes, or until fragrant. 2. Stir in the sweet potatoes, peas, brown rice, and coconut aminos. Sauté for 5 minutes. 3. Transfer the hash to a serving dish and garnish with the cilantro and cashews.
Per serving: Calories: 424; Total fat 11.8g; Sodium 419mg; Total carbs 71.9g; Fiber 6.6g; Sugars 2.4g; Protein 9g

Mushroom Risotto in Vegetable Broth

Prep time: 15 minutes | Cook time: 20 minutes | Serves: 4

2 tablespoons extra-virgin olive oil
1 large shallot, sliced
1 garlic clove, minced
1 pint sliced mushrooms
1½ cups arborio rice
3 cups vegetable broth, warmed
1 teaspoon salt
½ teaspoon black pepper
Pinch ground nutmeg
1 tablespoon chopped fresh thyme leaves
Balsamic vinegar, for garnish

1. In a suitable skillet over high heat, heat the olive oil. Add the shallot and garlic. Sauté for 3 minutes. 2. Add the mushrooms and rice. Sauté for 3 minutes more. Reduce its heat to medium-high. 3. Add the vegetable broth to the rice, constantly stirring until the rice has absorbed the liquid before adding another cup of broth. 4. Once all the broth is absorbed, add salt, pepper, and nutmeg. Taste the risotto to see if the rice is cooked through; it should be tender but not mushy. 5. Transfer the risotto to a serving dish. Garnish with the thyme leaves and drizzle with balsamic vinegar.
Per serving: Calories: 357; Total fat 8.6g; Sodium 1161mg; Total carbs 59.4g; Fiber 2.6g; Sugars 1.2g; Protein 9.6g

Butternut Squash and Spinach Gratin

Prep time: 15 minutes | Cook time: 20 minutes | Serves: 4 to 6

1 tablespoon coconut oil
1 onion, peeled and chopped
2 garlic cloves, minced
1 small butternut squash, peeled, and diced
4 cups spinach
1 teaspoon salt
½ teaspoon black pepper
1 (13.5-ounce) can coconut milk
1½ or 2 cups vegetable broth
1 (15-ounce) can lentils, drained and rinsed
¼ cup fresh parsley, chopped
2 tablespoons chopped fresh sage
½ cup chopped toasted walnuts

1. At 375 degrees F, preheat your oven. Cut the butternut squash into ½-inch cubes. 2. In a suitable ovenproof skillet over high heat, melt the coconut oil. Add the onion and garlic. Sauté for 3 minutes. 3. Add the butternut squash, spinach, salt, and pepper. Sauté for 3 minutes more. 4. Stir in the coconut milk and just enough vegetable broth to cover the squash. Bring the liquid to a boil. 5. Add the lentils, parsley, and sage. Stir to combine. 6. Place the lentil skillet in the preheated oven and bake the casserole for 15 to 20 minutes, or until the squash is tender. 7. Transfer the casserole to a serving dish and garnish it with walnuts.
Per serving: Calories: 568; Total fat 26.4g; Sodium 1602mg; Total carbs 58g; Fiber 27.5g; Sugars 5.7g; Protein 30.6g

Basic Quinoa

Prep time: 15 minutes | Cook time: 6 hours | Serves: 4

2 cups quinoa, rinsed well
4 cups vegetable broth

1. In your slow cooker, combine the quinoa and broth. 2. Cover the cooker and set to low. Cook for almost 4 to 6 hours. 3. Fluff with a fork, cool, and serve.
Per serving: Calories 234; Fat 4.3g; Sodium 512mg; Carbs 37g; Fiber 4g; Sugars 0.5g; Protein 11.2g

Mushroom and Peas Risotto

Prep time: 15 minutes | Cook time: 3 hours | Serves: 4

½ cups arborio rice
cup English peas
small shallot, minced
¼ cup dried porcini mushrooms
1½ cups broth (choose vegetable

to keep it vegan)
1 tablespoon lemon juice
½ teaspoon garlic powder
½ teaspoon sea salt

1. In your slow cooker, combine the rice, peas, shallot, mushrooms, broth, lemon juice, garlic powder, and salt. Stir to mix well. 2. Cover the cooker and set to high. Cook for almost 2 to 3 hours and serve.
Per serving: Calories 223; Fat 1.4g; Sodium 734mg; Carbs 42.5g; Fiber 2.6g; Sugars 2g; Protein 8.2g

Ritzy Wild Rice Stuffed Sweet Potatoes

Prep time: 1 hour 15 minutes | Cook time: 20 minutes | Serves: 4

2 cups cooked wild rice
½ cup chopped hazelnuts
½ cup dried blueberries
1 teaspoon chopped fresh thyme
½ cup shredded Swiss chard

1 scallion, white and green parts, peeled and thinly sliced
Sea salt and black pepper, to taste
4 sweet potatoes, baked, cut the top off lengthwise, hollowed

1. At 400 degrees F, preheat your oven. 2. Combine the wild rice, hazelnuts, blueberries, thyme, Swiss chard, and scallion in a suitable bowl. 3. Sprinkle with salt and pepper. Stir to mix well. 4. Fill the hollowed sweet potatoes with the wild rice mixture, then arrange the stuffed sweet potato on a parchment paper-lined baking sheet. 5. Bake in the preheated oven for 20 minutes or until the skin of the sweet potato is lightly charred. 6. Remove the stuffed sweet potato from the oven and serve on a suitable plate.
Per serving: Calories: 535; Total fat 6.9g; Sodium 30mg; Total carbs 106.6g; Fiber 12.7g; Sugars 5.1g; Protein 15.8g

Whole-Wheat Pasta with Tomato Sauce

Prep time: 15 minutes | Cook time: 10 minutes | Serves: 4

2 tablespoons extra-virgin olive oil
1 onion, minced
6 garlic cloves, minced
2 (28-ounce) cans crushed tomatoes, undrained

½ teaspoon sea salt
¼ teaspoon black pepper
¼ cup basil leaves, chopped
1 (8-ounce) package whole-wheat pasta

1. In a suitable pot over medium-high heat, heat the olive oil until it shimmers. 2. Add the onion. Cook for almost 5 minutes, occasionally stirring, until soft. Add the garlic. Cook for 30 seconds, stirring constantly. 3. Stir in the tomatoes, salt, and pepper. Bring to a simmer. Reduce its heat to medium and cook for 5 minutes, stirring occasionally. 4. Remove from the heat and stir in the basil. Toss with the pasta.
Per serving: Calories: 644; Total fat 9.4g; Sodium 1001mg; Total carbs 126.3g; Fiber 26g; Sugars 23.5g; Protein 18.7g

Grain-Free Salad Bowl

Prep time: 10 minutes | Cook time: 5 minutes | Serves: 4

½ cup chopped walnuts
¼ cup chopped pistachios
¼ cup raw pumpkin seeds or sunflower seeds
4 cups baby arugula or spinach leaves
2 cups riced cauliflower (not frozen)
1 large seedless cucumber, peeled and chopped

4 roma tomatoes, seeded and chopped
½ cup chopped parsley or cilantro
¼ cup chopped red onion
¼ cup extra-virgin olive oil
2 tablespoons apple cider vinegar
1 teaspoon salt
¼ teaspoon black pepper, freshly ground

1. In a large dry skillet, toast the walnuts, pistachios, and pumpkin seeds over medium-low heat for almost 5 minutes, until the nuts and seeds are golden and fragrant. 2. Remove from this skillet and set aside to cool. 3. In a suitable bowl, combine the arugula, cauliflower, cucumber, tomatoes, parsley, and onion. 4. In a suitable bowl, whisk together the olive oil, vinegar, salt, and pepper. Add the cooled nuts and seeds to the vegetable bowl, drizzle with the oil mixture, and toss to coat well. 5. Divide among bowls and serve chilled or at room temperature.
Per serving: Calories 364; Fat 33.4g; Sodium 652mg; Carbs 14.5g; Fiber 5.6g; Sugars 6.4g; Protein 7.8g

Spinach, Butternut Squash, and Lentils Gratin

Prep time: 15 minutes | Cook time: 25 minutes | Serves: 4 to 6

1 tablespoon coconut oil
2 garlic cloves, minced
1 onion, peeled and chopped
4 cups spinach
1 small butternut squash, peeled, deseeded, diced
1 teaspoon sea salt
½ teaspoon black pepper

1 (13.5-ounce) can coconut milk
1½ or 2 cups vegetable broth
¼ cup fresh parsley, chopped
1 (15-ounce) can lentils, drained and rinsed
2 tablespoons chopped fresh sage
½ cup chopped toasted walnuts

1. Cut the butternut squash into ½-inch cubes. 2. At 375 degrees F, preheat your oven. Heat the coconut oil in a suitable oven-safe skillet over high heat until melted. 3. Add the garlic and onion to the skillet and sauté for 3 minutes or until fragrant and the onion is translucent. 4. Add the spinach, butternut squash, salt, and ground black pepper to the skillet and sauté for an additional 3 minutes or until the spinach is lightly wilted. 5. Pour in the coconut milk and enough vegetable broth to cover the butternut squash. Bring to a boil. 6. Then add the parsley, lentils, and sage. Stir to combine well. Arrange the skillet in the preheated oven and bake for 15 minutes or until the butternut squash is soft. 7. Remove the lentil skillet from the oven and transfer them to a suitable plate. Garnish with walnuts and serve immediately.
Per serving: Calories: 299; Total fat 8.1g; Sodium 109mg; Total carbs 49.6g; Fiber 12.1g; Sugars 24g; Protein 11g

Tofu and Spinach Sauté

Prep time: 10 minutes | Cook time: 10 minutes | Serves: 4

2 tablespoons extra-virgin olive oil
1 onion, chopped
4 cups fresh baby spinach
8 ounces tofu

3 garlic cloves, minced
Juice of 1 orange
Zest of 1 orange
½ teaspoon sea salt
⅛ teaspoon black pepper

1. In a suitable skillet over medium-high heat, heat the olive oil until it shimmers. 2. Add the onion, spinach, and tofu. Cook for almost 5 minutes, occasionally stirring, until the onion is soft. 3. Add the garlic. Cook for 30 seconds, stirring constantly. Add the orange juice, orange zest, salt, and pepper. Cook for 3 minutes, stirring until heated through.
Per serving: Calories: 161; Total fat 12.7g; Sodium 355mg; Total carbs 7.1g; Fiber 2.4g; Sugars 2.2g; Protein 7.9g

Sweet Potato Curry with Spinach

Prep time: 10 minutes | Cook time: 20 minutes | Serves: 4

2 tablespoons extra-virgin olive oil
1 onion, chopped
4 cups cubed peeled sweet potato
4 cups fresh baby spinach
3 cups no-salt-added vegetable

broth
1 cup lite coconut milk
2 tablespoons curry powder
½ teaspoon sea salt
⅛ teaspoon black pepper

1. In a suitable pot over medium-high heat, heat the olive oil until it shimmers. 2. Add the onion. Cook for almost 5 minutes, stirring, until soft. Stir in the sweet potato, spinach, vegetable broth, coconut milk, curry powder, salt, and pepper. 3. Bring to a simmer and reduce its heat to medium. Cook for almost 15 minutes, occasionally stirring, until the sweet potatoes are soft.
Per serving: Calories: 263; Total fat 10.6g; Sodium 718mg; Total carbs 43g; Fiber 7.1g; Sugars 9.9g; Protein 4.3g

Coconutty Brown Rice

Prep time: 15 minutes | Cook time: 3 hours | Serves: 4 to 6

2 cups brown rice, soaked in water overnight, drained, and rinsed
3 cups water

1½ cups full-fat coconut milk
1 teaspoon sea salt
½ teaspoon ground ginger
Black pepper

1. In your slow cooker, combine the rice, water, coconut milk, salt, and ginger. Season with pepper and stir to incorporate the spices. 2. Cover the cooker and set to high. Cook for almost 3 hours and serve.
Per serving: Calories 230; Fat 1.7g; Sodium 318mg; Carbs 48.4g; Fiber 2.2g; Sugars 0g; Protein 4.8g

Sweet Potato and Butternut Squash Curry

Prep time: 15 minutes | Cook time: 15 minutes | Serves: 4 to 6

1 tablespoon coconut oil	2 cups no-salt-added vegetable broth
1 onion, chopped	1 (13.5-ounce) can coconut milk
1 large sweet potato, peeled and cut into ½-inch cubes	2 teaspoons curry powder
2 cups (½-inch) butternut squash cubes	1 teaspoon sea salt
2 garlic cloves, sliced	2 tablespoons chopped fresh cilantro

1. Heat the coconut oil in a Dutch oven over high heat. 2. Add the onion and sauté for almost 3 minutes until softened. 3. Stir in the sweet potato, butternut squash, and garlic and sauté for 3 minutes more. Add the vegetable broth, coconut milk, curry powder, and salt to the vegetables, and bring to a boil. 4. Reduce its heat and bring to a simmer and continue cooking for almost 5 minutes, or until the vegetables are fork-tender. 5. Sprinkle the cilantro on top for garnish and serve.
Per serving: Calories: 145; Total fat 5.2g; Sodium 772mg; Total carbs 23.3g; Fiber 3.9g; Sugars 6.7g; Protein 3.5g

Hummus Burgers

Prep time: 10 minutes | Cook time: 30 minutes | Serves: 4

1 tablespoon extra-virgin olive oil	2 teaspoons lemon zest
2 (15-ounce) cans garbanzo beans, drained and rinsed	2 garlic cloves, minced
¼ cup tahini	2 tablespoons chickpea flour
1 tablespoon lemon juice	4 scallions, minced
	1 teaspoon salt

1. At 375 degrees F, preheat your oven. Brush a baking sheet with olive oil. 2. In a suitable food processor, combine the garbanzo beans, tahini, lemon juice, lemon zest, garlic, and the remaining 1 tablespoon of olive oil. Pulse until smooth. 3. Add the chickpea flour, scallions, and salt. Pulse to combine. 4. Form the mixture into four patties and place them on the prepared baking sheet. 5. Place the patties baking sheet in the preheated oven and bake for 30 minutes.
Per serving: Calories: 495; Total fat 13g; Sodium 334mg; Total carbs 73.7g; Fiber 20.7g; Sugars 12.9g; Protein 24.6g

Sweet Potato and Bell Pepper Hash

Prep time: 5 minutes | Cook time: 25 minutes | Serves: 4

4 tablespoons extra-virgin olive oil	4 cups cubed, peeled sweet potato
1 onion, chopped	1 teaspoon sea salt
1 red bell pepper, chopped	⅛ teaspoon black pepper
	4 eggs

1. In a suitable nonstick skillet over medium-high heat, heat 2 tablespoons of the olive oil until it shimmers. 2. Add the onion, red bell pepper, and sweet potato. Season with ½ teaspoon of salt and pepper. Cook for 15 to 20 minutes, occasionally stirring, until the sweet potatoes are soft and browned. Divide the potatoes among 4 plates. 3. Return the skillet to the heat, reduce its heat to medium-low, and heat the remaining 2 tablespoons of olive oil, swirling to coat the bottom of the pan. 4. Carefully crack the eggs into the pan and sprinkle with the remaining ½ teaspoon of salt. Cook for almost 3 to 4 minutes until the whites are set. 5. Gently flip the eggs and turn off the heat. Let the eggs sit in the hot pan for 1 minute. Place 1 egg on top of each serving of hash.
Per serving: Calories: 333; Total fat 18.5g; Sodium 576mg; Total carbs 38.2g; Fiber 5g; Sugars 10g; Protein 8.1g

Mushroom Pesto Burgers

Prep time: 5 minutes | Cook time: 20 minutes | Serves: 4

4 portobello mushroom caps, stemmed, gills removed	4 onion slices
½ cup pesto	4 tomato slices
	4 whole-wheat hamburger buns

1. At 400 degrees F, preheat your oven. 2. Brush all the Portobello mushroom caps on both sides with the pesto to coat and place them on a rimmed baking sheet. 3. Bake for almost 15 to 20 minutes until soft. Layer the mushrooms on the buns with tomatoes and onions.
Per serving: Calories: 259; Total fat 14.9g; Sodium 325mg; Total carbs 26.2g; Fiber 4.9g; Sugars 7.4g; Protein 8.5g

Kale Frittata

Prep time: 10 minutes | Cook time: 17 minutes | Serves: 4

2 tablespoons extra-virgin olive oil	8 eggs
4 cups stemmed and chopped kale	½ teaspoon sea salt
3 garlic cloves, minced	¼ teaspoon black pepper
	2 tablespoons sunflower seeds

1. Preheat the broiler to high. 2. In a suitable ovenproof skillet over medium-high heat, heat the olive oil until it shimmers. Add the kale. Cook for almost 5 minutes, stirring, until soft. 3. Add the garlic. Cook for 30 seconds, stirring constantly. 4. In a suitable bowl, beat the eggs, salt, and pepper. Carefully pour them over the kale. Reduce its heat to medium. Cook the eggs for almost 3 minutes until set around the edges. 5. Using a rubber spatula, carefully pull the eggs away from the edges of the skillet and tilt the pan to let the uncooked eggs run into the edges. Cook for almost 3 minutes until the edges set again. 6. Sprinkle with the sunflower seeds. Transfer this pan to the preheated broiler and cook for 3 to 5 minutes until puffed and brown. Cut into wedges to serve.
Per serving: Calories: 231; Total fat 16.5g; Sodium 387mg; Total carbs 8.8g; Fiber 1.2g; Sugars 0.7g; Protein 13.5g

Broccoli and Egg Muffins

Prep time: 10 minutes | Cook time: 20 minutes | Serves: 4

Nonstick cooking spray	8 eggs, beaten
2 tablespoons extra-virgin olive oil	1 teaspoon garlic powder
1 onion, chopped	½ teaspoon sea salt
1 cup broccoli florets, chopped	¼ teaspoon black pepper

1. At 350 degrees F, preheat your oven. 2. Spray a suitable muffin tin with nonstick cooking spray. 3. In a suitable nonstick skillet over medium-high heat, heat the olive oil until it shimmers. 4. Add the onion and broccoli. Cook for 3 minutes. Spoon the vegetables evenly into 4 muffin cups. 5. In a suitable bowl, beat the eggs, garlic powder, salt, and pepper. Pour them over the vegetables in the muffin cups. 6. Bake for 15 to 17 minutes until the eggs are set.
Per serving: Calories: 207; Total fat 15.9g; Sodium 366mg; Total carbs 5.4g; Fiber 1.3g; Sugars 2.4g; Protein 12.1g

Sweet Potatoes and Pea Hash

Prep time: 10 minutes | Cook time: 10 minutes | Serves: 4

2 tablespoons coconut oil	in their skins, peeled and chopped
3 garlic cloves, minced	2 cups cooked brown rice
4 scallions, sliced	1 cup frozen peas
2 teaspoons minced fresh ginger	1 tablespoon coconut aminos
1 teaspoon curry powder	¼ cup chopped fresh cilantro, for garnish
½ teaspoon ground turmeric	
1 teaspoon sea salt	½ cup chopped cashews, for garnish
2 medium sweet potatoes, roasted	

1. In a suitable skillet, melt the coconut oil over medium-high heat. 2. Add the garlic, scallions, ginger, curry powder, turmeric, and salt, and stir well. Sauté for 2 minutes until fragrant. 3. Fold in the sweet potatoes, brown rice, peas, and coconut aminos, and sauté for 5 minutes, stirring occasionally. 4. Sprinkle the cilantro and cashews on top for garnish and serve warm.
Per serving: Calories: 423; Total fat 11.8g; Sodium 343mg; Total carbs 71.7g; Fiber 6.6g; Sugars 2.4g; Protein 9g

Black Bean Chili with Garlic and Tomatoes

Prep time: 10 minutes | Cook time: 20 minutes | Serves: 4

2 tablespoons extra-virgin olive oil	2 (14-ounce) cans of black beans, drained
1 onion, chopped	1 tablespoon chili powder
2 (28-ounce) cans chopped tomatoes, undrained	1 teaspoon garlic powder
	½ teaspoon sea salt

1. In a suitable pot over medium-high, heat the olive oil until it shimmers. 2. Add the onion. Cook for almost 5 minutes, occasionally stirring, until soft. 3. Stir in the tomatoes, black beans, chili powder, garlic powder, and salt. Bring to a simmer. 4. Reduce its heat to medium and cook for 15 minutes, stirring occasionally.
Per serving: Calories: 552; Total fat 7.3g; Sodium 189mg; Total carbs 95.5g; Fiber 24.2g; Sugars 10.7g; Protein 31.3g

Tomato Asparagus Frittata

Prep time: 10 minutes | Cook time: 10 minutes | Serves: 4

2 tablespoons extra-virgin olive oil
10 asparagus spears, trimmed
10 cherry tomatoes
5 eggs
1 tablespoon chopped, fresh thyme
½ teaspoon sea salt
⅛ teaspoon black pepper

1. Preheat the broiler to high. 2. In a suitable ovenproof skillet over medium-high heat, heat the olive oil until it shimmers. Add the asparagus. Cook for 5 minutes, stirring occasionally. 3. Add the tomatoes. Cook 3 minutes, stirring occasionally. 4. In a suitable bowl, whisk together the eggs, thyme, salt, and pepper. Carefully pour over the asparagus and tomatoes, moving the vegetables around, so they are evenly spread in the pan. 5. Reduce its heat to medium. Cook the eggs for almost 3 minutes until set around the edges. 6. Using a rubber spatula, carefully pull the eggs away from the edges of the skillet and tilt the pan to let the uncooked eggs run into the edges. Cook for almost 3 minutes until the edges set again. 7. Carefully transfer the pan to the broiler and cook for 3 to 5 minutes until puffed and brown. Cut into wedges to serve.
Per serving: Calories: 222; Total fat 14.3g; Sodium 343mg; Total carbs 14.8g; Fiber 5g; Sugars 9.7g; Protein 12.3g

Tofu Sloppy Joes

Prep time: 10 minutes | Cook time: 15 minutes | Serves: 4

2 tablespoons extra-virgin olive oil
1 onion, chopped
10 ounces tofu, chopped
2 (14-ounce) cans of crushed tomatoes
¼ cup apple cider vinegar
1 tablespoon chilli powder
1 teaspoon garlic powder
½ teaspoon sea salt
⅛ teaspoon black pepper

1. In a suitable pot over medium-high heat, heat the olive oil until it shimmers. 2. Add the onion and tofu. Cook for almost 5 minutes, occasionally stirring, until the onion is soft. 3. Stir in the tomatoes, cider vinegar, chilli powder, garlic powder, salt, and pepper. 4. Simmer for 10 minutes to let the flavors blend, stirring occasionally.
Per serving: Calories: 211; Total fat 10.3g; Sodium 645mg; Total carbs 21.3g; Fiber 8.3g; Sugars 13.1g; Protein 11.2g

Roasted Rainbow Cauliflower

Prep time: 10 minutes | Cook time: 20 minutes | Serves: 4 to 6

1½ cups white cauliflower florets
1½ cups yellow cauliflower florets
1½ cups purple cauliflower florets
¼ cup fresh lemon juice
3 tablespoons extra-virgin olive oil
1 teaspoon sea salt
¼ teaspoon black pepper

1. At 400 degrees F, preheat your oven. 2. Add the cauliflower, lemon juice, and olive oil to a suitable bowl, and toss to combine. 3. Spread out the coated cauliflower on a rimmed baking sheet and season with salt and pepper. 4. Wrap in aluminum foil and bake in the preheated oven for 15 minutes. 5. Remove the foil and bake for an additional 5 minutes, or until the tips and edges of the cauliflower are beginning to brown. 6. Let the cauliflower cool for 5 minutes before serving.
Per serving: Calories: 144; Total fat 10.6g; Sodium 528mg; Total carbs 11.8g; Fiber 1.2g; Sugars 4.9g; Protein 4.3g

Lentils Stew with Tomatoes

Prep time: 10 minutes | Cook time: 10 minutes | Serves: 4

2 tablespoons extra-virgin olive oil
1 tablespoon ground turmeric
1 onion, chopped
1 (14-ounce) can lentils, drained
1 (14-ounce) can chopped tomatoes, drained
1 teaspoon garlic powder
½ teaspoon sea salt
¼ teaspoon black pepper

1. Heat the olive oil in a suitable skillet over medium-high heat until shimmering. 2. Toss in the turmeric and onion and sauté for almost 5 minutes, stirring occasionally, or until the onion is translucent. 3. Add the lentils, tomatoes, garlic powder, salt, and pepper and mix well. Continue cooking for 5 minutes until heated through. 4. Remove from the heat to a plate and garnish with additional olive oil, if desired.
Per serving: Calories: 299; Total fat 5.6g; Sodium 165mg; Total carbs 45.2g; Fiber 21.7g; Sugars 4g; Protein 18g

Quinoa Florentine

Prep time: 5 minutes | Cook time: 25 minutes | Serves: 4

2 tablespoons extra-virgin olive oil
1 onion, chopped
3 cups fresh baby spinach
3 garlic cloves, minced
2 cups quinoa, rinsed well
4 cups no-salt-added vegetable broth
½ teaspoon sea salt
⅛ teaspoon black pepper

1. In a suitable pot over medium-high heat, heat the olive oil until it shimmers. 2. Add the onion and spinach. Cook for 3 minutes, stirring occasionally. Add the garlic and cook for 30 seconds, stirring constantly. 3. Stir in the quinoa, vegetable broth, salt, and pepper. Bring to a boil and reduce its heat to low. 4. Cover this quinoa and simmer for 15 to 20 minutes until the liquid is absorbed. Fluff with a fork.
Per serving: Calories: 423; Total fat 12.3g; Sodium 1318mg; Total carbs 64.7g; Fiber 9.1g; Sugars 5.3g; Protein 13.1g

Sweet Potato and Spinach

Prep time: 10 minutes | Cook time: 20 minutes | Serves: 4

2 tablespoons extra-virgin olive oil
1 onion, chopped
4 cups fresh baby spinach
4 cups cubed, peeled sweet potato
3 cups no-salt-added vegetable
broth
1 cup unsweetened coconut milk
2 tablespoons curry powder
½ teaspoon sea salt
⅛ teaspoon black pepper

1. Heat the olive oil in a suitable skillet over medium-high heat until shimmering. 2. Add the onion and cook for almost 5 minutes, stirring occasionally, or until the onion is tender. 3. Stir in the spinach, sweet potatoes, vegetable broth, coconut milk, curry powder, salt, and pepper, and bring to a boil. 4. Reduce its heat to medium and bring to a simmer for almost 15 minutes, stirring occasionally, or until the vegetables are softened. 5. Remove from the heat and serve on a plate.
Per serving: Calories: 371; Total fat 21.9g; Sodium 727mg; Total carbs 43.3g; Fiber 7.6g; Sugars 11.9g; Protein 6.4g

Baby Bok Choy Stir-Fry

Prep time: 12 minutes | Cook time: 12 minutes | Serves: 6

2 tablespoons coconut oil
1 large onion, diced
2 teaspoons ground cumin
1-inch piece fresh ginger, grated
1 teaspoon ground turmeric
½ teaspoon sea salt
12 baby bok choy heads, ends trimmed and sliced lengthwise
3 cups cooked brown rice

1. Heat the coconut oil in a suitable skillet over medium heat. 2. Add the onion and sauté for 5 minutes, stirring occasionally. 3. Fold in the cumin, ginger, turmeric, and salt, and stir until the onion is coated in the spices. 4. Add the bok choy and stir-fry for almost 6 to 7 minutes, or until the bok choy is tender but still crisp. 5. Remove from the heat to a plate and serve with cooked brown rice.
Per serving: Calories: 462; Total fat 8g; Sodium 941mg; Total carbs 83.9g; Fiber 15.5g; Sugars 15.7g; Protein 24.6g

Sautéed Tofu and Spinach

Prep time: 10 minutes | Cook time: 10 minutes | Serves: 4

2 tablespoons extra-virgin olive oil
1 onion, chopped
8 ounces tofu
4 cups fresh baby spinach
3 garlic cloves, minced
Juice and zest of 1 orange
½ teaspoon sea salt
⅛ teaspoon black pepper

1. Heat the olive oil in a suitable skillet over medium-high heat until shimmering. 2. Add the onion, tofu, and spinach and mix well. Cook for almost 4 to 5 minutes, stirring occasionally, or until the onion is soft. 3. Stir in the garlic and cook for almost 30 seconds until fragrant. 4. Add the lemon juice and zest, salt, and pepper. Stir to combine and continue cooking for 3 minutes until heated through. 5. Remove from the heat and serve on a plate.
Per serving: Calories: 121; Total fat 9.5g; Sodium 266mg; Total carbs 5.4g; Fiber 1.8g; Sugars 1.7g; Protein 5.9g

Zucchini Stuffed with White Beans

Prep time: 15 minutes | Cook time: 20 minutes | Serves: 4

4 large zucchinis, halved lengthwise
2 tablespoons extra-virgin olive oil
½ teaspoon salt, plus additional for seasoning
Black pepper
Pinch ground rosemary

1 (15-ounce) can white beans, drained
½ cup chopped pitted green olives
2 garlic cloves, minced
1 cup chopped arugula
¼ cup fresh parsley, chopped
1 tablespoon apple cider vinegar

1. At 375 degrees F, preheat your oven. 2. Brush a suitable rimmed baking sheet with olive oil. 3. Using a small spoon or melon baller, carefully scoop out and discard the seeds from the zucchini halves. 4. Brush the scooped-out section of each zucchini boat with olive oil and lightly season the inside of each boat with salt, pepper, and rosemary. 5. Transfer the prepared zucchini to the prepared baking sheet, cut-side up. 6. Place the zucchini sheet in the preheated oven and roast for 15 to 20 minutes, or until the zucchini are tender and lightly browned. 7. In a suitable bowl, lightly mash the white beans with a fork. 8. Add the olives, garlic, arugula, parsley, cider vinegar, the remaining ½ teaspoon of salt, and the remaining 2 tablespoons of olive oil. Season with pepper and mix well. 9. Spoon the bean mixture into the zucchini boats and serve.
Per serving: Calories: 330; Total fat 7.1g; Sodium 408mg; Total carbs 51.6g; Fiber 13.8g; Sugars 5.3g; Protein 19.5g

Buckwheat Noodle Pad Thai

Prep time: 15 minutes | Cook time: 15 minutes | Serves: 4

1 (8-ounce) package buckwheat soba noodles
1 tablespoon coconut oil
1 red onion, chopped
2 garlic cloves, minced
2 teaspoons minced fresh ginger
1 zucchini, chopped
2 bok choy, sliced thin
1 tablespoon coconut aminos
1 tablespoon apple cider vinegar

3 tablespoons almond butter or cashew butter
2 tablespoons toasted sesame oil
1 tablespoon raw honey or coconut sugar
¼ cup vegetable broth, or water
Salt
2 scallions, sliced thin
¼ cup chopped fresh cilantro
2 tablespoons sesame seeds

1. Cook the soba noodles as per the box's directions, drain and set aside. 2. In a suitable pan over high heat, melt the coconut oil. Add the red onion, garlic, ginger, zucchini, and bok choy. Sauté for 5 minutes. 3. Add the coconut aminos, cider vinegar, almond butter, sesame oil, honey, and vegetable broth. Cook for 2 minutes, stirring constantly. 4. Add the soba noodles to the pan and sauté them, using a suitable spatula to scoop the mixture from the bottom of the pan to the top to combine the vegetables with the noodles. 5. Season with salt, and transfer the Pad Thai to a serving dish. Garnish with scallions, cilantro, and sesame seeds.
Per serving: Calories: 427; Total fat 15g; Sodium 49mg; Total carbs 60.2g; Fiber 5g; Sugars 5g; Protein 14.1g

Vegetable Cabbage Cups

Prep time: 20 minutes | Cook time: 15 minutes | Serves: 4

1 tablespoon extra-virgin olive oil
1 sweet onion, chopped
1 teaspoon grated fresh ginger
1 teaspoon minced garlic
1 cup shredded sweet potato
2 cups shredded broccoli stalks
1 carrot, shredded
2 cups chopped cauliflower

1 cup chopped fresh spinach
1 cup fresh peas
1 teaspoon ground cumin
½ teaspoon ground coriander
2 tablespoons apple cider vinegar
¼ cup dried cherries
¼ cup pumpkin seeds
4 large cabbage leaves

1. Heat the olive oil in a nonstick skillet over medium-high heat until shimmering. 2. Add the onion, ginger, and garlic to the skillet and sauté for 3 minutes or until fragrant and the onion is translucent. 3. Add the sweet potato, broccoli, carrot, and cauliflower to the skillet and sauté for 8 minutes or until soft. 4. Add the spinach, peas, cumin, coriander, and cider vinegar to the skillet and sauté for an additional 2 minutes or until the spinach is wilted. 5. Turn off its heat and stir in the cherries and pumpkin seeds. Unfold the cabbage leaves on four serving plates, then divide the mixture over the leaves and serve warm.
Per serving: Calories: 199; Total fat 5.4g; Sodium 73mg; Total carbs 33.1g; Fiber 8g; Sugars 16g; Protein 7.4g

Lentils with Tomatoes and Turmeric

Prep time: 10 minutes | Cook time: 10 minutes | Serves: 4

2 tablespoons extra-virgin olive oil
1 onion, chopped
1 tablespoon ground turmeric
1 teaspoon garlic powder

1 (14-ounce) can lentils, drained
1 (14-ounce) can chopped tomatoes, drained
½ teaspoon sea salt
¼ teaspoon black pepper

1. In a suitable pot over medium-high heat, heat the olive oil until it shimmers. 2. Add the onion and turmeric, and cook for almost 5 minutes, occasionally stirring, until soft. 3. Add the garlic powder, lentils, tomatoes, salt, and pepper. Cook for 5 minutes, stirring occasionally. 4. Garnish with additional olive oil, if desired and serve.
Per serving: Calories: 448; Total fat 8.5g; Sodium 247mg; Total carbs 67.7g; Fiber 32.5g; Sugars 6g; Protein 27g

Zucchini Spaghetti with Almonds and Peas

Prep time: 15 minutes | Cook time: 0 | Serves: 4

1 cup fresh oregano leaves
½ cup almonds
Juice and zest of 1 lemon
1 cup fresh basil leaves, plus more for garnish
2 teaspoons minced garlic

Sea salt and black pepper, to taste
2 tablespoons extra-virgin olive oil
1 cup fresh peas
2 large green zucchinis, julienned or spiralized

1. Put the oregano, almonds, lemon juice and zest, basil, garlic, salt, and ground black pepper in a suitable food processor. Pulse to combine well until smooth. 2. While the food processor is processing, gently mix the olive oil in the mixture until the mixture performs a thick consistency. 3. Combine the peas and spiralized zucchini in a suitable bowl, then pour in the mixture. Toss to coat well. 4. Garnish with more fresh basil leaves and serve immediately.
Per serving: Calories: 170; Total fat 13.1g; Sodium 2mg; Total carbs 10.3g; Fiber 4.4g; Sugars 3.6g; Protein 5.1g

Tahini Brown Rice Spaghetti with Kale

Prep time: 5 minutes | Cook time: 10 minutes | Serves: 4

12 cups water
1¼ teaspoons sea salt
8 ounces brown rice spaghetti
4 cups kale

½ cup tahini
¾ cup hot water
½ cup fresh parsley, chopped

1. Bring 12 cups of water to a boil, sprinkle with 1 teaspoon of salt, then add the brown rice spaghetti. 2. Cook for 10 minutes or until the pasta is al dente. Keep stirring during the cooking time. 3. During the last minute of the cooking time, add the kale to blanch. 4. When the cooking is complete, transfer the pasta and kale to a colander to drain, then put them in a suitable bowl. Set aside. 5. Combine the tahini, remaining salt, and hot water in a suitable bowl. Stir to mix well. 6. Add the tahini sauce with parsley to the pasta. Toss to coat well. Serve warm.
Per serving: Calories: 297; Total fat 16.7g; Sodium 1376mg; Total carbs 31.3g; Fiber 4.8g; Sugars 0.5g; Protein 9.1g

Roasted Root Vegetables

Prep time: 10 minutes | Cook time: 25 to 35 minutes | Serves: 4 to 6

2 small sweet potatoes, peeled and cut into 1-inch cubes
1 bunch beets, peeled and cut into 1-inch cubes
4 carrots, peeled and sliced
3 parsnips, peeled and sliced

¼ cup coconut oil, melted
1 tablespoon olive oil
1 tablespoon raw honey or maple syrup
1 teaspoon salt
½ teaspoon black pepper

1. At 400 degrees F, preheat your oven. Layer two rimmed baking sheets with parchment paper. 2. In a suitable bowl, combine the sweet potatoes, beets, carrots, and parsnips. Add the coconut oil, olive oil, honey, salt, and pepper. Toss to coat the vegetables. 3. Divide the vegetables between the two baking sheets, spreading them into a single layer. 4. Place the sheets in the preheated oven and bake the vegetables for 10 to 15 minutes. 5. Turn them, so they brown on the other side. Continue to bake the vegetables for 10 to 15 minutes more, or until brown and tender. 6. Serve warm or at room temperature.
Per serving: Calories: 240; Total fat 11.8g; Sodium 440mg; Total carbs 33.9g; Fiber 6.7g; Sugars 8.8g; Protein 2.2g

Braised Bok Choy with Mushrooms

Prep time: 10 minutes | Cook time: 5 to 10 minutes | Serves: 4

1 tablespoon coconut oil	½ cup water
8 baby bok choy, halved lengthwise	1 tablespoon coconut aminos
1 cup shiitake mushrooms, stemmed and thinly sliced	Sea salt and black pepper, to taste
	1 scallion, sliced thin
	1 tablespoon toasted sesame seeds

1. Melt the coconut oil in a suitable skillet over high heat. 2. Add the bok choy, mushrooms, water, and coconut aminos to the skillet. Braise the vegetables for almost 5 to 10 minutes, covered, or until the bok choy is softened. 3. Remove from the heat and sprinkle the salt and pepper to season. 4. Divide the bok choy and mushrooms among plates. Scatter each plate evenly with the scallions and sesame seeds. 5. Serve immediately.

Per serving: Calories: 162; Total fat 9.8g; Sodium 359mg; Total carbs 17.7g; Fiber 5.1g; Sugars 6.1g; Protein 6.3g

Harvest Rice

Prep time: 15 minutes | Cook time: 3 hours | Serves: 4

2 cups brown rice, soaked in water overnight, drained, and rinsed	oil
	½ teaspoon dried thyme leaves
½ small onion, chopped	½ teaspoon garlic powder
4 cups vegetable broth	½ cup cooked sliced mushrooms
2 tablespoons extra-virgin olive	½ cup dried cranberries
	½ cup toasted pecans

1. In your slow cooker, combine the rice, onion, broth, olive oil, thyme, and garlic powder. Stir well. 2. Cover the cooker and set to high. Cook for almost 3 hours. 3. Stir in the mushrooms, cranberries, and pecans, and serve.

Per serving: Calories 313; Fat 8.2g; Sodium 512mg; Carbs 50.8g; Fiber 2.8g; Sugars 1.2g; Protein 8.4g

Spanish Rice

Prep time: 15 minutes | Cook time: 6 hours | Serves: 4 to 6

2 cups white rice	½ medium onion, diced
2 cups vegetable broth	1 teaspoon sea salt
2 tablespoons extra-virgin olive oil	½ teaspoon ground cumin
	½ teaspoon garlic powder
1 (15-ounce) can crushed tomatoes	½ teaspoon chili powder
	½ teaspoon dried oregano
1 (4-ounce) can hatch green chiles	Black pepper

1. In your slow cooker, combine the rice, broth, olive oil, tomatoes, chiles, onion, salt, cumin, garlic powder, chili powder, and oregano, and season with pepper. 2. Cover the cooker and set to low. Cook for almost 5 to 6 hours, fluff, and serve.

Per serving: Calories 313; Fat 5.6g; Sodium 709mg; Carbs 56.6g; Fiber 3.5g; Sugars 4.8g; Protein 7.9g

Ratatouille with Fennel

Prep time: 15 minutes | Cook time: 30 minutes | Serves: 4

½ cup extra-virgin olive oil	½ teaspoon black pepper
1 onion, sliced	½ teaspoon ground turmeric
1 fennel bulb, white part only, bottom trimmed and sliced	1 eggplant, cut into 1-inch cubes
4 garlic cloves, minced	2 zucchini or yellow squash, cut into ½-inch thick rounds
1 teaspoon smoked paprika	4 roma tomatoes, quartered
1 teaspoon salt	½ cup chopped parsley

1. In a large soup pot or Dutch oven, heat the olive oil over medium heat. 2. Add the onion and fennel and sauté for 8 to 10 minutes, until they are softened and fragrant. 3. Add the garlic, paprika, salt, pepper, and turmeric and sauté for almost 2 minutes, until fragrant. 4. Add the eggplant, zucchini, and tomatoes and sauté for almost 4 to 5 minutes, until the vegetables are just tender. 5. Reduce its heat to low, cover, and cook, while stirring occasionally, for almost 10 to 12 minutes until the vegetables are very tender. 6. Remove from the heat and stir in the parsley. Season to taste with black pepper and salt and serve warm.

Per serving: Calories 322; Fat 26.2g; Sodium 636mg; Carbs 23.7g; Fiber 9.6g; Sugars 9.7g; Protein 5g

Buckwheat and Sweet Potatoes

Prep time: 15 minutes | Cook time: 20 minutes | Serves: 4 to 6

1 tablespoon coconut oil	1 cup lentils, rinsed
2 cups cubed sweet potatoes	6 cups vegetable broth
1 yellow onion, chopped	1 teaspoon salt
2 garlic cloves, minced	½ teaspoon black pepper
2 teaspoons ground cumin	2 cups chopped kale, washed and stemmed
½ cup buckwheat groats	

1. In a suitable pot over medium-high heat, melt the coconut oil. Stir in the sweet potatoes, onion, garlic, and cumin. Sauté for 5 minutes. 2. Add the buckwheat groats, lentils, vegetable broth, salt, and pepper. Bring to a boil. 3. Reduce its heat to simmer, and cover the pot. 4. Cook for 15 minutes, or until the sweet potatoes, buckwheat, and lentils are tender. 5. Remove the pot from the heat. Add the kale and stir to combine. 6. Cover this cooking pot and let it sit for 5 minutes before serving.

Per serving: Calories: 406; Total fat 6.7g; Sodium 1771mg; Total carbs 64.5g; Fiber 19.4g; Sugars 7.1g; Protein 24.2g

Stuffed Sweet Potatoes

Prep time: 15 minutes | Cook time: 7 hours | Serves: 4

4 medium sweet potatoes	(both white and green parts)
1 cup hatch chile "refried" beans	1 avocado, peeled, pitted, and quartered
4 tablespoons chopped scallions	

1. Wash the sweet potatoes, but do not dry them. The water left on the skins from washing is the only moisture needed for cooking. 2. Put the damp sweet potatoes in your slow cooker. Cover the cooker and set to low. Cook for almost 6 to 7 hours. A fork should easily poke through when they are done. 3. Carefully remove the hot sweet potatoes from the slow cooker. Slice each one lengthwise about halfway through. 4. Mash the revealed flesh with a fork, and fill the opening with ¼ cup of beans. 5. Top each with 1 tablespoon of scallions and a quarter of the avocado and serve.

Per serving: Calories 281; Fat 10.1g; Sodium 17mg; Carbs 46.6g; Fiber 9.7g; Sugars 1.1g; Protein 3.4g

Rice-Stuffed Peppers

Prep time: 15 minutes | Cook time: 5 hours | Serves: 4

1 tablespoon avocado oil	2 cups Spanish rice
4 bell peppers, any color, washed, tops cut off, and seeded	1 (15-ounce) can black beans, rinsed and drained well
½ cup water	

1. Layer the bottom of your slow cooker with the avocado oil. 2. Set the peppers, upright, in the cooker. Add the water to the bottom of your slow cooker, around the outside of the peppers. 3. In a suitable bowl, stir together the rice and black beans. Stuff each pepper with one-quarter of the prepared mixture. 4. Cover the cooker and set to low. Cook for almost 4 to 5 hours and serve. Cooking tip: choose peppers that are the same size and shape so they cook evenly and fit properly into your slow cooker. Cut a thin slice from the bottoms of the peppers if they are uneven and won't stand properly in your cooker.

Per serving: Calories 286; Fat 1g; Sodium 6mg; Carbs 61.3g; Fiber 3.4g; Sugars 4.3g; Protein 7.3g

Fried Quinoa

Prep time: 15 minutes | Cook time: 6 hours | Serves: 4 to 6

2 cups quinoa, rinsed well	¼ cup diced scallion
4 cups vegetable broth	1 tablespoon sesame oil
¼ cup sliced carrots	1 teaspoon garlic powder
¼ cup corn kernels	1 teaspoon sea salt
¼ cup green peas	Dash red pepper flakes

1. In your slow cooker, combine the quinoa, broth, carrots, corn, peas, scallion, sesame oil, garlic powder, salt, and red pepper flakes. 2. Cover the cooker and set to low. Cook for almost 4 to 6 hours, fluff, and serve.

Per serving: Calories 270; Fat 6.7g; Sodium 829mg; Carbs 40.2g; Fiber 4.7g; Sugars 1.5g; Protein 12g

Wild Rice Mushroom Soup

Prep time: 15 minutes | Cook time: 8 hours | Serves: 4

1½ cups uncooked wild rice
6 cups vegetable broth
2 carrots, diced
1 celery stalk, diced
½ medium onion, diced
¼ cup dried porcini mushrooms

1 tablespoon extra-virgin olive oil
1 teaspoon sea salt
½ teaspoon garlic powder
½ teaspoon dried thyme leaves
1 bay leaf
Black pepper

1. In your slow cooker, combine the rice, broth, carrots, celery, onion, mushrooms, olive oil, salt, garlic powder, thyme, and bay leaf, and season with pepper. 2. Cover the cooker and set to low. Cook for almost 6 to 8 hours. 3. Remove and discard the bay leaf before serving.
Per serving: Calories 240; Fat 4.2g; Sodium 1095mg; Carbs 37.4g; Fiber 5g; Sugars 3.2g; Protein 12.8g

Boiled Beans

Prep time: 10 minutes | Cook time: 8 hours | Serves: 6

1 pound dried beans, any kind   Water

1. Rinse the beans, and pick out any broken ones or possible rocks or dirt particles. 2. Put the beans in a suitable bowl or in your slow cooker and cover with water. Let soak for a minimum of 8 hours, or overnight. 3. Drain and rinse the beans well. Put them in your slow cooker and cover with 2 inches of fresh water. 4. Cover your slow cooker with its lid. Slow cook for 8 hours until soft and cooked through. Drain and serve. Cooking tip: Add a strip of kombu seaweed to your cooking beans to help make them more digestible, especially if you don't have time to presoak. Kombu contains the enzymes needed to break down some of the oligosaccharides, called raffinose, in the beans. Look for it in the Asian foods section of your grocery store.
Per serving: Calories 140; Fat 5g; Sodium 10mg; Carbs 23g; Fiber 7g; Sugars 0g; Protein 8g

Baked Navy Beans

Prep time: 15 minutes | Cook time: 8 hours | Serves: 4 to 6

2 cups dried navy beans, soaked in water overnight, drained, and rinsed
6 cups vegetable broth
¼ cup dried cranberries
1 medium sweet onion, diced
½ cup sugar-free ketchup

3 tablespoons olive oil
2 tablespoons maple syrup
2 tablespoons molasses
1 tablespoon apple cider vinegar
1 teaspoon Dijon mustard
1 teaspoon sea salt
½ teaspoon garlic powder

1. In your slow cooker, combine the beans, broth, cranberries, onion, ketchup, olive oil, maple syrup, molasses, vinegar, mustard, salt, and garlic powder. 2. Cover the cooker and set to low. Cook for 7 to 8 hours and serve. Cooking tip: it's extremely important to soak your beans before using them in a recipe. It reduces the phytic acid, reduces cooking time, ensures an even cooking experience, and allows your tummy the best (and least painful) experience as it digests them. You can even use the bowl of your slow cooker the night before to soak your beans in cool water with a dash of salt. Make sure it's at room temperature and the beans get at least an 8-hour bath. Rinse them well before using, and discard the soaking water.
Per serving: Calories 380; Fat 9.5g; Sodium 1092mg; Carbs 54.8g; Fiber 17.5g; Sugars 12.1g; Protein 20.6g

Spaghetti Squash

Prep time: 15 minutes | Cook time: 8 hours | Serves: 4 to 6

1 spaghetti squash, washed well   2 cups water

1. Using a fork, poke 10 to 15 holes all around the outside of the spaghetti squash. Put the squash and the water in your slow cooker. 2. Cover the cooker and set to low. Cook for 8 hours. 3. Transfer the squash from the slow cooker to a cutting board. Let sit for almost 15 minutes to cool. 4. Halve the squash lengthwise. Using a spoon, scrape the seeds out of the center of the squash. 5. Then, using a fork, scrape at the flesh until it shreds into a spaghetti-like texture. Serve warm.
Per serving: Calories 26; Fat 0.3g; Sodium 10mg; Carbs 5.4g; Fiber 1.8g; Sugars 3.6g; Protein 2g

Refried Beans

Prep time: 15 minutes | Cook time: 8 hours | Serves: 4

2 cups dried pinto beans, soaked in water overnight, drained, and rinsed
7 cups vegetable broth
½ medium onion, minced

1 (4-ounce) can hatch green chiles
1 tablespoon lime juice
½ teaspoon ground cumin
½ teaspoon garlic powder
½ teaspoon sea salt

1. In your slow cooker, combine the beans, broth, onion, chiles, lime juice, cumin, garlic powder, and salt. 2. Cover the cooker and set to low. Cook for almost 6 to 8 hours, until the beans are soft. 3. Using an immersion blender, mash the beans to your desired consistency before serving. If you don't own an immersion blender, mash the beans by hand with a fork or a potato masher.
Per serving: Calories 413; Fat 11.1g; Sodium 1215mg; Carbs 46.4g; Fiber 10.9g; Sugars 3.3g; Protein 30.9g

Quinoa with Pepperoncini

Prep time: 15 minutes | Cook time: 8 hours | Serves: 4 to 6

1½ cups quinoa, rinsed well
3 cups vegetable broth
½ teaspoon sea salt
½ teaspoon garlic powder
¼ teaspoon dried oregano
¼ teaspoon dried basil leaves

Black pepper
3 cups arugula
½ cup diced tomatoes
⅓ cup sliced pepperoncini
¼ cup lemon juice
3 tablespoons olive oil

1. In your slow cooker, combine the quinoa, broth, salt, garlic powder, oregano, and basil, and season with pepper. 2. Cover the cooker and set to low. Cook for almost 6 to 8 hours. In a suitable bowl, toss together the arugula, tomatoes, pepperoncini, lemon juice, and olive oil. 3. When the quinoa is done, add it to the arugula salad, mix well, and serve.
Per serving: Calories 245; Fat 10.5g; Sodium 567mg; Carbs 29.2g; Fiber 3.4g; Sugars 1.2g; Protein 8.9g

Butter Chickpeas

Prep time: 15 minutes | Cook time: 8 hours | Serves: 4

1 tablespoon coconut oil
1 medium onion, diced
1 pound dried chickpeas, soaked in water overnight, drained, and rinsed
2 cups full-fat coconut milk
1 (15-ounce) can crushed tomatoes

2 tablespoons almond butter
2 tablespoons curry powder
1½ teaspoons garlic powder
1 teaspoon ground ginger
½ teaspoon sea salt
½ teaspoon ground cumin
½ teaspoon chili powder

1. Layer the slow cooker with coconut oil. 2. Layer the onion along the bottom of your slow cooker. 3. Add the chickpeas, coconut milk, tomatoes, almond butter, curry powder, garlic powder, ginger, salt, cumin, and chili powder. Gently stir to ensure the spices are mixed into the liquid. 4. Cover the cooker and set to low. Cook for almost 6 to 8 hours, until the chickpeas are soft, and serve.
Serving tip: for a complete meal, serve these over coconutty brown rice.
Per serving: Calories 478; Fat 19.6g; Sodium 316mg; Carbs 59.9g; Fiber 17.7g; Sugars 13.8g; Protein 18.4g

Sweet Potato Leek Soup

Prep time: 15 minutes | Cook time: 5 hrs | Serves: 4 to 6

5 medium sweet potatoes, peeled and chopped
1 leek, washed and sliced
1½ teaspoons garlic powder
1 teaspoon sea salt

½ teaspoon ground turmeric
¼ teaspoon ground cumin
4 cups vegetable broth
Black pepper

1. In your slow cooker, combine the sweet potatoes, leek, garlic powder, salt, turmeric, cumin, and broth, and season with pepper. 2. Cover the cooker and set to low. Cook for almost 4 to 5 hours. 3. Using an immersion blender, purée the soup until smooth and serve.
Per serving: Calories 192; Fat 1.2g; Sodium 836mg; Carbs 39.6g; Fiber 5.7g; Sugars 2.3g; Protein 5.8g

Vegetarian Pad Thai

Prep time: 15 minutes | Cook time: 25 minutes | Serves: 4

3 large zucchinis, spiralized
4 large eggs
¼ cup, plus 2 tablespoons tamari
3 tablespoons sesame oil
¼ cup avocado oil
½ cup unsweetened almond or cashew butter
Grated zest and juice of 1 lime
4 celery stalks, sliced
1 carrot, peeled and sliced into rounds
4 ounces shiitake mushrooms,
sliced
1 cup snow peas, trimmed
1 (2-inch) piece fresh ginger, peeled and minced
½ cup chopped scallions, white and green parts
2 garlic cloves, minced
¼ cup chopped fresh cilantro
¼ cup chopped fresh mint
¼ cup chopped cashews
1 lime, quartered

1. Set the zucchini in a suitable bowl. 2. In a suitable bowl, whisk together the eggs, 2 tablespoons of tamari, and 2 tablespoons of sesame oil. 3. In a large nonstick skillet, heat 2 tablespoons of avocado oil over medium-high heat. Add the prepared egg mixture. Reduce its heat to medium, and cook undisturbed for almost 2 to 3 minutes, until the eggs begin to set. 4. Using a rubber spatula, scramble the eggs for almost 2 to 3 minutes, until cooked through. Transfer the eggs to a plate or bowl to keep warm, reserving this skillet. 5. In another small bowl, combine the almond butter, lime zest and juice, the rest of the ¼ cup of tamari, and the rest of the 1 tablespoon of sesame oil and whisk until smooth. 6. In the reserved skillet, heat the rest of the 2 tablespoons of avocado oil over medium heat. Add the celery, carrot, mushrooms, snow peas, and ginger and sauté for almost 4 to 5 minutes, until the vegetables are just tender. 7. Add the scallions and garlic and sauté for almost 2 to 3 minutes. Add the almond butter mixture, reduce its heat to low, and cook, while stirring constantly, for almost 3 to 4 minutes, until heated through. 8. Pour the vegetable and sauce mixture over the zucchini, add the cooked egg, cilantro, mint, and cashews and toss to coat well. 9. Serve warm garnished with the lime wedges.
Per serving: Calories 339; Fat 23.4g; Sodium 195mg; Carbs 23.8g; Fiber 6.8g; Sugars 9g; Protein 13.9g

Vegetable Broth

Prep time: 15 minutes | Cook time: 8 hours | Serves: 12

Olive oil, for coating the slow cooker
6 cups veggie scraps (peels and pieces of carrots, celery, onions, garlic)
12 cups filtered water
½ medium onion, chopped
2 garlic cloves, chopped
1 parsley sprig
¾ teaspoon sea salt
½ teaspoon dried oregano
½ teaspoon dried basil leaves
2 bay leaves

1. Layer the slow cooker with a thin layer of olive oil. 2. In the slow cooker, combine the veggie scraps, water, onion, garlic, parsley, salt, oregano, basil, and bay leaves. 3. Cover the cooker and set to low. Cook for almost 6 to 8 hours. 4. Pour the broth through a fine-mesh sieve. Set over a suitable bowl, discarding the veggie scraps. 5. Refrigerate the broth in airtight containers for up to 5 days, or freeze for up to 3 months.
Per serving: Calories 104; Fat 0.4g; Sodium 129mg; Carbs 23.1g; Fiber 1.6g; Sugars 0.9g; Protein 4.4g

Split Pea Carrot Soup

Prep time: 15 minutes | Cook time: 8 hours | Serves: 4 to 6

2 cups dried split peas, soaked in water overnight, drained, and rinsed well
3 carrots, chopped
1 celery stalk, diced
½ medium onion, diced
1 tablespoon extra-virgin olive oil
1 tablespoon lemon juice, freshly
squeezed
2 teaspoons dried thyme leaves
1 teaspoon garlic powder
½ teaspoon dried oregano
2 bay leaves
8 cups broth (choose vegetable to keep it vegan)

1. In your slow cooker, combine the split peas, carrots, celery, onion, olive oil, lemon juice, thyme, garlic powder, oregano, bay leaves, and broth. 2. Cover the cooker and set to low. Cook for 7 to 8 hours. 3. Remove and discard the bay leaves. For a smoother soup, blend with an immersion blender and serve.
Per serving: Calories 315; Fat 5g; Sodium 1052mg; Carbs 45.5g; Fiber 18g; Sugars 8.3g; Protein 23.1g

Tofu Tikka

Prep time: 10 minutes | Cook time: 25 minutes | Serves: 4

¼ cup coconut oil
2 tablespoons extra-virgin olive oil
½ onion, chopped
1 (2-inch) piece fresh ginger, peeled and minced
4 garlic cloves, minced
1½ tablespoons garam masala
1 teaspoon fennel seed
1 (15-ounce) can full-fat coconut milk
½ cup vegetable broth
2 tablespoons tomato paste
1 teaspoon salt
1 (14-ounce) package extra-firm tofu, drained and cut into 1-inch cubes
Grated zest and juice of 1 lime
Perfect riced cauliflower or steamed spinach, for serving
½ cup chopped fresh cilantro

1. In a large saucepan or Dutch oven, heat the coconut and olive oils over medium heat. Add the onion and ginger and sauté for almost 4 to 5 minutes, until the onion is lightly browned and just soft. 2. Add the garlic, garam masala, and fennel and sauté for almost 2 to 3 minutes, until a thick paste has formed. 3. Whisk in the coconut milk, broth, tomato paste, and salt and bring to a boil over high heat. 4. Reduce its heat to low, add the tofu, and simmer, covered, for almost 10 to 15 minutes until the flavors have developed. Remove from the heat and stir in the lime zest and juice. 5. Serve warm over riced cauliflower or steamed spinach, garnished with the cilantro.
Per serving: Calories 311; Fat 26.9g; Sodium 711mg; Carbs 9.9g; Fiber 3.4g; Sugars 2.3g; Protein 12.2g

French Onion Soup

Prep time: 15 minutes | Cook time: 4 hours | Serves: 4

2 large onions, sliced
¼ cup extra-virgin olive oil
¾ teaspoon sea salt
2 (14-ounce) cans cannellini beans, rinsed and drained well
4 cups vegetable broth
½ teaspoon garlic powder
½ teaspoon dried thyme leaves
1 bay leaf
Black pepper

1. In your slow cooker, combine the onions, olive oil, and salt. 2. Cover the cooker and set to high. Cook for almost 3 hours, allowing the onions to caramelize. 3. Stir the onions well and add the beans, broth, garlic powder, thyme, and bay leaf, and season with pepper. 4. Re-cover the cooker and set to low. Cook for almost 4 hours. 5. Remove and discard the bay leaf before serving.
Per serving: Calories 225; Fat 14.2g; Sodium 1121mg; Carbs 16.8g; Fiber 5.2g; Sugars 4.3g; Protein 9.1g

Cauliflower Rice Risotto

Prep time: 15 minutes | Cook time: 5 hours | Serves: 4

1 pound riced cauliflower
1 celery stalk, minced
1 small shallot, minced
¼ cup vegetable broth
½ teaspoon garlic powder
½ teaspoon sea salt
Black pepper

1. In your slow cooker, combine the riced cauliflower, celery, shallot, broth, garlic powder, and salt, and season with pepper. Stir well. 2. Cover the cooker and set to low. Cook for almost 4 to 5 hours and serve.
Per serving: Calories 27; Fat 0.2g; Sodium 619mg; Carbs 4.2g; Fiber 1.2g; Sugars 1.4g; Protein 1.9g

Broccolini and Quinoa Sauté

Prep time: 10 minutes | Cook time: 10 minutes | Serves: 4

1 tablespoon coconut oil
2 garlic cloves, chopped
2 leeks, white part only, sliced
4 cups chopped broccolini
½ cup vegetable broth, low-
sodium
2 cups cooked quinoa
1 tablespoon coconut aminos
1 teaspoon curry powder

1. In a suitable skillet, melt the coconut oil over high heat. Stir in the garlic and leeks and sauté for 2 minutes until fragrant. 2. Add the broccolini and vegetable broth. Cover and cook for 5 minutes until the broccolini softens. 3. Add the cooked quinoa, coconut aminos, and curry powder and stir to incorporate. 4. Cook uncovered for almost 2 to 3 minutes until warmed through, stirring occasionally. 5. Divide the mixture among four plates and serve warm.
Per serving: Calories: 393; Total fat 8.9g; Sodium 124mg; Total carbs 64.7g; Fiber 8.1g; Sugars 2.6g; Protein 14.7g

Chapter 5 Poultry Recipes

Lemony Roasted Chicken

Prep time: 10 minutes | Cook time: 1 hour 45 minutes | Servings: 4-6

1 tablespoon extra-virgin olive oil	½ cup chicken broth
1 (3½- to 4-pound) chicken	½ cup dry white wine
1 teaspoon salt	1 (15-ounce) can white beans,
¼ teaspoon black pepper	drained and rinsed
1 onion, sliced	2 tablespoons fresh lemon juice
2 garlic cloves, sliced	

1. At 375 degrees F, preheat your oven. 2. Heat the olive oil in the Dutch oven over high heat. 3. Pat the chicken dry with a paper towel and season with the salt and pepper. 4. Place the chicken in the Dutch oven and brown the skin for 5 minutes, breast-side down. Turn the chicken over and brown the back. 5. Scatter the onion and garlic slices around the chicken and add the broth and white wine. Cover the Dutch oven and bake for almost 1 hour. 6. Add the white beans and lemon juice, cover and cook for an additional 30 minutes. 7. Uncover and let the chicken cool for 10 minutes before serving.
Per Serving: Calories 386; Total Fat 11.42g; Sodium 859mg; Total Carbs 3.22g; Fiber 1g; Sugars 0.71g; Protein 64.25g

Chicken and Apple Salad with Walnuts

Prep time: 10 minutes | Cook time: 0 | Servings: 2

2 cooked boneless and skinless chicken breasts, cut into ½-inch diced	1 romaine lettuce heart, chopped
	3 scallions, chopped
	½ cup canned chickpeas
½ cup chopped celery	½ cup Lemony Mustard Dressing
1 large green apple, cored and coarsely chopped	½ cup chopped toasted walnuts

1. Mix the chicken, celery, apple, romaine, scallions and chickpeas in a suitable bowl. 2. Add the prepared dressing and toss to mix. 3. Divide the prepared salad among four serving bowls, top with the toasted walnuts and serve.
Per Serving: Calories 733; Total Fat 24.69g; Sodium 424mg; Total Carbs 63.37g; Fiber 17.7g; Sugars 22.73g; Protein 73.11g

Balsamic-Glazed Chicken Breasts

Prep time: 10 minutes | Cook time: 20 minutes | Servings: 4

¼ cup balsamic vinegar	1 teaspoon salt
2 tablespoons honey	4 boneless, skinless chicken
1 shallot, minced	breasts

1. At 350 degrees F, preheat your oven. 2. Mix the balsamic vinegar, honey, shallot and salt in a 9-by-13-inch baking pan and stir until the honey has dissolved. 3. Add the chicken, turning to coat. 4. Bake the food for 20 minutes until the chicken is cooked through. 5. Let rest for almost 5 minutes before serving.
Per Serving: Calories 303; Total Fat 7.08g; Sodium 994mg; Total Carbs 11.79g; Fiber 0.1g; Sugars 11.2g; Protein 48.13g

Tasty Chicken Stew

Prep time: 10 minutes | Cook time: 4 hrs | Servings: 4-6

1 tablespoon extra-virgin olive oil	lightly crushed
3 pounds boneless, skinless chicken thighs	1 teaspoon salt
	¼ teaspoon freshly ground black pepper
1 large onion, thinly sliced	2 cups chicken broth
2 garlic cloves, thinly sliced	1 cup unsweetened coconut milk
1 teaspoon minced fresh ginger root	¼ cup chopped fresh cilantro (optional)
2 teaspoons ground turmeric	
1 teaspoon whole coriander seeds,	

1. Drizzle the oil into a slow cooker. 2. Add the chicken, onion, garlic, ginger root, turmeric, coriander, salt, pepper, chicken broth and coconut milk to the slow cooker, toss them to combine. 3. Cover and cook on high for 4 hours. 4. Garnish with the chopped cilantro and serve.
Per Serving: Calories 331; Total Fat 12.17g; Sodium 950mg; Total Carbs 5.92g; Fiber 0.8g; Sugars 3.53g; Protein 46.97g

Coconut Chicken Thighs

Prep time: 10 minutes | Cook time: 4 hrs | Servings: 4-6

¼ cup white miso	root
2 tablespoons coconut oil, melted	1 cup chicken broth
2 tablespoons honey	8 boneless, skinless chicken
1 tablespoon unseasoned rice wine vinegar	thighs
	2 scallions, sliced
2 garlic cloves, thinly sliced	1 tablespoon sesame seeds
1 teaspoon minced fresh ginger	

1. In a slow cooker, mix the miso, coconut oil, honey, rice wine vinegar, garlic and ginger root. 2. Add the chicken and toss to combine. Cover and cook on high for 4 hours. 3. Transfer the cooked chicken and sauce to a serving dish. 4. Add scallions and sesame seeds and serve.
Per Serving: Calories 409; Total Fat 16.74g; Sodium 828mg; Total Carbs 9.91g; Fiber 0.9g; Sugars 6.78g; Protein 52.65g

Scrambled Chicken Things with Broccoli

Prep time: 10 minutes | Cook time: 15 minutes | Servings: 4-6

2 tablespoons coconut oil	root
pound boneless chicken thighs, cut into thin strips	1 teaspoon salt
	¼ teaspoon red pepper flakes
2 cups broccoli florets	¾ cup chicken broth
2 garlic cloves, sliced	1 teaspoon toasted sesame oil
1 teaspoon minced fresh ginger	1 tablespoon sesame seeds

1. Heat the coconut oil in a Dutch oven over high heat. 2. Add the chicken and sauté for 5 to 8 minutes until it starts to brown. 3. Add the broccoli florets, garlic, ginger, salt, red pepper flakes, and broth. 4. Cover the cooking pot, lower the heat to medium and let the mixture steam for 5 minutes until the broccoli turns bright green. 5. Remove from the heat, add the sesame oil and sesame seeds and serve.
Per Serving: Calories 274; Total Fat 20.81g; Sodium 578mg; Total Carbs 1.52g; Fiber 0.6g; Sugars 0.17g; Protein 19.78g

Turkey Burgers with Onion

Prep time: 10 minutes | Cook time: 10 minutes | Servings: 4

1½ pounds ground turkey	2 teaspoons minced fresh ginger
1 large egg, lightly beaten	root
2 tablespoons coconut flour (or almond flour)	1 tablespoon fresh cilantro
	1 teaspoon salt
½ cup freshly chopped onion	¼ teaspoon black pepper
1 garlic clove, minced	1 tablespoon extra-virgin olive oil

1. Mix up the ground turkey, egg, flour, onion, garlic, ginger root, cilantro, salt and pepper in the bowl. 2. Form the turkey mixture into four patties. 3. Heat the olive oil in a suitable skillet over medium-high heat. 4. Cook the burgers for 4 minutes on each side, flipping once, until firm to the touch. 5. Serve and enjoy.
Per Serving: Calories 293; Total Fat 15.73g; Sodium 762mg; Total Carbs 3.31g; Fiber 0.5g; Sugars 1.34g; Protein 34.59g

Turkey Thighs with Mushrooms

Prep time: 15 minutes | Cook time: 4 hrs | Servings: 4

1 tablespoon extra-virgin olive oil	1 rosemary sprig
2 turkey thighs	1 teaspoon salt
2 cups button or cremini mushrooms, sliced	¼ teaspoon freshly ground black pepper
1 large onion, sliced	2 cups chicken broth
1 garlic clove, sliced	½ cup dry red wine

1. Drizzle the olive oil into a slow cooker; add the turkey thighs, mushrooms, onion, garlic, rosemary sprig, salt and pepper. 2. Pour in the chicken broth and wine. Cover and cook on high for almost 4 hours. 3. Remove and discard the rosemary sprig. Transfer the thighs to a plate and allow them to cool for several minutes for easier handling. 4. Cut the meat from the bones, stir the meat into the mushrooms and serve.
Per Serving: Calories 291; Total Fat 15.24g; Sodium 1764mg; Total Carbs 4.62g; Fiber 0.8g; Sugars 2.19g; Protein 30.92g

Satay Chicken Breast

Prep time: 15 minutes | Cook time: 8 minutes | Servings: 4

For the Sauce

½ cup almond butter
¼ cup water
2 tablespoons coconut aminos
1 tablespoon grated fresh ginger

1 tablespoon freshly squeezed lime juice
1 garlic clove
1 teaspoon raw honey

For the Satay

Juice of 2 limes
2 tablespoons olive oil
2 tablespoons raw honey
1 tablespoon finely chopped fresh cilantro

1 tablespoon bottled minced garlic
1½ pounds boneless and skinless chicken breast, cut into strips

To make the sauce: 1. Blend the almond butter, water, coconut aminos, ginger, lime juice, garlic and honey in the blender until smooth. Set aside for later use.
To make the satay: 1. In a suitable bowl, whisk the lime juice, olive oil, honey, cilantro and garlic until well mixed. 2. Add the cut chicken strips and toss well to coat. 3. Cover this bowl with plastic wrap and refrigerate for almost 1 hour to marinate. 4. Preheat the broiler. 5. Thread the chicken strips onto a wooden skewer, and lay them on a rimmed baking sheet. 6. Broil the chicken for 4 minutes per side until cooked through and golden, turning once. 10. Serve with the sauce.
Per Serving: Calories 486; Total Fat 29.26g; Sodium 307mg; Total Carbs 19.67g; Fiber 3.5g; Sugars 12.15g; Protein 41.53g

Herbed Whole Chicken

Prep time: 15 minutes | Cook time: 1 hr. 30 minutes | Servings: 4

2 lemons, halved
1 sweet onion, quartered
1 (4-pound) whole chicken, rinsed and patted dry
4 garlic cloves, crushed
5 fresh thyme sprigs

6 fresh rosemary sprigs
3 bay leaves
2 tablespoons olive oil
Sea salt
Freshly ground black pepper

1. At 400 degrees F, preheat your oven. 2. Place the chicken in a roasting pan. Stuff the lemons, onion, garlic, thyme, rosemary and bay leaves into the cavity. 3. Brush the prepared chicken with the olive oil and season lightly with sea salt and pepper. 4. Roast the chicken for 1½ hours until golden brown and cooked through. 5. Remove the cooked chicken strips from the oven and let it sit for almost 10 minutes. Remove the lemons, onion, and herbs from the cavity and serve.
Per Serving: Calories 365; Total Fat 13.46g; Sodium 206mg; Total Carbs 9.94g; Fiber 1.4g; Sugars 4.79g; Protein 49.59g

Turkey Meat Loaf with Gravy

Prep time: 15 minutes | Cook time: 20 minutes | Servings: 4

For the Meat Loaf

1½ pounds ground turkey
1 yellow onion, diced
¼ cup almond meal
2 large eggs
¼ cup fresh parsley, chopped

For the Gravy

1 cup vegetable broth, plus more as needed
5 tablespoons ghee

3 garlic cloves, minced
1 teaspoon dried oregano
2 tablespoons tomato paste
½ teaspoon sea salt
2 cups vegetable broth

½ teaspoon sea salt
¼ teaspoon cornstarch

To make the meat loaf: 1. Mix together the ground turkey, onion, almond meal, eggs, parsley, garlic, oregano, tomato paste and salt in the bowl. 2. Form the mixture into a loaf or oval shape 6 inches in diameter. Place the loaf on a suitable piece of aluminum foil. 3. Place a metal trivet or steam rack into the Instant pot and pour in the broth. 4. Lift the loaf using the edges of the foil and place it on the trivet. Lock the lid. 5. Set the pressure cook mode and cook at high pressure for almost 20 minutes. 6. When cooking is complete, use a quick release. 7. Remove the cooker's lid and then remove the trivet and transfer the meat loaf to a serving dish, leaving the juices in the pot. Select Cancel.
To make the gravy: 1. Select Sauté function, pour in the broth and add the ghee, salt, and cornstarch to the juices in the pot. Cook for 3 minutes, whisking continuously, until the gravy bubbles and thickens. If it needs to be thinned, whisk in more broth a little at a time to get the desired consistency. 2. Slice the meat loaf and drizzle with the gravy.
Per Serving: Calories 498; Total Fat 31.44g; Sodium 1119mg; Total Carbs 16.71g; Fiber 3.2g; Sugars 4.89g; Protein 39.11g

Coconut-Braised Chicken Thighs

Prep time: 10 minutes | Cook time: 35 minutes | Servings: 6

1½ cups canned lite coconut milk
2 tablespoons grated fresh ginger
Juice of 1 lime
Zest of 1 lime (optional)
1 tablespoon raw honey
½ teaspoon ground cardamom

1 tablespoon olive oil
1 pound bone-in skin-on chicken thighs
1 scallion, white and green parts, chopped

1. Whisk the coconut milk, ginger, lime juice, lime zest, honey and cardamom in the bowl. Set aside. 2. Heat the olive oil in the skillet over medium-high heat. 3. Add the chicken thighs and pan-sear for 20 minutes, or until golden, flipping halfway through. 4. Pour in the prepared coconut milk mixture over the chicken and bring the liquid to a boil. 5. Lower the heat to low, cover the skillet and simmer for almost 15 minutes, or until the chicken is tender and cooked through. 6. Serve garnished with the scallions.
Per Serving: Calories 315; Total Fat 26.9g; Sodium 70mg; Total Carbs 6.55g; Fiber 0.2g; Sugars 3.21g; Protein 13.8g

Sautéed Chicken Breasts with Mushroom

Prep time: 20 minutes | Cook time: 45 minutes | Servings: 6

1 tablespoon olive oil
3 (8-ounce) boneless and skinless chicken breasts, diced
1 sweet onion, chopped, or almost 1 cup precut packaged onion
2 cups sliced button mushrooms
2 teaspoons bottled minced garlic

1 cup uncooked buckwheat
1 cup chicken bone broth
1 cup canned lite coconut milk
½ teaspoon ground nutmeg
4 cups fresh spinach
Sea salt
Zest of 1 lemon (optional)

1. Heat the olive oil in the skillet over medium-high heat. 2. Add the chicken and sauté for almost 15 minutes until just cooked through, flipping halfway through. 3. Remove the cooked chicken and transfer to a plate and set it aside. 4. Return this skillet to the heat. 5. Sauté the mushrooms, onion and garlic in this skillet for 5 minutes. 6. Pour in the buckwheat and sauté for 1 minute. 7. Add coconut milk, chicken broth, and nutmeg. Bring the liquid to a boil. 8. Lower its heat to low, cover the skillet and simmer the food for almost 25 minutes, or until the buckwheat is tender. 9. Stir in the spinach and chicken and season with sea salt. 10. Serve sprinkled with lemon zest (optional).
Per Serving: Calories 330; Total Fat 15.83g; Sodium 269mg; Total Carbs 13.89g; Fiber 2.7g; Sugars 4.88g; Protein 33.9g

Lean Turkey Meatballs

Prep time: 20 minutes | Cook time: 15 minutes | Servings: 4

1½ pounds lean ground turkey
½ sweet onion, chopped, or about ½ cup precut packaged onion
¼ cup almond flour
1 tablespoon chopped fresh thyme

2 teaspoons bottled minced garlic
1 egg
¼ teaspoon ground nutmeg
Pinch sea salt

1. At 350 degrees F, preheat your oven. 2. Layer a suitable rimmed baking sheet with aluminum foil and set it aside. 3. Mix up the turkey, onion, almond flour, thyme, garlic, egg, nutmeg and sea salt in the bowl. 4. Roll the turkey mixture into 1½-inch meatballs. Arrange the meatballs on the prepared baking sheet. 5. Bake the meatballs for 15 minutes, or until browned and cooked through.
Per Serving: Calories 305; Total Fat 16.74g; Sodium 185mg; Total Carbs 4.08g; Fiber 0.5g; Sugars 2.26g; Protein 34.58g

Rosemary Chicken

Prep time: 15 minutes | Cook time: 20 minutes | Serves: 4

1½ pounds chicken breast tenders
2 tablespoons extra-virgin olive oil
2 tablespoons chopped fresh

rosemary leaves
½ teaspoon sea salt
⅛ teaspoon black pepper

1. At 425 degrees F, preheat your oven. 2. Set the chicken tenders on a rimmed baking sheet. 3. Brush them with the olive oil and sprinkle with the rosemary, salt, and pepper. 4. Bake for almost 15 to 20 minutes until the juices run clear.
Per serving: Calories 415; Fat 6.7g; Sodium 973mg; Carbs 0.7g; Fiber 0.5g; Sugars 0g; Protein 81.7g

Turkey Meatballs

Prep time: 10 minutes | Cook time: 20 minutes | Serves: 12 meatballs

1½ pounds ground turkey
1 small white onion, minced
1 egg, whisked
¼ cup fresh mushrooms, minced
1 teaspoon garlic powder
½ teaspoon salt

½ teaspoon dried oregano
¼ teaspoon black pepper
¼ teaspoon ground ginger
1 slice gluten-free bread, torn into small pieces

1. At 400 degrees F, preheat your oven. 2. In a suitable bowl, add the turkey, onion, egg, mushrooms, garlic powder, salt, oregano, pepper, ginger, and bread, and mix them with your hands. 3. Form the turkey mixture into 12 balls and place 1 in each cup of a 12-cup muffin tin. Bake the mixture for 20 minutes. 4. Serve immediately.
Per serving: Calories: 423; Total fat 23.2g; Sodium 340mg; Total carbs 2.7g; Fiber 0.5g; Sugars 0.5g; Protein 57.7g

Broccoli Chicken Meat

Prep time: 10 minutes | Cook time: 5 minutes | Servings: 4

1½ pounds boneless and skinless chicken breasts or thighs, cut into bite-size pieces
¼ cup water
6 tablespoons reduced-sodium tamari
2 teaspoons grated peeled fresh

ginger
3 garlic cloves, minced
4 cups broccoli florets
1 tablespoon apple cider vinegar
2 tablespoons sesame seeds
1 tablespoon toasted sesame oil (optional)

1. Mix the chicken, water, tamari, ginger, garlic and broccoli in the Instant Pot; lock the lid. 2. Select the Pressure Cook mode and cook at high pressure for 3 minutes. 3. When cooking is complete, use a quick release. 4. Press the Cancel button and remove the cooker's lid. 5. Select Sauté function. Stir in the vinegar, sesame seeds, and sesame oil, cook them for 2 minutes, stirring frequently. 6. Press the Cancel button and serve warm.
Per Serving (including the toasted sesame oil): Calories 293; Total Fat 10.59g; Sodium 743mg; Total Carbs 5.81g; Fiber 1.7g; Sugars 1.49g; Protein 42.36g

Turmeric Chicken

Prep time: 10 minutes | Cook time: 7 minutes | Servings: 6

1 tablespoon avocado oil
1 medium yellow onion, chopped
3 garlic cloves, minced
1½ pounds boneless and skinless chicken breasts or thighs, cut into bite-size pieces
2 teaspoons ground turmeric

1 teaspoon sea salt
½ teaspoon ground cumin
¼ teaspoon freshly ground black pepper
1½ cups quinoa, rinsed
3 cups low-sodium chicken broth

1. Select Sauté function and let the Instant Pot preheat. 2. Pour in the oil, add the onion, garlic and cook them for 3 minutes, or until the onion is translucent. 3. Stir in the chicken, turmeric, salt, cumin, pepper and cook for 3 minutes longer. 4. Add the quinoa and broth and stir to combine. Press the Cancel button. 5. Lock the lid. Select the pressure cook mode and cook the food at high pressure for 1 minute. 6. When cooking is complete, use a quick release. 7. Remove the cooker's lid, stir well and serve warm.
Per Serving: Calories 346; Total Fat 8.71g; Sodium 478mg; Total Carbs 31.74g; Fiber 3.6g; Sugars 0.99g; Protein 34.35g

Chicken Salad with Green Apples and Grapes

Prep time: 15 minutes | Cook time: 0 | Serves: 4

1 large avocado, diced
2 tablespoons Dijon mustard
½ teaspoon garlic powder
Dash salt
Dash black pepper
2 (8-ounce) grilled boneless,

skinless chicken breasts, chopped
2 small green apples, diced
1 cup grapes, halved
¼ cup sliced scallions
2 tablespoons minced celery

1. In a suitable bowl, add the avocado, mustard, garlic powder, salt, and pepper, stirring until creamy. 2. Add the chicken, apples, grapes, scallions and celery. Stir well to combine. 3. Serve chilled, if desired.
Per serving: Calories: 314; Total fat 13.3g; Sodium 194mg; Total carbs 24.9g; Fiber 6.8g; Sugars 16g; Protein 26g

Chicken with Brown Rice

Prep time: 10 minutes | Cook time: 25 minutes | Servings: 4

1½ pounds boneless and skinless chicken breasts or thighs, cut into bite-size chunks
1½ cups chicken broth
1 cup brown rice
1 pound cremini mushrooms,

sliced
2 carrots, chopped
2 celery stalks, chopped
1 yellow onion, chopped
1 teaspoon sea salt

1. Mix the chicken, broth, brown rice, mushrooms, carrots, celery, onion and salt in the Instant Pot. Lock the lid. 2. Select the pressure cook mode and cook the food at high pressure for 25 minutes. 3. When cooking is complete, use a natural release for almost 10 minutes, then quick release any remaining pressure. 4. Remove the cooker's lid, stir well, and serve.
Per Serving: Calories 431; Total Fat 6.5g; Sodium 1042mg; Total Carbs 45.57g; Fiber 4.2g; Sugars 5.77g; Protein 46.69g

Chicken Pho

Prep time: 30 minutes | Cook time: 3 hours| Serves: 6

5-lbs chicken, quartered, backbone reserved
2 yellow onions, peeled and halved
2-in [5-cm] piece fresh ginger, peeled and smashed
Kosher salt

1 lb. Dried brown rice noodles
2 teaspoon light brown sugar
4.7 L water
¼ cup fish sauce
1 bunch green onions, sliced
2 cups mung bean sprouts
2 jalapeños, sliced

1. Mix the chicken pieces with backbone, ginger, onions, 2 teaspoon of salt, brown sugar, and water in a stockpot with at least an 8-qt [7.5-L] capacity. 2. Slowly cook to a boil over medium-high heat. Turn the heat to medium-low and simmer gently, uncovered, for 1 hour, skimming off any impurities that come to the surface. 3. Transfer the cooked chicken to a cutting board using a tong. Remove all the chicken meat from the skin and bones and transfer to a suitable bowl. 4. Return those skin and bones to the stockpot. Shred the meat, then cover and refrigerate until ready to serve. 5. Return the stock to a simmer and continue to cook for 1½ to 2 hours. 6. Strain the cooked stock into another stockpot using a fine mesh sieve and cook over high heat until reduced to 12 cups [3 l], about 20 minutes. Stir in the fish sauce. 7. Cook the dried rice noodles according to their package instructions. 8. While the noodles cook, add half of the shredded chicken to the stock and simmer until the chicken is warmed through. 9. Divide the cooked rice noodles among six large soup bowls and sprinkle them evenly with green onions, bean sprouts, and jalapeños. 10. Ladle the cooked stock and chicken over the prepared noodles and garnish with the torn herbs. 11.Serve.
Per serving: Calories 384; Fat 12.5g; Sodium 621mg; Carbs 58.3g; Fiber 4.1g; Sugars 7.2g; Protein 10.1g

Blackened Chicken with Sautéed Vegetable

Prep time: 15 minutes | Cook time: 20 minutes | Serves: 4

For the Vegetable Sauté
1 tablespoon avocado oil
3 garlic cloves, minced
2 cups organic sweet corn kernels
1-pint cherry tomatoes halved
For the Chicken
2 teaspoons avocado oil
2 pounds boneless, skinless chicken breasts

4 scallions, sliced
¼ cup fresh cilantro leaves, minced

2 teaspoons ancho chili powder
1 teaspoon salt

1. To make the vegetable sauté: In a suitable skillet, heat the avocado oil over medium heat. Add the garlic and cook for 2 minutes, stirring frequently. 2. Add the corn, tomatoes, and scallions, cook for 5 to 7 minutes until the corn is cooked. Remove the skillet from heat and stir in the cilantro. 3. To make the chicken: In another large skillet, heat the avocado oil over medium heat. 4. Pat the chicken dry with paper towels and season with the ancho chili powder and salt.
5. Add the chicken to the skillet and cook for 4 to 5 minutes on each side, until the spices have crusted and blackened to your liking. 6. Remove this skillet from the heat when the chicken is cooked through. 7. Serve the blackened chicken alongside the vegetable sauté.
Per serving: Calories: 389; Total fat 12.7g; Sodium 685mg; Total carbs 20.9g; Fiber 3.5g; Sugars 6.5g; Protein 47.2g

Turkey-Pepper Cups

Prep time: 10 minutes | Cook time: 5 minutes | Servings: 4

1 tablespoon avocado oil	2 tablespoons tamari
1½ pounds ground turkey	1 teaspoon red pepper flakes
2 garlic cloves, minced	1 teaspoon apple cider vinegar
½ cup chicken broth	1 head romaine lettuce
3 scallions, white and green parts, minced	1 teaspoon toasted sesame oil
1 tablespoon minced peeled fresh ginger	1 tablespoon toasted sesame seeds (optional)

1. Select Sauté and let the Instant Pot preheat. 2. Pour in the avocado oil and add the ground turkey and garlic, cook for 3 minutes, or until the garlic is lightly browning. 3. Spoon the turkey mixture onto a cutting board and using a suitable knife, mince the turkey. Toss the minced turkey back into the pot. 4. Stir in the broth, scallions, ginger, tamari, red pepper flakes, and vinegar. Select Cancel. 5. Lock the lid. Set the pressure cook mode and cook at high pressure until the display reads 0 minutes. 6. While the pressure builds, make the lettuce cups. Cut off the core of the romaine lettuce and chop off any wilted green tops so the cups are almost 5 inches long. 7. Separate the individual leaves and set aside on a serving plate. 8. When cooking is complete, use a quick release. 9. Remove the cooker's lid and select Cancel. 10. Stir in the sesame oil (optional). 11. Transfer the prepared mixture to a serving bowl and sprinkle with the sesame seeds. Serve with the romaine lettuce cups on the side.
Per Serving: Calories 391; Total Fat 21.21g; Sodium 752mg; Total Carbs 8.05g; Fiber 4.1g; Sugars 2.37g; Protein 43.47g

Yellow Chicken Curry

Prep time: 10 minutes | Cook time: 35 minutes | Serves: 6

2 tablespoons coconut oil	½ cup canned diced tomatoes, with their juice
2 (4-ounce) boneless chicken breasts, cut into bite-size pieces	1 (5.4-ounce) can unsweetened coconut cream
4 garlic cloves, minced	¼ cup filtered water
2 medium carrots, diced	1 tablespoon fish sauce
1 small white onion, diced	1 tablespoon Indian curry powder
1 tablespoon minced peeled fresh ginger	¼ teaspoon salt
1 cup sugar snap peas, diced	Pinch cayenne pepper
1 cup chicken broth	Black pepper

1. In a suitable skillet, heat 1 tablespoon of coconut oil over medium-high heat. 2. Add the chicken and cook for almost 15 minutes, until cooked through. Set aside. 3. In another large skillet, heat the remaining 1 tablespoon of coconut oil over medium heat. 4. Add the garlic, carrots, onion, and ginger, sauté for 5 minutes or until the onions soften. 5. Stir in the snap peas, broth, tomatoes, coconut cream, water, fish sauce, curry powder, salt, and cayenne pepper, and season with black pepper. 6. Bring to a simmer, Reduce its heat to medium-low, and cook for 10 minutes. Add the cooked chicken and cook for 2 minutes until reheated. 7. Serve hot over rice or quinoa, if desired.
Per serving: Calories: 441; Total fat 33.9g; Sodium 759mg; Total Carbs 14.9g; Fiber 2.2g; Sugars 3.6g; Protein 21.4g

Chicken with Fennel and Zucchini

Prep time: 15 minutes | Cook time: 15 minutes | Serves: 4

2 tablespoons olive oil	rounds
4 boneless chicken breasts, cut into strips	½ cup chicken broth
1 leek, white part only, sliced thin	1 teaspoon salt
1 fennel bulb, sliced into ¼-inch rounds	½ teaspoon black pepper
3 zucchinis, sliced into ½-inch	½ cup sliced green olives
	2 tablespoons fresh dill, chopped

1. In a suitable pan, heat the olive oil over high heat. 2. Add the chicken strips. Brown them for 1 to 2 minutes, stirring constantly. Transfer the chicken and its juices to a plate or bowl and set aside. 3. Add the leek, fennel, and zucchini to the pan, sauté the food for 5 minutes. 4. Return the chicken and juices to the pan. Pour in the broth, add the salt and pepper. Cover the pan and simmer for 5 minutes almost. 5. Remove this pan from the heat, and stir in the olives and dill.
Per serving: Calories: 418; Total fat: 20g; Sodium: 1121mg; Total Carbs: 15g; Sugars: 5g; Fiber: 4g; Protein: 45g

Baked Chicken Breast with Lemon & Garlic

Prep time: 5 minutes | Cook time: 20 to 25 minutes | Serves: 4

Juice of 1 lemon	3 tablespoons avocado oil
Zest of 1 lemon	2 (8-ounce) boneless, skinless chicken breasts
1 teaspoon garlic powder	
½ teaspoon salt	

1. At 375 degrees F, preheat your oven. 2. In a suitable bowl, mix the lemon juice, lemon zest, garlic powder and salt. Set aside. 3. With a basting brush, spread 1½ tablespoons of avocado oil on the bottom of a glass or ceramic baking dish and brush them with the chicken breasts in the dish. 4. Brush the remaining 1½ tablespoons of avocado oil. With the brush, coat the chicken with the lemon-garlic mixture. 5. Bake for almost 20 to 25 minutes, until the chicken reaches an internal temperature of 165 degrees F. 6. Serve.
Per serving: Calories: 232; Total fat 9.7g; Sodium 389mg; Total carbs 1.1g; Fiber 0.5g; Sugars 0.2g; Protein 33.1g

Creamy Chicken Pesto Pasta

Prep time: 10 minutes | Cook time: 10 minutes | Serves: 6

3 cups brown rice fusilli	1 tablespoon minced shallot
1 cup diced cooked chicken breast	2 teaspoons lemon juice
1 cup pistachio pesto	½ teaspoon salt
1 cup yogurt	¼ teaspoon black pepper
1 red bell pepper, diced	

1. Cook the pasta according to the package instructions and drain. 2. Transfer to a suitable bowl. 3. Add the chicken, pistachio pesto, yogurt, red bell pepper, shallot, lemon juice, salt, and pepper. Stir well. 4. Serve chilled, if desired.
Per serving: Calories: 305; Total fat 5.7g; Sodium 307mg; Total carbs 40g; Fiber 1.8g; Sugars 4.4g; Protein 20.8g

General Tso's Chicken

Prep time: 15 minutes | Cook time: 15 minutes | Serves: 4

For the Sauce

1 tablespoon ghee	3 tablespoons coconut aminos
¼ teaspoon ground ginger	2 tablespoons rice vinegar
2 garlic cloves, minced	1 tablespoon arrowroot powder
3 tablespoons coconut sugar	½ teaspoon red pepper flakes

For the Chicken

2 tablespoons avocado oil	¼ teaspoon garlic powder
1 cup brown rice flour	1 pound boneless chicken thighs, diced
¼ teaspoon salt	

1. To make the sauce: In a suitable saucepan, stir together the ghee and ginger, cook them for 2 minutes over medium heat, stirring frequently. 2. Add the garlic, coconut sugar, coconut aminos, vinegar, arrowroot powder, and red pepper flakes. Stir well and bring to a simmer. 3. Reduce its heat to medium-low and cook for 5 minutes until the sauce begins to thicken and reduce slightly. 4. To make the chicken: In a suitable skillet, heat the avocado oil over medium-high heat. 5. In a suitable bowl, mix the rice flour, salt and garlic powder. 6. Dredge the chicken in the flour mixture and put it in the hot skillet. Cook for almost 3 to 4 minutes on each side. 7. Transfer to a serving dish. Pour the sauce over the chicken, and serve immediately.
Per serving: Calories: 456; Total fat 26.2g; Sodium 119mg; Total carbs 23.5g; Fiber 1.5g; Sugars 2.3g; Protein 28.8g

Chicken Bell Pepper Sauté

Prep time: 5 minutes | Cook time: 15 minutes | Serves: 4

3 tablespoons extra-virgin olive oil	breasts, boneless, diced
1 red bell pepper, chopped	5 garlic cloves, minced
1 onion, chopped	½ teaspoon sea salt
1½ pounds skinless chicken	¼ teaspoon black pepper, freshly ground

1. In a suitable skillet over medium-high heat, heat the olive oil until it shimmers. 2. Add the red bell pepper, onion, and chicken. Cook for almost 10 minutes, while stirring it occasionally. 3. Add the garlic, salt, and pepper. Cook for almost 30 seconds, while stirring constantly.
Per serving: Calories 440; Fat 23.2g; Sodium 383mg; Carbs 6.1g; Fiber 1.1g; Sugars 2.7g; Protein 50.1g

Ground Turkey and Spinach Stir-Fry

Prep time: 15 minutes | Cook time: 10 minutes | Serves: 4

2 tablespoons extra-virgin olive oil	1 onion, chopped
1½ pounds ground turkey breast	4 cups fresh baby spinach
	1 recipe stir-fry sauce

1. In a suitable skillet over medium-high heat, heat the olive oil until it shimmers. 2. Add the turkey, onion, and spinach. Cook for almost 5 minutes, breaking up the turkey with a spoon, until the meat is browned. 3. Add the stir-fry sauce. Cook for almost 3 to 4 minutes, while stirring constantly, until it thickens.
Per serving: Calories 399; Fat 19.8g; Sodium 132mg; Carbs 3.7g; Fiber 1.3g; Sugars 1.3g; Protein 50g

Chicken Stir-Fry

Prep time: 15 minutes | Cook time: 15 minutes | Serves: 4

3 tablespoons extra-virgin olive oil	1 pound skinless chicken breasts, boneless, diced
6 scallions, white and green parts, chopped	2 tablespoons toasted sesame seeds
1 cup broccoli florets	

1. Cut the chicken breast into bite-size pieces. 2. In a suitable skillet over medium-high heat, heat the olive oil until it shimmers. 3. Add the scallions, broccoli, and chicken. Cook for almost 5 to 7 minutes, while stirring occasionally, until the chicken is cooked and the vegetables are tender. 4. Add the stir-fry sauce. Cook for almost 5 minutes, while stirring, until the sauce reduces. 5. Garnish with sesame seeds, if using.
Per serving: Calories 320; Fat 19g; Sodium 109mg; Carbs 3.2g; Fiber 1.2g; Sugars 0.9g; Protein 33.9g

Chicken Chile Verde

Prep time: 15 minutes | Cook time: 2 hours 20 minutes | Serves: 4–6

8 bone-in, skin-on chicken thighs	½ cup chicken stock
Kosher salt	2 cups tomatillo and jalapeño
Black pepper	Salsa Verde
2 tablespoons olive oil	

1. Season all the chicken thighs with black pepper and salt. 2. In a suitable sauté pan over medium-high heat, warm the olive oil. 3. Add the chicken and cook for 10 minutes on each side until the skin is golden brown. 4. Once all the chicken thighs have been seared, and return the pan to medium-high heat. 5. Stir in the prepared chicken stock and salsa Verde and cook to a boil, scraping up any browned bits from the bottom of the pan. 6. Pour the prepared mixture into a slow cooker and place the chicken thighs in it. Cover and cook for almost 2 hours on the high setting. 7. Serve.
Per serving: Calories: 370; Total fat 30.2g; Sodium 185mg; Total carbs 2.6g; Fiber 0.9g; Sugars 0.1g; Protein 22.9g

Chicken Bites with Aioli

Prep time: 10 minutes | Cook time: 10 minutes | Serves: 4

For the Aioli

½ cup paleo mayonnaise	Dash cayenne pepper
1 tablespoon lemon juice	Dash salt
¼ teaspoon garlic powder	

For the Chicken

1 pound boneless chicken breast, diced	½ teaspoon salt
2 tablespoons avocado oil	½ teaspoon garlic powder

1. To make the aioli: In a suitable bowl, mix up the mayonnaise, lemon juice, garlic powder, cayenne, and salt. 2. To make the chicken: Preheat your broiler. 3. Layer a baking sheet with aluminum foil. 4. Spread out the chicken pieces on a plate. Brush with the avocado oil, and sprinkle with salt and garlic powder. 5. Arrange the chicken on the prepared pan, so the pieces are not touching. Broil the chicken for 7 to 10 minutes, turning halfway through. 6. Serve the chicken bites alongside the aioli sauce for dipping.
Per serving: Calories: 238; Total fat 10.6g; Sodium 149mg; Total carbs 0.6g; Fiber 0.4g; Sugars 0.2g; Protein 33g

Mediterranean Chicken Bake

Prep time: 10 minutes | Cook time: 20 minutes | Serves: 4

4 (4-ounce) boneless, skinless chicken breasts	1 cup sliced cremini mushrooms
2 tablespoons avocado oil	½ red onion, thinly sliced
1-pint cherry tomatoes halved	½ cup chopped fresh basil
1 cup chopped fresh spinach	4 garlic cloves, minced
	2 teaspoons balsamic vinegar

1. At 400 degrees F, preheat your oven. 2. Place the chicken breasts in a glass baking dish. Brush with the avocado oil. 3. In a suitable bowl, stir together the tomatoes, spinach, mushrooms, red onion, basil, garlic, and vinegar. 4. Top each chicken breast with one-fourth of the vegetable mixture. 5. Bake the chicken breasts for almost 20 minutes or until them are cooked through.
Per serving: Calories: 259; Total fat 9.6g; Sodium 111mg; Total carbs 7.3g; Fiber 2.1g; Sugars 3.4g; Protein 34.8g

Chicken Lettuce Wraps

Prep time: 20 minutes | Cook time: 0 | Serves: 4

2 heads butter lettuce	½ cup toasted sesame oil
1 pound grilled boneless chicken breast, cut into ½-inch cubes	3 tablespoons lime juice
1 cup shredded carrots	1 tablespoon coconut aminos
½ cup thinly sliced radishes	1 garlic clove
2 scallions, sliced thin	1 thin slice of fresh ginger
2 tablespoons chopped fresh cilantro	1 teaspoon lime zest
	1 tablespoon sesame seeds

1. Place all the lettuce cups on a serving platter. 2. Evenly divide the chicken, carrots, radishes, scallions, and cilantro among the lettuce cups. 3. In a suitable blender, combine the sesame oil, lime juice, coconut aminos, garlic, ginger, and lime zest. Blend until smooth. 4. Drizzle the chicken and vegetables with the dressing and sprinkle each with sesame seeds.
Per serving: Calories: 342; Total fat: 30g; Sodium: 40mg; Total Carbs: 13g; Sugars: 4g; Fiber: 3g; Protein: 7g

Turkey Larb Lettuce Wraps

Prep time: 10 minutes | Cook time: 20 minutes | Serves: 4

1 pound ground turkey	2 tablespoons minced fresh cilantro
1 small red onion, diced	1 tablespoon minced fresh mint
2 garlic cloves, minced	1 tablespoon coconut sugar
4 scallions, sliced	¼ teaspoon red pepper flakes
2 tablespoons lime juice	8 small romaine lettuce leaves
2 tablespoons fish sauce	

1. In a suitable skillet, cook the turkey for 10 minutes over medium-high heat, stirring and breaking up the meat. 2. Add the onion and garlic, cook for almost 10 minutes, stirring, until the onions soften and the meat is cooked. 3. Remove the skillet from the heat. Stir in the scallions, lime juice, fish sauce, cilantro, mint, coconut sugar, and red pepper flakes until well incorporated. 4. Fill each romaine leaf with the meat mixture. Serve warm or cold.
Per serving: Calories: 265; Total fat 12.7g; Sodium 826mg; Total carbs 9.9g; Fiber 1.5g; Sugars 5.6g; Protein 32.6g

Broccoli, Carrot and Chicken Stir-Fry

Prep time: 15 minutes | Cook time: 15 minutes | Serves: 4 to 6

1 pound boneless chicken thighs, cut into thin strips	1 teaspoon salt
1 tablespoon coconut oil	¼ teaspoon red pepper flakes
2 cups broccoli florets	½ cup chicken broth
2 carrots, cut into matchsticks	1 teaspoon toasted sesame oil
1 garlic clove, minced	1 teaspoon coconut aminos
1 teaspoon minced fresh ginger	1 tablespoon sesame seeds

1. In a suitable pan, melt the coconut oil over high heat. Add the chicken and sauté for 5 to 8 minutes, or until the chicken browns. 2. Stir in the broccoli, carrots, garlic, ginger, salt, red pepper flakes, and chicken broth. Cover the pan and cook for 5 minutes, or until the broccoli turns bright green. 3. Remove this pan from the heat and stir in the sesame oil, coconut aminos, and sesame seeds.
Per serving: Calories: 305; Total fat: 14g; Sodium: 812mg; Total Carbs: 8g; Sugars: 2g; Fiber: 2g; Protein: 35g

Chicken and Vegetables

Prep time:5 minutes | Cook time: 15 minutes | Serves: 4

2 large bone-in chicken breasts (about 2 pounds)
1 teaspoon kosher salt
½ teaspoon black pepper
½ cup chicken stock
6 large carrots
8 medium whole new potatoes

1. Season the chicken breasts with ½ teaspoon salt and ¼ teaspoon pepper. 2. Pour the stock into the insert of the Instant pot and then add the chicken breasts. Set the carrots and potatoes on top of the chicken and season them with the rest of the black pepper and salt. 3. Close the lid and secure it well. Pressure cook for 15 minutes. 4. Once cooked, release the pressure naturally then remove the lid. 5. Transfer to plates to serve and spoon the juices on top.
Per serving: Calories 398; Fat 4.3g; Sodium 1320mg; Carbs 40.8g; Fiber 4.7g; Sugars 7.4g; Protein 45.5g

Coconut Lime Chicken with Cauliflower

Prep time:15 minutes | Cook time: 11 minutes | Serves: 4

1 tablespoon coconut oil
1 small yellow onion, peeled and diced
2 heaping cups large cauliflower florets
1½ pounds chicken breasts, boneless, cut into 1½" chunks
1 (13.66-ounce) can full-fat
coconut milk, unsweetened
1 cup chicken broth
Juice from 1 medium lime
1 teaspoon kosher salt
1 teaspoon ground cumin
½ teaspoon ground ginger
2 cups baby spinach leaves

1. Heat the oil in the inner pot. When the oil melts, add the onion and cook until it's softened, about 5 minutes. 2. Add the cauliflower, chicken, coconut milk, broth, lime juice, salt, cumin, and ginger and stir well to combine. 3. Close the lid and secure it well. Pressure cook for 6 minutes approximately. 4. Once cooked, release the pressure naturally then remove the lid. Stir in the spinach until it is wilted and then serve.
Per serving: Calories 351; Fat 20.6g; Sodium 634mg; Carbs 5.4g; Fiber 2.1g; Sugars 2.7g; Protein 35.7g

Chicken Cacciatore

Prep time: 5 minutes | Cook time: 20 minutes | Serves: 4

2 tablespoons olive oil
1½ pounds skinless, boneless chicken breasts, diced
2 (28-ounce) cans crushed tomatoes, drained
½ cup black olives, chopped
1 teaspoon garlic powder
1 teaspoon onion powder
½ teaspoon sea salt
⅛ teaspoon black pepper, freshly ground

1. In a suitable skillet over medium-high heat, heat the olive oil until it shimmers. 2. Add the chicken and cook for 7 to 10 minutes, while stirring occasionally, until it is browned. Stir in the tomatoes, olives, garlic powder, onion powder, salt, and pepper. 3. Simmer for almost 10 minutes, while stirring occasionally.
Per serving: Calories 432; Fat 21.4g; Sodium 647mg; Carbs 7g; Fiber 2.6g; Sugars 3.9g; Protein 51g

Russian Kotleti

Prep time: 10 minutes | Cook time: 10 minutes | Serves: 4

¼ cup filtered water
1 pound ground chicken
½ small white onion, diced
1 egg, whisked
1 teaspoon salt
½ teaspoon garlic powder
½ teaspoon dried dill
½ teaspoon black pepper
1 slice gluten-free bread
2 teaspoons ghee

1. In a suitable bowl, combine the chicken, onion, egg, salt, garlic powder, dill, and pepper. Mix well with your hands. 2. In a suitable bowl, soak the bread in the water for 1 minute. 3. Add the soaked bread to the chicken mixture. With your hands, break it up as you mix it in. If you prefer, mix the ingredients in a stand mixer. 4. Divide the chicken mixture into 8 portions and roll each into a ball. Press them slightly to form short, thick patties. 5. In a suitable skillet, heat the ghee over medium heat. Place the patties in the pan so they do not touch and cook for 5 minutes per side. 6. Cut into one to check for doneness (no longer pink) before removing from the heat.
Per serving: Calories: 256; Total fat 11.6g; Sodium 695mg; Total carbs 1.4g; Fiber 0.3g; Sugars 0.5g; Protein 34.4g

Garlic Chicken Thighs

Prep time:10 minutes | Cook time: 11 minutes | Serves: 4

1 tablespoon avocado oil
1½ pounds boneless chicken thighs
1 small onion, peeled and diced
1 tablespoon minced garlic
Juice and zest from 1 large lemon
1 tablespoon Italian seasoning blend
⅓ cup chicken stock
1 tablespoon arrowroot powder

1. Add the oil to the inner pot. Heat oil for 2 minutes. 2. Set the chicken thighs in the insert of the Instant pot and brown 2 minutes per side. Remove the chicken thighs from the pot and set aside. 3. Add the onion to the pot and sauté 2 minutes. Add the garlic and sauté another 30 seconds. 4. Add the lemon juice, lemon zest, and Italian seasoning. Scrape up any brown bits from the bottom of the pot. Turn off the heat. 5. Put the chicken thighs back in the pot along with stock. 6. Close the lid and secure it well. Pressure cook for 7 minutes. 7. Once done, release the pressure naturally then remove the lid. 8. Remove the chicken from the pot and then stir in the arrowroot powder. 9. When the sauce is thickened, serve on top of the chicken thighs.
Per serving: Calories 339; Fat 13.1g; Sodium 211mg; Carbs 2.6g; Fiber 0.6g; Sugars 0.8g; Protein 49.

Southwest Turkey-Stuffed Bell Peppers

Prep time: 10 minutes | Cook time: 35 minutes | Serves: 6

6 bell peppers, tops removed, seeded
1 tablespoon avocado oil
1 pound ground turkey
1 small white onion, diced
2 garlic cloves, minced
1 (16-ounce) can diced tomatoes,
drained
½ teaspoon ground cumin
½ teaspoon paprika
½ teaspoon dried oregano
½ teaspoon salt
Black pepper

1. At 400 degrees F, preheat your oven Layer a baking sheet with aluminum foil. Arrange the bell peppers on the prepared pan. Drizzle with the avocado oil. 2. Bake the bell peppers for 20 minutes, or until softened and cooked. 3. While baking the bell peppers, in a suitable skillet, brown the turkey for 5 minutes over medium-high heat, breaking up the meat with a spoon. 4. Add the onion and garlic. Cook for 10 minutes, frequently stirring, until the turkey is cooked. Stir in the tomatoes, cumin, paprika, oregano, and salt, and season with pepper. 5. Fill each cooked pepper with the meat mixture. Enjoy warm.
Per serving: Calories: 210; Total fat 9.1g; Sodium 282mg; Total carbs 13.8g; Fiber 3g; Sugars 8.5g; Protein 22.8g

Country Captain's Chicken with Curry and Raisins

Prep time: 30 minutes | Cook time: 1 hour 20 minutes | Serves: 4–6

5-lbs. Chicken, cut into 8 pieces
Kosher salt
2 tablespoons olive oil
1 large red onion, thinly sliced
3 celery stalks, sliced
1½ tablespoon curry powder
Black pepper
2 tablespoon tomato paste
1 (28-oz.) Can diced tomatoes
1 cup chicken stock
½ cup raisins
½ cup raw almonds, toasted and chopped
4 cups cooked brown rice
2 tablespoon chopped parsley

1. In a suitable Dutch oven over medium-high heat, warm the olive oil. Sear the chicken for 8 to 10 minutes per batch. 2. Transfer the seared chicken to a platter and remove all but 2 tablespoons of the leftover fat. 3. Turn the heat of the stove to medium and toss in the onion and celery. Sauté them for 5 to 7 minutes. 4. Stir in the curry powder, ½ teaspoon of black pepper, and tomato paste and cook them for 30 seconds, constantly stirring, until fragrant. Add the tomatoes with their juices, chicken stock, and raisins and bring to a simmer. 5. Place the chicken thighs into the pot, cover, and turn the heat to medium-low. Simmer the chicken thighs for 45 minutes or until them are fork-tender. 6. Transfer the chicken thighs to a platter; turn the heat to medium-high, and cook for 7 minutes, stirring occasionally, until the sauce had reduced slightly. 7. Stir the toasted almonds into the brown rice. Spoon on plates and top with the chicken and sauce. Finish with the parsley.
Per serving: Calories 339; Fat 13.1g; Sodium 211mg; Carbs 2.6g; Fiber 0.6g; Sugars 0.8g; Protein 49.

Chicken Souvlaki with Tzatziki Sauce

Prep time: 15 minutes | Cook time: 15 minutes | Serves: 4

For the Tzatziki

1 cup plain whole-milk Greek yogurt	1 garlic clove, minced
½ cucumber, peeled and grated	1 teaspoon fresh lemon zest
1 tablespoon lemon juice	½ teaspoon minced fresh dill
	¼ teaspoon salt

For the Souvlaki

1 pound boneless chicken breasts, diced	2 teaspoons fresh lemon zest
2 small white onions, diced	2 teaspoons dried oregano
2 green bell peppers, diced	2 teaspoons garlic powder
2 tablespoons olive oil	1 teaspoon salt

1. To make the tzatziki: In a suitable bowl, mix up the yogurt, cucumber, lemon juice, garlic, lemon zest, dill, and salt. Set aside. 2. To make the souvlaki: Soak 8 bamboo skewers in water for 10 to 30 minutes before cooking. 3. Preheat a grill to medium-high heat, or place a grill pan over medium-high heat on the stove top. 4. In a suitable bowl, gently toss the chicken, onions, green bell peppers, and olive oil until coated. 5. In a suitable bowl, combine the lemon zest, oregano, garlic powder, and salt. 6. On each skewer, alternate pieces of chicken, onion, and bell pepper. Sprinkle with the lemon-spice mixture. Transfer them to the grill. 7. Cook the food for 10 to 15 minutes or until the chicken is cooked through. Serve with the tzatziki dip.

Per serving: Calories: 351; Total fat 15.8g; Sodium 271mg; Total carbs 15.9g; Fiber 2.3g; Sugars 9.1g; Protein 35.7g

Turkey Scaloppine with Rosemary and Lemon Sauce

Prep time: 15 minutes | Cook time: 15 minutes | Serves: 4

¼ cup whole-wheat flour	¼ cup olive oil
1 teaspoon sea salt	Juice of 3 lemons
¼ teaspoon black pepper	Zest of 1 lemon
4¼ to 4½ pounds skinless, boneless turkey breast cutlets, pounded ¼ inch thick	1 tablespoon chopped fresh rosemary leaves

1. At 400 degrees F, preheat your oven. Layer a baking sheet with parchment paper. 2. In a shallow dish, whisk the flour, ½ teaspoon salt, and the pepper. 3. Working with one piece at a time, dip each cutlet in the flour and pat off any excess. 4. In a suitable skillet over medium-high heat, use 1 tablespoon olive oil for each cutlet in the batch and heat until it shimmers. Add the cutlets to the hot oil and cook for almost 2 minutes per side. 5. Transfer each cutlet to the prepared baking sheet when cooked. When they are all cooked, put the baking sheet in the oven to keep them warm. 6. When all the cutlets are cooked and warming in the oven, return this skillet to the heat. Add the lemon juice and zest to this pan. Use a spoon to scrape any browned bits from the bottom of this pan. 7. Add the rest of the ½ teaspoon of salt and the rosemary. Cook for almost 2 minutes, while stirring constantly, until the sauce thickens. 8. Serve the sauce spooned over the cutlets.

Per serving: Calories 410; Fat 13.8g; Sodium 694mg; Carbs 6.6g; Fiber 0.6g; Sugars 0g; Protein 64.1g

Spicy Spinach-Turkey Burgers

Prep time: 10 minutes | Cook time: 12 minutes | Serves: 4

2 cups fresh spinach, washed	½ teaspoon red pepper flakes
½ small white onion, diced	½ teaspoon salt
1 egg, whisked	¼ teaspoon dried thyme
1 pound ground turkey	¼ teaspoon black pepper
1 teaspoon garlic powder	Dash cayenne pepper
½ teaspoon dried oregano	1 tablespoon avocado oil
½ teaspoon dried basil	

1. In your food processor, combine the spinach, onion, and egg. Pulse for almost 15 seconds until the vegetables are minced. 2. Add the turkey, garlic powder, oregano, basil, red pepper flakes, salt, thyme, black pepper, and cayenne pepper. Pulse them for 20 to 30 seconds until well combined. 3. Form the turkey mixture into 4 patties. 4. In a suitable skillet, add the avocado oil over medium heat, and then cook the patties for almost 6 minutes on each side.

Per serving: Calories: 253; Total fat 14.1g; Sodium 440mg; Total carbs 2.5g; Fiber 0.9g; Sugars 0.7g; Protein 33.2g

Garlic Turkey Breast

Prep time:10 minutes | Cook time: 17 minutes | Serves: 4

1 (1½-pound) turkey breast, boneless and skinless	minced
2 tablespoons avocado oil	1 large garlic clove, minced
Zest from ½ large lemon	½ teaspoon kosher salt
½ medium shallot, peeled and	¼ teaspoon black pepper

1. Dry the turkey breast with a towel. Cut the turkey breast in half to fit in your instant pot. Brush both sides of the turkey breast with 1 tablespoon oil. 2. In a suitable bowl, mix together the lemon zest, shallot, garlic, salt, and pepper. Rub this mixture onto both sides of the turkey breast. 3. Heat the rest of the 1 tablespoon oil in the insert of the Instant pot 2 minutes. Add the turkey breast and sear it on both sides, about 3 minutes per side. 4. Turn off the heat. Remove the turkey from the insert of the Instant pot and place it on a plate. 5. Add 1 cup water to the insert of the Instant pot and use a spatula to scrape up any brown bits that are stuck. 6. Set the steam rack in the pot and the turkey breast on top of it. Close the lid and secure it well. Pressure cook for 10 minutes. 7. Once cooked, release the pressure naturally then remove the lid. Slice and serve.

Per serving: Calories 439; Fat 7.5g; Sodium 4414mg; Carbs 17.8g; Fiber 2.3g; Sugars 14.6g; Protein 71.1g

Strawberry Avocado Salad

Prep time:10 minutes | Cook time: 6 minutes approximately | Serves: 4

1 pound chicken breasts, boneless,	⅛ teaspoon white pepper
½ cup chicken stock	8 cups baby spinach
13 large strawberries, hulled	1 medium avocado, peeled, pitted, and cut into slices
2 tablespoons extra-virgin olive oil	⅓ cup sliced almonds
2 tablespoons fresh lemon juice	½ teaspoon salt
¼ teaspoon ground ginger	¼ teaspoon black pepper

1. Add the chicken breasts and stock to the insert of your Instant Pot. 2. Close the lid and secure it well. Pressure cook for 6 minutes approximately. 3. Meanwhile, make the dressing. In a suitable blender, place five hulled strawberries, oil, lemon juice, ginger, and white pepper and blend until smooth. Set aside. 4. Slice the rest eight strawberries, set aside. Once cooked, release the pressure naturally then remove the lid. 5. Remove the chicken from the instant pot and let it cool down completely. Once it is cool, chop the chicken. 6. In a large serving bowl, set the baby spinach, avocado slices, almonds, and strawberry slices. Add the chopped chicken. 7. Drizzle with the salad dressing, add black pepper and salt, and toss to combine.

Per serving: Calories 460; Fat 29.7g; Sodium 536mg; Carbs 13.1g; Fiber 6.9g; Sugars 4g; Protein 37.7g

Turkey Meatloaf

Prep time:15 minutes | Cook time: 25 minutes | Serves: 4

1 tablespoon avocado oil	1 pound lean ground turkey
1 small onion, peeled and diced	¼ cup almond flour
2 garlic cloves, minced	1 large egg
3 cups mixed baby greens, chopped	¾ teaspoon salt
	½ teaspoon black pepper

1. Add the oil to the inner pot. Heat the oil 1 minute. 2. Add the onion and sauté until softened, 3 minutes. Add the garlic and greens and sauté 1 more minute. Turn off heat. 3. In a suitable bowl, combine the turkey, flour, egg, salt, and pepper. Add the onion and greens mixture to the turkey mixture and stir to combine. 4. Rinse out the insert of the Instant pot and then add 2 cups water. 5. Make an aluminum foil sling by folding a large piece of foil in half and bending the edges upward. 6. Form the turkey mixture into a rectangular loaf and place it on the aluminum foil sling. Set the sling onto the steam rack with handles, and lower it into the inner pot. 7. Close the lid and secure it well. Pressure cook for 20 minutes. 8. When cooked, release the pressure quickly until the float valve drops and then unlock lid. 9. Carefully remove the meatloaf from the insert of the Instant pot and allow it to rest for almost 10 minutes before slicing to serve.

Per serving: Calories 263; Fat 13.2g; Sodium 575mg; Carbs 9.4g; Fiber 3.6g; Sugars 0.9g; Protein 28g

Whole Roasted Chicken

Prep time:5 minutes | Cook time: 28 minutes | Serves: 6

¼ cup water
1 medium lemon
1 (4-pound) whole chicken
1 tablespoon salt
2 teaspoons black pepper

1. Add water to the inner pot. 2. Cut the lemon in half. Squeeze the juice of half the lemon onto the chicken and sprinkle with black pepper and salt. Stuff the other half of the lemon inside the bird. 3. Set the chicken in the pot breast side down. Close the lid and secure it well. Pressure cook for 28 minutes. 4. Once cooked, release the pressure naturally then remove the lid. 5. Carefully remove the chicken from the insert of the Instant pot and allow it to rest 10 minutes before slicing to serve.
Per serving: Calories 576; Fat 22.4g; Sodium 1424mg; Carbs 0.5g; Fiber 0.2g; Sugars 0g; Protein 87.6g

Chicken and Cauliflower Bake

Prep time:5 minutes | Cook time: 5 minutes | Serves: 4

4 cups riced cauliflower
8 ounces white mushrooms, chopped
8 ounces shiitake mushrooms, stems removed and chopped
8 ounces oyster mushrooms, chopped
1½ pounds chicken breasts,
boneless, cut into bite-sized pieces
¼ cup chicken stock
1 tablespoon minced garlic
1 teaspoon salt
1 teaspoon dried thyme
Juice from 1 large lemon

1. Set the cauliflower, mushrooms, and chicken in the insert of your Instant Pot. 2. In a suitable bowl, whisk together the stock, garlic, salt, thyme, and lemon juice. 3. Pour the liquid over the ingredients in the instant pot and stir to combine. 4. Close the lid and secure it well. Pressure cook for 5 minutes. 5. Once cooked, release the pressure naturally then remove the lid. Stir and serve.
Per serving: Calories 386; Fat 3.5g; Sodium 911mg; Carbs 45.5g; Fiber 9g; Sugars 4.1g; Protein 41.7g

Tuscan Chicken

Prep time: 5 minutes | Cook time: 20 minutes | Serves: 4

4 skinless, boneless chicken breast halves, pounded to ½- to ¼-inch thickness
½ teaspoon sea salt
⅛ teaspoon black pepper
1 teaspoon garlic powder
2 tablespoons extra-virgin olive oil
1 zucchini, chopped
2 cups cherry tomatoes
½ cup sliced green olives
¼ cup dry white wine

1. Rub the chicken breasts with the salt, pepper, and garlic powder. 2. In a suitable skillet over medium-high heat, heat the olive oil until it shimmers. Stir in the chicken and cook 7 to 10 minutes per side, until it reaches an internal temperature of 165°F. 3. Remove the cooked chicken and set aside on a platter, tented with foil. 4. In the same skillet, add the zucchini, tomatoes, and olives. Cook for almost 4 minutes, while stirring occasionally, until the zucchini is tender. 5. Add the white wine and use a spoon to scrape any browned bits from the bottom of this pan. Simmer for almost 1 minute. 6. Return the cooked chicken and any juices that have collected on the platter to this pan and stir to coat with the sauce and vegetables.
Per serving: Calories 366; Fat 17.8g; Sodium 381mg; Carbs 6.2g; Fiber 1.7g; Sugars 3.5g; Protein 42g

Chicken Adobo

Prep time: 5 minutes | Cook time: 15 minutes | Serves: 4

3 tablespoons extra-viegin olive oil
1½ pounds skinless, boneless chicken breasts, diced
2 teaspoons ground turmeric
¼ cup low-sodium soy sauce
1 teaspoon garlic powder
1 teaspoon onion powder
½ teaspoon sea salt
¼ teaspoon black pepper

1. In a suitable skillet over medium-high heat, heat the olive oil until it shimmers. 2. Add the chicken and turmeric. Cook for almost 7 to 10 minutes, while stirring occasionally, until the chicken is cooked through. 3. Stir in the soy sauce, garlic powder, onion powder, salt, and pepper. Cook for almost 3 minutes, while stirring.
Per serving: Calories 427; Fat 23.2g; Sodium 1261mg; Carbs 2.8g; Fiber 0.4g; Sugars 1.4g; Protein 50.5g

Jerk Chicken

Prep time:15 minutes | Cook time: 22 minutes | Serves: 8

1 large onion, peeled
1 tablespoon peeled and chopped fresh ginger
3 small hot chili peppers, deveined and deseeded
½ teaspoon ground allspice
2 tablespoons dry mustard
1 teaspoon black pepper
2 tablespoons red wine vinegar
2 tablespoons coconut aminos
2 garlic cloves, minced
½ cup chicken stock
4 pounds skinless chicken breasts, boneless, cut in 1" pieces

1. Cut the onion into 8 pieces. 2. Combine all the recipe ingredients except the chicken in a food processor or blender and process until liquefied. 3. Add the chicken to the insert of the instant pot, top with the sauce, and stir to combine. Close the lid and secure it well. Pressure cook for 12 minutes. 4. When cooked, release the pressure quickly until the float valve drops and then unlock lid. 5. Remove the chicken from instant pot and spread on a baking sheet lined with parchment paper or a silicone baking mat. Drizzle sauce over the chicken. 6. Serve as is, or for a golden-browned finish, set broiler to high and broil 6–10 minutes, turning once until chicken is nicely browned.
Per serving: Calories 455; Fat 17.7g; Sodium 244mg; Carbs 3.3g; Fiber 0.9g; Sugars 1.1g; Protein 66.7g

Chopped Kale Salad with Chicken

Prep time:20 minutes | Cook time: 6 minutes approximately | Serves: 4

1 pound skinless, boneless chicken breast
½ cup chicken stock
2 bunches kale (about 12 ounces total), deveined and diced
1 medium red bell pepper, seeded and diced
1 cup diced carrot
3 cups chopped cabbage
¼ cup pure sesame oil
¼ cup almond butter
¼ cup raw honey
Juice from 2 medium limes
1 tablespoon reduced-sodium tamari
¼ teaspoon minced garlic
⅓ cup sesame seeds

1. Add the chicken and stock to the insert of your Instant Pot. Close the lid and secure it well. Pressure cook for 6 minutes approximately. 2. Once cooked, release the pressure naturally then remove the lid. 3. Remove the chicken from the instant pot and let it cool down completely. Once it is cool, chop the chicken. 4. In a suitable bowl, mix together the kale, bell peppers, carrots, cabbage, and chopped chicken. 5. In a suitable blender, blend together the oil, lime juice, tamari, almond butter, honey, and garlic until smooth. 6. Pour the dressing onto the kale salad and toss to coat. Stir in the sesame seeds and lightly toss. Serve.
Per serving: Calories 441; Fat 23.2g; Sodium 199mg; Carbs 32.1g; Fiber 4.5g; Sugars 22.1g; Protein 28.7g

Italian Seasoned Turkey Breast

Prep time:10 minutes | Cook time: 18 minutes | Serves: 4

1½ pounds boneless, turkey breast
2 tablespoons avocado oil
1 teaspoon sweet paprika
1 teaspoon Italian seasoning blend
½ teaspoon kosher salt
½ teaspoon thyme
¼ teaspoon garlic salt
¼ teaspoon black pepper

1. Dry the turkey breast with a towel. Cut the turkey breast in half to fit in your instant pot. Brush both sides of the turkey breast with 1 tablespoon oil. 2. In a suitable bowl, mix together the paprika, Italian seasoning, kosher salt, thyme, garlic salt, and pepper. Rub this mixture onto both sides of the turkey breast. 3. Press the sauté button and heat the rest of the 1 tablespoon oil in the insert of the Instant pot 2 minutes. 4. Add the turkey breast and sear it on both sides, about 3 minutes per side. Turn off the heat. 5. Remove the turkey from the insert of the Instant pot and place it on a plate. Add 1 cup water to the insert of the Instant pot and use a spatula to scrape up any brown bits that are stuck. 6. Set the steam rack in the pot and the turkey breast on top of it. Close the lid and secure it well. Pressure cook for 10 minutes. 7. Once cooked, release the pressure naturally then remove the lid. Slice and serve.
Per serving: Calories 189; Fat 3.8g; Sodium 2018mg; Carbs 8.1g; Fiber 1.5g; Sugars 6.1g; Protein 29.3g

Spiced Chicken Vegetables

Prep time: 15 minutes | Cook time: 15 minutes | Serves: 4

1 teaspoon dried thyme
¼ teaspoon ground ginger
¼ teaspoon ground allspice
1 teaspoon kosher salt
½ teaspoon black pepper
2 large bone-in chicken breasts

(about 2 pounds)
½ cup chicken stock
2 medium onions, peeled and cut in fourths
4 medium carrots

1. In a suitable bowl, mix together the thyme, ginger, allspice, salt, and pepper. 2. Use half of the spice mixture to season the chicken breasts. 3. Pour the chicken stock into the insert of the Instant pot and then add the chicken breasts. Set the onions and carrots on top of the chicken and sprinkle them with the rest of the seasoning blend. 4. Close the lid and secure it well. Pressure cook for 15 minutes. 5. Once cooked, release the pressure naturally then remove the lid. 6. Remove the chicken and the vegetables and serve alone or with rice or lentils.
Per serving: Calories 156; Fat 2.3g; Sodium 766mg; Carbs 11.7g; Fiber 2.9g; Sugars 5.4g; Protein 21.6g

Chicken, Mushrooms, and Quinoa

Prep time: 15 minutes | Cook time: 5 minutes | Serves: 6

1 tablespoon avocado oil
1 small yellow onion, diced
6 garlic cloves, minced
1½ pounds boneless, chicken thighs, cut into bite-sized pieces

2 (8-ounce) packages sliced white mushrooms
3 cups chicken stock
1½ cups quinoa, rinsed well
1 cup nondairy Greek-style yogurt

1. Add the oil to the inner pot. Heat the oil for 1 minute. Add the onion and sauté 5 minutes. Add the garlic and sauté an additional 30 seconds. Turn off the heat. 2. Add the chicken, mushrooms, stock, quinoa, and yogurt and stir to combine. 3. Close the lid and secure it well. Pressure cook for 3 minutes. 4. When cooked, release the pressure quickly until the float valve drops and then unlock lid. 5. Spoon onto plates or into bowls to serve.
Per serving: Calories 434; Fat 12.3g; Sodium 516mg; Carbs 35.2g; Fiber 4.2g; Sugars 5.1g; Protein 44.2g

Turkey Sweet Potato Hash

Prep time: 10 minutes | Cook time: 17 minutes | Serves: 4

1½ tablespoons avocado oil
1 medium yellow onion, peeled and diced
2 garlic cloves, minced
1 medium sweet potato, cut into

cubes (peeling not necessary)
½ pound lean ground turkey
½ teaspoon salt
1 teaspoon Italian seasoning blend

1. Heat the oil. Allow the oil to heat 1 minute and then add the onion and cook until softened, about 5 minutes. Add the garlic and cook an additional 30 seconds. 2. Add the sweet potato, turkey, salt, and Italian seasoning and cook another 5 minutes. Turn off the heat. 3. Close the lid and secure it well. Pressure cook for 5 minutes. 4. When cooked, release the pressure quickly until the float valve drops and then unlock lid. 5. Spoon onto plates and serve.
Per serving: Calories 146; Fat 6.6g; Sodium 346mg; Carbs 10.1g; Fiber 2.4g; Sugars 3.1g; Protein 12.4g

Easy Chicken and Broccoli

Prep time: 10 minutes | Cook time: 7 minutes | Serves: 4

3 tablespoons extra-virgin olive oil
1½ pounds skinless chicken breasts, boneless, diced
1½ cups broccoli florets, or chopped broccoli stems

½ onion, chopped
½ teaspoon sea salt
⅛ teaspoon black pepper, freshly ground
3 garlic cloves, minced
2 cups cooked brown rice

1. Cut the chicken breasts into bite-size pieces. 2. In a suitable skillet over medium-high heat, heat the olive oil until it shimmers. 3. Add the chicken, broccoli, onion, salt, and pepper. Cook for almost 7 minutes, while stirring occasionally, until the chicken is cooked. 4. Add the garlic. Cook for almost 30 seconds, while stirring constantly. 5. Toss with the brown rice to serve.
Per serving: Calories 389; Fat 12.9g; Sodium 198mg; Carbs 38.3g; Fiber 2.2g; Sugars 0.6g; Protein 28.8g

Chicken Salad Sandwiches

Prep time: 5 minutes | Cook time: 0 minutes | Serves: 4

2 cups chopped, cooked, chicken from a rotisserie chicken, skinless
¼ cup anti-inflammatory mayonnaise
1 red bell pepper, minced

2 tablespoons chopped fresh tarragon leaves
2 teaspoons Dijon mustard
½ teaspoon sea salt
8 slices whole-wheat bread

1. In a suitable bowl, stir together the chicken, mayonnaise, red bell pepper, tarragon, mustard, and salt. 2. Spread on top of 4 slices of bread and top with the rest of the bread.
Per serving: Calories 258; Fat 4.3g; Sodium 572mg; Carbs 26g; Fiber 4.4g; Sugars 4.6g; Protein 28.2g

Chicken Breast with Cherry Sauce

Prep time: 10 minutes | Cook time: 30 minutes | Serves: 4

1 tablespoon coconut oil
4 boneless skinless chicken breasts
Salt
Black pepper

2 scallions, sliced
¾ cup chicken broth
1 tablespoon balsamic vinegar
½ cup dried cherries

1. At 375 degrees F, preheat your oven. 2. In a suitable ovenproof skillet over medium-high heat, melt the coconut oil. 3. Season the chicken with salt and pepper. Place the chicken in the pan and brown it on both sides, about 3 minutes per side. 4. Add the scallions, chicken broth, balsamic vinegar, and dried cherries. Cover with an ovenproof lid or aluminum foil and place the pan in the preheated oven. 5. Bake the food for almost 20 minutes, or until the chicken is cooked through.
Per serving: Calories: 379; Total fat: 14g; Sodium: 308mg; Total Carbs: 17g; Sugars: 9g; Fiber: 5g; Protein: 43g

Taco Lettuce Boats

Prep time: 10 minutes | Cook time: 24 minutes | Serves: 4

1 tablespoon avocado oil
1 medium onion, peeled and diced
2 large carrots, peeled and diced
2 medium stalks celery, ends removed and diced
2 garlic cloves, minced
1 pound lean ground turkey
1 teaspoon chili powder

1 teaspoon paprika
1 teaspoon cumin
½ teaspoon salt
¼ teaspoon black pepper
1 cup chipotle salsa
12 large romaine leaves
1 medium avocado, peeled, pitted, and sliced

1. Heat the oil. Allow the oil to heat 1 minute and then add the onion, carrots, celery, and garlic. Cook until softened, about 5 minutes. 2. Add the turkey and cook until browned, about 3 minutes. 3. Add the chili powder, paprika, cumin, salt, pepper, and salsa and stir to combine. Turn off heat. 4. Close the lid and secure it well. Pressure cook for 15 minutes. 5. When cooked, release the pressure quickly until the float valve drops and then unlock lid. 6. To serve, spoon a portion of the taco meat into a romaine lettuce leaf and then top with sliced avocado.
Per serving: Calories 241; Fat 9g; Sodium 430mg; Carbs 17.4g; Fiber 4.1g; Sugars 6.4g; Protein 24.7g

Turkey Burgers

Prep time: 15 minutes | Cook time: 10 minutes | Serves: 4

1 pound ground turkey patties
½ teaspoon sea salt
⅛ teaspoon black pepper
2 tablespoons extra-virgin olive

oil
1 cup ginger-teriyaki sauce
4 pineapple rings

1. Form the ground turkey breast into 4 patties. 2. Season the turkey burgers with black pepper and salt. 3. In a suitable skillet over medium-high heat, heat the olive oil until it shimmers. 4. Add the burgers and cook for almost 7 minutes, turning once, until cooked through and browned on both sides. 5. While the burgers cook, in a small saucepan over medium-high heat, bring the teriyaki sauce to a simmer, while stirring constantly. Cook for almost 1 to 2 minutes until the sauce thickens. 6. Spoon the warmed sauce over the cooked burgers and top with the pineapple rings.
Per serving: Calories 549; Fat 30.8g; Sodium 611mg; Carbs 0g; Fiber 0g; Sugars 0g; Protein 65.1g

Chicken Sandwiches with Roasted Red Pepper Aioli

Prep time: 15 minutes | Cook time: 10 minutes | Serves: 4

tablespoons extra-virgin olive oil	⅛ teaspoon black pepper, freshly ground
pound skinless chicken breasts, boneless, cut into 4 equal pieces and pounded ½ inch thick	6 roasted red pepper slices ¼ cup anti-inflammatory mayonnaise
½ teaspoon sea salt	4 whole-wheat buns

1. In a suitable skillet over medium-high heat, heat the olive oil until it shimmers. 2. Season the chicken with black pepper and salt. Add it to this skillet and cook for almost 4 minutes per side until the juices run clear. 3. While the chicken cooks, in a suitable blender or food processor, combine the mayonnaise and 2 red pepper pieces. Blend until smooth. 4. Spread the sauce on the buns and top with the rest of the roasted red pepper slices. Top with the chicken.
Per serving: Calories 275; Fat 15.4g; Sodium 332mg; Carbs 0g; Fiber 0g; Sugars 0g; Protein 32.8g

Avocado Chicken Salad

Prep time:10 minutes | Cook time: 6 minutes approximately | Serves: 4

pound skinless chicken breasts, boneless	1 tablespoon lemon juice
cup chicken stock	1 tablespoon chopped fresh parsley
½ medium avocados, peeled, pitted, and mashed	½ teaspoon dried dill weed
medium stalk celery, ends removed and diced	2 teaspoons Dijon mustard ½ teaspoon kosher salt
scallion, sliced	¼ teaspoon black pepper

1. Add the chicken breasts and stock to the insert of your Instant Pot. 2. Close the lid and secure it. Pressure cook for 6 minutes approximately. 3. Once cooked, release the pressure naturally then remove the lid. 4. Remove the chicken from the instant pot and let it cool down completely. Once it is cool, chop the chicken. 5. Set the chopped chicken in a suitable bowl and add the rest of the ingredients. Stir to combine.
Per serving: Calories 336; Fat 19.6g; Sodium 518mg; Carbs 5.6g; Fiber 4.1g; Sugars 0.6g; Protein 34.3g

Gingered Turkey Meatballs

Prep time: 10 minutes | Cook time: 10 minutes | Serves: 4

½ pounds ground turkey	1 teaspoon garlic powder
cup shredded cabbage	1 teaspoon onion powder
¼ cup chopped fresh cilantro leaves	½ teaspoon sea salt ⅛ teaspoon black pepper
tablespoon grated fresh ginger	2 tablespoons olive oil

1. In a suitable bowl, combine the turkey, cabbage, cilantro, ginger, garlic powder, onion powder, salt, and pepper. Mix well. 2. Form the turkey mixture into about 20 (¾-inch) meatballs. 3. In a suitable skillet over medium-high heat, heat the olive oil until it shimmers. 4. Add the meatballs and cook for almost 10 minutes, turning as they brown.
Per serving: Calories 270; Fat 17.2g; Sodium 280mg; Carbs 2g; Fiber 0.5g; Sugars 0.7g; Protein 31.4g

Turkey Kale Fry

Prep time: 10 minutes | Cook time: 10 minutes | Serves: 4

tablespoons extra-virgin olive oil	2 tablespoons fresh thyme leaves
½ pounds ground turkey breast	½ teaspoon sea salt ⅛ teaspoon black pepper
cups stemmed and chopped kale	5 garlic cloves, minced
½ onion, chopped	

1. In a suitable skillet over medium-high heat, heat the olive oil until it shimmers. 2. Add the turkey, kale, onion, thyme, salt, and pepper. Cook for almost 5 minutes, crumbling the turkey with a spoon until it browns. 3. Add the garlic. Cook for almost 30 seconds, while stirring constantly.
Per serving: Calories 396; Fat 19.7g; Sodium 343mg; Carbs 3.4g; Fiber 0.9g; Sugars 0.6g; Protein 49.4g

Lime Chicken and Rice

Prep time:5 minutes | Cook time: 5 minutes | Serves: 4

1 cup jasmine rice	1 teaspoon salt
1 (13.66-ounce) can full-fat coconut milk, unsweetened	½ teaspoon ground cumin ¼ teaspoon ground ginger
½ cup chicken stock	Juice from 1 medium lime
1¼ pounds chicken breasts, boneless, cut into 1" cubes	½ cup chopped cilantro leaves and stems

1. Set the rice, coconut milk, stock, chicken, salt, cumin, and ginger in the insert of the Instant pot and stir to combine. 2. Close the lid and secure it well. Pressure cook for 5 minutes. Once cooked, release the pressure naturally then remove the lid. 3. Stir in the lime juice and spoon into four bowls. Top each bowl with an equal amount of cilantro and serve.
Per serving: Calories 532; Fat 21.5g; Sodium 701mg; Carbs 31.3g; Fiber 1.6g; Sugars 0.1g; Protein 49.6g

Turkey with Bell Peppers and Rosemary

Prep time: 15 minutes | Cook time: 10 minutes | Serves: 4

3 tablespoons extra-virgin olive oil	2 tablespoons chopped fresh rosemary leaves
2 red bell peppers, chopped	
1 onion, chopped	½ teaspoon sea salt
1½ pounds skinless, boneless turkey breasts, diced	⅛ teaspoon black pepper 3 garlic cloves, minced

1. In a suitable skillet over medium-high heat, heat the olive oil until it shimmers. 2. Add the red bell peppers, onion, turkey, rosemary, salt, and pepper. 3. Cook for 7 to 10 minutes, while stirring occasionally, until the turkey is cooked and the vegetables are tender. 4. Add the garlic. Cook for almost 30 seconds more, while stirring constantly.
Per serving: Calories 389; Fat 10.7g; Sodium 3284mg; Carbs 17.6g; Fiber 2.6g; Sugars 13g; Protein 53.8g

Chicken Breasts with Mushrooms

Prep time:10 minutes | Cook time: 18 minutes | Serves: 4

2 tablespoons avocado oil	8 cups chopped green cabbage
1 pound sliced baby bella mushrooms	1½ teaspoons dried thyme ½ cup chicken stock
1½ teaspoons salt	1½ pounds chicken breasts, boneless, skinless
2 garlic cloves, minced	

1. Heat the oil to the insert of the Instant pot and allow it to heat 1 minute. Add the mushrooms and ¼ teaspoon salt and sauté until they have cooked down and released their liquid, about 10 minutes. 2. Add the garlic and sauté another 30 seconds. Turn off heat. Add the cabbage, ¼ teaspoon salt, thyme, and stock to the insert of the Instant pot and stir to combine. 3. Dry the chicken breasts and sprinkle both sides with the rest of the salt. Place on top of the cabbage mixture. 4. Close the lid and secure it well. Pressure cook for 6 minutes approximately. 5. Once cooked, release the pressure naturally then remove the lid. Transfer to plates and spoon the juices on top.
Per serving: Calories 404; Fat 14g; Sodium 3473mg; Carbs 15.7g; Fiber 6.1g; Sugars 6.7g; Protein 54.3g

Chicken Tenders with Mustard Sauce

Prep time:5 minutes | Cook time: 7 minutes | Serves: 4

1 pound chicken tenders	1 tablespoon avocado oil
1 tablespoon fresh thyme leaves	1 cup chicken stock
½ teaspoon salt	¼ cup Dijon mustard
¼ teaspoon black pepper	¼ cup raw honey

1. Dry the chicken tenders with a towel and then season them with the thyme, salt, and pepper. 2. Press the sauté button and then use the adjust button to change to the more setting. 3. Add the oil to the insert of the Instant pot and let it heat 2 minutes. Add the chicken tenders and seer them until brown on both sides, about 1 minute per side. 4. Turn off heat. Remove the chicken tenders and set aside. Add the stock to the pot. 5. Use a spoon to scrape up any small bits from the bottom of the pot. Set the steam rack in the insert of the Instant pot and set the chicken tenders directly on the rack. 6. Close the lid and secure it well. Pressure cook for 3 minutes. 7. In a suitable bowl, combine the Dijon mustard and honey and stir to combine. 8. Once done, release the pressure naturally then remove the lid. Serve the chicken tenders with the honey mustard sauce.
Per serving: Calories 300; Fat 9.7g; Sodium 758mg; Carbs 19.2g; Fiber 1g; Sugars 17.7g; Protein 33.8g

Chapter 6 Meat Recipes

Lamb and Lentil Curry

Prep time: 10 minutes | Cook time: 20 minutes | Servings: 4

Marinade

½ cup coconut milk
1 (1-inch) piece fresh ginger, peeled and grated
4 garlic cloves, minced

¼ teaspoon sea salt
¼ teaspoon freshly ground black pepper

For the Curry

1½ pounds cubed lamb stew meat
1 yellow onion, chopped
3 carrots, chopped
1 head cauliflower, chopped into florets
1 (14.5-ounce) can diced tomatoes

½ cup dried lentils
½ cup water
1 tablespoon ghee
1½ tablespoons curry powder
Chopped fresh cilantro, for garnish

To make the marinade: 1. Mix the coconut milk, ginger, garlic, salt, pepper and the lamb in a suitable resealable plastic bag, and then seal the bag, turning to coat the lamb in the marinade. 2. Place the bag in the refrigerator to let the lamb to marinate for at least 30 minutes, or ideally overnight.
To make the curry: 1. Mix the marinated lamb and marinade, onion, carrots, cauliflower, tomatoes and their juices, lentils, water, ghee and curry powder in the Instant Pot. Lock the lid. 2. Select the pressure cook mode and cook the food at high pressure for 20 minutes. 3. When cooking is complete, use a natural release for 15 minutes, then quick release any remaining pressure. 4. Remove the cooker's lid and serve, garnished with cilantro.
Per Serving: Calories 427; Total Fat 22.34g; Sodium 444mg; Total Carbs 19.49g; Fiber 7.2g; Sugars 8.27g; Protein 39.28g

Beef Tenderloin with Savory Blueberry Sauce

Prep time: 10 minutes | Cook time: 15 minutes | Servings: 4

4 beef tenderloin filets, about ¾ inch thick
1 teaspoon sea salt
¼ teaspoon black pepper
2 tablespoons olive oil

1 shallot, minced
½ cup tawny port
2 cups fresh blueberries
3 tablespoons grass-fed butter, cut into pieces

1. Season the beef with ½ teaspoon of the salt and ⅛ teaspoon of the pepper. 2. In a suitable skillet over medium-high heat, heat the olive oil until it shimmers. 3. Add the seasoned steaks. Cook for almost 5 minutes per side until the beef registers an internal temperature of 130 degrees F. 4. Set aside on a platter, tented with aluminum foil. 5. Return this skillet to the heat. Add the shallot, port, blueberries, and the rest of the ½ teaspoon of salt, and the rest of the ⅛ teaspoon of pepper. 6. Use a spoon to scrape any browned bits from the bottom of this pan. Bring to a simmer and reduce its heat to medium-low. Simmer for almost 4 minutes, while stirring and smashing the blueberries slightly, until the liquid reduces by half. 7. One piece at a time, whisk in the butter. Return the meat to this skillet. Turn it once to coat with the sauce. 8. Serve with the rest of the sauce spooned over the meat.
Per serving: Calories 361; Fat 23.7g; Sodium 580mg; Carbs 10.9g; Fiber 1.8g; Sugars 7.2g; Protein 25.3g

Pork Chops with Kale

Prep time: 10 minutes | Cook time: 15 minutes | Servings: 4

4 thin-cut pork chops
1 teaspoon sea salt
¼ teaspoon black pepper
4 tablespoons Dijon mustard

3 tablespoons olive oil
½ red onion, chopped
4 cups stemmed and chopped kale
2 tablespoons apple cider vinegar

1. At 425 degrees F, preheat your oven. 2. Season the pork chops with ½ teaspoon of the salt and ⅛ teaspoon of the pepper. Spread 2 tablespoons of the mustard over them and put them on a rimmed baking sheet. 3. Bake for almost 15 minutes until the pork registers an internal temperature of 165 degrees F on an instant-read meat thermometer. 4. While the pork cooks, in a suitable skillet over medium-high, heat the olive oil until it shimmers. 5. Add the red onion and kale. Cook for almost 7 minutes, while stirring occasionally, until the vegetables soften. 6. In a suitable bowl, whisk the rest of the 2 tablespoons of mustard, the cider vinegar, the rest of the ½ teaspoon of salt, and the rest of the ⅛ teaspoon of pepper. 7. Add this to the kale. Cook for almost 2 minutes, while stirring.
Per serving: Calories 235; Fat 16.6g; Sodium 889mg; Carbs 9.7g; Fiber 1.8g; Sugars 0.9g; Protein 13.5g

Pulled Pork Tacos

Prep time: 15 minutes | Cook time: 7-8 hours | Servings: 4

1 teaspoon sea salt
1 teaspoon ground cumin
1 teaspoon garlic powder
½ teaspoon dried oregano
½ teaspoon black pepper
3 to 4 pounds pork shoulder or

butt
2 cups broth
Juice of 1 orange
1 small onion, chopped
4 to 6 corn taco shells

1. Shredded cabbage, lime wedges, avocado, and hot sauce, for topping. 2. In a suitable bowl, stir together the salt, cumin, garlic powder, oregano, and pepper. Rub the pork with the spice mixture, and put it in your slow cooker. 3. Pour the broth and orange juice around the pork. Scatter the onion around the pork. Cover the cooker and set on low. Cook for 7 to 8 hours. 4. Transfer the pork to a work surface, and shred it with a fork. 5. Serve in taco shells with any optional toppings you like.
Per serving: Calories 509; Fat 36.8g; Sodium 541mg; Carbs 0.7g; Fiber 0.1g; Sugars 0.3g; Protein 40.9g

Mustard Pork Tenderloin

Prep time: 10 minutes | Cook time: 15 minutes | Servings: 4

½ cup fresh parsley leaves
¼ cup Dijon mustard
6 garlic cloves
3 tablespoons fresh rosemary leaves

3 tablespoons olive oil
½ teaspoon sea salt
¼ teaspoon black pepper
1 (1½-pound) pork tenderloin

1. At 400 degrees F, preheat your oven. 2. In a suitable blender, combine the parsley, mustard, garlic, rosemary, olive oil, salt, and pepper. 3. Pulse in 1-second pulses, about 20 times, until a paste forms. Rub this paste all over the tenderloin and put the pork on a rimmed baking sheet. 4. Bake the pork for almost 15 minutes until it registers 165 degrees F on an instant-read meat thermometer. 5. Let rest for almost 5 minutes, slice, and serve.
Per serving: Calories 362; Fat 17.6g; Sodium 515mg; Carbs 4.5g; Fiber 2g; Sugars 0.2g; Protein 45.8g

Pork Chops with Applesauce

Prep time: 10 minutes | Cook time: 15 minutes | Servings: 4

4 thin-cut pork chops
½ teaspoon sea salt
⅛ teaspoon black pepper
6 apples, peeled, cored, and

chopped
¼ cup packed brown sugar
¼ cup water
1 tablespoon grated fresh ginger

1. At 425 degrees F, preheat your oven. 2. Season the pork chops with the black pepper and salt, put them on a rimmed baking sheet. 3. Bake them for almost 15 minutes until the pork registers an internal temperature of 165 degrees F on an instant-read meat thermometer. 4. While baking the pork chops, in a suitable pot over medium-high heat, stir together the apples, brown sugar, water, and ginger. 5. Cover and cook for almost 10 minutes, while stirring occasionally, until the apples have cooked into a sauce. 6. Serve the pork chops with the sauce.
Per serving: Calories 338; Fat 3.6g; Sodium 470mg; Carbs 56.1g; Fiber 8.1g; Sugars 44.6g; Protein 22.9g

Ground Beef Chili with Tomatoes

Prep time: 10 minutes | Cook time: 15 minutes | Servings: 4

1 pound extra-lean ground beef
1 onion, chopped
2 (28-ounce) cans chopped tomatoes, undrained
2 (14-ounce) cans kidney beans,

drained
1 tablespoon chili powder
1 teaspoon garlic powder
½ teaspoon sea salt

1. In a suitable pot, cook the beef and onion for almost 5 minutes over medium-high heat, crumbling the beef with a spoon until it browns. 2. Stir in the tomatoes, kidney beans, chili powder, garlic powder, and salt. 3. Bring to a simmer. Cook for almost 10 minutes, while stirring.
Per serving: Calories 564; Fat 10.1g; Sodium 366mg; Carbs 64g; Fiber 16.4g; Sugars 5.8g; Protein 55.3g

Beef Steak Tacos

Prep time: 10 minutes | Cook time: 14 minutes | Servings: 4

¼ cup fresh cilantro leaves	1½ pounds beef flank steak
6 tablespoons olive oil	½ teaspoon sea salt
4 garlic cloves, minced	⅛ teaspoon black pepper
1 jalapeño pepper, chopped	Jalapeno guacamole sauce

1. In a suitable blender or food processor, combine the cilantro, 4 tablespoons of the olive oil, the garlic, and jalapeño. 2. Pulse 10 to 20 (1-second) pulses to make a paste. Set aside 1 tablespoon of the paste and spread the remainder over the flank steak. 3. Let it rest for almost 5 minutes. 4. In a suitable skillet, heat the rest olive oil over medium-high heat until it shimmers. 5. Add the steak and cook the steak for almost 7 minutes on each side until it registers an internal temperature of 125 degrees F. 6. Transfer the cooked steak to a cutting board and let rest for almost 5 minutes. Slice it against the grain into ½-inch-thick slices. 7. Set the slices in a suitable bowl and toss with the reserved 1 tablespoon of herb paste. Serve with the guacamole sauce.
Per serving: Calories 502; Fat 31.7g; Sodium 347mg; Carbs 1.2g; Fiber 0.2g; Sugars 0.2g; Protein 51.9g

Fried Beef and Broccoli

Prep time: 10 minutes | Cook time: 10 minutes | Servings: 4

2 tablespoons olive oil	1 cup sugar snap peas
1 pound flank steak, sliced	1 zucchini, chopped
1 cup broccoli florets	¼ cup stir-fry sauce

1. In a suitable skillet, heat the olive oil over medium-high heat until it shimmers. 2. Add the beef and cook for almost 5 to 7 minutes, while stirring occasionally, until it browns. Remove with a slotted spoon and keep it aside on a platter. 3. Add the broccoli, sugar snap peas, and zucchini. Cook for almost 5 minutes, while stirring occasionally, until the vegetables are crisp-tender. 4. Return the beef to this pan. Add the stir-fry sauce. Cook for almost 3 minutes, while stirring, until heated through.
Per serving: Calories 318; Fat 17.3g; Sodium 310mg; Carbs 6.7g; Fiber 1.5g; Sugars 2.8g; Protein 33.5g

Fried Beef and Bell Pepper

Prep time: 5 minutes | Cook time: 10 minutes | Servings: 4

1 pound extra-lean ground beef	2 tablespoons grated fresh ginger
6 scallions, white and green parts, chopped	½ teaspoon sea salt
2 red bell peppers, chopped	3 garlic cloves, minced

1. In a suitable skillet over medium-high heat, cook the beef for almost 5 minutes, crumbling it with a spoon until it browns. 2. Add the scallions, red bell peppers, ginger, and salt. Cook for almost 4 minutes, while stirring, until the bell peppers are soft. 3. Add the garlic and cook for almost 30 seconds, while stirring constantly.
Per serving: Calories 203; Fat 6.8g; Sodium 313mg; Carbs 8.8g; Fiber 1.8g; Sugars 3.6g; Protein 26.2g

Macadamia-Dusted Pork Cutlets

Prep time: 10 minutes | Cook time: 10 minutes | Servings: 4

1 (1-pound) pork tenderloin, cut into ½-inch slices and pounded	½ cup macadamia nuts, crushed
1 teaspoon sea salt	1 cup full-fat coconut milk
¼ teaspoon black pepper	2 tablespoons olive oil

1. At 400 degrees F, preheat your oven. 2. Season the pork chops with ½ teaspoon of the salt and ⅛ teaspoon of the pepper. 3. In a shallow dish, mix up the macadamia nut powder, the rest of the ½ teaspoon of salt and the rest of the ⅛ teaspoon of pepper. 4. In another shallow dish, whisk the coconut milk and olive oil to combine. 5. Dip the pork into the coconut milk and into the macadamia nut powder. Put it on a rimmed baking sheet. Repeat with the rest of the pork slices. 6. Bake the pork for almost 10 minutes until it registers an internal temperature of 165 degrees F measured on an instant-read meat thermometer.
Per serving: Calories 364; Fat 23.8g; Sodium 534mg; Carbs 6.2g; Fiber 5g; Sugars 0.8g; Protein 32.2g

Beef Broth

Prep time: 15 minutes | Cook time: 18-24 hours | Servings: 4

2 pounds beef marrow bones	1 tablespoon apple cider vinegar
2 cups chopped onions, celery, carrots, garlic	Filtered water, to cover the ingredients
2 bay leaves	

1. In your slow cooker, combine the bones, onion, celery, carrots, garlic, bay leaves, and vinegar. Add enough water to cover the ingredients. 2. Cover the cooker and set to low. Cook for 18 to 24 hours. 3. Skim off and discard any foam from the surface. Pass the broth through a fine-mesh sieve or cheesecloth into a suitable bowl. Transfer to airtight containers to store. 4. The broth can be kept in refrigerator for almost 3 to 4 days. Freeze any excess for up to 3 months.
Per serving: Calories 96; Fat 3.6g; Sodium 53mg; Carbs 5.8g; Fiber 1.6g; Sugars 2.6g; Protein 10.4g

Hamburgers

Prep time: 10 minutes | Cook time: 10 minutes | Servings: 4

1 pound extra-lean ground beef patties	3 tablespoons low-; Sodium soy sauce
½ teaspoon sea salt	2 tablespoons brown sugar
⅛ teaspoon black pepper	2 tablespoons chopped fresh chives
½ cup garlic aioli	

1. Season the patties with the black pepper and salt. 2. In a suitable skillet over medium-high heat, cook the patties for almost 5 minutes per side until they register an internal temperature of 145 degrees F on an instant-read meat thermometer. 3. While the hamburgers cook, in a suitable bowl, whisk the aioli, soy sauce, brown sugar, and chives. 4. Serve the aioli on top of the hamburgers or anything else that tickles your taste buds.
Per serving: Calories 319; Fat 11.7g; Sodium 1026mg; Carbs 5.2g; Fiber 0g; Sugars 5.2g; Protein 45.7g

Garlicky Lamb Stew

Prep time: 15 minutes | Cook time: 15 minutes | Servings: 4

1 pound ground lamb	¼ teaspoon black pepper
1 tablespoon olive oil	1 (28-ounce) can chopped tomatoes, drained
1 onion, chopped	5 garlic cloves, minced
1 teaspoon dried oregano	
½ teaspoon sea salt	

1. In a suitable skillet over medium-high heat, cook the lamb for almost 5 minutes, crumbling with a spoon until it browns. Drain the fat and remove the lamb to a dish. 2. Return this skillet to the heat, add the olive oil, and heat it until it shimmers. 3. Add the onion, oregano, salt, and pepper. Cook for almost 5 minutes, while stirring, until the onions are soft. 4. Return the lamb to this skillet and stir in the tomatoes. Cook for almost 3 minutes, while stirring occasionally until heated through. 5. Add the garlic. Cook for almost 30 seconds, while stirring constantly.
Per serving: Calories 295; Fat 12.3g; Sodium 332mg; Carbs 11.9g; Fiber 3.2g; Sugars 6.5g; Protein 34.2g

Lamb Meatballs with Garlic Aioli

Prep time: 15 minutes | Cook time: 15 minutes | Servings: 4

1½ pounds ground lamb	1 teaspoon garlic powder
2 tablespoons dried rosemary leaves	½ teaspoon sea salt
1 tablespoon dried oregano	¼ teaspoon black pepper
1 teaspoon onion powder	½ cup garlic aioli

1. At 400 degrees F, preheat your oven. 2. In a suitable bowl, mix the lamb, rosemary, oregano, onion powder, garlic powder, salt, and pepper. 3. Roll the prepared mixture into about 20 (¾-inch) balls and put them on a rimmed baking sheet. 4. Bake the food for almost 15 minutes until the internal temperature registers 145 degrees F on an instant-read meat thermometer.
Serve with the aioli.
Per serving: Calories 525; Fat 23.2g; Sodium 698mg; Carbs 6g; Fiber 2.7g; Sugars 0.9g; Protein 69.7g

Beef Tenderloin

Prep time: 15 minutes | Cook time: 6-7 hours | Servings: 4

1 pound beef tenderloin, cut into 1-inch chunks	1 (14-ounce) can diced tomatoes
1 red bell pepper, seeded and chopped	1 cup beef bone broth or store-bought broth
1 yellow bell pepper, seeded and chopped	¼ cup coconut aminos
1 green bell pepper, seeded and chopped	1½ teaspoons garlic powder
1 medium onion, chopped	1 teaspoon coconut sugar
	½ teaspoon ground ginger
	Dash hot sauce
	Black pepper

1. In your slow cooker, mix and season the beef tenderloin chunks with other ingredients. 2. Cover the cooker and set the cooking temperature to low. Cook for almost 6 to 7 hours and then you can serve.
Per serving: Calories 190; Fat 7.1g; Sodium 50mg; Carbs 7.8g; Fiber 1.7g; Sugars 4.2g; Protein 23.3g

Bolognese Sauce

Prep time: 15 minutes | Cook time: 7-8 hours | Servings: 4

1 tablespoon olive oil	1 tablespoon white wine vinegar
3 garlic cloves, minced	⅛ teaspoon ground nutmeg
½ cup chopped onion	2 bay leaves
⅔ cup chopped celery	½ teaspoon red pepper flakes
⅔ cup chopped carrot	Dash sea salt
1 pound ground beef	Dash black pepper
1 (14-ounce) can diced tomatoes	

1. Layer the bottom of your slow cooker with the olive oil. 2. Add the garlic, onion, celery, carrot, ground beef, tomatoes, vinegar, nutmeg, bay leaves, red pepper flakes, salt, and black pepper. 3. Using a fork, break up the ground beef as much as possible. Cover your slow cooker with its lid. Slow cook for 7-8 hours. 4. Remove and discard the bay leaves. Stir, breaking up the meat completely, and serve.
Per serving: Calories 186; Fat 7.2g; Sodium 71mg; Carbs 5.6g; Fiber 1.6g; Sugars 3g; Protein 23.9g

Pot Roast

Prep time: 15 minutes | Cook time: 7-8 hours | Servings: 6-8

1 teaspoon sea salt	1 celery stalk, chopped
1½ teaspoons dried thyme leaves	6 garlic cloves, minced
1 teaspoon dried rosemary	2 cups broth
½ teaspoon black pepper	3 bay leaves
1 (4-pound) beef chuck roast	2 large sweet potatoes, peeled and cubed
1 medium onion, sliced	
5 carrots, chopped	

1. In a suitable bowl, stir together the salt, thyme, rosemary, and pepper. Rub the spices all over the roast. Set aside. 2. In your slow cooker, layer the onion, carrots, celery, and garlic on the bottom. 3. Add the broth and bay leaves. Put the meat on top of the vegetables. Put the sweet potatoes on top of the meat. 4. Cover your slow cooker with its lid and cook the food for 7 to 8 hours. 5. Remove and discard the bay leaves before serving.
Per serving: Calories 492; Fat 32g; Sodium 530mg; Carbs 16.8g; Fiber 3g; Sugars 2.9g; Protein 32.1g

Herbed Meatballs

Prep time: 15 minutes | Cook time: 7-8 hours | Servings: 6

1½ pounds ground beef	½ teaspoon dried oregano
1 large egg	¼ teaspoon black pepper
1 small white onion, minced	¼ teaspoon ground ginger
¼ cup minced mushrooms	Dash red pepper flakes
1 teaspoon garlic powder	1 (14-ounce) can crushed tomatoes
½ teaspoon sea salt	

1. In a suitable bowl, mix up the ground beef, egg, onion, mushrooms, garlic powder, salt, oregano, black pepper, ginger, and red pepper flakes. 2. Form 12 meatballs from the beef mixture.
Pour the tomatoes into the bottom of your slow cooker. 3. Gently arrange the meatballs on top.
Cover your slow cooker with its lid. Slow cook for 8 hours and serves.
Per serving: Calories 409; Fat 13.4g; Sodium 285mg; Carbs 3.6g; Fiber 1.3g; Sugars 2.2g; Protein 64.5g

Pork Ragù

Prep time: 15 minutes | Cook time: 8 hrs | Servings: 4-6

1 pound pork tenderloin	½ teaspoon ground cumin
1 medium yellow onion, diced	½ teaspoon smoked paprika
1 red bell pepper, diced	Dash red pepper flakes
1 (28-ounce) can diced tomatoes	1 cup fresh spinach leaves, minced
2 teaspoons chili powder	
1 teaspoon garlic powder	

1. In your slow cooker, combine the pork, onion, bell pepper, tomatoes, chili powder, garlic powder, cumin, paprika, red pepper flakes, and spinach. 2. Cover the cooker and set to low. Cook for 7 to 8 hours. 3. Transfer the cooked pork loin to a cutting board and shred with a fork. 4. Return it to the slow cooker, stir it into the sauce, and serve.
Per serving: Calories 227; Fat 4.8g; Sodium 90mg; Carbs 14g; Fiber 4g; Sugars 8.2g; Protein 32.4g

Beef Meatloaf

Prep time: 15 minutes | Cook time: 5-6 hours | Servings: 4

1 pound lean ground beef	½ cup sugar-free ketchup
1 small onion, diced	½ teaspoon sea salt
1 cup fresh spinach, minced well	½ teaspoon garlic powder
1 large egg, whisked well	½ teaspoon dried sage, minced
½ cup almond milk	½ teaspoon Dijon mustard

1. In your slow cooker, mix up the ground beef, onion, spinach, egg, almond milk, ketchup, salt, garlic powder, sage, and mustard. 2. Form the prepared meat mixture into a nice loaf shape, and position it in the center of your slow cooker. 3. Cover the cooker and set to low. Cook for almost 5 to 6 hours until the center of the meatloaf reaches an internal temperature of 160 degrees F, and then you can serve.
Per serving: Calories 244; Fat 8.8g; Sodium 363mg; Carbs 2.6g; Fiber 0.8g; Sugars 1g; Protein 36.6g

Chili-Lime Pork Loin

Prep time: 15 minutes | Cook time: 6-7 hours | Servings: 4

3 teaspoons chili powder	2 (1-pound) pork tenderloins
2 teaspoons garlic powder	1 cup broth
1 teaspoon ground cumin	¼ cup lime juice
½ teaspoon sea salt	

1. In a suitable bowl, stir together the chili powder, garlic powder, cumin, and salt. Rub the pork all over with the spice mixture, and put it in the slow cooker. 2. Pour the broth and lime juice around the pork in the cooker. 3. Cover the cooker and set to low. Cook for almost 6 to 7 hours. 4. Remove the pork from the slow cooker and let rest for almost 5 minutes. Slice the pork against the grain into medallions before serving.
Per serving: Calories 478; Fat 19.2g; Sodium 591mg; Carbs 2.6g; Fiber 0.9g; Sugars 0.7g; Protein 69.5g

Sesame-Ginger Bok Choy and Beef Stir-Fry

Prep time: 10 minutes | Cook time: 10 minutes | Serves: 4

12 ounces flank steak, cut into thin 2-inch strips	lengthwise
½ teaspoon salt	3 tablespoons coconut aminos
¼ teaspoon black pepper	2 tablespoons rice vinegar
2 teaspoons avocado oil	1 tablespoon grated peeled fresh ginger
1 tablespoon sesame oil	1 tablespoon coconut sugar
2 garlic cloves, minced	¼ teaspoon red pepper flakes
4 heads baby bok choy, quartered	

1. Place a suitable skillet over medium-high heat. 2. Season the sliced steak strips with salt and pepper. 3. In your skillet, adjust the heat to medium-high, heat avocado oil and then add the steak strips; stir-fry the steak strips for 3 to 4 minutes until just cooked. Transfer to a plate. 4. Wipe out the skillet. Reduce the heat to medium and add the sesame oil and garlic. Cook them for 2 to 3 minutes, occasionally stirring. 5. Stir in the bok choy, coconut aminos, vinegar, ginger, coconut sugar, and red pepper flakes until well combined. Cover and cook for 2 minutes. 6. Add the steak to the skillet. Toss gently to combine and warm through, about 1 minute. Serve hot.
Per serving: Calories: 319; Total fat 12.5g; Sodium 889mg; Total carbs 19.8g; Fiber 8.6g; Sugars 10g; Protein 36.4g

Beef Wraps

Prep time: 15 minutes | Cook time: 7-8 hours | Servings: 4

2 pounds beef chuck roast
1 small white onion, diced
1 cup broth
3 tablespoons coconut aminos
2 tablespoons coconut sugar
1 tablespoon rice vinegar
1 teaspoon garlic powder

1 teaspoon sesame oil
½ teaspoon ground ginger
¼ teaspoon red pepper flakes
8 romaine lettuce leaves
1 tablespoon sesame seeds
2 scallions (both white and green parts), diced

1. In your slow cooker, combine the beef, onion, broth, coconut aminos, coconut sugar, vinegar, garlic powder, sesame oil, ginger, and red pepper flakes. 2. Cover the cooker and set the cooking temperature to low. Cook for 7 to 8 hours. 3. Scoop spoonful of the beef mixture into each lettuce leaf. Garnish with sesame seeds and diced scallion and serve.
Per serving: Calories 580; Fat 43.8g; Sodium 225mg; Carbs 2.3g; Fiber 0.6g; Sugars 0.8g; Protein 40.9g

Lamb Meatballs with Sauce

Prep time: 15 minutes | Cook time: 7-8 hours | Servings: 6

1½ pounds ground lamb
1 small white onion, minced
1 large egg
1 teaspoon garlic powder
½ teaspoon sea salt

½ teaspoon ground cumin
½ teaspoon pumpkin pie spice
½ teaspoon paprika
¼ teaspoon black pepper
1 cup avocado-dill sauce

1. In a suitable bowl, combine the lamb, onion, egg, garlic powder, salt, cumin, pumpkin pie spice, paprika, and pepper. 2. Form the lamb mixture into about 12 meatballs. Arrange the meatballs along the bottom of your slow cooker. 3. Cover the cooker and set on low. Cook for 7 to 8 hours. Serve with the avocado-dill sauce.
Per serving: Calories 115; Fat 4.6g; Sodium 127mg; Carbs 0.9g; Fiber 0.2g; Sugars 0.4g; Protein 16.6g

Lamb and Quinoa Skillet Ragù

Prep time: 10 minutes | Cook time: 35 minutes | Serves: 6

1 cup quinoa, rinsed well
2 cups filtered water
1 pound ground lamb
3 garlic cloves, minced
1 yellow onion, diced
1 red bell pepper, diced

1 (28-ounce) can diced tomatoes
1 cup minced fresh spinach leaves
2 teaspoons chili powder
½ teaspoon ground cumin
½ teaspoon smoked paprika
Dash red pepper flakes

1. In your saucepan, turn the heat to high, bring the quinoa and the water to a boil. Cover the pan and reduce the heat to low. Simmer the quinoa for 15 minutes. Remove it from the heat and fluff with a fork. 2. While simmering, in a suitable skillet, cook the lamb for 10 minutes over medium heat, occasionally stirring to break up the meat. 3. Add the onion, garlic, and red bell pepper, cook them for 5 minutes. 4. Stir in the tomatoes, spinach, chili powder, cumin, paprika, and red pepper flakes. Cover and cook for almost 5 minutes, or until the lamb is fully cooked. 5. Remove the ragù from the heat and spoon over portions of quinoa.
Per serving: Calories: 265; Total fat 7.5g; Sodium 163mg; Total carbs 22.2g; Fiber 3.1g; Sugars 1.4g; Protein 26g

Garlicky Lamb Shoulder

Prep time: 10 minutes | Cook time: 15 minutes | Servings: 4

2 tablespoons olive oil
2 tablespoons apple cider vinegar
1 tablespoon dried oregano
2 teaspoons bottled minced garlic

½ teaspoon sea salt
pound lamb shoulder, cut into 1-inch cubes

1. Stir together the olive oil, cider vinegar, oregano, garlic and sea salt in the bowl until well mixed. 2. Stir in the lamb. Cover the bowl and refrigerate it for 1 hour to marinate. 3. Preheat the broiler. 4. Place one of the racks in the upper third of the oven. 5. Using 8 wooden skewers, thread 4 or 5 pieces of lamb on each and arrange them on a baking sheet. 6. Broil for almost 15 minutes total until the meat is browned evenly on all sides, flipping halfway through.
Per Serving: Calories 239; Total Fat 16.19g; Sodium 374mg; Total Carbs 0.84g; Fiber 0.2g; Sugars 0.06g; Protein 22.49g

Pork Chops with Gravy

Prep time: 10 minutes | Cook time: 15 minutes | Servings: 4

4 (½-inch-thick) boneless center-cut pork chops
½ teaspoon sea salt
¼ teaspoon freshly ground black pepper
⅓ cup raw honey
⅓ cup tamari

2 tablespoons tomato paste
1 tablespoon apple cider vinegar
2 tablespoons ghee
1 cup chicken broth
3 garlic cloves, minced
1 tablespoon cornstarch
1 tablespoon water

1. Season the prepared pork chops on both sides with the salt and pepper. 2. Combine the honey, tamari, tomato paste and vinegar in the bowl. Set aside. 3. Select Sauté function and let the Instant Pot preheat. 4. Place the ghee in the pot to melt and cook for 1 minute until it begins to bubble. 5. Working in two batches, two at a time, add the pork chops to the pot and sear for 2 minutes per side, or until lightly browned. Select Cancel. Remove the chops and set aside. 6. Deglaze the same pan by adding the broth and scraping any browned bits from the bottom of the pot with a wooden spoon. 7. Return the seared chops to the pot along with any accumulated juices on the plate and cover with the garlic. Lock the lid. 8. Set the pressure cook mode and cook at high pressure for almost 1 minute. 9. When cooking is complete, use a natural release for almost 5 minutes, then quick release any remaining pressure. 10. Remove the cooker's lid and transfer the pork chops to a serving platter, leaving the juices in the pot. 11. In a suitable bowl, whisk the cornstarch and water to blend. 12. Select Sauté on the Instant Pot and add the cornstarch mixture to the pot. Cook for almost 2 minutes, or until thickened. 13. Stir in the honey mixture and cook for 2 minutes, leaving no lumps. Select Cancel. 14. Immediately pour the gravy over the pork chops and serve.
Per Serving: Calories 399; Total Fat 12.57g; Sodium 1959mg; Total Carbs 28.88g; Fiber 0.7g; Sugars 24.66g; Protein 42.69g

Rosemary Pork Loin Roast

Prep time: 10 minutes | Cook time: 50 minutes | Servings: 4-6

1 cup water
1 (4-pounds) boneless pork loin roast
2 tablespoons olive oil

1½ teaspoons salt
½ teaspoon black pepper
1 teaspoon dried rosemary

1. At 375 degrees F, preheat your oven. Pour the water into a 9-by-13-inch roasting pan. 2. Coat the roast with the olive oil. 3. Heat a suitable skillet over high heat and then place the coated roast in the hot skillet. 4. Cook the roast for 3 minutes per side. 5. Transfer the browned roast to the roasting pan. Mix the salt, pepper, and rosemary in a suitable bowl and sprinkle the seasonings evenly over the meat. 6. Roast the pork loin for 30 to 40 minutes until a meat thermometer inserted in the center reads 150 degrees F. 7. Let the roast rest for almost 10 minutes before serving.
Per Serving: Calories 440; Total Fat 16.79g; Sodium 731mg; Total Carbs 0.18g; Fiber 0.1g; Sugars 0g; Protein 67.74g

Thai Ground Beef with Asparagus and Chiles

Prep time: 10 minutes | Cook time: 17 minutes | Serves: 6

1 tablespoon plus 1 teaspoon fish sauce
1 tablespoon plus 1 teaspoon coconut aminos
1 teaspoon coconut sugar
1 tablespoon coconut oil
1 bunch asparagus, shaved into ribbons

3 garlic cloves, minced
3 red jalapeño chile peppers, seeded and sliced into 2-inch matchsticks
1¼ pounds lean ground beef
1 cup loosely fresh basil leaves
Lime wedges, for garnish

1. In a suitable bowl, stir together the fish sauce, coconut aminos, and coconut sugar. Set aside. 2. In a suitable skillet, heat the coconut oil over medium heat. Add the asparagus and sauté for 1 minute. Transfer to a plate and set aside. 3. To the skillet, add the garlic and half of the jalapeño chiles peppers. Cook them for 15 seconds, stirring constantly. 4. Add the ground beef, and cook for almost 15 minutes until cooked through and browned, breaking the meat up with a wooden spoon. 5. Stir in the sauce and cook for 30 seconds. Add the basil, cooked asparagus, and the remaining half of the jalapeño chiles pepper, and stir to combine. 6. Serve hot, garnished with lime wedges.
Per serving: Calories: 418; Total fat 15.3g; Sodium 427mg; Total carbs 2.4g; Fiber 0.5g; Sugars 1.1g; Protein 64g

Boned Pork Loin with Fennel

Prep time: 10 minutes | Cook time: 1 hr. 15 minutes | Servings: 4

1 fennel bulb, fronds cut off, cut into ¼-inch slices	1 teaspoon bottled minced garlic
	Pinch sea salt
1 celeriac, peeled and diced	1 pound boned pork loin, trimmed of visible fat
2 tablespoons olive oil, divided	
1 tablespoon pure maple syrup	1 teaspoon chopped fresh thyme

1. At 375 degrees F, preheat your oven. 2. In a suitable bowl, toss the fennel, celeriac, 1 tablespoon of olive oil, maple syrup, garlic, and sea salt until well mixed. 3. Transfer the prepared vegetables to the baking dish and set it aside. 4. Place a suitable skillet over medium-high heat, and add the remaining 1 tablespoon of olive oil. 5. Add the pork loin and brown it for 15 minutes on all sides, turning once. 6. Place the browned pork on top on the vegetables and sprinkle with the thyme. 7. Roast the pork for 1 hour until cooked through but still juicy. 8. Transfer both the roast and vegetables to a serving platter and pour any pan juices over the top. 9. Let the meat rest for almost 10 minutes before serving.
Per Serving: Calories 329; Total Fat 19.42g; Sodium 133mg; Total Carbs 7.98g; Fiber 1.9g; Sugars 5.34g; Protein 29.84g

Herbed Lamb Fillets with Cauliflower Mash

Prep time: 10 minutes | Cook time: 20 minutes | Serves: 4

For the Cauliffower Mash

1 large head cauliflower, florets broken into small chunks	1 tablespoon ghee
	½ teaspoon garlic powder
Filtered water for cooking the cauliflower	½ teaspoon salt
	Dash cayenne pepper

For the Lamb

2 (8-ounce) grass-fed lamb fillets	2 tablespoons avocado oil
1 teaspoon salt	1 teaspoon dried rosemary
½ teaspoon black pepper	

1. To make the cauliflower mash: In a suitable pot, combine the cauliflower and enough water to cover. 2. Bring to a boil over high heat, and cook for almost 10 minutes. Drain, and transfer to a suitable food processor. 3. Add the ghee, garlic powder, salt, and cayenne pepper. Pulse them to a smooth consistency. Season the lamb with salt and pepper. 4. In a suitable skillet, heat the avocado oil and rosemary over medium-high heat. 5. Add the lamb fillets to the skillet, spaced, so they are not touching. Sear for 5 minutes, spooning the rosemary oil from the bottom of the pan over the lamb halfway through. 6. Flip and continue to cook the lamb for 5 minutes, basting with the rosemary oil after 2 minutes approximately. 7. Transfer to a plate, and let rest for 5 minutes. Slice the lamb into coins and serve with the cauliflower mash.
Per serving: Calories: 282; Total fat 21.8g; Sodium 399mg; Total carbs 2.4g; Fiber 1.2g; Sugars 0.7g; Protein 19.1g

Broiled Beef Sirloin Kebabs

Prep time: 20 minutes | Cook time: 10 minutes | Servings: 4

2 tablespoons olive oil	trimmed of visible fat and cut into 1½-inch chunks
1 tablespoon coconut aminos	
1 tablespoon apple cider vinegar	1 red onion, quartered and separated into layers
1 tablespoon bottled minced garlic	
1 tablespoon chopped fresh cilantro	1 sweet potato, peeled, halved lengthwise, each half cut into 8 pieces
pound boneless sirloin steak,	8 medium button mushrooms

1. Stir together 1 tablespoon of olive oil, the coconut aminos, cider vinegar, garlic and cilantro in the bowl until well mixed. 2. Add diced beef to the bowl and stir to coat the meat in the marinade. Cover the bowl and refrigerate for 1 hour to marinate. 3. Preheat the broiler. 4. Place an oven rack in the top quarter of the oven. 5. Assemble the kebabs on 4 skewers by alternating pieces of beef, onion, sweet potato and mushrooms. 6. Lightly brush the vegetables with the remaining olive oil and arrange the kebabs on the baking sheet. 7. Broil the kebabs for 10 minutes for medium, turning once or twice, or until the beef is cooked to your desired doneness. 8. Transfer the broiled kebabs to a plate, and let them rest for almost 5 minutes before serving.
Per Serving: Calories 326; Total Fat 19.56g; Sodium 86mg; Total Carbs 11.17g; Fiber 1.9g; Sugars 3.37g; Protein 25.54g

Spaghetti Bolognese

Prep time: 10 minutes | Cook time: 25 minutes | Serves: 8

1 pound brown rice spaghetti	1 (14-ounce) can diced tomatoes
2 tablespoons ghee	1 tablespoon white wine vinegar
3 garlic cloves, minced	½ teaspoon red pepper flakes
½ cup chopped white onion	⅛ teaspoon ground nutmeg
⅔ cup chopped celery	Dash salt
⅔ cup chopped carrot	Dash black pepper
1 pound lean ground beef	

1. Cook the spaghetti according to the package instructions. 2. In a suitable skillet, heat the ghee over medium heat. 3. Add the chopped garlic and onion, and sauté them for 5 minutes. Add the celery and carrot, and sauté for 5 minutes. Push the vegetables to the side of the skillet. 4. Add the ground beef next to the vegetables. Sauté for 10 minutes, breaking up the meat as it begins to brown. 5. Stir in the tomatoes, vinegar, red pepper flakes, nutmeg, salt, and pepper, and bring to a simmer for 5 minutes. 6. Serve over the cooked noodles.
Per serving: Calories: 201; Total fat 7g; Sodium 321mg; Total carbs 14g; Fiber 1.4g; Sugars 2.5g; Protein 18.9g

Lamb Burgers with Herbed Yogurt Sauce

Prep time: 40 minutes | Cook time: 20 minutes | Serves: 6

Pickled onions	½ teaspoon kosher salt
½ red onion, sliced	½ teaspoon raw cane sugar
6 tablespoon lime juice	
Herbed Yoghurt Sauce	
2 tablespoon lemon juice	2 tablespoon chopped herbs
1 cup Greek yogurt	Kosher salt
1 garlic clove, minced	
Lamb Burgers	
1 tablespoon olive oil	4 garlic cloves, minced
½ red onion, diced	1-½ teaspoons ground cumin
1 lb. Ground lamb	1 teaspoon ground coriander
8 oz. Ground pork	1 teaspoon kosher salt
3 tablespoon chopped mint	½ teaspoon black pepper
2 tablespoon chopped dill	Mixed greens, sliced tomatoes,
3 tablespoon chopped parsley	

1. Mix the onion, lime juice, salt, and sugar in a suitable bowl. 2. Cover, and let the onions sit at room temperature for almost 2 hours. 3. In a suitable bowl, stir together the lemon juice, yogurt, garlic, herbs, and ½ teaspoon of salt. Cover and refrigerate this yogurt sauce until ready to use. 4. To make the lamb burgers: In a suitable skillet over medium heat, warm the olive oil. Add the onion and cook for 7 minutes, stirring frequently stirring, until softened. Transfer to a small plate to cool. 5. In a suitable bowl, combine the pork, lamb, dill, parsley, garlic, cumin, mint, coriander, salt, pepper, and cooled onions. 6. Form the mixture into six equal-sized meatballs. Press each into a patty and transfer to a parchment-lined baking sheet. 7. Prepare a suitable grill for cooking over medium-high heat. Lightly grease its grill grate. Place the burgers on the preheat grill, and cook for 5 minutes per side. 8. Transfer the burgers to a plate to rest for 5 minutes before serving. 9. Top with a generous dollop of herbed yogurt sauce and some pickled onions. Add greens and sliced tomatoes or cucumbers. Serve.
Per serving: Calories 351; Fat 20.6g; Sodium 634mg; Carbs 5.4g; Fiber 2.1g; Sugars 2.7g; Protein 35.7g

Pork Tenderloin with Dijon-Cider Glaze

Prep time: 5 minutes | Cook time: 25 minutes | Serves: 4

¼ cup apple cider vinegar	2 teaspoons garlic powder
¼ cup coconut sugar	Dash salt
3 tablespoons Dijon mustard	1 (1½-pound) pork tenderloin

1. In a suitable bowl, stir together the vinegar, coconut sugar, mustard, garlic powder, and salt until the sugar dissolves. Brush this mixture over the pork loin. 2. Place a grill pan over medium-high heat and add the pork. Sear for 2 minutes per side. Spoon half of the vinegar mixture over the pork and reduce the heat to medium. 3. Cover this pan and cook for almost 10 minutes. 4. Spoon the remaining vinegar mixture over the pork. Cook for 5 minutes, or until the pork reaches an internal temperature of 145 degrees F. Transfer the pork to a plate. 5. Bring the vinegar mixture remaining in the pan to a simmer. Cook for almost 5 minutes to reduce and thicken. 6. Serve the pork drizzled with the glaze.
Per serving: Calories: 274; Total fat 6.5g; Sodium 270mg; Total carbs 5.8g; Fiber 0.5g; Sugars 4.5g; Protein 45.3g

Dijon Mustard-Crusted Lamb Racks

Prep time: 10 minutes | Cook time: 35 minutes | Servings: 4

¼ cup whole-grain Dijon mustard	2 (8-rib) frenched lamb racks,
2 tablespoons chopped fresh thyme	patted dry
	Sea salt
1 tablespoon chopped fresh rosemary	Freshly ground black pepper
	1 tablespoon olive oil

1. At 425 degrees F, preheat your oven. 2. Stir together the mustard, thyme and rosemary in the bowl. 3. Lightly season the lamb racks with sea salt and pepper. 4. Heat the olive oil in the ovenproof skillet over medium-high heat. 5. Add the lamb racks and pan-sear for 2 minutes per side, turning once. Remove the skillet from the heat. 6. Turn the racks upright in the skillet with the bones interlaced, and spread the mustard mixture over the outside surface of the lamb. Roast for almost 30 minutes for medium, or until your desired doneness. 7. Remove the lamb racks from the oven and let them rest for almost 10 minutes. Cut the racks into chops and serve 4 per person.
Per Serving: Calories 335; Total Fat 24.92g; Sodium 109mg; Total Carbs 6.3g; Fiber 1.2g; Sugars 0.03g; Protein 21.97g

Baked Beef Meatloaf

Prep time: 10 minutes | Cook time: 1 hour 10 minutes | Servings: 4

1½ pounds extra-lean ground beef	parsley
½ cup almond flour	1 teaspoon grated fresh
½ cup chopped sweet onion	horseradish, or prepared
1 egg	horseradish
1 tablespoon chopped fresh basil	⅛ teaspoon sea salt
1 tablespoon chopped fresh	

1. At 350 degrees F, preheat your oven. 2. Mix the ground beef, almond flour, onion, egg, basil, parsley, horseradish and sea salt in the bowl until well mixed. Press the meatloaf mixture into the loaf pan. 3. Bake the food for 1 hour until cooked through. 4. Remove the cooked meatloaf from the hot oven, and let it rest for 10 minutes before serving.
Per Serving: Calories 254; Total Fat 9.68g; Sodium 215mg; Total Carbs 3.45g; Fiber 0.5g; Sugars 2.23g; Protein 38.23g

Bibimbap

Prep time: 40 minutes | Cook time: 30 minutes | Serves: 4

8 oz. flank steak, sliced	2 small crookneck squash, cut
6½ teaspoon tamari	into matchsticks
2 teaspoon minced garlic	8 oz. baby spinach
3 teaspoon toasted sesame oil	8 oz. mung bean sprouts
2½ teaspoon raw cane sugar	1 tablespoon sesame seeds
9 teaspoon organic canola oil	8 oz. shiitake mushrooms, sliced
½ yellow onion, thinly sliced	4 cups steamed short-grain brown
1 carrot, peeled and julienned	rice
Kosher salt, to taste	4 fried eggs
1 red bell pepper, julienned	Kimchi and gochujang for serving

1. In a suitable bowl, combine the steak with 4 ½ teaspoons of the tamari, 1 teaspoon of the garlic, 1 teaspoon of the sesame oil, and 2 teaspoons of the sugar. Marinate at room temperature for 30 minutes. 2. In a suitable nonstick skillet, heat 1 teaspoon of the canola oil over medium-high heat. Add the onion and carrot, season with salt, and cook for 4 to 6 minutes, stirring occasionally stirring, until tender-crisp. Transfer to a suitable bowl. 3. Repeat the process to cook each vegetable separately until just tender, seasoning each with a pinch of salt and adding it to the onion and carrot when done. 4. Cook the bell pepper in 1 teaspoon canola oil; the squash in 1 teaspoon canola oil and 1 teaspoon of sesame oil; the spinach in 1 teaspoon canola oil, adding the remaining 1 teaspoon garlic during the last minute of cooking; and the bean sprouts and sesame seeds in 1 teaspoon of canola oil and the remaining sesame oil. 5. Add 2 teaspoon of canola oil to the skillet. Add the mushrooms and cook until browned, about 5 minutes. Add the remaining 2 teaspoon of tamari and remaining sugar and cook for 1 minute or until glazed. Transfer to the bowl of vegetables. 6. Add the remaining 2 teaspoon of canola oil to the skillet, turn the heat to high, add the steak, and cook for 3 to 4 minutes on each side or until browned on both sides. 7. Divide the rice among four bowls. Top evenly with the meat and vegetables, followed by a fried egg. Serve with kimchi and gochujang.
Per serving: Calories 386; Fat 3.5g; Sodium 911mg; Carbs 45.5g; Fiber 9g; Sugars 4.1g; Protein 41.7g

Buckwheat Cabbage Rolls in Beef Broth

Prep time: 30 minutes | Cook time: 1 hour 5 minutes | Servings: 4

8 large outer cabbage leaves with	1 egg
the hard core removed	2 teaspoons bottled minced garlic
pound lean ground beef	1 teaspoon chopped fresh oregano
½ cup cooked buckwheat	Pinch sea salt
½ sweet onion, chopped	½ cup beef bone broth

1. At 350 degrees F, preheat your oven. 2. Bring the water to boil in the saucepan over high heat. 3. Add the cabbage leaves and blanch them for 4 minutes, or until tender. Remove them from the water and set them aside. 4. Mix the ground beef, buckwheat, onion, egg, garlic, oregano and sea salt in the bowl until well combined. Divide the mixture into 8 portions. 5. Place one cabbage leaf at a time on a work surface, and place 1 meat portion in the center. 6. Fold the top and bottom of the cabbage leaf over the meat. 7. Roll the leaf from the nearest unfolded edge until the meat is completely enclosed in a roll. Place the roll seam-side down in the baking dish. Repeat with the remaining leaves and meat portions. 8. Pour the beef broth over the cabbage rolls. 9. Cover the prepared baking dish with aluminum foil and bake the food for 1 hour until the filling is cooked through.
Per Serving: Calories 245; Total Fat 9.57g; Sodium 233mg; Total Carbs 12.21g; Fiber 2.2g; Sugars 4.52g; Protein 28.69g

Stewed Lamb Leg with Greens

Prep time: 10 minutes | Cook time: 50 minutes | Servings: 6

1 (4-pound) whole boneless leg of	1 large yellow onion, chopped
lamb	4 garlic cloves, minced
1½ teaspoons sea salt	1 tablespoon fresh rosemary
2 tablespoons avocado oil,	leaves, chopped
divided	1 tablespoon fresh thyme leaves,
2 cups vegetable broth, divided	chopped
pound baby red potatoes, halved	1 cup frozen peas
2 large carrots, chopped	1 cup frozen pearl onions

1. Generously season the leg of lamb on all sides with the salt. 2. Select Sauté function, pour in 1 tablespoon of oil, and let the pot preheat. 3. Add the lamb to the pot and cook for 2 minutes per side, or until browned on every side. Select Cancel. 4. Transfer the seared lamb to a plate and set aside. 5. Deglaze the pot by pouring ½ cup of vegetable broth into the pot. 6. Pour in the remaining 1½ cups of broth, then add the potatoes, carrots, onion, garlic, rosemary, and thyme. Return the lamb to the pot, placing it on top of the vegetables. Lock the lid. 7. Set the pressure cook mode and cook at high pressure for almost 40 minutes. 8. When cooking is complete, use a natural release for almost 15 minutes, then quick release any remaining pressure. 9. Remove the cooker's lid and stir in the peas and pearl onions. Replace the lid without sealing it. Let sit for almost 5 minutes. 10. Transfer the cooked lamb and vegetables to a serving platter. Pour any juices over the lamb and vegetables to serve.
Per Serving: Calories 594; Total Fat 24.25g; Sodium 1048mg; Total Carbs 25.22g; Fiber 4.5g; Sugars 4.95g; Protein 66.22g

Pan-Fried Pork Chops with Apple Salsa

Prep time: 20 minutes | Cook time: 25 minutes | Servings: 4

For the Salsa

1 teaspoon olive oil	2 apples, peeled, cored, and diced
¼ cup finely chopped sweet onion	½ cup dried raisins
½ teaspoon grated fresh ginger	Pinch sea salt

For the Pork Chops

4 (4-ounce) boneless center-cut	1 teaspoon ground cinnamon
pork chops, trimmed and patted	Sea salt
dry	black pepper
1 teaspoon garlic powder	1 tablespoon olive oil

1. Heat the olive oil in the skillet over medium heat. 2. Add the onion and ginger, sauté them for almost 2 minutes or until softened. 3. Stir in the apples and raisins, sauté for almost 5 minutes or until the fruit is just tender. 4. Season the prepared salsa with sea salt and set it aside. 5. Season the prepared pork chops on both sides with the garlic powder, cinnamon, sea salt, and pepper. 6. Heat the olive oil in the skillet over medium-high heat. 7. Add the seasoned chops and panfry for 7 to 8 minutes per side until just cooked through and browned, turning once. 8. Serve the chops with the cooked apple salsa.
Per Serving: Calories 322; Total Fat 11.3g; Sodium 144mg; Total Carbs 14.8g; Fiber 2.9g; Sugars 9.85g; Protein 39.68g

Rosemary Lamb Chops

Prep time: 15 minutes | Cook time: 7-8 hours | Servings: 4

1 medium onion, sliced	Black pepper
2 teaspoons garlic powder	8 bone-in lamb chops (about 3
2 teaspoons dried rosemary	pounds)
1 teaspoon sea salt	2 tablespoons balsamic vinegar
½ teaspoon dried thyme leaves	

1. Layer the bottom of your slow cooker with the onion slices. 2. In a suitable bowl, stir together the garlic powder, rosemary, salt, thyme, and pepper. 3. Rub the chops evenly with the spice mixture, and gently place them in the slow cooker. 4. Drizzle the vinegar over the top. Cover your slow cooker with its lid. 5. Slow cook for 8 hours and serve.
Per serving: Calories 213; Fat 8.1g; Sodium 420mg; Carbs 2.8g; Fiber 0.7g; Sugars 1g; Protein 31.1g

Spinach-Pork Salad

Prep time: 15 minutes | Cook time: 0 | Servings: 2

2 cups baby spinach	1 green apple, cored and sliced
8 (½-inch-thick) slices Pan-	½ red bell pepper, sliced
Seared Pork Loin	¼ cup Ginger-Turmeric Dressing
4 leftover Roasted Fingerling	¼ cup toasted pecans, chopped
Potatoes, cut in half lengthwise	

1. In a suitable bowl, toss together the spinach, pork loin, potatoes, green apple and red bell pepper. 2. Pour the turmeric prepared dressing over and toss to combine. 3. Divide between two bowls, top with the pecans and serve.
Per Serving: Calories 554; Total Fat 15.61g; Sodium 584mg; Total Carbs 78.03g; Fiber 13.1g; Sugars 11.25g; Protein 30.05g

Grilled Rib-Eye and Summer Succotash with Lime-Herb Vinaigrette

Prep time: 45 minutes | Cook time: 20 minutes | Serves: 4

1-lb boneless rib-eye steak	as basil, mint, and chives
Olive oil for brushing	3 zucchini, ends trimmed, sliced
Kosher salt	lengthwise into strips
Black pepper	2 summer squash, ends trimmed,
1 small shallot, minced	sliced lengthwise into strips
3 tablespoon lime juice	2 red or yellow bell peppers,
1 tablespoon sherry vinegar	halved and seeds, cored
1 tablespoon Dijon mustard	2 cups cherry tomatoes, halved
1 tablespoon honey	1 cup Edamame, fava beans,
¼ cup olive oil	or other shelled fresh beans,
3 tablespoon chopped herbs, such	blanched

1. Rinse the steak and pat dry. Place on a plate and brush both sides with olive oil. Lightly season the steak with salt and pepper and let marinate at room temperature for 1 hour. 2. In a suitable bowl, whisk together the shallot, lime juice, vinegar, mustard, and honey. Slowly whisk in the olive oil to form a vinaigrette. Gently stir in the herbs, then taste and season with salt and pepper. Set aside. 3. Prepare a suitable grill for direct cooking over high heat. 4. Brush the zucchini strips, summer squash strips, and bell pepper halves on both sides with olive oil, then sprinkle with salt and pepper. Grill the zucchini and squash until just cooked through, about 2 minutes per side. 5. Transfer to a cutting board. Grill the bell peppers for 5 to 7 minutes, turning occasionally, until charred and blistered. Place in a suitable bowl and cover with plastic wrap. Allow the vegetables to cool. 6. While the vegetables cool, grill the steak for 3 to 4 minutes on each side or until well seared and an instant-read thermometer inserted into the center reads 130 degrees F for medium-rare, or grill longer to reach the desired doneness. 7. Allow the steak to sit on a cutting board for 5 to 10 minutes before slicing across the grain. Remove the skins from the cooled bell peppers. Cut the zucchini, squash, and peppers into ½-in dice. 8. Place the vegetables in a suitable bowl and add the tomatoes and Edamame. Pour half of the vinaigrette over the vegetables and toss to coat, adjusting with more vinaigrette as desired. 9. Place several generous spoonsful of the succotash on each plate, then pair with a fourth of the sliced steak. 10. Serve immediately.
Per serving: Calories 460; Fat 29.7g; Sodium 536mg; Carbs 13.1g; Fiber 6.9g; Sugars 4g; Protein 37.7g

Beef and Bell Pepper Fajitas

Prep time: 5 minutes | Cook time: 10 minutes | Servings: 4

3 tablespoons olive oil	1 cup store-bought salsa
1½ pounds flank steak, sliced	1 teaspoon garlic powder
2 green bell peppers, sliced	½ teaspoon sea salt
1 onion, sliced	

1. In a suitable skillet over medium-high heat, heat the olive oil until it shimmers. 2. Add the beef, bell peppers, onion and cook them for almost 6 minutes until the beef browns, stirring occasionally. 3. Stir in the salsa, garlic powder, and salt. Cook for almost 3 minutes, stirring occasionally.
Per serving: Calories 461; Fat 24.9g; Sodium 527mg; Carbs 9.6g; Fiber 2g; Sugars 5.3g; Protein 48.8g

Pork Tenderloin with Blueberry Sauce

Prep time: 10 minutes | Cook time: 20 minutes | Servings: 4

For the Pork

2 (10-ounce) pork tenderloins,	black pepper
trimmed and patted dry	1 tablespoon olive oil
Sea salt	

For the Sauce

1 tablespoon olive oil	1 cup fresh blueberries
¼ cup chopped sweet onion	¼ teaspoon ground nutmeg
½ cup chicken bone broth	1 teaspoon lemon zest
2 tablespoons apple cider vinegar	

To make the pork: 1. At 425 degrees F, preheat your oven. 2. Lightly season the tenderloins with sea salt and pepper. 3. Heat the olive oil in the ovenproof skillet over medium-high heat. 4. Add the pork and brown it on all sides, turning, about 5 minutes. 5. Place the skillet in the oven and roast the pork for almost 15 minutes until just cooked through. 6. Remove the pork's skillet from the oven and let the pork rest for almost 10 minutes. 7. Cut the cooked pork into medallions and serve with the berry sauce.
To make the sauce: 1. While the pork roasts, heat the olive oil in the saucepan over medium-high heat. 2. Add the onion and sauté for almost 3 minutes, or until softened. 3. Stir in the chicken broth and cider vinegar. Bring the liquid to a boil. Lower its heat to low and simmer for almost 4 minutes, or until the sauce has reduced by half. 4. Stir in the blueberries and nutmeg. Cook for almost 5 minutes, or until the berries break down. 5. Remove the prepared sauce from the heat and stir in the lemon zest. 15 Serve with the pork medallions.
Per Serving: Calories 283; Total Fat 15.73g; Sodium 207mg; Total Carbs 7.75g; Fiber 1.3g; Sugars 4.79g; Protein 26.68g

Stalks Celery-Braised Lamb Shoulder

Prep time: 10 minutes | Cook time: 2 hours 15 minutes | Servings: 4

2 tablespoons olive oil	½ teaspoon ground turmeric
pound lamb shoulder, trimmed	¼ teaspoon ground allspice
of visible fat and cut into 1-inch	2 cups beef bone broth
chunks	2 cups diced sweet potato
2 stalks celery, chopped	1 cup diced carrot
1 sweet onion, chopped	1 cup diced parsnip
1 tablespoon grated fresh ginger	2 cups fresh spinach
2 teaspoons bottled minced garlic	2 tablespoons chopped fresh
1 teaspoon ground cinnamon	parsley

1. At 325 degrees F, preheat your oven. 2. Heat 1 tablespoon of olive oil in the ovenproof skillet over medium-high heat. 3. Add the lamb in batches and brown for 8 minutes. 4. Remove the cooked lamb meat to a plate. Return the skillet to the heat. 5. Add the remaining olive oil, the celery, onion, ginger, and garlic, then sauté them for almost 3 minutes or until softened. 6. Stir in the cinnamon, turmeric, allspice and sauté for 1 minute. 7. Stir in the beef broth, sweet potato, carrot, parsnip, lamb and any accumulated juices on the plate, then bring the liquid to a boil. 8. Cover this skillet with a foil sheet and place it in the oven. 9. Braise the stew for 2 hours with occasional stirring, until the lamb is very tender. 10. Remove the cooked stew from the oven and stir in the spinach. Let the stew sit for almost 10 minutes. 11. Serve garnished with the parsley.
Per Serving: Calories 374; Total Fat 21.57g; Sodium 441mg; Total Carbs 21.4g; Fiber 5.8g; Sugars 8.54g; Protein 26.27g

Chapter 7 Fish and Seafood

Simple Baked Salmon

Prep time: 5 minutes | Cook time: 15 minutes | Servings: 4

Extra-virgin olive oil, for brushing the pan
4 (3- to 4-ounce) boneless salmon fillets
1 teaspoon salt
¼ teaspoon black pepper
2 tablespoons fresh lemon juice

1. At 375 degrees F, preheat your oven. Grease a suitable baking pan with oil. 2. Place the salmon in the pan, season the salmon with the salt and pepper, then drizzle with the lemon juice. 3. Bake the fish in the oven for 10 to 15 minutes. 4. Remove the fish from the oven and let rest for almost 5 to 10 minutes before serving.
Per Serving: Calories 53; Total Fat 2.83g; Sodium 595mg; Total Carbs 0.64g; Fiber 0.1g; Sugars 0.19g; Protein 6.17g

Fennel Baked Salmon Fillets

Prep time: 10 minutes | Cook time: 20 minutes | Servings: 4

1 tablespoon extra-virgin olive oil
1 fennel bulb, sliced
½ small red onion, sliced
4 (3- to 4-ounce) boneless salmon fillets
1 teaspoon salt
¼ teaspoon freshly ground black pepper
½ cup dry white wine

1. Preheat your oven to 375 degrees F. Grease a 9-inch square baking pan with the olive oil. 2. Scatter the fennel and red onion slices in the bottom of the pan. 3. Add the salmon fillets and the salt and pepper. Pour in the wine. 4. Bake the salmon for 20 minutes until the salmon is firm to the touch and flakes with a fork. 5. Let the salmon rest for almost 5 minutes before serving.
Per Serving: Calories 127; Total Fat 7.71g; Sodium 853mg; Total Carbs 5.45g; Fiber 2g; Sugars 2.74g; Protein 9.62g

White Fish Fillets with Mushrooms

Prep time: 15 minutes | Cook time: 18 minutes | Servings: 4

1 leek, sliced
1 teaspoon minced fresh ginger root
1 garlic clove, minced
½ cup sliced shiitake mushrooms
½ cup dry white wine
1 tablespoon toasted sesame oil
4 (6-ounce) white fish fillets
1 teaspoon salt
⅛ teaspoon freshly ground black pepper

1. Preheat your oven to 375 degrees F. 2. Mix the leek, ginger root, garlic, mushrooms, wine and sesame oil in a 9-by-13-inch baking pan. Toss them well to combine. 3. Bake the food for almost 10 minutes. Set the fish on top of the mushrooms. 4. Add the salt and pepper, cover with aluminum foil, and bake for 5 to 8 minutes until the fish is firm. 5. Serve.
Per Serving: Calories 195; Total Fat 7.17g; Sodium 652mg; Total Carbs 4.19g; Fiber 0.5g; Sugars 1.29g; Protein 27.23g

Coconut Milk–Baked Sole with Cilantro

Prep time: 20 minutes | Cook time: 30 minutes | Servings: 4

2 tablespoons warm water
Pinch saffron threads
2 pounds' sole fillets
Sea salt
2 tablespoons freshly squeezed lemon juice
1 tablespoon coconut oil
1 sweet onion, chopped, or 1 cup
precut packaged onion
2 teaspoons bottled minced garlic
1 teaspoon grated fresh ginger
1 cup canned full-fat coconut milk
2 tablespoons chopped fresh cilantro

1. Place the water in a suitable bowl and sprinkle the saffron threads on top. Let it stand for almost 10 minutes. 2. At 350 degrees F, preheat your oven. 3. Rub the fish with sea salt and the lemon juice, and place the fillets in the baking dish. 4. Roast the fish for 10 minutes. 5. While the fish is roasting, heat the coconut oil in the skillet over medium-high heat. 6. Add the onion, garlic, and ginger, sauté them for almost 3 minutes, or until softened. 7. Stir in the coconut milk and the saffron water. Bring to a boil. 8. Lower its heat to low and simmer the sauce for 5 minutes. Remove the skillet from the heat. 9. Pour the sauce over the fish. Cover the dish with foil and bake for 10 minutes, or until the fish flakes easily with a fork. 10. Serve the fish topped with the cilantro.
Per Serving: Calories 357; Total Fat 22.19g; Sodium 727mg; Total Carbs 10.78g; Fiber 2.1g; Sugars 6.38g; Protein 30.34g

Lemony Trout Fillets

Prep time: 10 minutes | Cook time: 15 minutes | Servings: 4

Extra-virgin olive oil, for brushing
½ red onion, sliced
1 (10-ounce) package frozen spinach, thawed
4 boneless trout fillets
1 teaspoon salt
¼ teaspoon chipotle powder
¼ teaspoon garlic powder
2 tablespoons fresh lemon juice

1. Preheat your oven to 375 degrees F. Grease a suitable baking pan with olive oil. 2. Scatter the red onion and spinach in the pan. 3. Lay the trout fillets over the spinach. 4. Sprinkle the salt, chipotle powder and garlic powder over the fish. 5. Cover with aluminum sheet and bake the food for 15 minutes. 6. Drizzle with the lemon juice and serve.
Per Serving: Calories 216; Total Fat 6.93g; Sodium 667mg; Total Carbs 2.83g; Fiber 1.5g; Sugars 0.56g; Protein 34.41g

Smoked Trout Fried Rice with Red Pepper

Prep time: 10 minutes | Cook time: 10 minutes | Servings: 6

2 tablespoons toasted sesame oil
4 scallions, sliced
1 teaspoon minced fresh ginger root
1 garlic clove, minced
⅛ teaspoon red pepper flakes
2 cups baby spinach
½ cup chicken or vegetable broth
4 cups cooked brown rice
1 teaspoon low-sodium soy sauce (optional)
8 ounces smoked trout, flaked
¼ cup toasted slivered almonds (optional)

1. Heat the sesame oil in the skillet over high heat; sauté the scallions, ginger root, garlic, red pepper flakes, spinach and broth in the hot oil for 2 minutes. 2. Add the rice and stir to combine. Stir in the soy sauce (optional) and the trout. 3. Garnish with the almonds and serve.
Per Serving: Calories 267; Total Fat 9.16; Sodium 107mg; Total Carbs 32.57g; Fiber 3g; Sugars 1.27g; Protein 13.43g

Salmon with Cucumber Salad

Prep time: 10 minutes | Cook time: 20 minutes | Servings: 4

1 tablespoon extra-virgin olive oil, plus more for brushing
4 (3- to 4-ounce) boneless salmon fillets
2 or 3 dill sprigs, plus 2 teaspoons minced dill fronds
1 shallot, sliced
½ cup dry white wine
2 teaspoons salt, divided
¼ teaspoon freshly ground black pepper
2 cups sliced escarole
8 radishes, quartered
1 English cucumber, seeded and chopped
1 tablespoon fresh lemon juice, plus extra sliced lemons for garnish

1. Preheat your oven to 375 degrees F. Grease a suitable 9-inch square baking pan with olive oil. 2. Place the salmon fillets in the pan, skin-side down. Scatter the dill sprigs and shallot over the fish, then add the wine, 1 teaspoon of salt and the black pepper. 3. Spread aluminum foil on top and bake for 20 to 25 minutes until the fish is firm. 4. Transfer the prepared salmon fillets to a plate and let them cool completely. Discard the remaining contents of the pan. 5. Mix up the escarole, radishes, cucumber and minced dill in a bowl. 6. Add 1 tablespoon of olive oil, the lemon juice, and the remaining 1 teaspoon of salt. Toss well. 7. Mound the salad on four plates, top with the salmon, and garnish with the lemon slices. 8. Serve.
Per Serving: Calories 215; Total Fat 5.59g; Sodium 1658mg; Total Carbs 33.29g; Fiber 13.9g; Sugars 18.62g; Protein 11.48g

Basic Shrimp

Prep time: 15 minutes | Cook time: 0 minutes | Serves: 4

12 frozen jumbo shrimp, in shells

1. Pour 1½ cups water into the insert of the Instant pot and set the steam rack inside. 2. Add the shrimp to the steamer basket and place it on the rack. 3. Close the lid and secure it well. Hit the the manual cook button and adjust the time to 0 minutes. 4. When cooked, release the pressure quickly until the float valve drops and then unlock lid.
Per serving: Calories 120; Fat 2g; Sodium 170mg; Carbs 1g; Fiber 0g; Sugars 0g; Protein 23g

White Miso Salmon

Prep time: 10 minutes | Cook time: 20 minutes | Servings: 4

¼ cup white miso
¼ cup apple cider
1 tablespoon unseasoned white rice vinegar
1 tablespoon toasted sesame oil

⅛ teaspoon ground ginger
4 (3 to 4-ounce) boneless salmon fillets
1 scallion, sliced
⅛ teaspoon red pepper flakes

1. At 375 degrees F, preheat your oven. 2. Mix the miso, cider, rice vinegar, sesame oil and ginger in the bowl. If the mixture is too thick, thin with a suitable amount of water. 3. Place the salmon fillets in a suitable 9-inch square baking pan, skin-side down. Pour the miso sauce over the salmon to coat evenly. 4. Bake the salmon for 15 to 20 minutes until the salmon is firm. 5. Top with the scallions and red pepper flakes and serve.
Per Serving: Calories 120; Total Fat 5.73g; Sodium 664mg; Total Carbs 9.12g; Fiber 1.2g; Sugars 2.72g; Protein 8.14g

Quinoa Salmon with Sauce

Prep time: 10 minutes | Cook time: 0 | Servings: 4

4 cups cooked quinoa
1 pound cooked salmon, flaked
3 cups arugula
6 radishes, sliced into half moons
1 zucchini, sliced into half moons
3 scallions, minced
½ cup almond oil

1 tablespoon apple cider vinegar
1 teaspoon Sriracha sauce or other hot sauce (you can add more if you like it spicy)
1 teaspoon salt
½ cup toasted slivered almonds (optional)

1. Mix the quinoa, salmon, arugula, radishes, zucchini and scallions in the bowl; add the vinegar, Sriracha, almond oil, salt and mix them well. 2. Divide the prepared mixture among four serving bowls, garnish with the toasted almonds; enjoy.
Per Serving: Calories 646; Total Fat 39.14g; Sodium 1102mg; Total Carbs 41.06g; Fiber 5.8g; Sugars 2.34g; Protein 32.22g

Shrimp Coleslaw with Avocado

Prep time: 10 minutes | Cook time: 0 | Servings: 4

1 pound frozen cooked shrimp, thawed
1 (8-ounce) package shredded cabbage
3 scallions, sliced
3 tangerines, peeled and sectioned
3 tablespoons toasted sesame oil
2 tablespoons unseasoned white rice vinegar

2 teaspoons grated fresh ginger root
⅛ teaspoon red pepper flakes
3 tablespoons chopped fresh cilantro
1 avocado, peeled, pitted and sliced
¼ cup toasted slivered almonds (optional)

1. Mix up the shrimp, cabbage, scallions, tangerines, sesame oil, vinegar, ginger root and red pepper flakes in the bowl. 2. Mix well and refrigerate the shrimp for at least 30 minutes for the prepared dressing to slightly wilt the cabbage. 3. Top with the cilantro, avocado and almonds (optional) just before serving.
Per Serving: Calories 318; Total Fat 19.05g; Sodium 654mg; Total Carbs 21.32g; Fiber 5.4g; Sugars 8.35g; Protein 17.9g

Seared Scallops with Greens

Prep time: 20 minutes | Cook time: 15 minutes | Servings: 4

1½ pounds sea scallops, cleaned and patted dry
Sea salt
Freshly ground black pepper

2 tablespoons olive oil
2 garlic cloves, sliced
2 cups chopped kale leaves
2 cups fresh spinach

1. Lightly season the scallops all over with sea salt and pepper. 2. Heat 1 tablespoon of olive oil in the skillet over medium-high heat. 3. Sear the scallops for 2 minutes on each side or until opaque and just cooked. 4. Place the scallops to a plate and cover loosely with aluminum foil to keep them warm. 5. Wipe the same skillet with a paper towel and place it back on the heat. 6. Heat the remaining olive oil and sauté the garlic for 4 minutes, or until caramelized. 7. Stir in the kale and spinach, sauté them for almost 6 minutes, or until the greens are tender and wilted. 8. Divide the greens with any juices equally among four plates and top each with the scallops.
Per Serving: Calories 258; Total Fat 8.32g; Sodium 1189mg; Total Carbs 10.96g; Fiber 0.7g; Sugars 0.26g; Protein 35.81g

Mussels in Chicken Bone Broth

Prep time: 10 minutes | Cook time: 15 minutes | Servings: 4

1 tablespoon olive oil
2 teaspoons bottled minced garlic
1 cup canned lite coconut milk
½ cup chicken bone broth
2 teaspoons chopped fresh thyme

1 teaspoon chopped fresh oregano
1½ pounds fresh mussels, scrubbed and debearded
1 scallion, white and green parts, sliced on an angle

1. Heat the olive oil in the skillet over medium-high heat. 2. Add the garlic and sauté for 3 minutes, or until softened. 3. Stir in the coconut milk, chicken broth, thyme and oregano. Bring the liquid to a boil and then add the mussels. 4. Cover the skillet and steam the food for 8 minutes, or until the shells open. 5. Discard any unopened shells and remove the skillet from the heat. 6. Stir in the scallion and serve.
Per Serving: Calories 320; Total Fat 21.59g; Sodium 612mg; Total Carbs 10.75g; Fiber 1.6g; Sugars 2.25g; Protein 22.02g

Lime Shrimp with Mango-Cucumber Salsa

Prep time: 15 minutes | Cook time: 10 minutes | Servings: 4

For the Shrimp
¼ cup extra-virgin olive oil
3 tablespoons fresh lime juice, plus extra lime wedges for garnish
1 teaspoon salt
For the Salsa
1 large mango, peeled, pitted, and cubed
1 small cucumber, diced
1 scallion, sliced

⅛ teaspoon chipotle powder
1½ pounds uncooked shrimp, peeled and deveined

1 tablespoon fresh lime juice
1 tablespoon olive oil
¼ teaspoon salt

1. Mix the olive oil, lime juice, salt, chipotle powder and the shrimps in the baking pan, let the shrimps marinate for at least 15 minutes. 2. Combine all the salsa ingredients in the bowl. 3. When ready to cook, skewer the shrimp, fitting as many as you can on each skewer. 4. Heat a stove top grill or skillet over high heat. 5. When the grill is hot, lay the skewers on the grill, being careful not to crowd them. Cook the shrimp for 3 minutes. 6. Serve the shrimp skewers over a bed of salsa, with lime wedges for squeezing.
Per Serving: Calories 385; Total Fat 19.6g; Sodium 2210mg; Total Carbs 16.81g; Fiber 1.9g; Sugars 12.73g; Protein 35.88g

Carrot Crab Cakes

Prep time: 10 minutes | Cook time: 15 minutes | Servings: 4

2 pounds cooked lump crabmeat, drained and picked over
½ cup shredded unsweetened coconut
½ cup coconut flour, plus more as needed
½ cup shredded carrot

2 scallions, white and green parts, finely chopped
2 eggs
1 teaspoon freshly grated lemon zest (optional)
2 tablespoons olive oil

1. Mix up the crab, coconut, coconut flour, carrot, scallions, eggs and lemon zest in the bowl until the mixture holds together when pressed. Add more coconut flour if the mixture is too wet. 2. Divide the prepared mixture into 8 portions and flatten them until they are almost 1 inch thick. Cover the crab cakes and refrigerate for about 1 hour to firm up. 3. Heat the olive oil in the skillet over medium-high heat; add the crab cakes and sear for 6 minutes on each side until cooked through and golden on both sides, turning just once. 4. Serve 2 crab cakes per person.
Per Serving: Calories 362; Total Fat 16.71g; Sodium 1372mg; Total Carbs 5.1g; Fiber 1.8g; Sugars 2.59g; Protein 45.85g

Pan-Seared Scallops with Vinaigrette

Prep time: 10 minutes | Cook time: 7 minutes | Serves: 4

2 tablespoons olive oil
1½ pounds sea scallops
½ teaspoon sea salt

⅛ teaspoon black pepper
¼ cup lemon-ginger vinaigrette

1. In a suitable nonstick skillet, heat the olive oil over medium-high heat until it shimmers. 2. Season the scallops with salt and pepper and add them to the skillet. Cook them for almost 3 minutes on each side until just opaque. 3. Serve with the vinaigrette spooned over the top.
Per serving: Calories: 304; Total fat 5.9g; Sodium 619mg; Total carbs 7.4g; Fiber 0g; Sugars 0g; Protein 52.3g

Avocado Tuna Melts

Prep time: 10 minutes | Cook time: 5 minutes | Serves: 4

4 slices sourdough bread
2 (5-ounce) cans of wild-caught albacore tuna
¼ cup pale mayonnaise
2 tablespoons minced shallot
1 teaspoon lemon juice

Dash garlic powder
Dash paprika
1 large avocado, cut into 8 slices
1 large tomato, cut in 8 slices
¼ cup shredded raw parmesan cheese

1. Preheat the broiler. Layer a baking sheet with aluminum foil. 2. Arrange the slices of bread in the prepared pan. 3. In a suitable bowl, mix the tuna, mayonnaise, shallot, lemon juice, garlic powder, and paprika. Spread one-fourth of the tuna mixture on each slice of bread. 4. Top each with 2 avocado slices and 2 tomato slices. Sprinkle each with a tablespoon of parmesan cheese. 5. Broil the food for 3 to 4 minutes, do not let them burn. Serve hot.
Per serving: Calories: 471; Total fat: 27g; saturated fat: 4g; cholesterol: 40mg; carbohydrates: 31g; Fiber: 4g; Protein: 27g

Fish Curry with Lemon Juice

Prep time: 10 minutes | Cook time: 15 minutes | Servings: 4

2 tablespoons avocado oil
6 large Thai basil leaves
1 large white onion, peeled and diced
1½ teaspoons salt
2 cloves garlic, minced
1 tablespoon peeled and grated fresh ginger
3 tablespoons curry powder

2 cups canned unsweetened full-fat coconut milk
2 green chilies, seeded and sliced into strips
1 cup whole cherry tomatoes
1½ pounds tilapia filet, cut into small pieces
2 tablespoons lemon juice

1. Select the Sauté function and add the oil to the inner pot. Allow it to heat 1 minute, and then add the basil leaves and cook for 1 minute until they turn golden around the edges. 2. Add the onion, salt, garlic, and ginger and sauté them for 5 minutes until the onion is soft. Add the curry powder and sauté with the onion for 2 minutes longer. 3. Add the coconut milk and stir, making sure to scrape any brown bits from the bottom of the pot. 4. Add the green chilies, tomatoes, and fish pieces. Stir until well combined. Press the Cancel button. Seal the cooker's lid. 5. Select the Manual or Pressure mode and adjust the pressure to low and adjust the time to 5 minutes. 6. Once the timer beeps, quick-release the pressure then unlock lid and remove it. 7. Add the lemon juice and then spoon into bowls to serve.
Per Serving: Calories 499; Total Fat 34.86g; Sodium 983mg; Total Carbs 14.2g; Fiber 4g; Sugars 4.08g; Protein 38.48g

Seared Cod with Mushroom Sauce

Prep time: 15 minutes | Cook time: 20 minutes | Serves: 4

1 pound cod fillet
½ teaspoon salt
¼ teaspoon black pepper
½ cup coconut oil
Grated zest and juice of 1 lime
4 ounces shiitake mushrooms, sliced
2 garlic cloves, minced

1 (15-ounce) can full-fat coconut milk
1 teaspoon ground ginger
1 teaspoon red pepper flakes
2 tablespoons tamari (or 1 tablespoon miso paste and 1 tablespoon water)
2 tablespoons toasted sesame oil

1. Cut the cod into four equal pieces and season with black pepper and salt. 2. In a suitable skillet, heat 4 tablespoons of coconut oil over high heat until just before smoking. 3. Add the cod, skin-side up, cover to prevent splattering and sear for almost 4 to 5 minutes, until it's golden brown. Remove the fish from this skillet, drizzle with the juice of ½ lime, and let rest. 4. In the same skillet, add the rest of the 4 tablespoons of coconut oil and heat over medium. 5. Add the mushrooms and sauté for almost 5 to 6 minutes, until they are just tender. Add the garlic and sauté for almost 1 minute, until fragrant. 6. Whisk in the coconut milk, ginger, red pepper flakes, tamari, and remaining lime zest and juice. 7. Reduce its heat to low. Return the cod to this skillet, skin-side down, cover and simmer for almost 3 to 4 minutes, until the fish is cooked through. 8. To serve, set the cod on rimmed plates or in shallow bowls and spoon the sauce over the fish. Drizzle with the sesame oil.
Per serving: Calories 470; Fat 41.2g; Sodium 940mg; Carbs 6.1g; Fiber 0.9g; Sugars 1.7g; Protein 22.2g

Crispy Fish Tacos with Mango Salsa

Prep time: 30 minutes | Cook time: 10 minutes | Serves: 4

Mango Salsa
2 mangoes, peeled, pitted, and diced
½ small red onion, diced
Avocado Crema
2 avocados, halved and pitted
Kosher salt
2 tablespoon mayonnaise
2 tablespoon lime juice
1 lb. tilapia fillets
Kosher salt
Black pepper
2 eggs

1 jalapeño, minced
2 tablespoon lime juice
2 tablespoon chopped cilantro
Kosher salt

1 cup gluten-free flour
1 cup grated Parmigiano-Reggiano
4 tablespoons olive oil
8 corn tortillas, warmed
½ head green cabbage, cored and shredded
Lime wedges for serving

1. To make the mango salsa: Combine the mangos, onion, jalapeño, lime juice, and cilantro in a bowl and stir to combine. Add salt and lime juice as desired. Set aside. 2. To make the avocado crema: Place the avocado flesh and ¼ teaspoon of salt in a suitable bowl. 3. Using a fork or a pastry blender, mash the food until very smooth. Stir in the mayonnaise and lime juice. You can add additional salt and lime juice as desired. (To store, with a piece of plastic wrap, pressed directly onto the surface, in the refrigerator for up to 2 days.) 4. Rinse the tilapia and pat dry. Halve each fillet lengthwise by slicing down the middle seam. Season them with salt and pepper. 5. Whisk the eggs in a shallow bowl. Place the flour, Parmigiano-Reggiano, and ½ teaspoon salt in another small bowl and stir to combine. 6. Dip the fish, one piece at a time, into the eggs, coating evenly and allowing any excess to drip off into the bowl. 7. Then place in the flour mixture and coat both sides evenly, gently tapping off any excess. Arrange the coated fish on a baking sheet in a single layer. 8. Layer another baking sheet with paper towels. In a suitable nonstick skillet over medium-high heat, warm 2 tablespoons of olive oil. 9. Working in two batches, place the fish pieces in the skillet and cook for 2 minutes on each side until golden brown and opaque in the center. 10. Transfer the fish pieces to the prepared sheet. Pour any remaining oil from the skillet, wipe clean with a paper towel, and add the remaining 2 tablespoons of olive oil. 11. Spread some avocado crema on each tortilla. Top with cabbage, a piece of fish, and a spoonful of mango salsa. 12. Serve with lime wedges and extra crema and salsa on the side.
Per serving: Calories: 412; Total fat 20.8g; Sodium 104mg; Total carbs 43.5g; Fiber 7.9g; Sugars 13.9g; Protein 17.2g

Salmon Bok Choy

Prep time: 15 minutes | Cook time: 25 minutes | Serves: 4

¼ cup miso paste
2 tablespoons rice wine vinegar or dry white wine
6 tablespoons toasted sesame oil
2 teaspoons ground ginger
1 teaspoon red pepper flakes
2 garlic cloves, minced

1 pound wild-caught salmon fillet, skin removed
½ cup extra-virgin olive oil
8 heads baby bok choy, quartered
2 tablespoons tamari or water
2 tablespoons sesame seeds

1. In a suitable bowl, combine the miso, vinegar, 2 tablespoons of sesame oil, ginger, red pepper flakes, and garlic and whisk until smooth. 2. In a glass baking dish or resealable storage bag, set the salmon and pour the marinade over it. Refrigerate for at least 30 minutes or up to overnight. 3. To cook the fish, in a suitable skillet heat 4 tablespoons of avocado oil over medium-high heat. 4. Remove the salmon from the marinade, reserving the liquid, and fry for almost 3 to 5 minutes per side, until the fish is crispy and golden brown. 5. The time depends on your desired doneness and the thickness of the fish. Transfer the fish to a large platter and keep warm. 6. In the same skillet, add the rest of the 4 tablespoons of avocado oil over medium-high heat. Add the bok choy and fry for almost 7 minutes, until it is crispy and just tender. Transfer it to the platter with the salmon. 7. Reduce its heat to low. Add the reserved miso marinade and tamari to the oil in this skillet and whisk to combine well. Simmer, uncovered, for almost 4 to 5 minutes, until slightly thickened. Whisk in the rest of the 4 tablespoons of sesame oil until smooth. 8. Serve the salmon and bok choy drizzled with the warm miso vinaigrette and sprinkled with the sesame seeds.
Per serving: Calories 511; Fat 28.1g; Sodium 1545mg; Carbs 29.4g; Fiber 12.4g; Sugars 14.1g; Protein 43.5g

Lemon Salmon Salad

Prep time: 20 minutes | Cook time: 5 minutes | Servings: 4

pound salmon
teaspoon salt, divided
½ teaspoon black pepper, divided
tablespoon lemon juice
1½ tablespoons olive oil
tablespoon fresh lemon juice
½ tablespoon apple cider vinegar
1 tablespoon chopped fresh parsley
2 teaspoons minced garlic
½ teaspoon dried oregano

4 cups chopped romaine lettuce
1 large cucumber, diced
2 Roma tomatoes, cored and diced
1 medium red onion, peeled and sliced
1 medium avocado, peeled, pitted, and sliced
⅓ cup pitted Kalamata olives, sliced

1. Season the salmon with ½ teaspoon of salt, ¼ teaspoon of pepper and the lemon juice. 2. Place 1 cup of water in the inner pot and place the steam rack inside. Place the salmon on top of the steam rack. Seal the cooker's lid. 3. Select the Manual or Pressure mode and adjust the time to 3 minutes. 4. Meanwhile, prepare the prepared dressing and salad ingredients. In a container with a tight lid, place the oil, lemon juice, vinegar, parsley, garlic, oregano, ½ teaspoon of salt and ¼ teaspoon of pepper. Shake well until combined and set aside.5. Place the lettuce, cucumber, tomatoes, red onion, avocado and olives in a suitable bowl. Set aside. 6. Release the pressure completely then remove its lid. 7. Remove the cooked salmon from the Instant Pot® and allow it to cool completely. Once it is cool, cut it into bite-sized pieces. 8. Add the salmon pieces to the salad bowl. Drizzle with the prepared dressing and gently toss to combine.
Per Serving: Calories 317; Total Fat 19.05g; Sodium 761mg; Total Carbs 12.24g; Fiber 6.2g; Sugars 3.98g; Protein 26.1g

Haddock with Beets

Prep time: 10 minutes | Cook time: 45 minutes | Servings: 4

8 beets, peeled and cut into eighths
2 shallots, sliced
1 teaspoon bottled minced garlic
2 tablespoons olive oil, divided

2 tablespoons apple cider vinegar
1 teaspoon chopped fresh thyme
Pinch sea salt
4 (5-ounce) haddock fillets, patted dry

1. At 400 degrees F, preheat your oven. 2. Mix up the beets, shallots, garlic and 1 tablespoon of olive oil in the bowl until well coated. Spread the beet mixture in the baking dish. 3. Roast the beet mixture for 30 minutes, or until the vegetables are caramelized and tender. 4. Remove the roasted and cooked beets from the oven and stir in the cider vinegar, thyme, and sea salt. 5. While the beets are roasting, place a suitable skillet over medium-high heat and add the remaining olive oil. 6. Panfry the fish for 15 minutes, turning once, until it flakes when pressed with a fork. 7. Serve the fish with roasted beets.
Per Serving: Calories 279; Total Fat 7.91g; Sodium 579mg; Total Carbs 16.87g; Fiber 4.8g; Sugars 11.52g; Protein 34.32g

Tomato Basil Tilapia

Prep time: 10 minutes | Cook time: 2 minutes | Servings: 4

1 cup dry quinoa
1 cup chicken stock
4 (4-ounce) tilapia filets
½ teaspoon salt, divided
¼ teaspoon black pepper, divided
3 Roma tomatoes, cored and

roughly chopped
2 cloves garlic, minced
5 large fresh basil leaves, chiffonade
2 tablespoons olive oil

1. Add the quinoa and stock to the inner insert and place the steam rack on top. Place the tilapia on top of the steam rack and season the filets with ¼ teaspoon of salt and ⅛ teaspoon of pepper. Seal the cooker's lid. 2. Select the Manual or Pressure mode and adjust the time to 2 minutes. 3. While cooking, mix the tomatoes, garlic, basil and oil in a suitable bowl. Set aside. 4. Release the pressure completely then remove its lid. Remove the rack and tilapia from the pot. 5. Use any fork to fluff the quinoa, and then divide it among four plates. Place one tilapia filet on top of the quinoa, and then add the tomato mixture on top of the fish and quinoa.
Per Serving: Calories 351; Total Fat 11.63g; Sodium 589mg; Total Carbs 31.75g; Fiber 4.2g; Sugars 2.71g; Protein 30.64g

Tilapia Fish Tacos with Cilantro-Lime Crema

Prep time: 15 minutes | Cook time: 25 minutes | Serves: 4

For the Cilantro-Lime Crema
½ cup plain whole-milk Greek yogurt
2 tablespoons lime juice
1 tablespoon minced fresh
For the Fish Tacos
8 small corn tortillas
1 teaspoon paprika
½ teaspoon salt
½ teaspoon garlic powder
½ teaspoon ground cumin

cilantro leaves
¼ teaspoon garlic powder
Dash salt

¼ teaspoon cayenne pepper
1 pound tilapia fillets
2 tablespoons avocado oil
1 large avocado, sliced

1. To make the cilantro-lime crema: In a suitable bowl, whisk the yogurt, lime juice, cilantro, garlic powder, and salt. Cover and chill until ready to serve. 2. To make the fish tacos: At 350 degrees F, preheat your oven. 3. Wrap the tortillas in a suitable aluminum foil and place them in the oven to warm for almost 15 minutes. 4. Meanwhile, in a suitable bowl, mix the paprika, salt, garlic powder, cumin, and cayenne pepper. 5. Put the fish fillets on a plate, and sprinkle them with the seasoning mixture. 6. In a suitable skillet over medium-high heat, heat the avocado oil. 7. Add the fish fillets to the skillet and cook them for almost 3 minutes on each side, or until flaky. 8. Lay the warm tortillas out on a work surface. Divide the fish among the tortillas. 9. Serve the fish tacos with the sliced avocado and cilantro-lime crema.
Per serving: Calories: 363; Total fat: 17g; saturated fat: 3g; cholesterol: 62mg; carbohydrates: 25g; Fiber: 6g; Protein: 27g

Easy-to-Make Salmon Patties

Prep time: 15 minutes | Cook time: 10 minutes | Servings: 4

pound skinless boned salmon fillets, minced
¼ cup minced sweet onion
½ cup almond flour
2 garlic cloves, minced
2 eggs, whisked
1 teaspoon Dijon mustard

1 tablespoon freshly squeezed lemon juice
Dash red pepper flakes
½ teaspoon sea salt
¼ teaspoon freshly ground black pepper
1 tablespoon avocado oil

1. Mix together the minced salmon, sweet onion, almond flour, garlic, whisked eggs, mustard, lemon juice, red pepper flakes, sea salt and pepper in a suitable bowl until well incorporated. 2. Allow the salmon mixture to rest for 5 minutes. 3. Scoop out the salmon mixture and shape into four ½-inch-thick patties with your hands. 4. Heat the avocado oil in the skillet over medium heat; add the patties and cook each side for 5 minutes until lightly browned and cooked through. 5. Serve on a plate.
Per Serving: Calories 258; Total Fat 12.43g; Sodium 776mg; Total Carbs 3.76g; Fiber 0.5g; Sugars 1.82g; Protein 33.22g

Salmon with Kale Salad

Prep time: 10 minutes | Cook time: 5 minutes | Servings: 4

pound salmon
1 teaspoon salt
2 bunches kale (almost 12 ounces total), deveined and chopped
½ teaspoon black pepper
1 tablespoon lemon juice
1 red bell pepper, seeded and diced
1 cup diced carrot

3 cups chopped cabbage
¼ cup pure sesame oil
¼ cup almond butter
¼ cup raw honey
Juice from 2 medium limes
1 tablespoon reduced-sodium tamari
¼ teaspoon minced garlic
⅓ cup sesame seeds

1. Season the salmon with ½ teaspoon of salt, ¼ teaspoon of pepper, and the lemon juice. 2. Place 1 cup water in the insert of the Instant Pot and place the steam rack inside. Place the salmon on top of the steam rack. Seal the cooker's lid. 3. Select the Manual or Pressure mode and adjust the time to 3 minutes. 4. Release the pressure completely then remove its lid. 5. Remove the prepared salmon from the Instant Pot® and allow it to cool completely. Once it is cool, cut it into bite-sized pieces. 6. In a suitable bowl, mix together the kale, bell peppers, carrots, and cabbage. Top with the salmon. 7. In a suitable blender, blend together the oil, almond butter, honey, lime juice, tamari and garlic until smooth. 8. Pour the prepared dressing onto the kale salad and toss to coat. Add the sesame seeds and lightly toss. Top with the remaining salt and pepper.
Per Serving: Calories 534; Total Fat 30.33g; Sodium 782mg; Total Carbs 39.68g; Fiber 7.5g; Sugars 25.61g; Protein 32.76g

Salmon Patties with Lime Wedges

Prep time: 10 minutes | Cook time: 10 minutes | Servings: 4

½ pound cooked boneless salmon fillet, flaked
2 eggs
¾ cup almond flour, plus more as needed
1 scallion, white and green parts, chopped

Juice of 2 limes (2-4 tablespoons, plus more as needed)
Zest of 2 limes (optional)
1 tablespoon chopped fresh dill
Pinch sea salt
1 tablespoon olive oil
1 lime, cut into wedges

1. In a suitable bowl, mix together the salmon, eggs, almond flour, scallion, lime juice, lime zest, dill, and sea salt until the mixture holds together when pressed. 2. If the mixture is too dry, add more lime juice; if it is too wet, add more almond flour. 3. Divide the salmon mixture into 4 equal portions, and press them into patties about ½ inch thick. Refrigerate them for 30 minutes to firm up. 4. Heat the olive oil in the skillet over medium-high heat. 5. Add the salmon patties and brown for almost 5 minutes on each side, turning once. 6. Serve the patties with lime wedges.
Per Serving: Calories 203; Total Fat 12.66g; Sodium 337mg; Total Carbs 6.37g; Fiber 0.7g; Sugars 1.35g; Protein 16.79g

Salmon and Spinach Mixture with Lemon Wedges

Prep time: 10 minutes | Cook time: 7 minutes | Servings: 4

1 pound small red potatoes, quartered
1 cup water
1¼ teaspoons salt, divided
¾ teaspoon black pepper, divided
4 (5-ounce) salmon filets

¼ teaspoon sweet paprika
½ teaspoon lemon zest
4 cloves garlic, minced
2 tablespoons avocado oil
4 cups packed baby spinach
4 lemon wedges

1. Place the quartered potatoes in the inner pot and add 1 cup of water, ¼ teaspoon of salt, and ¼ teaspoon of pepper. Set a steam rack on top of the potatoes. 2. Add the lemon zest, paprika, ½ teaspoon salt, and ¼ teaspoon black pepper on top of the salmon and set the salmon on the steam rack. Seal the cooker's lid. 3. Select the Manual or Pressure mode and adjust the time to 3 minutes. 4. Release the pressure completely then remove its lid. 5. Then transfer salmon to a plate and remove the rack and water from the pot. 6. Hit the Sauté button and cook the potatoes 1 minute. 7. Add the garlic and sauté for almost 2 minutes. Stir in the oil, black pepper and salt. 8. Mash the potatoes with a fork to make a chunky texture. 9. Stir in spinach and stir for 1–2 minutes until wilted. 10. Serve the salmon and spinach mixture with the lemon wedges.
Per Serving: Calories 208; Total Fat 8.78g; Sodium 791mg; Total Carbs 23.9g; Fiber 3g; Sugars 2.86g; Protein 10.58g

Fish Sticks with Avocado Dipping Sauce

Prep time: 15 minutes | Cook time: 5 minutes | Serves: 4

For the Avocado Dipping Sauce
2 avocados
¼ cup lime juice
2 tablespoons fresh cilantro leaves
2 tablespoons olive oil
For the Fish Sticks
1½ cups almond flour
1 teaspoon salt
½ teaspoon paprika
¼ teaspoon black pepper
3 eggs

1 teaspoon salt
1 teaspoon garlic powder
Dash ground cumin
Black pepper

¼ cup coconut oil
1 pound cod fillets, cut into 4-inch-long, 1-inch-thick strips
Juice of 1 lemon

1. In a suitable food processor, blend the avocados, lime juice, cilantro, olive oil, salt, garlic powder, and cumin, and season with pepper until smooth. 2. In a small shallow bowl, mix the almond flour, salt, paprika, and pepper. 3. Whisk the eggs in another small shallow bowl. Dip the fish sticks into the egg and then into the almond flour mixture until fully coated. 4. In a suitable skillet over medium-high heat, heat the coconut oil. 5. One at a time, place the fish sticks in the skillet. Cook for almost 2 minutes on each side until lightly browned. Apportion them between 2 plates. 6. To serve, sprinkle with the lemon juice and serve alongside the avocado dipping sauce.
Per serving: Calories: 583; Total fat: 50g; saturated fat: 17g; cholesterol: 200mg; carbohydrates: 14g; Fiber: 8g; Protein: 25g

Shrimp Balls over Garlicky Greens

Prep time: 15 minutes | Cook time: 25 minutes | Serves: 4

1 pound wild-caught shrimp, peeled, deveined, and chopped
¼ cup coconut or almond flour
1 large egg, lightly beaten
1 (2-inch) piece fresh ginger, peeled and minced
¼ cup minced scallion, green part only
1 teaspoon garlic powder
Grated zest of 1 lime

½ teaspoon salt
¼ to ½ teaspoon red pepper flakes
10 tablespoons extra-virgin olive oil, more for frying as needed
8 cups kale or spinach, torn into bite-size pieces
6 garlic cloves, minced
¼ cup soy sauce
2 tablespoons rice vinegar
2 tablespoons sesame oil

1. In a suitable bowl, combine the shrimp, coconut flour, egg, ginger, 2 tablespoons of scallion, garlic powder, lime zest, salt, and red pepper flakes, mixing well with a fork. 2. Using your hands, form the shrimp mixture into about a dozen (1-inch) balls and place them on a cutting board or baking sheet lined with parchment paper. Allow to rest for almost 10 minutes. 3. In a small skillet or saucepan, heat 4 tablespoons of olive oil over medium-high heat. Working in batches of three to four balls, panfry them for almost 5 to 7 minutes total, carefully turning to brown all sides. 4. Repeat until all the shrimp balls have been fried, adding additional oil with each batch as needed. Keep the shrimp balls warm. 5. In a suitable skillet, heat 2 tablespoons of olive oil over medium-high heat. Add the greens and sauté for almost 5 minutes. Add the garlic and sauté for almost 2 to 4 minutes until the greens are wilted. 6. In a suitable bowl, whisk together the soy sauce, vinegar, and sesame oil. 7. To serve, divide the sautéed greens between plates and top with three shrimp balls drizzled with the sauce.
Per serving: Calories 413; Fat 33.5g; Sodium 1542mg; Carbs 20g; Fiber 2g; Sugars 0.7g; Protein 4.9g

Salmon Fillets with Oregano

Prep time: 10 minutes | Cook time: 20 minutes | Servings: 4

For the Pistou
1 cup fresh oregano leaves
¼ cup almonds
2 garlic cloves
Juice of 1 lime (1-2 tablespoons)
For the Fish
4 (6-ounce) salmon fillets
Sea salt

Zest of 1 lime (optional)
1 tablespoon olive oil
Pinch sea salt

black pepper
1 tablespoon olive oil

1. Blend the oregano, almonds, garlic, lime juice, lime zest, olive oil and sea salt in the blender until very chopped. Transfer the pistou to a suitable bowl and set it aside. 2. At 400 degrees F, preheat your oven. 3. Lightly season the salmon with salt and black pepper. 4. Heat the olive oil in an ovenproof skillet over medium-high heat; add the salmon and sear for 4 minutes on each side. 5. Place the skillet in the oven and bake the fish for 10 minutes, or until it is just cooked through. 6. Serve the salmon topped with a spoonful of pistou.
Per Serving: Calories 120; Total Fat 8.43g; Sodium 100mg; Total Carbs 2.55g; Fiber 0.2g; Sugars 0.4g; Protein 8.79g

Skilled-Seared Trout Fillets with Salsa

Prep time: 20 minutes | Cook time: 10 minutes | Servings: 4

For the Salsa
1 English cucumber, diced
¼ cup unsweetened coconut yogurt
1 scallion, white and green parts,
For the Fish
1 tablespoon olive oil
4 (5-ounce) trout fillets, patted dry

chopped
2 tablespoons chopped fresh mint
1 teaspoon raw honey
Sea salt

Sea salt
Freshly ground black pepper

To make the salsa: 1. Mix up all the ingredients in the bowl and set aside.
To make the fish: 1. Season the trout fillets with sea salt and black pepper. 2. Heat the olive oil in the skillet over medium heat; add the seasoned trout fillets and panfry them for 5 minutes on each side, turning once, or until they are just cooked through. 3. Top the fillets with the cucumber salsa and serve.
Per Serving: Calories 238; Total Fat 9.07g; Sodium 106mg; Total Carbs 4.15g; Fiber 0.8g; Sugars 2.97g; Protein 33.11g

Honey Mustard–Glazed Salmon

Prep time: 15 minutes | Cook time: 8 minutes | Serves: 4

4 tablespoon honey
2 tablespoon Dijon mustard
4 (4-oz) salmon fillets, pin bones removed

Olive oil for brushing
Kosher salt
Black pepper

1. In a suitable bowl, whisk together the honey and mustard. Set aside. 2. Rinse the salmon and pat dry with a paper towel. Brush all sides of each fillet with olive oil and season with a pinch each of salt and pepper. 3. To grill the salmon, prepare a grill for direct cooking over medium-high heat. Fold a 24-by-12-in piece of aluminum foil to create a square. Crimp the edges upward to form a rim. 4. Place the foil directly on the grill grate, then set the salmon, skin-side down, on the foil, leaving 2.5-cm gap between each piece. 5. Close the lid and grill for 4 minutes. Lift the lid and generously brush the fish with the honey mustard. 6. Close the lid and grill for 2 to 3 minutes more for medium or until the salmon is cooked to the desired doneness. Remove the salmon from the grill. 7. To cook the salmon in the oven, place a rack in the top third of the oven and preheat the oven to broil. 8. Layer a baking sheet with aluminum foil and brush with olive oil. Place the salmon, skin-side down, on the foil, leaving 2.5-cm gap between each piece. 9. Broil for 2 minutes, and then liberally brush each fillet with the honey mustard. Continue broiling for 3 to 4 minutes more or until the salmon is cooked to the desired doneness. 10. Remove the salmon from the oven. Brush the salmon with more honey mustard and let rest for 3 to 5 minutes before serving. 11. Easy salmon skin removal. You'll notice that the salmon skin sticks to the foil, allowing the flesh to slide right off. If you like to eat the skin, you can peel it off, roll it up, and serve it alongside the fish.

Per serving: Calories: 219; Total fat 7.3g; Sodium 178mg; Total carbs 17.7g; Fiber 0.3g; Sugars 17.3g; Protein 22.4g

Spice-Rubbed Salmon

Prep time: 20 minutes | Cook time: 15 minutes | Servings: 4

Relish
4 tangerines, peeled, segmented, and chopped
½ cup chopped jicama
1 scallion, white and green parts, chopped

2 tablespoons chopped fresh cilantro
1 teaspoon lemon zest
Pinch sea salt

Fish
1 teaspoon ground cumin
1 teaspoon ground coriander
4 (6-ounce) skin-on salmon fillets,

patted dry
1 teaspoon olive oil

To make the relish: 1. Mix up all the relish ingredients in the bowl and then set aside for later use.
To make the fish: 1. Preheat your oven to 425 degrees F. 2. Whisk the cumin and coriander in another bowl. 3. Rub the flesh side of the fillets with the spice mixture. 4. Arrange the salmon fillets in the baking dish in a single layer, skin-side up. Brush the fillets with the olive oil. 5. Bake the salmon fillets for 15 minutes, or until just cooked through and lightly golden. 6. Serve the fish with the salsa.

Per Serving: Calories 120; Total Fat 3.41g; Sodium 75mg; Total Carbs 13.79g; Fiber 2.6g; Sugars 9.74g; Protein 9.73g

Baked Halibut Fillets with Salsa

Prep time: 20 minutes | Cook time: 15 minutes | Servings: 4

Salsa
1 avocado, peeled, pitted and diced
½ mango, diced, or about 1 cup frozen chunks, thawed

½ cup chopped fresh strawberries
1 teaspoon chopped fresh mint
Juice of 1 lemon (3 tablespoons)
Zest of 1 lemon (optional)

Fish
4 (6-ounce) boneless skinless halibut fillets, patted dry
Sea salt

Freshly ground black pepper
1 tablespoon olive oil

To make the salsa: Mix up all the salsa ingredients in the bowl; set aside for later use.
To make the fish: 1. Lightly season the halibut fillets with sea salt and pepper. 2. Heat the olive oil in the skillet over medium heat. 3. Add the fish and cook for 7 minutes on each side, turning once, or until it is just cooked through. 4. Top the fish with the avocado salsa and serve.

Per Serving: Calories 296; Total Fat 21.18g; Sodium 99mg; Total Carbs 10.78g; Fiber 4.3g; Sugars 4.64g; Protein 17.6g

Salade Niçoise with Salmon and Beets

Prep time: 30 minutes | Cook time: 45 minutes | Serves: 4

2 baby beets, peeled and cut into large dice
2 tablespoons olive oil
8 oz. green beans, trimmed
4 (4-oz) skin-on salmon fillets, pin bones removed
Kosher salt

French vinaigrette
Black pepper
1 cup halved cherry tomatoes
3 hard-boiled eggs, quartered
½ cup oil-cured niçoise olives, pitted
1 tablespoon minced chives

1. At 400 degrees F, preheat your oven. 2. In a small roasting pan, toss the beets with 1 tablespoon of olive oil. Roast the beets for 40 minutes, stirring every 10 to 15 minutes, until the beets are soft and caramelized. Set aside to cool. 3. Bring a cooking pot of salted water to a boil and fill a suitable bowl with ice water. Stir in the green beans to the boiling water and cook for 2 minutes. 4. With a slotted spoon, transfer the beans to the ice-water bath to stop the cooking. Be careful not to overcook the beans; they should still have some bite. 5. Dry the beans. Rinse the salmon and pat dry with a paper towel. Sprinkle each side with a small pinch of salt. 6. Place a suitable nonstick sauté pan over medium-high heat. When the pan is hot, add the remaining 1 tablespoon of olive oil. 7. Place the salmon fillets skin-side down in the pan and cook until the skin is crispy about 2 minutes. 8. For medium-rare salmon, turn the fillets and cook for 1 minute more. For medium salmon, also turn the salmon on its sides, cooking each side for 1 minute. 9. Remove and place on a wire rack, so the skin doesn't get soggy. Place the green beans in a suitable bowl, add 1 tablespoon of the vinaigrette, and toss to coat. 10. Arrange the beans in a pile on a serving platter. Repeat with the beets and cherry tomatoes. 11. Add the hard-boiled eggs and olives to the platter, and then top with the salmon fillets. Drizzle with a little vinaigrette and sprinkle with the chives. 12. Serve family-style.

Per serving: Calories: 403; Total fat 21.8g; Sodium 355mg; Total carbs 12.3g; Fiber 4.4g; Sugars 4.8g; Protein 43.5g

Vegetable and Fish Casserole

Prep time: 25 minutes | Cook time: 30 minutes | Servings: 4

2 cups diced sweet potato
2 cups diced carrot
2 cups diced parsnip
1 sweet onion, cut into eighths
1 cup (2-inch) asparagus pieces
2 teaspoons chopped fresh thyme

1 teaspoon bottled minced garlic
¼ teaspoon sea salt
1 tablespoon olive oil
4 (6-ounce) skinless tilapia fillets
Juice of 1 lemon (3 tablespoons)

1. At 350 degrees F, preheat your oven. 2. Tear off four 18-by-24-inch pieces of aluminum foil and fold each piece in half to make four 18-by-12-inch pieces. 3. Toss the sweet potato, carrot, parsnip, onion, asparagus, thyme, garlic, sea salt and olive oil well in the bowl. Place one-fourth of the vegetables in the center of each foil piece. 4. Top each vegetable mound with one tilapia fillet. 5. Sprinkle the fish with lemon juice. 6. Fold the foil to create sealed packages that have a bit of space at the top, and place the packets on a baking sheet. 7. Bake the food for almost 30 minutes, or until the fish begins to flake and the vegetables are tender. 8. Open the packets, serve and enjoy.

Per Serving: Calories 367; Total Fat 6.37g; Sodium 504mg; Total Carbs 52.88g; Fiber 14g; Sugars 23.18g; Protein 29.26g

Garlicky Cod Fillets

Prep time: 15 minutes | Cook time: 20 minutes | Servings: 4

1 garlic clove, minced
1 leek, sliced
1 teaspoon minced fresh ginger root
1 tablespoon olive oil

½ cup dry white wine
½ cup sliced shiitake mushrooms
4 (6-ounce / 170-g) cod fillets
1 teaspoon sea salt
⅛ teaspoon black pepper

1. At 375 degrees F, preheat your oven. 2. Mix together the garlic, leek, ginger root, wine, olive oil and mushrooms in a baking pan, and toss until the mushrooms are evenly coated. 3. Bake the food in the preheated oven for 10 minutes until lightly browned. 4. Remove the baking pan from the oven. Spread the cod fillets on top and season with sea salt and pepper. 5. Cover with aluminum foil and return to the oven. Bake for 5 to 8 minutes longer or until the fish is flaky. 6. Remove the aluminum foil and cool for 5 minutes before serving.

Per Serving: Calories 128; Total Fat 3.93g; Sodium 940mg; Total Carbs 4.19g; Fiber 0.5g; Sugars 1.29g; Protein 18.29g

Baked Miso Salmon

Prep time: 10 minutes | Cook time: 15 to 20 minutes | Servings: 4

Sauce:
¼ cup apple cider
¼ cup white miso
1 tablespoon olive oil
Fish:
4 (3-4 ounces/85-113g) boneless salmon fillets
1 sliced scallion, for garnish

1 tablespoon white rice vinegar
⅛ teaspoon ground ginger

⅛ teaspoon red pepper flakes, for garnish

At 375 degrees F, preheat your oven.
To make the sauce: Mix all the sauce ingredients in the bowl.
To make the fish: 1. Arrange the prepared salmon fillets in a baking pan, skin-side down. Spoon the prepared sauce over the fillets to coat evenly. 2. Bake in the preheated oven for almost 15 to 20 minutes, or until the fish flakes easily with a fork. 3. Garnish with the sliced scallion and red pepper flakes and serve.
Per Serving: Calories 135; Total Fat 6.06g; Sodium 664mg; Total Carbs 9.12g; Fiber 1.2g; Sugars 2.72g; Protein 10.89g

Salmon Ceviche

Prep time: 30 minutes | Cook time: 0 | Serves: 4

1 pound salmon, cut into bite-size pieces
½ cup lime juice
2 tomatoes, diced
¼ cup fresh cilantro leaves,

chopped
1 jalapeño pepper, seeded and diced
2 tablespoons olive oil
½ teaspoon sea salt

1. In a suitable bowl, stir together the salmon pieces and lime juice. Marinate the salmon pieces for 20 minutes. 2. Stir in the tomatoes, cilantro, jalapeño pepper, olive oil, and salt.
Per serving: Calories: 222; Total fat 14.2g; Sodium 288mg; Total carbs 2.6g; Fiber 0.9g; Sugars 1.8g; Protein 22.6g

Veggie Salmon Bowl

Prep time: 15 minutes | Cook time: 0 | Servings: 4

1 pound cooked salmon, flaked
4 cups cooked quinoa
6 radishes, thinly sliced
1 zucchini, sliced into half moons
3 cups arugula
3 scallions, minced

½ cup almond oil
1 teaspoon sugar-free hot sauce
1 tablespoon apple cider vinegar
1 teaspoon sea salt
½ cup toasted slivered almonds, for garnish (optional)

1. In a suitable bowl, mix together the flaked salmon, cooked quinoa, radishes, zucchini, arugula, and scallions until well. 2. Fold in the almond oil, hot sauce, apple cider vinegar and sea salt and toss to combine. 3. Divide the mixture into four bowls. Scatter each bowl evenly with the slivered almonds for garnish. Serve.
Per Serving: Calories 646; Total Fat 36.99g; Sodium 704mg; Total Carbs 40.98g; Fiber 5.8g; Sugars 2.29g; Protein 36.68g

Homemade Trout Fillets with Cucumber Salsa

Prep time: 20 minutes | Cook time: 10 minutes | Servings: 4

Salsa:
1 English cucumber, diced
¼ cup unsweetened coconut yogurt
2 tablespoons chopped fresh mint
Fish:
4 (5-ounce) trout fillets, patted dry
1 tablespoon olive oil

1 scallion, white and green parts, chopped
1 teaspoon raw honey
Sea salt

Sea salt and freshly ground black pepper, to taste

To make the salsa: Stir together all the salsa ingredients in a suitable bowl until completely mixed. Set aside.
To make the fish: 1. On a clean work surface, rub the trout fillets lightly with sea salt and pepper. 2. Heat the olive oil in the skillet over medium heat; add the trout fillets to the hot skillet and panfry for almost 10 minutes, flipping the fish halfway through, or until the fish is cooked to your liking. 3. Spread the salsa on top of the fish and serve.
Per Serving: Calories 253; Total Fat 13.42g; Sodium 111mg; Total Carbs 3.75g; Fiber 0.8g; Sugars 2.63g; Protein 27.9g

Ahi Tuna with Cucumber

Prep time: 10 minutes | Cook time: 0 | Servings: 4

pound sushi-grade ahi tuna, cut into 1-inch cubes
3 tablespoons coconut aminos
3 scallions, thinly sliced
1 serrano chili, deseeded and minced (optional)
1 teaspoon olive oil

1 teaspoon rice vinegar
1 teaspoon toasted sesame seeds
Dash ground ginger
1 large avocado, diced
1 cucumber, sliced into ½-inch-thick rounds

1. Toss the ahi tuna cubes with the coconut aminos, scallions, serrano chili (optional), olive oil, vinegar, sesame seeds, and ginger in a suitable bowl. 2. Cover this tuna bowl with plastic wrap and marinate in the fridge for almost 15 minutes. 3. Add the diced avocado to the bowl of ahi poke and stir to incorporate. 4. Arrange the cucumber rounds on a serving plate. Spoon the ahi poke over the cucumber and serve.
Per Serving: Calories 227; Total Fat 9.53g; Sodium 92mg; Total Carbs 6.41g; Fiber 4.2g; Sugars 0.98g; Protein 29.22g

Miso-Glazed Salmon

Prep time: 5 minutes | Cook time: 5 to 10 minutes | Serves: 4

4 (4-ounce) salmon fillets
3 tablespoons miso paste
2 tablespoons raw honey

1 teaspoon coconut aminos
1 teaspoon rice vinegar

1. Preheat the broiler. 2. Layer a suitable baking dish with aluminum foil and place the salmon fillets in it. 3. In a suitable bowl, stir together the miso, honey, coconut aminos, and vinegar. Brush the glaze evenly over the top of each fillet. 4. Broil for almost 5 minutes. The fish is done when it flakes easily (the cooking time depends on the thickness). 5. Brush any remaining glaze over the fish, and continue to broil for 5 minutes if needed.
Per serving: Calories: 264; Total fat: 9g; saturated fat: 1g; cholesterol: 80mg; carbohydrates: 13g; Fiber: 0g; Protein: 30g

Seared Haddock Fillets

Prep time: 20 minutes | Cook time: 40 minutes | Servings: 4

8 beets, peeled and cut into eighths
2 shallots, sliced
2 tablespoons apple cider vinegar
2 tablespoons olive oil

1 teaspoon bottled minced garlic
1 teaspoon chopped fresh thyme
Pinch sea salt
4 (5-ounce / 142-g) haddock fillets, patted dry

1. At 400 degrees F, preheat your oven. 2. Mix the beets, shallots, vinegar, garlic, thyme, sea salt and 1 tablespoon of olive oil in the bowl, and toss to coat well. Spread out the beet mixture in a baking dish. 3. Roast the mixture in the preheated oven for 30 minutes, turning once or twice with a spatula, or until the beets are tender. 4. Meanwhile, preheat the remaining olive oil in the skillet over medium-high heat. 5. Add the haddock and sear for 5 minutes per side, or until the flesh is opaque and it flakes apart easily. 6. Transfer the prepared fish to a plate and serve topped with the roasted beets.
Per Serving: Calories 279; Total Fat 7.91g; Sodium 579mg; Total Carbs 16.87g; Fiber 4.8g; Sugars 11.52g; Protein 34.32g

White Fish Chowder

Prep time: 10 minutes | Cook time: 35 minutes | Servings: 6 to 8

3 sweet potatoes, peeled and cut into ½-inch pieces
4 carrots, peeled and cut into ½-inch pieces
3 cups full-fat coconut milk
2 cups water

1 teaspoon dried thyme
½ teaspoon sea salt
10½ ounces white fish, skinless and firm, such as cod or halibut, cut into chunks

1. Add the sweet potatoes, carrots, coconut milk, water, thyme and sea salt in the saucepan over high heat, and cook to a boil. 2. Lower the heat to low, cover the pan and simmer the food for 20 minutes until the vegetables are tender with occasional stirring. 3. Pour half of the soup to a blender and purée until thoroughly mixed and smooth, then return it to the pot. 4. Stir in the fish chunks and continue cooking for 12 to 15 minutes longer. 5. Serve in bowls.
Per Serving: Calories 291; Total Fat 22.39g; Sodium 215mg; Total Carbs 16.71g; Fiber 4.1g; Sugars 5.84g; Protein 9.24g

Lemon Zoodles with Shrimp

Prep time: 25 minutes | Cook time: 0 | Servings: 4

Sauce:

½ cup packed fresh basil leaves	1 large yellow squash, julienned
Juice of 1 lemon	or spiralized
1 teaspoon minced garlic	1 large zucchini, julienned or
Pinch sea salt	spiralized
Pinch black pepper	pound shrimp, deveined, boiled,
¼ cup canned full-fat coconut	peeled, and chilled
milk	Zest of 1 lemon

1. Make the sauce: 2. Process the basil leaves, lemon juice, garlic, sea salt and pepper in a suitable food processor until chopped thoroughly. 3. Slowly pour in the coconut milk while the processor is still running. Pulse until smooth. 4. Transfer the sauce to a suitable bowl, along with the yellow squash and zucchini. Toss well. 5. Scatter the shrimp and lemon zest on top of the noodles. 6. Serve.
Per Serving: Calories 202; Total Fat 5.98g; Sodium 1381mg; Total Carbs 10.1g; Fiber 2.3g; Sugars 4.43g; Protein 27.57g

Seared Ahi Tuna with Peperonata

Prep time: 15 minutes | Cook time: 5 minutes | Serves: 4

1-lb ahi tuna fillet,	Black pepper
Olive oil for brushing	1 cup peperonata
Kosher salt	

1. At high heat, preheat your grill. 2. Rub the tuna fillet with olive oil and season with salt and pepper. Sear this seasoned tuna for 2 minutes per side. 3. Slice the tuna against the grain and divide it among four plates. 4. Spoon ¼ of the peperonata over each piece tuna slice and serve.
Per serving: Calories: 350; Total fat 9.5g; Sodium 523mg; Total carbs 4g; Fiber 1.5g; Sugars 5g; Protein 50.5g

Seared Large Scallops

Prep time: 10 minutes | Cook time: 15 minutes | Servings: 4

pound large scallops, rinsed and	¼ cup raw honey
patted dry	3 tablespoons coconut aminos
Dash sea salt	1 tablespoon apple cider vinegar
Dash black pepper	2 garlic cloves, minced
tablespoons avocado oil	

1. In a suitable bowl, toss the scallops, sea salt and pepper until coated well. 2. Heat the avocado oil in the skillet over medium-high heat. 3. Sear the scallops for 3 minutes on each side, or until the scallops turn milky white or opaque and firm. 4. Remove the scallops from the heat to a plate and loosely tent with foil to keep warm. Set aside. 5. Add the honey, coconut aminos, vinegar and garlic to the skillet and stir well. 6. Bring to a simmer and cook for 7 minutes until the liquid is reduced with occasional stirring. 7. Return the seared scallops to the skillet, stirring to coat them with the glaze. 8. Divide the scallops among four plates and serve warm.
Per Serving: Calories: 210; Total Fat 7.59g; Sodium 496mg; Total Carbs 22.04g; Fiber 0.2g; Sugars 17.73g; Protein 13.92g

Salmon Burgers

Prep time: 15 minutes | Cook time: 10 minutes | Serves: 4

pound skinless boned salmon	1 tablespoon lemon juice
fillets, minced	1 teaspoon Dijon mustard
½ cup almond flour	½ teaspoon salt
¼ cup minced sweet onion	¼ teaspoon black pepper
eggs, whisked	Dash red pepper flakes
garlic cloves, minced	1 tablespoon avocado oil

1. In a suitable bowl, mix the salmon, almond flour, onion, eggs, garlic, lemon juice, mustard, salt, black pepper, and red pepper flakes until combined. Let's rest for 5 minutes. 2. In a suitable skillet, heat the avocado oil over medium heat. 3. Form the salmon mixture into 4 patties, each about ½-inch thick. Place them in the skillet and for 4 to 5 minutes on each side, until lightly browned and firm.
Per serving: Calories: 250; Total fat: 9g; saturated fat: 5g; cholesterol: 28mg; carbohydrates: 4g; Fiber: 2g; Protein: 38g

Ahi Poke with Cucumber

Prep time: 25 minutes | Cook time: 0 | Serves: 4

1 pound sushi-grade ahi tuna,	1 teaspoon sesame oil
diced	1 teaspoon toasted sesame seeds
3 scallions, thinly sliced	Dash ground ginger
1 Serrano chili, seeded and minced	1 large avocado, diced
3 tablespoons coconut aminos	1 cucumber, sliced into ½-inch-
1 teaspoon rice vinegar	thick rounds

1. In a suitable bowl, gently mix the tuna, scallions, Serrano chili, coconut aminos, vinegar, sesame oil, sesame seeds, and ginger until well combined. 2. Cover and refrigerate to marinate for 15 minutes. Stir in the avocado, gently incorporating the chunks into the ahi mixture. 3. Arrange the cucumber slices on a plate. Place a spoonful of the ahi poke on each cucumber slice and serve immediately.
Per serving: Calories: 214; Total fat: 15g; saturated fat: 2g; cholesterol: 68mg; carbohydrates: 11g; Fiber: 4g; Protein: 10g

Easy Coconut Shrimp

Prep time: 10 minutes | Cook time: 6 minutes | Servings: 4

2 eggs	½ teaspoon sea salt
1 cup unsweetened dried coconut	Dash freshly ground black pepper
¼ cup coconut flour	¼ cup coconut oil
¼ teaspoon paprika	pound raw shrimp, peeled,
Dash cayenne pepper	deveined and patted dry

1. Beat the eggs in a suitable shallow bowl until frothy. Set aside. 2. In a separate bowl, mix the coconut flour, coconut, paprika, cayenne pepper, sea salt, and black pepper, and stir until well incorporated. 3. Dredge the shrimp in the beaten eggs, then coat the shrimp in the coconut mixture. Shake off any excess. 4. Heat the coconut oil in the skillet over medium-high heat. 5. Add the shrimp and cook for 3 to 6 minutes with occasional stirring, or until the flesh is totally pink and opaque. 6. Transfer the cooked coconut shrimp to a plate lined with paper towels to drain. Serve warm.
Per Serving: Calories 261; Total Fat 16.54g; Sodium 536mg; Total Carbs 3.29g; Fiber 1g; Sugars 2.1g; Protein 26.17g

Seared Honey-Garlic Scallops

Prep time: 10 minutes | Cook time: 15 minutes | Serves: 4

1 pound large scallops, rinsed	¼ cup raw honey
Dash salt	3 tablespoons coconut aminos
Dash black pepper	2 garlic cloves, minced
2 tablespoons avocado oil	1 tablespoon apple cider vinegar

1. Pat the scallops dry with paper towels and sprinkle with salt and pepper. 2. In a suitable skillet over medium-high heat, heat the avocado oil. 3. Place the scallops in the skillet, and cook for 2 to 3 minutes on each side until golden. Transfer to a plate, tent loosely with aluminum foil to keep warm, and set aside. 4. In the same skillet, stir together the honey, coconut aminos, garlic, and vinegar. Bring to a simmer, and cook for almost 7 minutes, occasionally stirring as the liquid reduces. 5. Return the scallops to the skillet with the glaze. Toss gently to coat and serve warm.
Per serving: Calories: 383; Total fat: 19g; saturated fat: 3g; cholesterol: 64mg; carbohydrates: 26g; Fiber: 1g; Protein: 21g

Orange Salmon

Prep time: 35 minutes | Cook time: 5 minutes | Servings: 4

1 teaspoon peeled and grated	1 tablespoon fresh orange juice
fresh ginger	1 tablespoon almond butter
2 cloves garlic, minced	½ teaspoon salt
1 tablespoon coconut aminos	pound salmon

1. Blend the garlic, ginger, orange juice, coconut aminos, almond butter and salt in the blender until smooth. 2. Set the salmon into a suitable glass bowl and pour the prepared marinade over the salmon. 3. Place this salmon in the refrigerator and allow to marinate 30 minutes. 4. Add 1 cup water to the inner insert and place the steam rack inside. 5. Set the bowl with the salmon on top of the steam rack. Seal the cooker's lid. 6. Select the Manual or Pressure mode and adjust the time to 3 minutes. 7. Release the pressure completely then remove its lid. 8. Remove the cooked salmon from the bowl and serve.
Per Serving: Calories 175; Total Fat 7.9g; Sodium 403mg; Total Carbs 1.13g; Fiber 0.1g; Sugars 0.45g; Protein 23.44g

Lemony Salmon with Asparagus

Prep time: 5 minutes | Cook time: 5 minutes | Servings: 2

1 medium lemon
2 (5-ounce) salmon filets
2 tablespoons avocado oil, divided
½ teaspoon salt, divided
¼ teaspoon black pepper, divided
10 large asparagus spears, woody ends removed

1. Zest the lemon and set the zest aside. Slice half of the lemon and juice the other half. 2. Brush each salmon filet with ½ tablespoon of avocado oil, then top with ⅛ teaspoon of salt and 1/16 teaspoon pepper. 3. Add the remaining oil, salt and pepper to the asparagus spears. 4. Place the salmon and asparagus in a steamer basket. 5. Add the lemon juice on top of the salmon and asparagus and sprinkle with the zest. 6. Place 1 cup of water in the inner pot and place the steam rack inside. Place the steamer basket with the salmon and asparagus on top of the rack. Seal the cooker's lid. 7. Select the Manual or Pressure mode and adjust the time to 3 minutes. 8. Release the pressure completely then remove its lid.
Per Serving: Calories 218; Total Fat 16.76g; Sodium 617mg; Total Carbs 2.56g; Fiber 0.5g; Sugars 0.94g; Protein 14.78g

Strawberry Shrimp Salad

Prep time: 15 minutes | Cook time: 0 minutes | Serves: 2

¼ cup extra-virgin olive oil
¼ cup apple cider vinegar
2 tablespoons fresh lemon juice
1 tablespoon raw honey
1 tablespoon Dijon mustard
1 garlic clove, minced
¼ teaspoon salt
¼ teaspoon black pepper
12 frozen jumbo shrimp
1 teaspoon Montreal steak seasoning
1 tablespoon avocado oil
8 cups mixed spring greens
⅔ cup chopped jicama
1½ cups sliced strawberries
⅔ cup pecans

1. In a small container or jar with a tight lid, add the olive oil, vinegar, lemon juice, honey, mustard, garlic, salt, and pepper and shake until the ingredients are well combined. Set aside. 2. Pour 1½ cups water into the insert of the Instant pot and set the steam rack inside. Add the shrimp to the steamer basket and place it on the rack. 3. Close the lid and secure it well. Hit the the manual cook button and adjust the time to 0 minutes. 4. When cooked, release the pressure quickly until the float valve drops and then unlock lid. 5. Carefully remove the steamer basket from the inner pot. 6. Peel the shrimp and place them in a suitable bowl. Add the steak seasoning and gently toss to layer the shrimp in the seasoning. 7. Remove the water from the insert of the Instant pot and wipe it dry. Press the sauté button and use the adjust button to change to the more setting. 8. Add the avocado oil to the insert of the Instant pot and allow it to heat 1 minute. Add the shrimp and cook to brown, 1 minute per side. 9. Put the greens, jicama, strawberries, pecans, and shrimp in a suitable bowl. Drizzle with the dressing and toss gently to coat.
Per serving: Calories 425; Fat 25g; Sodium 408mg; Carbs 33.3g; Fiber 10.8g; Sugars 15.1g; Protein 22.3g

Citrus Salmon with Greens

Prep time: 10 minutes | Cook time: 25 minutes | Serves: 4

¼ cup olive oil
1½ pounds salmon
1 teaspoon sea salt
½ teaspoon black pepper
Zest of 1 lemon
6 cups stemmed and chopped Swiss chard
3 garlic cloves, minced
Juice of 2 lemons

1. In a suitable nonstick skillet, heat 2 tablespoons of the olive oil over medium-high heat until it shimmers. 2. Season the salmon with ½ teaspoon of salt, ¼ teaspoon of pepper, and lemon zest. 3. Add the salmon to the skillet, skin-side up, and cook for almost 7 minutes until the flesh is opaque. 4. Flip the salmon and cook for 3 to 4 minutes to crisp the skin. Set aside on a plate, tented with aluminum foil. 5. Return the skillet to the heat, add the remaining olive oil, and heat it until it shimmers. 6. Add the Swiss chard. Cook for almost 7 minutes, occasionally stirring, until soft. 7. Add the garlic and cook for 30 seconds, stirring constantly. Sprinkle in the lemon juice, the remaining ½ teaspoon of salt, and the remaining pepper, cook them for 2 minutes. 8. Serve the salmon on the Swiss chard.
Per serving: Calories: 474; Total fat 25.6g; Sodium 430mg; Total carbs 1.5g; Fiber 0.5g; Sugars 0.3g; Protein 61.1g

Halibut Fillets with Pineapple Avocado Salsa

Prep time: 15 minutes | Cook time: 5 minutes | Servings: 4

1 cup pineapple, diced
2 tomatoes, seeded and diced
2 medium avocados, peeled, pitted, and diced
1 medium jalapeño pepper, seeded and diced
½ cup chopped cilantro
1 medium lime, juiced
1 teaspoon salt, divided
⅛ teaspoon cayenne pepper
4 (4-ounce) halibut filets
¼ teaspoon black pepper

1. Mix the avocado, pineapple, tomatoes, ½ teaspoon of salt, jalapeño, cilantro, lime juice and cayenne pepper in the bowl. 2. Rub the halibut with the remaining ½ teaspoon of salt and pepper. 3. Pour 1 cup water into the pot of the Instant Pot and set the steam rack inside. 4. Set the halibut on top of the steam rack. Seal the cooker's lid. 5. Select the Manual or Pressure mode and adjust the time to 3 minutes. 5. Release the pressure completely then remove its lid. 6. Place the cooked halibut filets in the plates and top each filet with Pineapple Avocado Salsa.
Per Serving: Calories 251; Total Fat 18.87g; Sodium 637mg; Total Carbs 17.95g; Fiber 8.1g; Sugars 5.51g; Protein 7.29g

Cod with Lentils

Prep time: 15 minutes | Cook time: 35 minutes | Serves: 4

Cooking spray
1 tablespoon slow-cooker ghee
4 (6-ounce) cod fillets
1 teaspoon salt
¼ teaspoon black pepper
2 shallots, sliced thin
1 garlic clove, sliced thin
2 carrots, diced
1 medium turnip, diced
2 cups shredded kale, washed
2 (15-ounce) cans lentils, drained and rinsed
1 tablespoon apple cider vinegar

1. At 375 degrees F, preheat your oven. Lightly coat a rimmed baking sheet with cooking spray. 2. In a suitable pan, melt the ghee over high heat. 3. While the ghee is melting, sprinkle the cod with salt and pepper. Place each fillet top-side down in the pan (the top side is the plumper, rounded side of the fillet). Sear the fillets for almost 4 minutes, or until golden. 4. Transfer the fillets to the prepared baking sheet, top-side up. Place the sheet in the preheated oven and bake for 15 to 20 minutes, or until firm and cooked through. 5. While the fish is baking, add the shallots and garlic to the pan used to sear the fish sauté them for 3 minutes. 6. Add the carrots and turnip, sauté them for 10 minutes more, or until tender. 7. Add the kale, lentils, and cider vinegar to the pan and cook for almost 1 minute to warm through. Remove this pan from the heat. 8. Divide the lentil mixture among four plates and top each with a cod fillet.
Per serving: Calories: 450; Total fat: 6g; Sodium: 1251mg; Total Carbs: 51g; Sugars: 7g; Fiber: 19g; Protein: 51g

Coconut-Crusted Cod with Herb-Tartar Sauce

Prep time: 15 minutes | Cook time: 20 minutes | Serves: 4

For the Fish
¼ cup melted coconut oil
¼ cup almond or coconut flour
½ teaspoon salt
¼ teaspoon black pepper
½ cup coconut flakes,
unsweetened
¼ cup ground flaxseed
1 large egg
1 pound cod fillet, skinned and cut into 4 equal pieces
For the Sauce
½ cup anti-inflammatory mayo
2 tablespoons lemon juice
2 tablespoons chopped capers
½ teaspoon red pepper flakes
½ teaspoon salt
¼ teaspoon black pepper

1. To make the fish: At 375 degrees F, preheat your oven. Layer a baking sheet with aluminum foil and coat with 2 tablespoons of coconut oil. 2. In a shallow bowl, combine the almond flour, salt, and pepper. 3. In a second shallow bowl, combine the coconut flakes and flaxseed. In a third shallow bowl, beat the egg. 4. Dredge each cod piece, one at a time, first in the almond flour, then the beaten egg, and then the coconut-flaxseed mixture, to coat well. Set the fish on the prepared baking sheet. 5.Drizzle with the rest of the 2 tablespoons of coconut oil and bake for almost 15 to 18 minutes until the fish is golden and crispy. 6. To make the sauce: While the fish cooks, in a suitable bowl, combine the mayo, lemon juice, capers, red pepper flakes, salt, and pepper and whisk well with a fork. 7. Serve each piece of fish with the sauce.
Per serving: Calories 492; Fat 13.6g; Sodium 595mg; Carbs 5.7g; Fiber 3.8g; Sugars 0.6g; Protein 85.7g

Honey-Balsamic Salmon

Prep time: 15 minutes | Cook time: 3 minutes | Serves: 4

2 tablespoons balsamic vinegar	1½ cups water
1 tablespoon raw honey	1 bunch asparagus, trimmed and
1 teaspoon sea salt	halved
½ teaspoon black pepper	2 tablespoons ghee
4 salmon fillets (about 2½ pounds	Juice of 1 lemon
total)	

1. In a suitable bowl, whisk the vinegar, honey, ½ teaspoon of salt, and the pepper to combine. Drizzle the honey-vinegar mixture over the salmon, and using the back of the spoon, spread it evenly across the salmon. 2. Place a metal trivet or steam rack in the instant pot and pour in 1 cup of water. Set the salmon on the trivet, skin-side down. 3. Lock the lid. Select pressure cook and cook at high pressure for almost 3 minutes. 4. When cooking is complete, use a quick release. Remove the lid. 5. Using potholders, remove the trivet and salmon fillets and transfer the fish to a serving platter or glass dish and cover with aluminum foil. Set aside. 6. Turn off the heat. Put the asparagus, the rest of the ½ cup of water, the ghee, and remaining ½ teaspoon of salt into the instant pot. 7. Lock the lid. Select pressure cook and cook at high pressure to 0 minutes. 8. When cooking is complete, use a quick release. Remove the lid and transfer the cooked asparagus to the serving platter with the fish. 9. Pour the lemon juice over the asparagus and fish and serve.

Per serving: Calories 311; Fat 17.4g; Sodium 557mg; Carbs 4.8g; Fiber 0.2g; Sugars 4.4g; Protein 34.7g

Lemon-Caper Trout with Caramelized Shallots

Prep time: 10 minutes | Cook time: 30 minutes | Serves: 2

For the Shallots

2 shallots, thinly sliced	Dash salt
1 teaspoon ghee	

For the Trout

1 tablespoon plus 1 teaspoon ghee	¼ teaspoon salt
2 (4-ounce) trout fillets	Dash black pepper
¼ cup lemon juice	1 lemon, thinly sliced
3 tablespoons capers	

1. To make the shallots: In a suitable skillet, cook the shallots, ghee, and salt for 20 minutes over medium heat, stirring every 5 minutes, until the shallots have fully wilted and caramelized. 2. To make the trout: While the shallots cook, in another large skillet over medium heat, heat 1 teaspoon of ghee. 3. Add the trout fillets and cook for almost 3 minutes on each side, or until the center is flaky. Transfer to a plate and set aside. 4. In the skillet used for the trout, add lemon juice, capers, salt, and pepper. Bring to a simmer. 5. Whisk in the remaining 1 tablespoon of ghee. Spoon the sauce over the fish. 6. Garnish the fish with lemon slices and caramelized shallots before serving.

Per serving: Calories: 399; Total fat: 22g; saturated fat: 10g; cholesterol: 46mg; carbohydrates: 17g; Fiber: 2g; Protein: 21g

Whitefish Curry

Prep time: 15 minutes | Cook time: 15 minutes | Serves: 4 to 6

2 tablespoons coconut oil	2 cups chopped broccoli
1 onion, chopped	1 (13.5-ounce) can coconut milk
2 garlic cloves, minced	1 cup vegetable broth or chicken
1 tablespoon minced fresh ginger	broth
2 teaspoons curry powder	1 pound firm whitefish fillets
1 teaspoon salt	¼ cup chopped fresh cilantro
¼ teaspoon black pepper	1 scallion, sliced thin
1 (4-inch) piece lemongrass	Lemon wedges, for garnish
2 cups cubed butternut squash	

1. In a suitable pot, melt the coconut oil over medium-high heat; add the onion, garlic, ginger, curry powder, salt, and pepper, sauté them for 5 minutes. 2. Add the lemongrass, butternut squash, and broccoli, sauté them for 2 minutes more. 3. Stir in the coconut milk and vegetable broth and bring to a boil. Reduce its heat to simmer and add the fish. 4. Cover the pot and simmer for 5 minutes, or until the fish is cooked through. 5. Remove and discard the lemongrass. Ladle the curry into a serving bowl. 6. Garnish with the cilantro and scallion and serve with the lemon wedges.

Per serving: Calories: 553; Total fat: 39g; Total Carbs: 22g; Sugars: 7g; Fiber: 6g; Protein: 34g; Sodium: 881mg

Thai Seafood Chowder

Prep time: 15 minutes | Cook time: 15 minutes | Serves: 4

2 tablespoons coconut oil	miso paste and 2 tablespoons
1 red bell pepper, chopped	water)
1 (2-inch) piece fresh ginger,	1 to 2 teaspoons monk fruit
peeled and minced	extract
6 garlic cloves, sliced	8 ounces wild-caught shrimp,
1 jalapeño, chopped (seeded for	peeled and deveined
less heat, if preferred)	8 ounces cod fillet, skinned and
2 teaspoons Thai green curry paste	cut into bite-size chunks
2 (15-ounce) cans full-fat coconut	Grated zest and juice of 1 lime
milk	½ to 1 cup sliced fresh basil
¼ cup tamari (or 2 tablespoons	Sliced jalapeño, for garnish

1. In a large stockpot, heat the coconut oil over medium heat. 2. Add the bell pepper, ginger, garlic, and jalapeño and sauté for almost 4 to 5 minutes, until the vegetables are tender. 3. Add the curry paste and sauté for almost 1 minute, then add the coconut milk and tamari and whisk to combine well. Stir in the monk fruit extract. 4. Bring the prepared mixture to a boil. Reduce its heat to low, add the shrimp and cod, cover and simmer for almost 3 to 4 minutes, until the seafood is cooked through but not overly done. 5. Remove from the heat and stir in the lime zest and juice and basil. 6. Serve warm, garnished with the jalapeño.

Per serving: Calories 439; Fat 38.8g; Sodium 813mg; Carbs 11.5g; Fiber 3.7g; Sugars 6g; Protein 16.8g

Herbed Salmon Orzo Antipasto

Prep time: 15 minutes | Cook time: 7 minutes | Serves: 4

2 tablespoons avocado oil	1 teaspoon Italian seasoning
1½ cups orzo	1 cup water
1 small yellow onion, diced	1 pound salmon fillets
3 garlic cloves, minced	½ teaspoon black pepper
2¾ cups vegetable broth	1 tablespoon extra-virgin olive oil
1 cup diced tomatoes	2 tablespoons chopped fresh
¼ cup fresh basil, chopped	parsley
2 teaspoons sea salt	

1. Select sauté on the instant pot and let the pot preheat. 2. Add the avocado oil, orzo, onion, and garlic. Cook for almost 3 minutes. 3. Stir in the broth, tomatoes, basil, 1 teaspoon of salt, and the Italian seasoning to combine. 4. Turn off the heat. Lock the lid. Pressure cook at high for almost 3 minutes. 5. When cooked, use a quick release. 6. Remove the lid and transfer the cooked orzo to a suitable bowl, cover, and set aside. 7. Place a metal trivet or steam rack in the instant pot and pour in the water. Set the salmon fillets on the trivet in a single layer and season with the rest of the 1 teaspoon of salt and the pepper. 8. Lock the lid. Pressure cook at high for almost 1 minute. 9. When cooked, use a quick release. 10. Remove the lid and, using a spatula, transfer the cooked salmon to a cutting board. 11. Using two forks, shred the salmon and let cool. Once cooled, add the salmon to the orzo and stir well to combine. 11. Drizzle with the olive oil and top with the parsley to serve.

Per serving: Calories 46; Fat 13.6g; Sodium 1326mg; Carbs 53g; Fiber 3.6g; Sugars 5.8g; Protein 32.9g

Coconut-Crusted Shrimp

Prep time: 10 minutes | Cook time: 6 minutes | Serves: 4

2 eggs	Dash cayenne pepper
1 cup unsweetened dried coconut	Dash black pepper
¼ cup coconut flour	¼ cup coconut oil
½ teaspoon salt	1 pound raw shrimp, peeled and
¼ teaspoon paprika	deveined

1. In a small shallow bowl, beat all the eggs. 2. In another small shallow bowl, mix the coconut, coconut flour, salt, paprika, cayenne pepper, and black pepper. 3. In a suitable skillet, heat the coconut oil over medium-high heat. 4. Pat the shrimp dry with a paper towel. 5. Working one at a time, hold each shrimp by the tail, dip it into the egg mixture, and then into the coconut mixture until coated. Place into the hot skillet. Cook for almost 3 minutes on each side. 6. Transfer the hot shrimp to a paper towel-lined plate to drain excess oil. Serve immediately.

Per serving: Calories: 279; Total fat: 2 0g; saturated fat: 15g; cholesterol: 258mg; carbohydrates: 6g; Fiber: 3g; Protein: 19g

Lemon Dill Salmon

Prep time: 15 minutes | Cook time: 3 minutes | Serves: 4

4 (4", 6-ounce) salmon filets	1 teaspoon dried dill weed
1 teaspoon avocado oil	½ teaspoon salt
Juice of 1 medium lemon	

1. Brush the salmon filets with oil, then top with the lemon juice, dill weed, and salt. 2. Add 1 cup water to the instant pot and set the steam rack inside. 3. Set the salmon filets on top of the steam rack. Close the lid and secure it well. 4. Hit the manual cook button and adjust the time to 3 minutes. 5. When cooked, release the pressure quickly until the float valve drops and then unlock lid. 6. Serve immediately.
Per serving: Calories 282; Fat 12.7g; Sodium 378mg; Carbs 0.2g; Fiber 0.1g; Sugars 0g; Protein 39.2g

Trout with Sweet-And-Sour Chard

Prep time: 10 minutes | Cook time: 15 minutes | Serves: 4

4 boneless trout fillets	2 garlic cloves, minced
Salt	2 bunches chard, sliced
Black pepper	¼ cup golden raisins
1 tablespoon olive oil	1 tablespoon apple cider vinegar
1 onion, chopped	½ cup vegetable broth

1. At 375 degrees F, preheat your oven. 2. Season the trout with salt and pepper. 3. In a suitable ovenproof pan over medium-high heat, heat the olive oil. Add the onion and garlic, sauté them for 3 minutes; add the chard and sauté for 2 minutes more. 4. Add the raisins, cider vinegar, and broth to the pan. Layer the trout fillets on top. 5. Cover the pan and cook it in the preheated oven for almost 10 minutes, or until the trout is cooked through.
Per serving: Calories: 231; Total fat: 10g; Total Carbs: 13g; Sugars: 7g; Fiber: 2g; Protein: 24g; Sodium: 235mg

Coconut-Crusted Cod with Mango-Pineapple Salsa

Prep time: 15 minutes | Cook time: 7 minutes | Serves: 4

For the Salsa

1 cup diced mango	Juice of 1 lime
1 cup diced pineapple	Dash salt
½ large avocado, diced	Dash chili powder

For the Cod

1 egg	1 teaspoon salt
1 cup unsweetened dried coconut	½ teaspoon garlic powder
2 tablespoons avocado oil	¼ teaspoon cayenne pepper
4 (4-ounce) cod fillets	

1. To make the salsa: In a suitable bowl, gently stir together the mango, pineapple, avocado, lime juice, salt, and chili powder. 2. To make the cod: In a small shallow bowl, beat the egg. Put the coconut in another small shallow bowl. 3. Dip each cod fillet into the egg, then into the coconut until well coated, and place on a plate. 4. Sprinkle each fillet with salt, garlic powder and cayenne pepper. 5. In a suitable skillet, heat the avocado oil over medium-high heat. Cook each fillet one at a time in the hot skillet for 4 to 5 minutes. 6. Flip and cook on the other side for 1 to 2 minutes until the flesh begins to flake. Transfer to a plate. 7. Top each fillet with salsa and serve.
Per serving: Calories: 379; Total fat: 27g; saturated fat: 14g; cholesterol: 107mg; carbohydrates: 18g; Fiber: 5g; Protein: 18g

Baked Spice Salmon Steaks

Prep time: 5 minutes | Cook time: 15 to 20 minutes | Serves: 4

Cooking spray	1 tablespoon olive oil
4 (6-ounce) salmon steaks	1 tablespoon spice rub

1. At 375 degrees F, preheat your oven. 2. Lightly spray a suitable rimmed baking sheet with cooking spray. 3. Place the salmon steaks on the baking sheet and brush both sides with olive oil. Season both sides of the steaks with the spice rub. 4. Place the sheet in the preheated oven and bake the salmon for 15 to 20 minutes, or until the steaks are firm and cooked through.
Per serving: Calories: 255; Total fat: 14g; Sodium: 210mg; Total Carbs: 0g; Sugars: 0g; Fiber: 0g; Protein: 33g

Salmon with Gremolata

Prep time: 10 minutes | Cook time: 20 minutes | Serves: 4

4 (5-ounce) skin-on salmon fillets	1 bunch basil
1 tablespoon plus	1 garlic clove
2 teaspoons olive oil	1 tablespoon lemon zest
¼ cup lemon juice	1 (8-ounce) bag mixed greens
1 teaspoon salt, plus additional for seasoning	1 small cucumber, sliced
¼ teaspoon black pepper, plus additional for seasoning	1 cup sprouts (radish, or sunflower)

1. At 375 degrees F, preheat your oven. 2. In a suitable shallow baking dish, place the salmon fillets, brush them with 2 teaspoons of olive oil and add the lemon juice, season the fillets with 1 teaspoon of salt and ¼ teaspoon of pepper. 3. Place the dish in the preheated oven and bake the fillets for almost 20 minutes, or until firm and cooked through. 4. In a suitable food processor, combine the basil, garlic, and lemon zest. Process until chopped. 5. Arrange the greens, cucumber, and sprouts on a serving platter. Drizzle the greens with the remaining olive oil and season with salt and pepper. 6. Set the salmon fillets on top of the greens and spoon the gremolata over the salmon.
Per serving: Calories: 274; Total fat: 12g; Sodium: 908mg; Total Carbs: 11g; Sugars: 5g; Fiber: 5g; Protein: 32g

Sole with Vegetables

Prep time: 15 minutes | Cook time: 15 minutes | Serves: 4

4 (5-ounce) sole fillets	2 tablespoons snipped fresh chives
Salt	
Black pepper	4 teaspoons olive oil
1 zucchini, sliced thin	½ cup vegetable broth or water
1 carrot, sliced thin	Lemon wedges, for garnish
2 shallots, sliced thin	

1. At 425 degrees F, preheat your oven. 2. Tear off four 12-by-20-inch pieces of aluminum foil. 3. Place one fillet on one half of a foil piece. Season the fillet with salt and pepper. 4. Top the fillet with one-quarter each of the zucchini, carrot, and shallots. Sprinkle with 1½ teaspoon of chives. 5. Drizzle 1 teaspoon of olive oil and 2 tablespoons of vegetable broth over the vegetables and fish. 6. Cover the other half of the foil over the fish and vegetables, sealing the edges, so the ingredients are completely encased in the packet and the contents won't leak. Place the packet on a suitable baking sheet. 7. Repeat steps 3 through 6 with the remaining ingredients. 8. Place the sheet in the preheated oven and bake the packets for 15 minutes, or until the fish is cooked through and the vegetables are tender. 9. Carefully peel back the foil (the escaping steam will be hot) and transfer the contents—the liquid, too—to a plate. Serve garnished with lemon wedges.
Per serving: Calories: 224; Total fat: 7g; Sodium: 205mg; Total Carbs: 4g; Sugars: 2g; Fiber: 1g; Protein: 35g

Mediterranean Poached Cod

Prep time: 15 minutes | Cook time: 25 minutes | Serves: 4

1 pound cod fillet, cut into 4 equal pieces	or black olives, drained and halved
1 teaspoon salt	4 large garlic cloves, peeled and crushed
½ teaspoon black pepper	
½ cup extra-virgin olive oil	2 tablespoons chopped fresh rosemary, or 2 teaspoons dried
1 red bell pepper, sliced	
1 (14-ounce) can artichoke hearts, drained and quartered	¼ cup white wine vinegar or rice vinegar
1 (6-ounce) can large pitted green	

1. Sprinkle the cod with black pepper and salt. 2. In a suitable skillet, heat 2 tablespoons of olive oil over medium-high heat. Sear the cod for almost 1 to 2 minutes per side. Transfer the fish to a serving dish and keep warm. 3. In the same skillet, add the rest of the 6 tablespoons of olive oil over medium heat. Add the bell pepper, artichokes, olives, garlic, and rosemary and sauté for almost 2 to 3 minutes until very fragrant. 4. Reduce its heat to low, stir in the vinegar, return the cod to this skillet, cover and poach for almost 10 to 12 minutes, until the fish is cooked through and the vegetables are tender. 5. Serve the cod and vegetables warm, drizzled with the cooking oil.
Per serving: Calories 419; Fat 31g; Sodium 1118mg; Carbs 16.6g; Fiber 7.3g; Sugars 2.6g; Protein 24.1g

Shrimp Scampi and Vegetables

Prep time: 15 minutes | Cook time: 35 minutes | Serves: 4

1½ cups wild rice, rinsed	1 pound raw shrimp, peeled and
1½ cups water	deveined
1 teaspoon sea salt	1 cup frozen peas
2 tablespoons avocado oil	⅛ teaspoon red pepper flakes
1 red bell pepper, chopped	Juice of 1 lemon
5 garlic cloves, minced	Black pepper
2 tablespoons ghee	¼ cup fresh parsley, chopped

1. In the instant pot, combine the wild rice, water, and salt. 2. Lock the lid. Select pressure cook and cook at high pressure for almost 28 minutes. 3. When cooked, use a natural release for almost 10 minutes, then quick release any remaining pressure. 4. Turn off the heat. Remove the lid and transfer the cooked rice to a dish and set aside. 5. Select sauté on the instant pot, pour in the oil, and add the bell pepper and garlic. Cook for almost 2 minutes, while stirring. Stir in the ghee and shrimp and cook for almost 2 minutes. 6. Add the peas, red pepper flakes, and lemon juice. Cook for almost 2 minutes. 7. Return the cooked rice to the pot. Cook for almost 3 minutes until the shrimp are completely pink. Turn off the heat. 8. Season with black pepper and top with the parsley to serve.
Per serving: Calories 463; Fat 10.1g; Sodium 784mg; Carbs 56.8g; Fiber 6.9g; Sugars 5g; Protein 37.5g

Power Poke Bowl

Prep time: 15 minutes | Cook time: 0 minutes | Serves: 4

¼ cup tamari	1 to 2 teaspoons sriracha or other
¼ cup sesame oil	hot sauce
1 tablespoon minced fresh ginger,	4 cups mixed greens
or ½ teaspoon ground ginger	¼ cup chopped fresh cilantro or
1 to 2 teaspoons red pepper flakes	basil
8 ounces sashimi-grade tuna or	1 avocado, sliced
smoked salmon, cut into bite-size	8 thin slices cucumber
cubes	¼ cup sliced scallions, white and
¼ cup anti-inflammatory mayo	green parts
2 tablespoons rice vinegar or lime	2 teaspoons sesame seeds
juice	

1. In a suitable bowl, whisk together the tamari, sesame oil, ginger, and red pepper flakes. Add the tuna, toss to coat, cover and refrigerate for at least 30 minutes or up to overnight. 2. While the tuna marinates, in a suitable bowl whisk together the mayo, vinegar, and sriracha. Set aside. 3. To prepare the bowls, divide the salad greens and cilantro between bowls. Top with the avocado, cucumber, and scallions. 4. Add half of the marinated tuna mixture and the liquid to each bowl. 5. Drizzle with the spicy mayonnaise mixture and sesame seeds. Serve immediately.
Per serving: Calories 352; Fat 18.4g; Sodium 1486mg; Carbs 35g; Fiber 10g; Sugars 11.1g; Protein 15.2g

Snapper Piccata

Prep time: 15 minutes | Cook time: 20 minutes | Serves: 4

¼ cup almond flour	2 tablespoons minced shallot or
1 teaspoon salt	red onion
½ teaspoon black pepper	2 tablespoons dry white wine
1 pound red snapper fillet, skinned	3 tablespoons chopped capers
and cut into 4 equal pieces	Juice of 1 lemon (about 2
2 tablespoons extra-virgin olive	tablespoons)
oil	¼ cup chopped parsley
½ cup unsalted butter	

1. In a shallow dish, combine the almond flour, salt, and pepper. Dredge the fish in the flour, shaking off any excess. 2. In a suitable skillet, heat the olive oil and 2 tablespoons of butter over medium-high heat. 3. Sear the fish for almost 2 to 3 minutes on each side, until browned and cooked through. Transfer to a serving dish and keep warm. 4. In the same skillet, melt 2 tablespoons of butter. Add the shallot and sauté for almost 1 to 2 minutes, until just tender. 5. Whisk in the wine, bring to a simmer, then reduce its heat to low. Add the capers and lemon juice and simmer for almost 1 to 2 minutes. 6. Remove this skillet from the heat and whisk in the rest of the 4 tablespoons of butter until melted. Stir in the parsley. 7. To serve, spoon the sauce over each piece of fish.
Per serving: Calories 461; Fat 35.4g; Sodium 815mg; Carbs 2.6g; Fiber 1.1g; Sugars 0.3g; Protein 31.8g

Halibut in Parchment

Prep time: 5 minutes | Cook time: 3 minutes | Serves: 2

¼ teaspoon dried dill weed	1 teaspoon avocado oil
1 tablespoon Dijon mustard	1 medium lemon
1 tablespoon chicken stock	2 (5-ounce, 1"-thick) halibut filets

1. Cut two large pieces of parchment paper (about 15" by 16") and fold them in half width-wise. Set aside. 2. In a suitable bowl, whisk together the dill weed, mustard, stock, and oil. 3. Cut the lemon in half. Slice half of it and juice the other half; set the juice aside. 4. Unfold a piece of parchment paper and place one halibut filet on one side of the crease. 5. Pour 1 tablespoon lemon juice over the halibut and then top with half of the mustard-dill sauce and then add half of the lemon slices. 6. Fold the opposite side of the parchment paper over the side with the fish. Make small overlapping pleats to seal the open sides and create a half-moon-shaped packet. 7. Make sure to press each crease as you fold. Repeat so you have two parchment packs. 8. Pour 1 cup water into the instant pot and set the steam rack inside. 9. Set the parchment packets in a 7-cup round bowl and add aluminum foil to the top and set the bowl on top of the steam rack. Close the lid and secure it well. 10. Hit the manual cook button and adjust the time to 3 minutes. 11. When cooked, release the pressure quickly until the float valve drops and then unlock lid. Serve the halibut in the parchment packets.
Per serving: Calories 209; Fat 1.8g; Sodium 187mg; Carbs 3.3g; Fiber 1.2g; Sugars 0.8g; Protein 43.4g

Mediterranean Halibut over Quinoa

Prep time: 15 minutes | Cook time: 2 minutes | Serves: 4

1 cup quinoa, rinsed	¼ cup chopped black olives
1 cup sliced shiitake mushrooms	2 cups fresh spinach
1½ cups vegetable broth	1 cup water
1 teaspoon sea salt	4 halibut fillets, 6 ounces each
½ cup shredded carrot	Black pepper
½ cup chopped tomatoes	1 tablespoon extra-virgin olive oil
¼ cup sliced red onion	

1. In the instant pot, combine the quinoa, mushrooms, broth, and ½ teaspoon of salt. 2. Lock the lid. Select pressure cook and cook at high pressure for almost 1 minute. 3. When cooking is complete, use a natural release for almost 10 minutes, then quick release any remaining pressure. 4. Remove the lid. Add the carrot, tomatoes, red onion, olives, and spinach to the pot. Stir to combine with the quinoa. 5. Turn off the heat. Transfer the quinoa and vegetable mixture to a serving dish and cover with aluminum foil. 6. Place a metal trivet or steam rack in the instant pot and pour in the water. Set the halibut fillets on the trivet in an even layer and season with the rest of the ½ teaspoon of black pepper and salt to taste. 7. Lock the lid. Select pressure cook and cook at high pressure for almost 1 minute. 8. When cooking is complete, use a quick release. 9. Remove the lid and set the cooked halibut on the quinoa and vegetables. 10. Drizzle with olive oil to serve.
Per serving: Calories 573; Fat 12.3g; Sodium 1860mg; Carbs 37.5g; Fiber 5.1g; Sugars 3.9g; Protein 74.6g

Mediterranean Fish Stew

Prep time: 15 minutes | Cook time: 15 minutes | Serves: 4

1 tablespoon olive oil	1 teaspoon ground oregano
1 white onion, sliced thin	1 teaspoon salt
1 fennel bulb, sliced thin	½ teaspoon black pepper
2 garlic cloves, minced	2 pounds firm white fish fillets,
1 (28-ounce) can crushed	cut into 2-inch pieces
tomatoes	2 tablespoons fresh parsley,
Pinch saffron threads	chopped
1 teaspoon ground cumin	½ lemon, for garnish

1. In a suitable pot or pan, heat 1 tablespoon of olive oil over medium-high heat. Add the onion, fennel, and garlic, sauté them for 5 minutes. 2. Stir in the crushed tomatoes, saffron threads, cumin, oregano, salt, and pepper. Bring the mixture to a simmer. 3. Lay the prepared fish fillets in a single layer over the vegetables, cover the pan, and simmer for 10 minutes. 4. Transfer the fish and vegetables to a serving platter. Garnish with the parsley, a drizzle of olive oil, and a generous squeeze of lemon juice.
Per serving: Calories: 535; Total fat: 21g; Sodium: 1144mg; Total Carbs: 24g; Sugars: 12g; Fiber: 9g; Protein: 62g

Salmon and Asparagus Skewers

Prep time: 15 minutes | Cook time: 10 minutes | Serves: 8 skewers

2 tablespoons ghee, melted
1 teaspoon Dijon mustard
1 teaspoon garlic powder
½ teaspoon salt
¼ teaspoon red pepper flakes
1½ pounds boned skinless

salmon, cut into 2-inch chunks
2 lemons, thinly sliced
1 bunch asparagus spears, tough
ends trimmed, cut into 2-inch
pieces

1. Preheat the broiler. Layer a baking sheet with aluminum foil. 2. In a suitable saucepan, melt the ghee over medium heat. 3. Stir in the mustard, garlic powder, salt, and red pepper flakes. 4. On each skewer, thread 1 chunk of salmon, 1 lemon slice folded in half, and 2 pieces of asparagus. Repeat with the remaining skewers until all the recipe ingredients are used. 5. Place the salmon skewers on the prepared pan and brush each with the ghee-seasoning mixture. 6. Broil the skewers for 4 minutes. Turn the skewers and broil on the other side for almost 4 minutes.
Per serving: (2 skewers): Calories: 250; Total fat: 9g; saturated fat: 5g; cholesterol: 68mg; carbohydrates: 4g; Fiber: 2g; Protein: 38g

Curried Poached Halibut

Prep time: 5 minutes | Cook time: 25 minutes | Serves: 4

1 tablespoon avocado oil
½ cup diced white onion
2 garlic cloves, minced
1 tablespoon red curry paste
1½ cups chicken broth

1 (14-ounce) can coconut milk
½ teaspoon coconut sugar
1 teaspoon salt
½ teaspoon black pepper
4 (4-ounce) halibut fillets

1. In a suitable skillet, heat the avocado oil over medium heat. 2. Add the onion and garlic, and sauté for 2 to 3 minutes until the onions are translucent. Stir in the curry paste until incorporated. 3. Add the broth, coconut milk, coconut sugar, salt, and pepper and stir to combine. Reduce its heat to medium-low and gently simmer for 10 minutes. 4. Pat the halibut dry with a paper towel. Place each fillet into the curried broth. Cover and poach for 10 minutes. Check the fish for doneness; if it flakes, it should be done. 5. To speed the cooking time, occasionally spoon some broth over the halibut as it cooks. 6. Serve the fillets in four bowls with the curried broth spooned on top.
Per serving: Calories: 358; Total fat: 22g; saturated fat: 17g; cholesterol: 68mg; carbohydrates: 10g; Fiber: 1g; Protein: 28g

Orange and Maple-Glazed Salmon

Prep time: 15 minutes | Cook time: 15 minutes | Serves: 4

Juice of 2 oranges
Zest of 1 orange
¼ cup pure maple syrup
2 tablespoons low-sodium soy

sauce
1 teaspoon garlic powder
4 (4 to 6-ounce) salmon fillets,
pin bones removed

1. At 400 degrees F, preheat your oven. 2. In a suitable dish, mix up the orange juice and zest, maple syrup, soy sauce, and garlic powder. 3. Put the salmon pieces, flesh-side down, into the dish. Let it marinate for 10 minutes. 4. Transfer the salmon, skin-side up, to a rimmed baking sheet and bake for almost 15 minutes until the flesh is opaque.
Per serving: Calories: 416; Total fat 22.1g; Sodium 642mg; Total carbs 14.2g; Fiber 0.1g; Sugars 12.4g; Protein 40.6g

Shrimp with Cinnamon Sauce

Prep time: 10 minutes | Cook time: 10 minutes | Serves: 4

2 tablespoons olive oil
1½ pounds peeled shrimp
2 tablespoons Dijon mustard
1 cup no-salt-added chicken broth

1 teaspoon ground cinnamon
1 teaspoon onion powder
½ teaspoon sea salt
¼ teaspoon black pepper

1. In a suitable nonstick skillet, heat the olive oil until it shimmers over medium-high heat. 2. Add the shrimp and cook for almost 4 minutes, stirring occasionally, until the shrimp is opaque. 3. In a suitable bowl, whisk the mustard, chicken broth, cinnamon, onion powder, salt, and pepper. 4. Pour this into the skillet and continue to cook for 3 minutes, stirring occasionally.
Per serving: Calories: 281; Total fat 10.6g; Sodium 929mg; Total carbs 4.3g; Fiber 0.6g; Sugars 0.5g; Protein 40.4g

Mediterranean Baked Salmon

Prep time: 5 minutes | Cook time: 20 minutes | Serves: 4

4 (4-ounce) salmon fillets
3 tablespoons pistachio pesto
¼ cup chopped sun-dried
tomatoes
¼ cup pitted, diced olives

2 tablespoons minced red onion
2 garlic cloves, minced
Dash salt
Fresh ground black pepper
1 tablespoon minced fresh basil

1. At 400 degrees F, preheat your oven. Layer a baking sheet with aluminum foil. 2. Put the salmon fillets in the prepared pan, skin-side down. 3. Spread a thin layer of the pistachio pesto over the top of each fillet. 4. In a suitable bowl, mix the sun-dried tomatoes, olives, red onion, garlic, and salt, and season with pepper. Spread one-fourth of the tomato mixture over the pesto on each fillet. 5. Bake the food for 20 minutes almost. Remove it from the oven and let rest for 5 minutes. 6. Sprinkle with the basil and serve immediately.
Per serving: Calories: 301; Total fat: 17g; saturated fat: 2g; cholesterol: 80mg; carbohydrates: 6g; Fiber: 1g; Protein: 31g

Whitefish with Spice Rub

Prep time: 3 minutes | Cook time: 15 minutes | Serves: 4

2 tablespoons slow-cooker ghee,
melted
4 (6-ounce) whitefish fillets
1 tablespoon paprika
2 teaspoons ground cumin

2 teaspoons onion powder
2 teaspoons salt
1 teaspoon ground turmeric
½ teaspoon black pepper
1 tablespoon coconut sugar

1. At 400 degrees F, preheat your oven. 2. Brush a shallow baking dish with 1 tablespoon of ghee. 3. Place the fish fillets in the dish and brush them with the remaining 1 tablespoon of ghee. 4. In a suitable bowl, combine the paprika, cumin, onion powder, salt, turmeric, pepper, and coconut sugar. 5. Use 1 tablespoon of the spice rub on the fillets, making sure the surface of the fish is covered with rub. Store the remaining rub for future use. 6. Place the baking dish in the preheated oven and bake the fish for 12 to 15 minutes, or until firm and cooked through.
Per serving: Calories: 364; Total fat: 20g; Total Carbs: 3g; Sugars: 1g; Fiber: 1g; Protein: 42g; Sodium: 1277mg

Pecan-Crusted Trout

Prep time: 15 minutes | Cook time: 15 minutes | Serves: 4

Olive oil, for brushing
4 large boneless trout fillets
Salt
Black pepper
1 cup pecans, ground

1 tablespoon coconut oil, melted
2 tablespoon chopped fresh thyme
leaves
Lemon wedges, for garnish

1. At 375 degrees F, preheat your oven. 2. Brush a suitable rimmed baking sheet with olive oil. 3. Place the trout fillets on the baking sheet skin-side down. Season the fillets with salt and pepper. 4. Gently press ¼ cup of ground pecans into the flesh of each fillet. 5.Drizzle the melted coconut oil over the nuts and then sprinkle the thyme over the fillets. Give each fillet another sprinkle of salt and pepper. 6. Place the sheet in the preheated oven and bake for 15 minutes, or until the fish is cooked through.
Per serving: Calories: 672; Total fat: 59g; Total Carbs: 13g; Sugars: 3g; Fiber: 9g; Protein: 30g; Sodium: 110mg

Sea Bass Baked with Capers

Prep time: 10 minutes | Cook time: 15 minutes | Serves: 4

2 tablespoons olive oil
4 (5-ounce) sea bass fillets
1 small onion, diced
½ cup vegetable or chicken broth
1 cup canned dice tomatoes
½ cup pitted and chopped

kalamata olives
2 tablespoons capers, drained
2 cups spinach
1 teaspoon salt
¼ teaspoon black pepper

1. At 375 degrees F, preheat your oven. 2. In a baking dish, add olive oil. Place the fish fillets in the dish, turning to coat both sides with the oil. 3. Top the fish with onion, vegetable broth, tomatoes, olives, capers, spinach, salt, and pepper. 4. Cover the baking dish with aluminum foil and place it in the preheated oven. 5. Bake the fish for almost 15 minutes, or until the fish is cooked through.
Per serving: Calories: 273; Total fat: 12g; Sodium: 1038mg; Total Carbs: 5g; Sugars: 2g; Fiber: 2g; Protein: 35g

Grilled Salmon Packets with Asparagus

Prep time: 10 minutes | Cook time: 20 minutes | Serves: 4

4 (4-ounce) skinless salmon fillets
6 asparagus spears, tough ends trimmed
4 tablespoons avocado oil

1 teaspoon garlic powder
½ teaspoon salt
Black pepper
1 lemon, thinly sliced

1. At 400 degrees F, preheat your oven. 2. Cut 4 squares out of parchment sheet or foil and put it on a work surface. 3. Place 1 salmon fillet in the center of each square and 4 asparagus spears next to each fillet. Brush the fish and asparagus with 1 tablespoon of avocado oil. 4. Sprinkle each fillet with ¼ teaspoon of garlic powder and ⅛ teaspoon of salt, and season with pepper. 5. Place the thinly sliced lemon slices on top of the fillets. Close and seal the parchment around each fillet, so it forms a sealed packet. 6. Place the parchment packets on a suitable baking sheet and bake the fillets for almost 20 minutes. 7. Place a sealed parchment packet on each of the 4 plates and serve hot.
Per serving: Calories: 339; Total fat: 23g; saturated fat: 3g; cholesterol: 80mg; carbohydrates: 1g; Fiber: 1g; Protein: 30g

Salmon Baked with Fennel

Prep time: 10 minutes | Cook time: 20 minutes | Serves: 4

1 tablespoon olive oil
1 leek, white part only, sliced thin
1 fennel bulb, sliced thin
4 (5 to 6-ounce) salmon fillets

1 teaspoon salt
¼ teaspoon black pepper
½ cup vegetable broth or water
1 fresh rosemary sprig

1. At 375 degrees F, preheat your oven. 2. In a shallow roasting pan, add 1 tablespoon of olive oil. Add the leek and fennel. Stir to coat with the oil. 3. Place the salmon fillets over the vegetables and sprinkle with salt and pepper. 4. Pour in the vegetable broth and add the rosemary sprig to the pan. Cover tightly with aluminum foil. 5. Place this pan in the preheated oven and bake the dish for 20 minutes or until the salmon is cooked through. 6. Remove and discard the rosemary sprig. Transfer the salmon and vegetables to a platter and serve.
Per serving: Calories: 288; Total fat: 14g; Sodium: 692mg; Total Carbs: 8g; Sugars: 1g; Fiber: 2g; Protein: 34g

Shrimp Scampi

Prep time: 10 minutes | Cook time: 15 minutes | Serves: 4

¼ cup olive oil
1 onion, chopped
1 red bell pepper, chopped
1½ pounds shrimp, peeled and tails removed

6 garlic cloves, minced
Juice of 2 lemons
Zest of 2 lemons
½ teaspoon sea salt
⅛ teaspoon black pepper

1. In a suitable nonstick skillet, heat the olive oil until it shimmers over medium-high heat. 2. Add the onion and red bell pepper, cook them for almost 6 minutes, stirring occasionally, until soft. 3. Add the shrimp and cook for almost 5 minutes until pink. Add the garlic and cook for 30 seconds, stirring constantly. 4. Add the lemon juice and zest, salt, and pepper. Simmer for 3 minutes.
Per serving: Calories: 345; Total fat: 16g; Sodium: 424mg; Total carbs: 10g; sugar: 3g; Fiber: 1g; Protein: 40g

Manhattan-Style Salmon Chowder

Prep time: 10 minutes | Cook time: 15 minutes | Serves: 4

¼ cup olive oil
1 red bell pepper, chopped
1 pound skinless salmon, pin bones removed, chopped into ½-inch pieces
2 (28-ounce) cans crushed tomatoes, 1 drained and 1 undrained

6 cups no-salt-added chicken broth
2 cups diced (½ inch) sweet potatoes
1 teaspoon onion powder
½ teaspoon sea salt
¼ teaspoon black pepper

1. In a suitable pot, heat the olive oil until it shimmers over medium-high heat. 2. Add the red bell pepper and salmon, cook them for almost 5 minutes, stirring occasionally, until the fish is opaque and the bell pepper is soft. 3. Stir in the tomatoes, chicken broth, sweet potatoes, onion powder, salt, and black pepper. Bring to a simmer and reduce the heat to medium. 4. Cook them for almost 10 minutes, stirring occasionally, until the sweet potatoes are soft.
Per serving: Calories: 293; Total fat 11g; Sodium 1510mg; Total carbs 35g; Fiber 10.1g; Sugars 19g; Protein 16g

Grilled Chipotle Shrimp Skewers

Prep time: 35 minutes | Cook time: 15 minutes | Serves: 4

½ cup canola oil
¼ cup lime juice
2 to 3 tablespoon chipotles in adobo
1 tablespoon honey
¼ red onion, chopped
2 garlic cloves, chopped
2 to 3 teaspoon hot sauce

2 teaspoon ancho chili powder
1 teaspoon ground cumin
1 teaspoon dried oregano
1 teaspoon kosher salt
½ teaspoon black pepper
1 ½ lb. Shrimp, peeled and deveined, tails on

1. Place the canola oil, lime juice, 2 tablespoons of the chipotles in adobo, honey, onion, garlic, 2 teaspoons of the hot sauce, chili powder, cumin, oregano, salt, and pepper in a suitable blender. 2. Puree until smooth to make a marinade. Taste and adjust with more chipotle or hot sauce as desired. 3. Place the shrimp in a nonreactive dish, such as ceramic or glass, or in a sealable plastic bag. 4. Pour half of the marinade over the shrimp. Toss the shrimp to evenly coat. Cover and refrigerate for 2 hours or up to 12 hours. 5. Preheat a grill pan over medium-high heat. When the grill or pan is hot, use a folded paper towel to lightly oil the grill rack or pan. Soak eight 9-in [23-cm] bamboo skewers in water for at least 30 minutes before cooking. 6. Thread the shrimp onto the skewers, allowing the marinade to drip off over the bowl, and set on a baking sheet. 7. Place the shrimp skewers on the grill or grill pan and cook until they are just pink and opaque, about 2 minutes per side. 8. Serve warm or at room temperature.
Per serving: Calories: 504; Total fat 19g; Sodium 1084mg; Total carbs 7.8g; Fiber 0.2g; Sugars 2.4g; Protein 71.2g

Shrimp Paella

Prep time: 15 minutes | Cook time: 14 minutes | Serves: 4

2 tablespoons avocado oil
1 medium white onion, peeled and chopped
4 garlic cloves, chopped
1 teaspoon paprika
1 teaspoon turmeric
½ teaspoon salt
¼ teaspoon black pepper

Pinch saffron threads
¼ teaspoon red pepper flakes
1 cup jasmine rice
1 cup chicken stock
1 pound frozen jumbo shrimp, shell and tail on
¼ cup chopped fresh cilantro

1. Press the sauté button and add the oil to the inner pot. Allow it to heat 2 minutes, and then add the onion and cook until softened, about 5 minutes. 2. Add the garlic, paprika, turmeric, salt, black pepper, saffron, and red pepper flakes and sauté another 30 seconds. Add the rice, stir, and cook 1 more minute. 3. Add the stock and stir, and use a spoon to make sure there are no brown bits stuck to the bottom of the pot. Add the shrimp. 4. Close the lid and secure it well. Hit the the manual cook button and adjust the time to 5 minutes. 5. When cooked, release the pressure quickly until the float valve drops and then unlock lid. 6. Remove the prepared mixture from the pot and peel the shrimp if desired. 7. Serve garnished with cilantro.
Per serving: Calories 312; Fat 3.2g; Sodium 654mg; Carbs 42g; Fiber 3.4g; Sugars 1.5g; Protein 26.9g

Buckwheat Ramen with Cod

Prep time: 15 minutes | Cook time: 2 minutes | Serves: 4

For the Ramen
6 ounces buckwheat ramen
5 ounces shiitake or cremini mushrooms, sliced
4 garlic cloves, minced
1 yellow onion, diced
For Serving
4 soft-boiled eggs

4 cups low-sodium vegetable broth
¼ cup tamari
2 tablespoons apple cider vinegar
3 cups chopped cod fillet

2 teaspoons toasted sesame seeds

1. To make the ramen: in the instant pot, combine the noodles, mushrooms, garlic, onion, broth, tamari, and vinegar. 2. Lock the lid. Select pressure cook and cook at high pressure for almost 2 minutes. 3. When cooked, use a natural release for almost 4 minutes, then quick release any remaining pressure. 4. Remove the lid and add the cod. Cook, while stirring, for almost 2 minutes in keep warm mode until the fish is cooked to your desired doneness. 5. To serve: divide the noodles, fish, and broth into serving bowls. Top each with a soft-boiled egg and a sprinkle of the sesame seeds.
Per serving: Calories 481; Fat 4.1g; Sodium 1150mg; Carbs 70.5g; Fiber 8.7g; Sugars 3.7g; Protein 40.5g

Swordfish with Pineapple

Prep time: 15 minutes | Cook time: 20 minutes | Serves: 4

1 tablespoon coconut oil
2 pounds swordfish, cut into 2-inch pieces
1 cup fresh pineapple chunks
¼ cup chopped fresh cilantro
2 tablespoons fresh parsley, chopped
2 garlic cloves, minced
1 tablespoon coconut aminos
1 teaspoon salt
¼ teaspoon black pepper

1. At 400 degrees F, preheat your oven 2. Grease a baking dish with coconut oil. 3. Add the swordfish, pineapple, cilantro, parsley, garlic, coconut aminos, salt, and pepper to the dish. Gently mix the ingredients together. 4. Place the dish in the preheated oven and bake for 15 to 20 minutes, or until the fish feels firm to the touch. 5. Serve warm.
Per serving: Calories: 408; Total fat: 16g; Sodium: 858mg; Total Carbs: 7g; Sugars: 4g; Fiber: 1g; Protein: 60g

Sesame-Tuna Skewers

Prep time: 20 minutes | Cook time: 15 minutes | Serves: 4 to 6

Cooking spray
¾ cup sesame seeds
1 teaspoon salt
½ teaspoon ground ginger
¼ teaspoon black pepper
2 tablespoons toasted sesame oil
4 (6-ounce) thick tuna steaks, cut into 1-inch cubes

1. At 400 degrees F, preheat your oven. Lightly coat a rimmed baking sheet with cooking spray. 2. Soak 12 (6-inch) wooden skewers in water so they won't burn while the tuna bakes. 3. In a shallow dish, combine the sesame seeds, salt, ground ginger, and pepper. 4. In a suitable bowl, toss the tuna with the sesame oil to coat. Press the oiled cubes into the sesame seed mixture. Put three cubes on each skewer. 5. Place the prepared skewers on the prepared baking sheet and place the sheet into the preheated oven. 6. Bake the skewers for 10 to 12 minutes, turning once halfway through.
Per serving: Calories: 395; Total fat: 22g; Sodium: 649mg; Total Carbs: 7g; Sugars: 0g; Fiber: 3g; Protein: 45g

Cod with Black Beans

Prep time: 10 minutes | Cook time: 15 minutes | Serves: 4

2 tablespoons olive oil
4 (6-ounce) cod fillets
1 tablespoon grated fresh ginger
1 teaspoon sea salt
¼ teaspoon black pepper
5 garlic cloves, minced
1 (14-ounce) can black beans, drained
¼ cup chopped fresh cilantro leaves

1. In a suitable nonstick skillet, heat the olive oil over medium-high heat until it shimmers. 2. Season the cod with ginger, ½ teaspoon of salt, and pepper. Place it in the hot oil and cook for almost 4 minutes on each side until the fish is opaque. 3. Remove the cod from the pan and set it aside on a platter tented with aluminum foil. 4. Return this skillet to heat and add the garlic, cook them for 30 seconds, stirring constantly. 5. Stir in the black beans and the remaining salt, cook them for 5 minutes, stirring occasionally. 6. Stir in the cilantro and spoon the black beans over the cod.
Per serving: Calories: 499; Total fat 9.5g; Sodium 545mg; Total carbs 64.2g; Fiber 15.4g; Sugars 2.2g; Protein 41.8g

Roasted Salmon and Asparagus

Prep time: 5 minutes | Cook time: 15 minutes | Serves: 4

1 pound asparagus spears, trimmed
2 tablespoons olive oil
1 teaspoon sea salt
1½ pound salmon, cut into four fillets
⅛ teaspoon freshly cracked black pepper
Zest and slices from 1 lemon

1. At 425 degrees F, preheat your oven. 2. Toss the asparagus with olive oil and ½ teaspoon of salt. Spread in a single layer in the bottom of a roasting pan. 3. Season the salmon with the pepper and remaining salt. Place skin-side down on top of the asparagus. 4. Sprinkle the salmon and asparagus with the lemon zest and place the lemon slices over the fish. 5. Roast the dish in the preheated oven for almost 12 to 15 minutes until the flesh is opaque.
Per serving: Calories: 454; Total fat 22.8g; Sodium 373mg; Total carbs 2.2g; Fiber 1.2g; Sugars 1.1g; Protein 61.8g

Miso Steamed Black Cod

Prep time: 15 minutes | Cook time: 28 minutes | Serves: 4

4 black cod fillets
1½ cups water, ¼ cup
2 tablespoons tamari
1 tablespoon brown rice miso paste
1 tablespoon raw honey, melted
½ teaspoon ground ginger
1½ cups wild rice
Pinch sea salt

1. Set the cod fillets in a large resealable plastic bag. 2. In a suitable blender, combine the ¼ cup of water, the tamari, miso, honey, and ginger and blend until smooth. Pour the marinade over the cod. 3. Seal the bag, turning to layer the cod in the marinade, and refrigerate overnight. 4. In the instant pot, combine the wild rice, the rest of the 1½ cups of water, and the salt. Lock the lid. 5. Select pressure cook and cook at high pressure for almost 28 minutes. 6. When cooking is complete, use a quick release. Turn off the heat. 7. Remove the lid and set the marinated cod on the rice in an even layer. 8. Lock the lid. Select pressure cook and cook at high pressure for 0 minutes. 9. When cooking is complete, use a quick release. 10. Remove the lid and serve the cod over the wild rice.
Per serving: Calories 516; Fat 23.7g; Sodium 577mg; Carbs 50.9g; Fiber 3.8g; Sugars 6g; Protein 26.8g

New England Clam Chowder

Prep time: 15 minutes | Cook time: 8 minutes | Serves: 4

3 (6.5-ounce) cans clams, drained, juice reserved, and chopped
½ cup water
2 tablespoons ghee
2 garlic cloves, minced
2 celery stalks, chopped
1 yellow onion, diced
1 teaspoon sea salt
¼ teaspoon black pepper, freshly ground
1½ pounds Yukon gold potatoes, diced
¼ teaspoon dried thyme
1⅓ cups coconut milk

1. In a glass measuring cup, combine the reserved clam juice and water, adding more water as needed to equal 2 cups total. Set aside. 2. Select sauté on the instant pot and let the pot preheat. 3. Set the ghee in the pot to melt and add the garlic, celery, onion, salt, and pepper. Cook for almost 3 minutes. 4. Add the clam juice-water mixture and the potatoes and stir to combine. Turn off the heat. 5. Lock the lid. Select the pressure cook and cook at high pressure for almost 5 minutes. When cooked, use a quick release. 6. Remove the lid and stir in the clams, thyme, and coconut milk. Cook for almost 2 minutes with the residual heat from the pot to warm, then serve.
Per serving: Calories 414; Fat 17.9g; Sodium 912mg; Carbs 59.5g; Fiber 4.5g; Sugars 6.4g; Protein 7.3g

Rainbow Trout

Prep time: 15 minutes | Cook time: 2 minutes | Serves: 4

2 carrots, chopped
2 celery stalks, chopped
1 cup broccoli florets, diced
1 cup cauliflower florets, diced
1 pound rainbow trout fillets
¼ cup water
1 teaspoon sea salt
¼ teaspoon paprika
¼ teaspoon black pepper
2 tablespoons ghee
1 lemon, cut into wedges
1 tablespoon chopped fresh parsley

1. In the instant pot, combine the carrots, celery, broccoli, and cauliflower. Put a metal trivet or steam rack on top of the vegetables so it lies flat. 2. Set the trout on the trivet and pour the water over the fish. Sprinkle the fish with the salt, paprika, and pepper. Set the ghee and lemon wedges on top of the fish. 3. Lock the lid. Select pressure cook and cook at high pressure for almost 2 minutes. 4. When cooking is complete, use a quick release. Remove the lid. 5. Using potholders, remove the trivet and transfer the steamed trout to a serving dish. 6. Spoon the vegetables onto the dish and sprinkle with the parsley to serve.
Per serving: Calories 219; Fat 14.6g; Sodium 872mg; Carbs 10.7g; Fiber 2.6g; Sugars 4g; Protein 14.7g

Fish with Tomatoes and Asparagus

Prep time: 30 minutes | Cook time: 20 minutes | Serves: 4

4 (4-oz) fish fillets
Kosher salt
Black pepper
Olive oil for drizzling
2 lemons, cut into 12 slices

Kernels from 2 ears of corn
16 asparagus spears, trimmed, sliced
1 cup cherry tomatoes
2 tablespoon chopped herbs

1. At 400 degrees F, preheat your oven. Cut the parchment paper into four, each 18 in [46 cm] long. 2. Place a fish fillet on the center of a piece of parchment. Place three lemon slices on top of the fish fillet. 3. Add ¼ of the asparagus, corn, and tomatoes around the fish. Drizzle oil, black pepper and salt on top. 4. Wrap the parchment sheet over the fish and place the packets in a suitable baking sheet. 5. Bake until the packets are lightly browned and have puffed up for about 15 minutes. 6. Transfer each fish packet to a plate and let them stand for 5 minutes. 7. Using sharp scissors, cut an x into the center of each packet and carefully pull back the parchment and sprinkle with the herbs. 8. Serve immediately.

Per serving: Calories: 211; Total fat 11.2g; Sodium 523mg; Total carbs 15.5g; Fiber 0.5g; Sugars 0g; Protein 13.3g

Green Tea Poached Salmon

Prep time: 15 minutes | Cook time: 40 minutes | Serves: 4

2 cups water
2 tablespoons coconut oil
1 (2-inch) piece fresh ginger, peeled and minced, or 2 teaspoons ground ginger
4 garlic cloves, very sliced

1 teaspoon salt
4 green tea bags
1 pound wild-caught salmon fillet, skinned and cut into 4 equal pieces
¼ cup olive oil

1. In a medium skillet over medium-high, combine the water, coconut oil, ginger, garlic, and salt. 2. Bring to a boil, cover. Reduce its heat to low, and simmer for almost 10 minutes. 3. Remove from the heat, add the tea bags, cover and steep for almost 10 minutes. 4. Remove the tea bags from the liquid and discard. Cover and bring to a simmer over medium-low heat. 5. Carefully set the salmon pieces into the simmering liquid, cover and cook for almost 15 to 18 minutes, until poached through. 6. Using a slotted spoon, remove the salmon pieces from the liquid and serve warm, drizzled with the avocado oil.

Per serving: Calories 353; Fat 21.8g; Sodium 665mg; Carbs 1g; Fiber 0.1g; Sugars 0g ; Protein 36.2g

Tuna Salad with Brown Rice

Prep time: 15 minutes | Cook time: 15 minutes | Serves: 4

1 cup brown rice
1 cup water
Pinch sea salt
1 ripe avocado, peeled, halved, and pitted
2 (3-ounce) cans water-packed tuna, drained and rinsed

1 red bell pepper, diced
1 cucumber, seeded and diced
1 scallion, white and green parts, sliced, then minced
2 tablespoons capers, drained
Juice of 1 small lemon

1. In the instant pot, combine the brown rice, water, and salt. Lock the lid. Pressure cook at high for almost 15 minutes. 2. In a suitable bowl, using a fork, mash the avocado until creamy. Add the tuna to the bowl, then add the bell pepper, cucumber, scallion, and capers. Mix until combined well. 3. When cooked, use a natural release for almost 5 minutes, then quick release any remaining pressure. 4. Turn off the heat. Remove the lid and pour the tuna mixture into the pot and stir to combine with the rice. 5. Stir in the lemon juice and serve immediately, or refrigerate in an airtight container for up to 4 days.

Per serving: Calories 347; Fat 11.6g; Sodium 217mg; Carbs 46g; Fiber 6g; Sugars 3.1g; Protein 16.3g

Fish Curry with Quinoa

Prep time: 15 minutes | Cook time: 5 minutes | Serves: 6

1 tablespoon coconut oil
1 yellow onion, chopped
2 garlic cloves, minced
1 tablespoon ground ginger
1 teaspoon ground coriander
1 teaspoon sea salt
½ teaspoon ground turmeric
½ teaspoon black pepper, freshly

ground
1 cup coconut milk
1 cup quinoa, rinsed
4 cod fillets or any whitefish (about 2½ pounds total)
1 teaspoon lime juice
¼ cup fresh cilantro, chopped

1. Select sauté on the instant pot and let the pot preheat. 2. Set the coconut oil in the pot and add the onion, garlic, and ginger. Cook for almost 3 minutes until the onion is translucent. 3. Stir in the coriander, salt, turmeric, and pepper to combine. Stir in the coconut milk and quinoa. 4. Set the cod fillets in the pot on top of the vegetable and quinoa mixture. Turn off the heat. 5. Lock the lid. Select pressure cook and cook at high pressure for almost 2 minutes. 6. When cooking is complete, use a quick release. 7. Remove the lid and stir in the lime juice. Top with the cilantro to serve.

Per serving: Calories 289; Fat 14.3g; Sodium 368mg; Carbs 23.3g; Fiber 3.5g; Sugars 2.2g; Protein 18.6g

Seafood Stew

Prep time: 15 minutes | Cook time: 18 minutes | Serves: 4

1½ pounds Yukon gold potatoes, diced
1 (15-ounce) can diced tomatoes
2 red bell peppers, chopped
1 yellow onion, chopped
4 garlic cloves, minced
2 teaspoons sea salt

1 cup water
½ cup apple cider vinegar
2 cups chopped cod or halibut
10 raw shrimp, peeled and deveined
1 cup bay scallops
6 ounces clam meat, rinsed

1. In the instant pot, combine the potatoes, tomatoes with their juices, bell peppers, onion, garlic, salt, water, and vinegar. 2. Lock the lid. Select pressure cook and cook at high pressure for almost 15 minutes. 3. When cooking is complete, use a natural release for almost 10 minutes, then quick release any remaining pressure. 4. Turn off the heat. Remove the lid. Select sauté on the instant pot and add the cod, shrimp, scallops, and clam meat. 5. Cook for almost 3 minutes, while stirring frequently. 6. Remove and serve.

Per serving: Calories 402; Fat 5.7g; Sodium 964mg; Carbs 21.8g; Fiber 2.4g; Sugars 5g; Protein 62.3g

Garlic Shrimp and Broccoli

Prep time: 15 minutes | Cook time: 5 minutes | Serves: 4

2 tablespoons avocado oil
2 medium shallots, peeled and diced
1 tablespoon minced garlic
¾ cup chicken stock
1½ tablespoons lemon juice

½ teaspoon kosher salt
½ teaspoon black pepper
1½ pounds peeled, deveined jumbo shrimp
2½ cups small broccoli florets

1. Press the sauté button and add the oil to the inner pot. 2. Allow it to heat 1 minute and then add the shallots. Cook the shallots 3 minutes and then add the garlic and continue to cook an additional 1 minute. 3. Add the stock and use a spoon to remove any brown bits that are stuck to the pot. 4. Add the lemon juice, salt, pepper, and shrimp. Then add the broccoli to the top layer and do not stir. 5. Close the lid and secure it well. Hit the manual cook button and adjust the time to 0 minutes. 6. When cooked, release the pressure quickly until the float valve drops and then unlock lid.

Per serving: Calories 335; Fat 2.2g; Sodium 451mg; Carbs 84.6g; Fiber 8.6g; Sugars 63.6g; Protein 3.7g

Salmon Cakes with Mango Salsa

Prep time: 15 minutes | Cook time: 20 minutes | Serves: 4

2 tablespoons coconut oil, melted
1 egg
2 teaspoons Dijon mustard
1 teaspoon
Worcestershire sauce
Dash hot sauce

2 scallions, sliced
1½ pounds salmon fillets, cut into
1-inch pieces
1 teaspoon salt
¼ teaspoon white pepper
1 cup mango salsa

1. At 400 degrees F, preheat your oven. 2. Brush a rimmed baking sheet with 1 tablespoon of melted coconut oil. 3. In a suitable food processor, combine the egg, Dijon mustard, Worcestershire sauce, hot sauce, scallions, salmon, salt and white pepper. 4. Pulse the ingredients until the salmon is chopped and the resulting mixture can be shaped into patties. Shape the mixture into four large patties of equal size. 5. Place the patties on the prepared baking sheet and brush them with the remaining melted coconut oil. 6. Place the sheet in the preheated oven and bake for 15 to 20 minutes, or until lightly browned and firm to the touch. Serve warm with mango salsa.
Per serving: Calories: 385; Total fat: 19g; Sodium: 762mg; Total Carbs: 20g; Sugars: 17g; Fiber: 3g; Protein: 35g

Seared Citrus Scallops with Mint and Basil

Prep time: 15 minutes | Cook time: 10 minutes | Serves: 4

1 pound sea scallops, patted dry
1 teaspoon salt
½ teaspoon black pepper
¼ cup extra-virgin olive oil
4 tablespoons grass-fed butter

Grated zest and juice of 1 orange
Grated zest and juice of 1 lemon
2 tablespoons chopped fresh mint
2 tablespoons chopped fresh basil

1. Sprinkle the scallops with ½ teaspoon of salt and the pepper. 2. In a suitable skillet, heat the olive oil over medium-high heat. 3. Set the scallops, one by one, into the hot oil and sear for almost 2 to 3 minutes on each side until the scallops are lightly golden. 4. Using a slotted spoon, remove from this skillet and keep warm. 5. Add the butter to this skillet and reduce its heat to medium low. 6. Once the butter has melted, whisk in the citrus zests and juices, mint, basil, and the rest of the ½ teaspoon of salt. Cook for almost 1 minute. 7. Remove from the heat and return the seared scallops to this skillet, tossing to layer them in the butter sauce. 8. Serve the scallops warm, drizzled with sauce.
Per serving: Calories 312; Fat 25g; Sodium 847mg; Carbs 3.1g; Fiber 0.3g; Sugars 0g; Protein 19.3g

Salmon and Cauliflower Rice Soup

Prep time: 15 minutes | Cook time: 7 minutes | Serves: 4

1 tablespoon sesame oil
1 large yellow onion, chopped
2 pounds salmon fillets, skin removed, cut into 2-inch pieces
6 cups water
Cauliflower rice
3 cups vegetable broth

1½ cups chopped fresh cilantro
2 tablespoons minced peeled fresh ginger
½ teaspoon sea salt
1 avocado, peeled, halved, pitted, and sliced

1. Select sauté on the instant pot and let the pot preheat. 2. Pour in the oil and add the onion. Sauté for almost 3 minutes until the onion is translucent. 3. Add the salmon, water, cauliflower rice, broth, 1 cup of cilantro, the ginger, and salt to the pot. 4. Turn off the heat. Lock the lid. Pressure cook at high for almost 4 minutes. 5. When done, use a quick release. 6. Remove the lid and serve the soup topped with avocado slices and the rest of the ½ cup of cilantro.
Per serving: Calories 481; Fat 28.4g; Sodium 932mg; Carbs 9.3g; Fiber 4.8g; Sugars 2.6g; Protein 49.5g

Shrimp with Spicy Spinach

Prep time: 10 minutes | Cook time: 15 minutes | Serves: 4

¼ cup olive oil
1½ pounds peeled shrimp
1 teaspoon sea salt
4 cups fresh baby spinach

6 garlic cloves, minced
½ cup orange juice
1 tablespoon sriracha sauce
⅛ teaspoon black pepper

1. In a suitable nonstick skillet, heat 2 tablespoons of the olive oil over medium-high heat until it shimmers. 2. Add the shrimp and ½ teaspoon of salt, cook for almost 4 minutes, stirring occasionally, until the shrimp are pink. 3. Transfer the shrimp to a plate, tent with aluminum foil to keep warm, and set aside. 4. Return the skillet to heat and heat the remaining olive oil until it shimmers. 5. Add the spinach and cook for 3 minutes; add the garlic and cook for 30 seconds. 6. In a suitable bowl, whisk the orange juice, sriracha, remaining ½ teaspoon of salt, and pepper. 7. Add this to the spinach and cook for 3 minutes. Serve the shrimp with spinach on the side.
Per serving: Calories: 338; Total fat 15.7g; Sodium 908mg; Total carbs 8.4g; Fiber 0.8g; Sugars 2.8g; Protein 40.1g

Salmon with Quinoa

Prep time: 10 minutes | Cook time: 25 minutes | Serves: 4

1 tablespoon olive oil
1 pound salmon fillets
Salt
Black pepper
1 red onion, diced

2 cups cooked quinoa
1-pint cherry tomatoes halved
½ cup chopped fresh basil
¼ cup chopped green olives
1 tablespoon apple cider vinegar

1. At 375 degrees F, preheat your oven. 2. Brush a suitable rimmed baking sheet with olive oil. 3. Place the salmon fillets on the prepared sheet and brush the top of each with olive oil. Season the fillets with salt and pepper. 4. Place the sheet in the preheated oven and bake the food for 20 minutes. 5. In a suitable pan over medium-high heat, heat 1 tablespoon of olive oil. Add the onion and sauté for almost 3 minutes. 6. Stir in the quinoa, cherry tomatoes, basil, olives, and cider vinegar. Cook for 1 to 2 minutes or until the tomatoes and quinoa are warmed through. 7. Transfer the tomatoes, quinoa, and salmon to a serving platter and serve.
Per serving: Calories: 396; Total fat: 16g; Sodium: 395mg; Total Carbs: 36g; Sugars: 4g; Fiber: 6g; Protein: 30g

Oven-Roasted Cod with Mushrooms

Prep time: 10 minutes | Cook time: 25 minutes | Serves: 4 to 6

1½ pounds cod fillets
½ teaspoon salt
Black pepper
1 tablespoon olive oil
1 leek, white part only, sliced thin
8 ounces shiitake mushrooms,

stemmed, sliced
1 tablespoon coconut aminos
1 teaspoon sweet paprika
½ cup vegetable broth, or chicken broth

1. At 375 degrees F, preheat your oven. 2. Season the cod with salt and pepper. Set aside. 3. In a suitable shallow baking dish, combine the olive oil, leek, mushrooms, coconut aminos, paprika, and ½ teaspoon of salt. Season with pepper, and give everything a gentle toss to coat with the oil and spices. 4. Place the dish in the preheated oven and bake the vegetables for 10 minutes. Stir the vegetables and place the cod fillets on top in a single layer. 5. Pour in the vegetable broth. Return the dish to the oven and bake for an additional 10 to 15 minutes, or until the cod is firm but cooked through.
Per serving: Calories: 221; Total fat: 6g; Sodium: 637mg; Total Carbs: 12g; Sugars: 3g; Fiber: 2g; Protein: 32g

Chapter 8 Dessert Recipes

Cinnamon Coconut Cake

Prep time: 10 minutes | Cook time: 40 minutes | Servings: 4

cup almond flour
½ cup unsweetened shredded
coconut
⅓ cup erythritol
1 teaspoon baking powder
1 teaspoon ground cinnamon

½ teaspoon ground ginger
2 large eggs lightly whisked
¼ cup coconut oil, melted
½ cup unsweetened full-fat
canned coconut milk

1. In a suitable bowl, mix up the flour, coconut, erythritol, baking powder, cinnamon, ginger, eggs, coconut oil, and coconut milk. 2. Grease a suitable spring-form pan with nonstick cooking spray. 3. Pour the cake batter into the pan. 4. Add 2 cups water to the inner pot and place a steam rack inside. 5. Set the pan on top of the steam rack. Seal the cooker's lid. 6. Select the Manual or Pressure mode and adjust the time to 40 minutes. 7. Once done, release the pressure completely then remove the cooker's lid. 8. Allow the cake to cool 5–10 minutes before slicing to serve.
Per Serving: Calories 254; Total Fat 23.39g; Sodium 82mg; Total Carbs 9.7g; Fiber 1.4g; Sugars 6.84g; Protein 4.19g

Coconut Ice Cream Sandwiches

Prep time: 45 minutes | Cook time: 20 minutes | Serves: 6

For the Coconut
Ice cream
4 cups full-fat coconut milk
For the Cookies
2 cups almond flour
3 tablespoons coconut sugar
1 teaspoon salt
½ teaspoon baking soda
¼ teaspoon ground cardamom
For the Finished
Ice cream sandwiches

¾ cup coconut sugar
2 teaspoons vanilla extract

6 tablespoons coconut oil, melted
and cooled
¼ cup maple syrup
1 tablespoon almond milk
1 teaspoon vanilla extract

½ cup shredded coconut

1. To make the coconut ice cream: In a suitable saucepan, add the coconut milk and coconut sugar, cook them for almost 5 minutes over medium heat, stirring constantly, or until the sugar dissolves. 2. Remove this pan from the heat and stir in the vanilla. Chill the mixture for at least 4 hours or overnight. 3. Make the ice cream according to the manufacturer's instructions for your ice cream maker. Freeze the ice cream in an airtight container. 4. To make the cookies: At 325 degrees F, preheat your oven. Line two baking sheets with parchment paper. 5. In a suitable bowl, combine the almond flour, coconut sugar, salt, baking soda, and cardamom. 6. Add the coconut oil, maple syrup, almond milk, and vanilla. Mix until a thick dough forms. 7. Using a spoon, place scoops of dough on the prepared sheets, leaving about 2 inches between each cookie. There should be enough dough for 12 cookies. 8. Gently flatten the cookies with your hand or the back of the spoon. Place the sheets in the preheated oven and bake for 10 to 12 minutes, or until golden brown. 9. Cool the cookies well before making the ice cream sandwiches. 10. To assemble the ice cream sandwiches: Place a generous scoop of coconut ice cream on the bottom of one cookie and top it with a second cookie, pressing together gently. 11. Individually wrap the cookies and freeze until ready to eat. When ready to serve, press shredded coconut into the ice cream along the edges of each sandwich.
Per serving: Calories: 179; Total fat 14.3g; Sodium 493mg; Total carbs 12.3g; Fiber 2.4g; Sugars 8.7g; Protein 0.9g

Tasty Coconut Pancakes

Prep time: 10 minutes | Cook time: 20 minutes | Servings: 4

½ cup coconut flour
½ teaspoon baking soda
¼ teaspoon salt
1 cup unsweetened coconut milk

4 large eggs, lightly beaten
½ teaspoon vanilla extract
3 tablespoons olive oil

1. Mix up the coconut flour, baking soda and salt in the bowl; add the eggs, coconut milk, vanilla and stir them well until smooth. 2. If the prepared batter is too thick, thin with additional coconut milk or water. 3. Heat 1 tablespoon of the oil in the skillet over medium heat. 4. Add the prepared batter in ½-cup scoops and cook for 3 minutes until golden brown on the bottom; flip and cook for 2 minutes longer. 5. Stack the pancakes on a plate while cooking the remaining batter. 6. Serve.
Per Serving: Calories 205; Total Fat 16.94g; Sodium 432mg; Total Carbs 4.46g; Fiber 0.3g; Sugars 4.11g; Protein 8.42g

Banana Nice Cream Sundae

Prep time: 10 minutes | Cook time: 1 minute | Servings: 6

1 pound strawberries, hulled and
chopped
2 tablespoons fresh lemon juice
½ cup erythritol

1 teaspoon arrowroot powder
½ teaspoon water
6 large ripe bananas, sliced and
frozen

1. Add the strawberries, lemon juice and erythritol to the inner pot. Seal the cooker's lid. 2. Select the Manual or Pressure mode and adjust the time to 1 minute. 3. Mix the arrowroot powder with water in a bowl to create a slurry. 4. Release the pressure completely then remove the cooker's lid. 5. Allow the strawberries to sit 5 minutes, and then stir in the arrowroot slurry and give it a few minutes to thicken. 6. Blend the frozen bananas in your food processor. 7. Process the bananas until you have a thick and creamy mixture. 8. Spoon the mixture into six bowls, and spoon some strawberry sauce on the top of each bowl.
Per Serving: Calories 206; Total Fat 0.69g; Sodium 27mg; Total Carbs 52.64g; Fiber 5.1g; Sugars 34.14g; Protein 2.12g

Almond-Pistachio Cake

Prep time: 30 minutes | Cook time: 40–45 minutes | Serves: 6–8

Cake
1 ¼ cup raw almonds or almond
meal
½ cup pistachios
½ teaspoon salt
6 eggs, separated
Coconut Whipped Cream
1 (13 ½-oz) can full-fat coconut
milk
Citrus Salad
2 oranges, quartered
2 grapefruits, quartered
1 tablespoon mint leaves, cut into

1¼ cup raw cane sugar
1 tablespoon grated lemon zest
1 teaspoon grated orange zest
1 teaspoon vanilla extract
¼ teaspoon almond extract

1 tablespoon confectioner's sugar

strips
1 tablespoon honey

1. At 350 degrees F, preheat your oven. Layer a 9-in round spring-form pan with nonstick cooking spray. 2. In a suitable food processor, combine the pistachios, almonds, and salt and pulse until ground. 3. In a suitable bowl, combine the egg yolks and 1 cup of the raw cane sugar. 4. Beat until fluffy. Stir in the orange zest, lemon zest, vanilla, and almond extract and beat. 5. In another bowl of a stand mixer fitted with the whisk attachment, beat the egg whites and the remaining ¼ cup cane sugar until it makes stiff peaks. 6. Add the egg whites and the almond mixture into the egg yolk mixture, and then mix well. 7. Pour into the prepared pan. Bake the mixture for almost 40 to 45 minutes. Allow the cake to cool completely. 8. Place the coconut cream in a stand mixer fitted with the whisk attachment. Stir in the confectioner's sugar and whip on high speed until light and fluffy, 3 to 4 minutes. 9. Toss the orange and grapefruit segments with the mint and honey in a suitable bowl. 10. Spread the prepared coconut cream into an even layer over the cake. Cut the cake into, then top with the citrus salad and serve.
Per serving: Calories 177; Fat 9.5g; Sodium 20mg; Carbs 21.4g; Fiber 0.1g; Sugars 16.8g; Protein 5.9g

Orange Coffee Cake

Prep time: 15 minutes | Cook time: 40 minutes | Servings: 4

3 large eggs
4 tablespoons pure maple syrup
plus ½ tablespoons
Zest from 1 medium orange
1 tablespoon fresh orange juice
1 teaspoon pure vanilla extract

1⅓ cups almond flour
1 teaspoon baking powder
¾ teaspoon ground cinnamon,
divided
½ teaspoon salt
½ cup walnut pieces

1. Add the eggs, orange zest, orange juice, vanilla, flour, baking powder, salt, 4 tablespoons of maple syrup and ½ teaspoon of cinnamon to a bowl and then mix them well. 2. Transfer the prepared mixture to a 6" cake pan. 3. Mix the walnuts, ¼ teaspoon of cinnamon and ½ tablespoon of maple syrup in another bowl. 4. Sprinkle on the top of the cake and cover it with aluminum foil. 5. Pour 1 cup of water into the inner pot and place a steam rack inside. 6. Set the cake pan on top of the steam rack. Seal the cooker's lid. 7. Select the Manual or Pressure mode and adjust the time to 40 minutes. 8. Once the timer beeps, quick-release the pressure then unlock lid and remove it. 9. Slice and serve.
Per Serving: Calories 197; Total Fat 10.36g; Sodium 348mg; Total Carbs 20.57g; Fiber 1.1g; Sugars 16.3g; Protein 6.53g

Chocolate-Cinnamon Gelato

Prep time: 15 minutes | Cook time: 0 | Serves: 4–6

2 teaspoon cornstarch
3 cups almond milk
¼ cup raw cane sugar
¼ teaspoon kosher salt
4 oz. dark chocolate, chopped

1 teaspoon ground cinnamon
½ teaspoon vanilla extract
Chocolate shavings, crushed walnuts, or crushed fresh raspberries for garnish

1. Put the cornstarch in a suitable bowl, add 1 tablespoon of the almond milk, and stir with a fork to dissolve the cornstarch. 2. Pour the rest of the almond milk into a suitable saucepan. Bring to a simmer over medium heat, and then turn the heat to low. 3. Whisk in the cornstarch mixture, sugar, and salt to dissolve. 4. Add the chocolate and cinnamon and whisk until the mixture is completely smooth. Cook the mixture for 5 minutes, stirring occasionally, until the mixture starts to thicken. 5. Pour the milk mixture through a fine-mesh strainer into a suitable bowl. Stir in the vanilla. 6. Refrigerate the mixture for 3 hours or until chilled. 7. Whisk the chilled mixture. Freeze in an ice-cream maker according to the manufacturer's instructions. 8. When ready, the gelato should be the consistency of soft-serve ice cream. Transfer to an airtight container and freeze for up to 1 week. 9. To serve, scoop into serving bowls and garnish as desired.
Per serving: Calories 124; Fat 6.8g; Sodium 7mg; Carbs 15.4g; Fiber 0.6g; Sugars 11.3g; Protein 1.1g

Vanilla Apple Wedges

Prep time: 10 minutes | Cook time: 17 minutes | Servings: 4

For the Filling
4 large apples, peeled, cut into wedges
2 tablespoons lemon juice
¼ cup erythritol
For the Topping
1 cup almond flour
⅓ cup erythritol
1 cup old fashioned rolled oats
½ cup chopped pecans

¼ teaspoon ground cinnamon
1 teaspoon pure vanilla extract
2 tablespoons almond flour

¾ teaspoon ground cinnamon
1½ teaspoons vanilla extract
¼ cup coconut oil
2 tablespoons water

To make the Filling: Mix the filling ingredients in a large bowl. Transfer the mixture to a suitable cake pan and set aside.
To make the Topping: 1. Mix the almond flour, erythritol, oats, pecans, cinnamon, vanilla extract, oil and water in a bowl to incorporate the coconut oil into other ingredients evenly. 2. Pour the topping over the apple filling. 3. Pour 2 cups water into the inner pot and place the steam rack inside. Seal the cooker's lid. 4. Select the Manual or Pressure mode and adjust the time to 17 minutes. 5. Once the timer beeps, quick-release the pressure then unlock lid and remove it. Spoon into four bowls and serve.
Per Serving: Calories 421; Total Fat 25.04g; Sodium 16mg; Total Carbs 56.88g; Fiber 10.7g; Sugars 31.15g; Protein 6.08g

Banana Pudding Cake

Prep time: 10 minutes | Cook time: 20 minutes | Servings: 6

3 tablespoons ground golden flaxseed meal
10 tablespoons water
1¾ cups mashed banana (about 3 bananas)
¼ cup avocado oil
1 teaspoon pure vanilla extract

2 cups almond flour
½ cup erythritol
1 teaspoon baking powder
¼ teaspoon salt
½ cup chopped pecans
½ teaspoon ground cinnamon

1. Mix the flaxseed with 9 tablespoons water in the bowl and give the mixture time to gel. 2. In another bowl, mix the flaxseed mixture, banana, vanilla and oil. 3. Add the erythritol, flour, baking powder and salt and stir them to combine well. 4. Spray the cake pan with nonstick cooking spray. Pour the prepared batter into the pan. 5. In the third bowl, mix the chopped pecans, cinnamon and 1 tablespoon water. 6. Sprinkle on top of the cake batter. 7. Pour 1 cup water into the inner pot and place a steam rack inside. 8. Set the pan on top of the steam rack. Seal the cooker's lid. 9. Select the Manual or Pressure mode and adjust the time to 20 minutes. 10. Once the timer beeps, quick-release the pressure then unlock lid and remove it. Spoon into six bowls and serve.
Per Serving: Calories 257; Total Fat 17.61g; Sodium 112mg; Total Carbs 25.57g; Fiber 4.1g; Sugars 15.11g; Protein 2.56g

Delicious Blueberry Crisp

Prep time: 10 minutes | Cook time: 17 minutes | Servings: 4

For the Filling
1 (10-ounce) bag frozen blueberries
2 tablespoons fresh orange juice
¼ cup erythritol
For the Topping
1 cup almond flour
⅓ cup erythritol
1 cup old fashioned rolled oats
½ cup sliced almonds

1 teaspoon pure vanilla extract
2 tablespoons almond flour
1 teaspoon orange zest

1½ teaspoons pure vanilla extract
¼ cup coconut oil
2 tablespoons fresh orange juice

To make the Filling: Mix the filling ingredients in a bowl and then transfer them to the cake pan. To make the Topping: 1. In another suitable bowl, mix the almond flour and rest of the topping ingredients. Use your hands to incorporate the oil into the rest of the ingredients evenly. 2. Pour the topping over the blueberry filling. 3. Pour 2 cups water into the inner pot and place the steam rack inside. 4. Set the cake pan on top of the steam rack. Seal the cooker's lid. 5. Select the Manual or Pressure mode and adjust the time to 17 minutes. 6. Once the timer beeps, quick-release the pressure then unlock lid and remove it. 7. Spoon into four bowls and serve.
Per Serving: Calories 258; Total Fat 15.94g; Sodium 13mg; Total Carbs 33.29g; Fiber 6.9g; Sugars 12.03g; Protein 4.44g

Cinnamon Pineapple Pieces

Prep time: 10 minutes | Cook time: 2 minutes | Servings: 6

2 tablespoons coconut oil
1 large pineapple, cored and cut

into 2" pieces
1½ teaspoons ground cinnamon

1. Select the Sauté function and add the oil to the inner pot. 2. When the oil is melted, add the pineapple and cinnamon and stir to combine. Press the Cancel button. Seal the cooker's lid. 3. Select the Manual or Pressure mode and adjust the time to 2 minutes. 4. Once the timer beeps, quick-release the pressure then unlock lid and unlock lid.
Per Serving: Calories 116; Total Fat 4.72g; Sodium 2mg; Total Carbs 20.31g; Fiber 2.5g; Sugars 14.87g; Protein 0.84g

Warm Caramel Apple Dip

Prep time: 10 minutes | Cook time: 1 minute | Servings: 10

2 cups pitted dates
½ cup tahini

¼ cup maple syrup
¼ cup water, plus more if needed

1. Add the dates, tahini, maple syrup and ¼ cup water in the inner pot and stir to combine. 2. Seal the cooker's lid. 3. Select the Manual or Pressure mode and adjust the time to 1 minute. 4. Once the timer beeps, quick-release the pressure then unlock lid and remove it. 5. Allow the tahini mixture to cool slightly and then transfer to a blender. 6. Blend the mixture on high until super smooth, adding additional water if needed, 1 tablespoon at a time. 7. Serve.
Per Serving: Calories 175; Total Fat 6.57g; Sodium 15mg; Total Carbs 29.88g; Fiber 3.5g; Sugars 23.45g; Protein 2.76g

Vanilla Pumpkin Pudding

Prep time: 10 minutes | Cook time: 5 minutes | Servings: 6

1 (13.66-ounces) can unsweetened full-fat coconut milk
1 large egg
½ cup canned pumpkin purée

½ cup pure maple syrup
1 tablespoon pure vanilla extract
2 teaspoons pumpkin pie spice
2 teaspoons arrowroot powder

1. Beat the coconut milk, egg, pumpkin purée, maple syrup and vanilla in a bowl until smooth. 2. Stir in the pumpkin pie spice and arrowroot powder. 3. Transfer the prepared mixture to a suitable 6" cake pan. 4. Pour 2 cups water into the inner pot and place the steam rack inside. 5. Set the cake pan on top of the steam rack. Seal the cooker's lid. 6. Select the Manual or Pressure mode and adjust the time to 5 minutes. 7. Quick-release the pressure completely then remove the cooker's lid. 8. Stir the pudding and then transfer it to a glass container with a lid. 9. Chill in the refrigerator 1 hour or more before serving.
Per Serving: Calories 296; Total Fat 21.09g; Sodium 50mg; Total Carbs 24.13g; Fiber 2.2g; Sugars 18.5g; Protein 5.51g

Banana Chocolate Chip

Prep time: 15 minutes | Cook time: 55 minutes | Servings: 8

½ cup room temperature coconut oil
1 cup monk fruit sweetener
2 large eggs, room temperature
3 medium bananas, mashed

2 cups oat flour
1½ teaspoons baking soda
½ teaspoon salt
½ cup stevia-sweetened chocolate chips

1. Add the oil, sweetener, and eggs to a large bowl of a stand mixer with a paddle attachment, then beat them together on medium speed until combined. 2. Stir in mashed banana and beat until combined. 3. Add baking soda, the flour, salt and beat again until combined. 4. Remove the paddle attachment and stir in the chocolate chips. 5. Spray a suitable 6" Bundt cake pan with cooking oil and then transfer the mixture to the pan. 6. Set a paper towel over the top of the batter and then cover with aluminum foil. 7. Add 1½ cups water to the Instant Pot inner pot and then place a steam rack inside. 8. Place the pan on the steam rack. Seal the cooker's lid. 9. Select the Manual or Pressure mode and adjust the time to 55 minutes. 10. Quick-release the pressure completely then remove the lid. 11. Slice and serve.
Per Serving: Calories 321; Total Fat 18.14g; Sodium 431mg; Total Carbs 34.41g; Fiber 2.9g; Sugars 7.25g; Protein 7.48g

Vanilla Blueberry Pudding Cake

Prep time: 10 minutes | Cook time: 20 minutes | Servings: 6

3 tablespoons ground golden flaxseed meal
9 tablespoons water
1¼ cups unsweetened cinnamon applesauce
¼ cup avocado oil
1 teaspoon pure vanilla extract

2 cups almond flour plus ¼ cups
¾ cup erythritol, divided
1 teaspoon baking powder
¼ teaspoon salt
½ cup sliced almonds
½ teaspoon ground cinnamon
1½ cups blueberries

1. Mix the flaxseed and water in a bowl and give it time to gel; add the applesauce, oil, vanilla and stir well. 2. Add the baking powder, salt, 2 cups of flour and ½ cup of erythritol, stir to combine well. 3. Spray a 7" cake pan with nonstick cooking spray. Add the prepared batter to the pan. 4. Mix the almonds, cinnamon, blueberries, the remaining ¼ cup flour, and ¼ cup of erythritol in a bowl. 5. Sprinkle mixture on top of the cake batter. 6. Pour 1 cup water into the inner pot and place a steam rack inside. 7. Set the pan on top of the steam rack. Seal the cooker's lid. 8. Select the Manual or Pressure mode and adjust the time to 20 minutes. 9. Once the timer beeps, quick-release the pressure then unlock lid and remove it. Spoon into six bowls and serve.
Per Serving: Calories 432; Total Fat 35.28g; Sodium 105mg; Total Carbs 24.04g; Fiber 9g; Sugars 11.2g; Protein 11.42g

Creamy Strawberry-Blueberry Ice Pops

Prep time: 5 minutes | Freeze time: 3 hours | Serves: 4

1 cup strawberries, fresh or frozen
1 cup blueberries, fresh or frozen
2 cups plain whole-milk yogurt

¼ cup filtered water
2 tablespoons raw honey
1 teaspoon lemon juice

1. In a blender, add the strawberries, blueberries, yogurt, water, honey, and lemon juice, blend them until smooth. 2. Pour the mixture into the ice pop molds and freeze for 3 hours or until solid.
Per serving: Calories: 120; Total fat 0.3g; Sodium 44mg; Total carbs 26.4g; Fiber 1.7g; Sugars 21.1g; Protein 3.1g

Chia Pudding with Oats

Prep time: 25 minutes | Cook time: 0 | Servings: 2

2 cups unsweetened almond milk
⅓ cup chia seeds
¼ cup maple syrup
½ teaspoon vanilla extract

½ cup toasted oats
4 large strawberries, sliced
1 kiwi, peeled and sliced

1. In a jar with a tight-fitting lid, mix up the milk, chia seeds, maple syrup and vanilla. 2. Cover the jar and shake well, then set aside for at least 15 minutes for the pudding to thicken. 3. Divide the pudding between two serving dishes, top with the toasted oats, strawberries and kiwi; enjoy.
Per Serving: Calories 355; Total Fat 9.2g; Sodium 138mg; Total Carbs 58.79g; Fiber 11.3g; Sugars 37.88g; Protein 14.82g

Chilled Lemon Custard

Prep time: 15 minutes | Cook time: 10 minutes | Servings: 4

2½ cups nondairy milk
½ cup raw honey
⅔ cup tapioca starch
1 tablespoon grated lemon zest
¼ teaspoon sea salt
2 large eggs

2 large egg yolks
1 tablespoon ghee
¼ cup freshly squeezed lemon juice
2 cups water

1. Select Sauté function. 2. Add the starch, lemon zest, salt and pour in the honey and milk to the inner pot. 3. Cook the mixture for almost 3 minutes or until the mixture boils. Pour the milk mixture into a heatproof pitcher and set aside. Press Cancel. 4. Whisk the eggs and egg yolks to combine in the bowl. A little at a time, slowly whisk in the hot milk mixture to prevent the eggs from cooking. Whisk in the ghee and lemon juice until smooth. 5. Pour the prepared mixture into four individual ramekins and cover each with aluminum foil. 6. Place a metal trivet or steam rack into the Instant Pot and pour in the water. 7. Set the ramekins on top of the trivet. Lock the lid. 8. Set the pressure cook mode and cook at high pressure for 5 minutes. 9. When cooking is complete, use a quick release. Select Cancel. 10. Allow the ramekins to cool before removing them from the pot. Refrigerate the food for at least 2 hours before serving.
Per Serving: Calories 358; Total Fat 7.72g; Sodium 239mg; Total Carbs 66.9g; Fiber 0.4g; Sugars 43.72g; Protein 8.22g

Pecan Pears

Prep time: 10 minutes | Cook time: 3 minutes | Servings: 4

2 ripe but firm d'Anjou pears, peeled and sliced
1½ tablespoons coconut oil, melted

1 tablespoon pure maple syrup
½ teaspoon ground cinnamon
¼ cup chopped pecans

1. Select the Sauté function and add the oil to the inner pot. 2. Once the oil heated, place the pears in the inner pot, cut side down, and cook them for 2 to 3 minutes until they are get browned. Press the Cancel button. 3. Transfer the pears to the steamer basket. 4. Add ½ cup of water to the inner insert. Set the steam rack inside, and place the steamer basket with the pears on top. 5. Seal the cooker's lid. Select the Manual or Pressure mode and adjust the time to 3 minutes. 6. Once the timer beeps, quick-release the pressure then unlock lid and remove it. transfer the pears to a platter. 7. Remove the water and dry the inner pot. Press Sauté button and add the maple syrup and cinnamon. 8. Stir to combine and heat for 1 minute to warm. 9. Drizzle the heated maple syrup and cinnamon onto the pears and then sprinkle with chopped pecans and serve.
Per Serving: Calories 151; Total Fat 9.69g; Sodium 2mg; Total Carbs 18.03g; Fiber 3.5g; Sugars 11.95g; Protein 0.9g

Coconut Chocolate Pudding

Prep time: 15 minutes | Cook time: 30 minutes | Servings: 4

4 large egg yolks
½ cup raw honey
2 tablespoons unsweetened cocoa powder
1 teaspoon vanilla extract
¼ teaspoon sea salt

1 (14-ounce) can full-fat coconut milk
6 ounces unsweetened chocolate chips
1½ cups water

1. Whisk the egg yolks in the bowl for 2 minutes; add the honey, vanilla, cocoa powder and salt, combine well and then set aside. 2. Select Sauté function; pour in the coconut milk to the pot and cook for 3 minutes until it bubbles. Press Cancel button. 3. Pour in the chocolate chips and whisk for 5 minutes, or until the chocolate chips melt. 4. Add the prepared egg mixture and whisk until combined well and smooth. 5. Transfer the pudding into four individual ramekins and cover each with aluminum foil. 6. Set a metal trivet or steam rack into the Instant Pot and pour in the water. Place the ramekins on the trivet. Lock the lid. 7. Set the pressure cook mode and cook at low pressure for 20 minutes. 8. When cooking is complete, use a natural release for 5 minutes, then quick release any remaining pressure. 9. Remove the cooker's lid. Remove the foil from the ramekins and let cool before removing them from the Instant Pot. 10. Refrigerate for at least 2 hours before serving.
Per Serving: Calories 663; Total Fat 39.96g; Sodium 414mg; Total Carbs 71.72g; Fiber 4.2g; Sugars 51.85g; Protein 11.51g

Almond Butter Fudge

Prep time: 5 minutes | Cook time: 7 minutes | Serves: 9 pieces

For the Chocolate Sauce
3 tablespoons coconut oil
3 tablespoons cocoa powder
1½ tablespoons raw honey
Dash salt
For the Fudge
¼ cup coconut oil
2 tablespoons coconut sugar
1 cup natural almond butter
½ teaspoon vanilla extract
½ teaspoon salt

1. To make the chocolate sauce: In a suitable saucepan over medium heat, stir together the coconut oil, cocoa powder, honey, and salt until dissolved and combined into a sauce, about 5 minutes. 2. Remove from the heat. Bring to room temperature before drizzling over the fudge. 3. To make the fudge: Layer a 9-by-5-inch loaf pan with parchment paper. In a suitable saucepan, warm the coconut oil over medium heat just until melted. 4. Remove from the heat, add the coconut sugar, and stir until dissolved. 5. In a suitable bowl, stir together the almond butter, warm coconut oil–coconut sugar mixture, vanilla, and salt until well combined. 6. Spread the fudge evenly over the bottom of the prepared pan. 7. Put this fudge freezer for 15 minutes or until solid. Cut into 9 pieces and serve drizzled with the chocolate sauce.
Per serving: Calories: 122; Total fat 10.7g; Sodium 40mg; Total carbs 8.8g; Fiber 1.2g; Sugars 6.6g; Protein 0.8g

Honey Panna Cotta

Prep time: 10 minutes | Cook time: 5 minutes | Serves: 6

2 ½ cups canned coconut milk
2 teaspoon gelatins
¼ cup honey
1 vanilla bean, split and seeds scraped
Kosher salt
Blackberry-lime sauce
2 cups blackberries
Grated zest of ½ lime, plus 2 teaspoon lime juice
1 teaspoon raw cane sugar

1. Add about ½ cup of coconut milk in a suitable bowl. 2. Sprinkle the gelatin over the top and allow it to sit for almost 2 minutes. 3. Place the remaining 2 cups of coconut milk, the honey, vanilla bean and its seeds, and a pinch of salt in a suitable saucepan. 4. Warm the liquid over low heat, occasionally whisking, until bubbles form around the edge of the pan. 5. Remove it from the heat and let the mixture steep for 5 minutes. Pour the coconut milk mixture through a fine-mesh strainer into a suitable bowl. 6. Discard the vanilla bean. Whisk the gelatin mixture slowly into the warm coconut mixture until there are no lumps of gelatin. Divide evenly among six ½-cup ramekins. 7. Then cover it and refrigerate until set, at least 4 hours or up to overnight. 8. To make the blackberry-lime sauce: place the blackberries, lime zest, lime juice, and sugar in a suitable bowl. 9. Using a fork or pastry blender, gently mash the berries, leaving some large pieces of berry while allowing some of the juices to make a sauce. 10. Set aside for at least for 10 minutes, or cover and refrigerate up to overnight. Spoon the sauce over each chilled panna cotta. Serve immediately.
Per serving: Calories 150; Fat 3.2g; Sodium 9mg; Carbs 31.1g; Fiber 3g; Sugars 24.4g; Protein 1.6g

Strawberry Mason Jar Cakes

Prep time: 10 minutes | Cook time: 15 minutes | Servings: 4

4 large eggs
2 teaspoons pure vanilla extract
1⅓ cups almond flour
¼ cup erythritol
1 teaspoon baking powder
¼ teaspoon salt
1 cup strawberry chunks
½ cup dark chocolate chips

1. Beat eggs with vanilla in a suitable bowl. 2. Stir in erythritol, flour, baking powder, and salt, and stir to combine. 3. Fold in the strawberries and chocolate chips. 4. Grease four (6-ounces) Mason jars with cooking oil. 5. Divide the prepared batter into the jars and cover them with aluminum foil. 6. Pour 1 cup water into the inner insert. Place the steam rack inside and place the Mason jars on the rack. Seal the cooker's lid. 7. Select the Manual or Pressure mode and adjust the time to 15 minutes. 8. Once the timer beeps, quick-release the pressure and then unlock lid. 9. Allow the dish to cool before serving.
Per Serving: Calories 219; Total Fat 9.87g; Sodium 232mg; Total Carbs 28.8g; Fiber 0.8g; Sugars 12.4g; Protein 4.03g

Apple Bundt Cake

Prep time: 10 minutes | Cook time: 55 minutes | Servings: 8

½ cup room temperature coconut oil
1 cup monk fruit sweetener
2 large eggs, room temperature
1 cup unsweetened apple sauce
2 cups oat flour
1½ teaspoons baking soda
1 teaspoon ground cinnamon
½ teaspoon salt
1 large apple, peeled, cored, and diced

1. In a suitable bowl of a stand mixer with a paddle attachment, beat together the oil, sweetener, and eggs on medium speed until well combined. 2. Add the applesauce and beat until combined. 3. Stir in the flour, baking soda, cinnamon, and salt and beat again; remove the paddle attachment and stir in the diced apple. 4. Spray a 6" cake pan with cooking oil. Transfer the prepared batter into the pan. 5. Spread a paper towel over the batter in the pan and cover with aluminum sheet. 6. Pour 1½ cups water to the inner pot and then place a steam rack inside. 7. Set the cake pan on the steam rack. Seal the cooker's lid. 8. Select the Manual or Pressure mode and adjust the cooking time to 55 minutes. 9. Once the timer beeps, let pressure release naturally for 10 minutes. 10. Allow the dish to cool before serving.
Per Serving: Calories 275; Total Fat 17.29g; Sodium 650mg; Total Carbs 25.9g; Fiber 3.1g; Sugars 4.55g; Protein 6.03g

Cherry Ice Cream

Prep time: 10 minutes | Cook time: 0 | Serves: 4-6

1 (10-ounce) package frozen sugar-free cherries
3 cups unsweetened almond milk
1 teaspoon vanilla extract
½ teaspoon almond extract

1. In a suitable blender, combine the cherries, almond milk, vanilla extract, and almond extract. 2. Process until mostly smooth; a few chunks of cherries are fine. 3. Pour the mixture into a container with an airtight lid. Freeze well before serving.
Per serving: Calories: 113; Total fat 1.9g; Sodium 68mg; Total carbs 24.6g; Fiber 3.5; Sugars 16.3g; Protein 2.4g

Vanilla Zucchini Cake

Prep time: 10 minutes | Cook time: 40 minutes | Servings: 4

½ cup almond flour
¼ cup coconut flour
⅓ cup erythritol
¼ teaspoon salt
1 teaspoon ground cinnamon
¾ teaspoon baking powder
3 large eggs
¼ cup avocado oil
1 teaspoon pure vanilla extract
½ cup shredded zucchini

1. Mix up the almond flour, coconut flour, erythritol, salt, cinnamon and baking powder in a bowl. 2. Mix the eggs with oil and vanilla in another bowl, then add the flour mixture and stir to combine. 3. Fold in the zucchini. 4. Transfer the prepared batter to a 6" cake pan and cover with aluminum foil. 5. Pour 1 cup of water into the inner pot and add the steam rack inside. Place the cake pan on the rack. Seal the cooker's lid. 6. Select the Manual or Pressure mode and adjust the time to 40 minutes. 7. Once the timer beeps, quick-release the pressure then unlock lid and remove it. 8. Allow the dish to cool before serving.
Per Serving: Calories 236; Total Fat 17.31g; Sodium 238mg; Total Carbs 15.52g; Fiber 0.6g; Sugars 13g; Protein 5.01g

Brown Rice Pudding

Prep time: 10 minutes | Cook time: 10 minutes | Servings: 4-6

1 cup brown rice
2 cups full-fat coconut milk
1 cup water
½ cup pitted dates, chopped
2 tablespoons raw honey
1 tablespoon ghee
1 teaspoon vanilla extract
1 teaspoon ground cinnamon
½ teaspoon ground nutmeg
½ teaspoon sea salt

1. In the Instant Pot, stir together the brown rice, coconut milk, water, dates, honey, ghee, vanilla, cinnamon, nutmeg and salt. 2. Lock the lid, select the Pressure Cook mode and cook at high pressure for 10 minutes. 3. When cooking is complete, use a natural release for 10 minutes, then quick release any remaining pressure. 4. Open the lid and stir the pudding well before serving warm or chilled.
Per Serving: Calories 297; Total Fat 21.4g; Sodium 209mg; Total Carbs 27.38g; Fiber 3.6g; Sugars 16.4g; Protein 3.04g

Mango-Peach Yogurt

Prep time: 15 minutes | Cook time: 0 minutes | Servings: 6

2 ½ cups whole milk vanilla yogurt

1 ½ cups frozen peaches

1 cup frozen mango chunks

½ medium orange, zested

1. Layer an 8" × 8" baking pan with parchment paper. Spread yogurt onto pan. Place yogurt in freezer at least 4 hours or overnight. 2. Remove from freezer and break into big chunks with a fork. 3. In a food processor, combine yogurt, peaches, mango, and orange zest. Pulse until a thick purée is made with fruit evenly distributed. 4. Serve.

Per serving: Calories 127; Fat 3.5g; Sodium 54mg; Carbs 20.6g; Fiber 1g; Sugars 19.7g; Protein 3.9g

Blueberry Mason Jar Cakes

Prep time: 10 minutes | Cook time: 15 minutes | Servings: 4

4 large eggs

2 teaspoons pure vanilla extract

1⅓ cups almond flour

¼ cup erythritol

1 teaspoon baking powder

¼ teaspoon salt

1 cup blueberries

¼ cup sliced almonds

1. Beat the eggs with vanilla in a suitable bowl. 2. Add the erythritol, the flour, baking powder and salt and stir to combine. Fold in the blueberries. 3. Spray four (6-ounce) Mason jars with cooking oil. 4. Divide the prepared batter into the jars, top each jar with some of the almonds, and cover them with aluminum foil. 5. Pour 1 cup water into the inner insert. Place the steam rack inside and place the Mason jars on the rack. Seal the cooker's lid. 6. Select the Manual or Pressure mode and adjust the time to 15 minutes. 7. Once the timer beeps, quick-release the pressure then unlock lid and remove it. 8. Allow the dish to cool before serving.

Per Serving: Calories 146; Total Fat 5.12g; Sodium 237mg; Total Carbs 17.94g; Fiber 1g; Sugars 14.42g; Protein 6.74g

Blueberry Chia Pudding

Prep time: 10 minutes | Cook time: 5 minutes | Servings: 6

1 (14-ounce) can full-fat coconut milk

1 cup water

1 cup chia seeds

1 cup certified gluten-free rolled

oats

12 ounces frozen blueberries

½ cup maple syrup

½ teaspoon vanilla extract

1. In the Instant Pot, stir together the coconut milk, water, chia seeds, oats, blueberries, maple syrup and vanilla. Lock the lid. 2. Set the pressure cook mode and cook at high pressure for 3 minutes. 3. When cooking is complete, use a natural release for 5 minutes, then quick release any remaining pressure. Select Cancel. 4. Remove the cooker's lid and pour the pudding into a suitable bowl. Cover the bowl and refrigerate the mixture for at least 1 hour, ideally overnight. 5. Serve chilled.

Per Serving: Calories 418; Total Fat 25.45g; Sodium 19mg; Total Carbs 49.81g; Fiber 14.6g; Sugars 23.14g; Protein 8.88g

Almond and Quinoa Crisps

Prep time: 5 minutes | Cook time: 0 | Servings: 8

Coconut oil, for greasing the baking dish

½ cup almond butter

¼ cup raw honey

¼ cup carob powder

4 cups puffed quinoa

¼ cup chopped almonds

1. Lightly grease an 8-by-8-inch baking dish with coconut oil and set it aside. 2. In a suitable saucepan over low heat, add the almond butter, honey, and carob powder, stir them until they are thoroughly mixed, melted and smooth. 3. Remove the saucepan from the heat. 4. In a suitable bowl, toss together the quinoa and almonds. 5. Add the almond butter mixture. Stir everything together until well mixed and the cereal and nuts are completely coated. 6. Press the mixture into the prepared dish and refrigerate for 1 hour until firm. 7. Cut the bars into 16 pieces and serve.

Per Serving: Calories 250; Total Fat 11.27g; Sodium 156mg; Total Carbs 32g; Fiber 4.3g; Sugars 10.6g; Protein 7.62g

Gluten-Free Apple Cobbler

Prep time: 15 minutes | Cook time: 2 minutes | Servings: 4

Crumb Topping

½ cup gluten-free flour

½ cup certified gluten-free rolled oats

½ cup maple syrup

2 tablespoons ghee

½ teaspoon ground cinnamon

½ teaspoon sea salt

Filling

2 tablespoons ghee

¼ cup maple syrup

1 tablespoon freshly squeezed lemon juice

½ teaspoon vanilla extract

½ teaspoon ground cinnamon

½ teaspoon sea salt

4 Granny Smith apples, cut into bite-size dice

1 cup water

To make the topping: Mix all the topping ingredients in the bowl. Using a fork, blend the mixture into crumbs. Set aside.

To make the filling: 1. Select Sauté on the instant pot and then melt the ghee. 2. Dip a paper towel into the melted ghee and coat the inside of the pot. Select Cancel. 3. Pour in the maple syrup, lemon juice, vanilla, cinnamon and salt and stir to combine. 4. Add the apples and water and stir until well coated. 5. Sprinkle the topping over the apples. Lock the lid. 6. Set the pressure cook mode and cook at high pressure for 1 minute. 7. When cooking is complete, use a quick release. 8. Remove the cooker's lid and serve hot.

Per Serving: Calories 399; Total Fat 12.8g; Sodium 617mg; Total Carbs 74.07g; Fiber 6.9g; Sugars 52.23g; Protein 3.24g

Banana Tapioca Pudding with Walnuts

Prep time: 10 minutes | Cook time: 12 minutes | Servings: 6

5 overripe bananas, peeled and sliced into ¼-inch disks

4 cups water

½ cup raw honey

½ cup tapioca pearls, rinsed and drained

1 teaspoon vanilla extract

¼ teaspoon sea salt

2 (14-ounce) cans full-fat coconut milk

¼ cup crushed walnuts

1. In the Instant Pot, stir together the bananas, water, honey, tapioca, vanilla and salt. Lock the lid. 2. Set the pressure cook mode and cook at low pressure for 7 minutes. When cooking is complete, use a quick release. Select Cancel. 3. Open the lid and stir in the coconut milk. 4. Select Sauté and bring the mixture to a boil. Cook for 5 minutes, stirring continuously. Select Cancel. 5. Top the pudding with the crushed walnuts and serve.

Per Serving: Calories 395; Total Fat 18.27g; Sodium 112mg; Total Carbs 61.18g; Fiber 4.4g; Sugars 38.03g; Protein 3.2g

Vanilla Granola with Pumpkin Seeds

Prep time: 15 minutes | Cook time: 3 hours 15 minutes | Servings: 8

1 cup coconut oil

4 cups certified gluten-free rolled oats

2 cups shredded unsweetened coconut

1 cup walnuts, chopped

1 cup almonds, chopped

¼ cup pumpkin seeds

½ teaspoon ground cinnamon

¼ teaspoon sea salt

½ cup raw honey

1 teaspoon vanilla extract

4 cups unsweetened coconut yogurt

1. Select Sauté function and heat the coconut oil in the inner pot. 2. When heated, select Cancel. Pour the oil into a suitable bowl and set aside. 3. Use a paper towel to spread the remaining oil around the pot to coat it well. 4. Combine the oats, coconut, walnuts, almonds, pumpkin seeds, cinnamon and salt in the pot. 5. Pour the honey, vanilla and melted coconut oil over the dry ingredients and stir well to combine. 6. Cover the Instant Pot with a lid that fits over it, or with aluminum foil, leaving a 2-inch gap to vent. 7. Set Slow Cook mode and set the time for 3 hours. Stir the granola every 30 minutes. The granola will begin to brown and smell nutty. 8. Transfer the granola onto a baking sheet in a single layer. Let cool completely. 9. Set aside ½ cup granola for this recipe and store the rest in an airtight container at room temperature for up to 7 days. 10. Spoon 1 cup of coconut yogurt into each serving bowl and top each with 2 tablespoons granola.

Per Serving: Calories 593; Total Fat 40.98g; Sodium 225mg; Total Carbs 61.58g; Fiber 9g; Sugars 28.66g; Protein 17.72g

Lemon Blackberry Granita

Prep time: 5 minutes | Cook time: 0 | Servings: 4

1 pound fresh blackberries
½ cup water
½ cup raw honey
¼ cup freshly squeezed lemon juice
1 teaspoon chopped fresh thyme

1. In the food processor, pulse the blackberries, water, honey, lemon juice and thyme until puréed. 2. Pour the purée through a fine-mesh sieve into an 8-by-8-inch metal baking dish. Discard the seeds. 3. Place the baking dish in the freezer for 2 hours. 4. Remove the dish and stir the granita to break up any frozen sections, scraping along the sides. 5. Return to the freezer for almost 1 hour. Stir and scrape again. 6. Return the mixture to the freezer until completely frozen, almost 4 hours total. 7. Cover the granita until you serve it. Use a fork to scrape off portions to serve.
Per Serving: Calories 181; Total Fat 0.6g; Sodium 4mg; Total Carbs 46.92g; Fiber 6.2g; Sugars 40.72g; Protein 1.77g

Stone Fruit Cobbler

Prep time: 10 minutes | Cook time: 20 minutes | Serves: 8

1 teaspoon coconut oil plus ¼ cup melted
2 cups sliced fresh peaches
2 cups sliced fresh nectarines
2 tablespoons lemon juice
¾ cup almond flour
¾ cup rolled oats
¼ cup coconut sugar
1 teaspoon ground cinnamon
½ teaspoon vanilla extract
Dash salt
Filtered water for mixing

1. At 425 degrees F, preheat your oven. 2. Coat the bottom of a suitable cast-iron skillet with 1 teaspoon of coconut oil. 3. In the skillet, mix the peaches, nectarines, and lemon juice. 4. In a suitable food processor or blender, add the almond flour, oats, coconut sugar, ¼ cup of melted coconut oil, cinnamon, vanilla, and salt. Pulse until the oats are broken up, and the mixture resembles a dry dough. 5. Pour the dough into a suitable bowl. With your fingers, break the dough into large chunks and sprinkle across the top of the fruit. 6. Bake the food for 20 minutes. Serve warm.
Per serving: Calories: 110; Total fat 3.4g; Sodium 3mg; Total carbs 17.8g; Fiber 3.2g; Sugars 8.7g; Protein 3.1g

Blueberry Crisp

Prep time: 15 minutes | Cook time: 20 minutes | Serves: 4

½ cup coconut oil, melted
1 quart fresh blueberries
¼ cup maple syrup
Juice of ½ lemon
2 teaspoons lemon zest
1 cup gluten-free rolled oats
½ teaspoon ground cinnamon
½ cup chopped pecans
Pinch salt

1. At 350 degrees F, preheat your oven. 2. Brush a shallow baking dish with melted coconut oil. Stir together the blueberries, maple syrup, lemon juice, and lemon zest in the dish. 3. In a suitable bowl, combine the oats, ½ cup of melted coconut oil, cinnamon, pecans, and salt. 4. Mix the ingredients well to evenly distribute the coconut oil. Sprinkle the oat mixture over the berries. 5. Place the dish in the preheated oven and bake for 20 minutes, or until the oats are lightly browned.
Per serving: Calories: 374; Total fat 27.9g; Sodium 3mg; Total carbs 35.1g; Fiber 3.8g; Sugars 26.1g; Protein 1.3g

Blueberry Parfait with Coconut Cream

Prep time: 10 minutes | Cook time: 0 | Serves: 4

For the Cream
2 (14-ounce) cans coconut milk, chilled
1 tablespoon pure maple syrup
1 tablespoon fresh lemon zest
½ teaspoon vanilla extract
Dash salt
For the Parfait
2½ cups fresh blueberries

1. To make the cream: In a suitable bowl, whip the coconut cream with an electric hand mixer for 2 minutes until small peaks form. 2. Add the maple syrup, lemon zest, vanilla, and salt, and whip for a few more seconds. 3. In 4 small glasses, alternate layers of whipped coconut cream and blueberries until the ingredients are all used. 4. Serve immediately.
Per serving: Calories: 345; Total fat 24.3g; Sodium 36mg; Total carbs 34.9g; Fiber 6.8g; Sugars 23.8g; Protein 3.7g

Cheese Berries Salad

Prep time: 10 minutes | Cook time: 0 | Serves: 4

5 oz. goat cheese
1 ½ tablespoon honey
1 tablespoon lemon juice
½ teaspoon grated orange zest
Kosher salt
2 cups blueberries
2 cups blackberries
¼ cup pistachios, chopped

1. Place the goat cheese, honey, lemon juice, orange zest, and a pinch of salt in a suitable bowl. 2. Whisk until the goat cheese is fluffy and smooth. 3. Divide the goat cheese mixture among bowls or wineglasses, reserving about four spoonsful. 4. Top each portion with berries, pistachios, and a spoonful of whipped goat cheese. 5. Drizzle with additional honey. Serve immediately.
Per serving: Calories 271; Fat 11g; Sodium 8mg; Carbs 46.7g; Fiber 3.2g; Sugars 32.8g; Protein 4.2g

Walnut Crumble

Prep time: 15 minutes | Cook time: 15 to 20 minutes | Serves: 6

For the Topping
1 cup chopped walnuts
¼ cup chopped hazelnuts
1 tablespoon ghee or melted
For the Filling
1 cup fresh blueberries
6 fresh figs, quartered
2 nectarines, pitted and sliced
coconut oil
1 teaspoon ground cinnamon
Pinch salt
½ cup coconut sugar
2 teaspoons lemon zest
1 teaspoon vanilla extract

1. To make the topping: In a suitable bowl, mix together the walnuts, hazelnuts, ghee, cinnamon, and salt. Set aside. 2. To make the filling: At 375 degrees F, preheat your oven. 3. In a suitable bowl, combine the blueberries, figs, nectarines, coconut sugar, lemon zest, and vanilla. 4. Divide the fruit among six ovenproof single-serving bowls or ramekins. Spoon equal amounts of the nut topping over each serving. 5. Place the bowls in the preheated oven and bake for 15 to 20 minutes, or until the nuts brown and the fruit is bubbly.
Per serving: Calories: 207; Total fat 6g; Sodium 32mg; Total carbs 39.5g; Fiber 3.9g; Sugars 31.1g; Protein 2.2g

Mini Dark Chocolate–Almond Butter Cups

Prep time: 10 minutes | Cook time: 5 minutes | Serves: 9 cups

6 ounces dark chocolate, chopped
½ cup natural almond butter
2 tablespoons raw honey
½ teaspoon vanilla extract
Dash salt

1. Line 9 cups of a mini muffin tin with mini paper liners. 2. In a suitable saucepan, slowly melt the chocolate over low heat. Use half of the chocolate among the mini muffin cups. Set the rest of the chocolate aside. 3. In a suitable bowl, stir together the almond butter, honey, and vanilla. Divide the mixture into 9 portions and roll each into a small ball. Drop 1 ball into each muffin cup. 4. Drizzle the remaining chocolate into each cup, covering the almond butter balls. Sprinkle each lightly with the salt. 5. Refrigerate until solid.
Per serving: Calories: 170; Total fat 9.8g; Sodium 49mg; Total carbs 17.4g; Fiber 1.5g; Sugars 15.5g; Protein 3.2g

Ginger Jam Dots

Prep time: 5 minutes | Cook time: 0 minutes | Servings: 12

¼ cup melted coconut oil
3 tablespoons pure maple syrup
½ teaspoon vanilla extract
2 cups almond flour
1 teaspoon ground cinnamon
⅛ teaspoon salt
⅓ cup berry ginger jam

1. At 325 degrees F, preheat your oven. Layer a baking sheet with parchment paper. 2. In a suitable bowl, combine oil, maple syrup, and vanilla. Add flour, cinnamon, and salt. Stir into a thick batter. 3. Roll cookies into ¾" balls. Place on baking sheet 1"–1 ½" apart. Flatten slightly into a disk shape. 4. Using thumb, press an indentation into middle of each cookie. Place about 1 teaspoon jam into each indentation. 5. Bake 12–15 minutes until cookies are golden brown. Remove from oven and cool. Cookies will firm up once completely cool.
Per serving: Calories 124; Fat 6.8g; Sodium 7mg; Carbs 15.4g; Fiber 0.6g; Sugars 11.3g; Protein 1.1g

Lime Sorbet

Prep time: 10 minutes | Cook time: 0 | Serves: 4

cup water
½ cup raw cane sugar

1 cup lime juice,
Grated zest from ½ lime

1. Fill a suitable bowl with ice water. 2. Combine the 1 cup water and sugar in a suitable saucepan. 3. Warm over low heat until the sugar is dissolved. Remove the simple syrup from the heat, place the pan in the ice-water bath, and stir to chill rapidly. 4. Alternatively, refrigerate the syrup for 3 hours or until chilled. 5. Combine the lime juice with 1 cup of simple syrup in a suitable bowl. Whisk in the lime zest. Freeze the sorbet in an ice-cream maker according to the manufacturer's instructions. 6. Transfer the ice cream to a freezer-safe container and place it in the freezer for 3 hours to set or store for up to 2 weeks.
Per serving: Calories 220; Fat 13.1g; Sodium 1mg; Carbs 29.1g; Fiber 2g; Sugars 22.2g; Protein 3.2g

Double Chocolate Chip Cookies

Prep time: 15 minutes | Cook time: 10 minutes | Serves: 12 cookies

¾ cup creamy almond butter
½ cup coconut sugar
¼ cup cocoa powder
2 teaspoons vanilla extract
1 egg

1 egg yolk
1 teaspoon baking soda
¼ teaspoon salt
½ cup semi-sweet chocolate chips
Dash sea salt

1. At 350 degrees F, preheat your oven. Line 2 baking sheets with parchment paper. 2. In a suitable bowl, cream together the almond butter, coconut sugar, cocoa powder, and vanilla. 3. In a suitable bowl, whisk the egg and egg yolk. Add the eggs to the almond butter mixture, and stir to combine. 4. Stir in the baking soda, salt, and chocolate chips until well mixed. Divide the dough into 12 pieces. Roll the dough into balls and put 6 on each prepared pan. 5. Bake the food for 9 to 10 minutes. Let the baked cookies rest on the pans for 5 minutes, where they'll continue to cook. 6. Drizzle a dash of sea salt. Remove to a cooling rack.
Per serving: Calories: 226; Total fat: 15g; saturated fat: 4g; cholesterol: 31mg; carbohydrates: 20g; Fiber: 3g; Protein: 6g

Melon with Berry-Yogurt Sauce

Prep time: 15 minutes | Cook time: 0 | Serves: 6

1 cantaloupe, peeled and sliced
1 pint fresh raspberries
½ teaspoon vanilla extract

1 cup plain coconut yogurt
½ cup toasted coconut

1. Arrange the melon slices on a serving plate. 2. In a suitable bowl, mash the berries with vanilla. Add the yogurt and stir until just mixed. 3. Spoon the berry-yogurt mixture over the melon slices and sprinkle with the coconut.
Per serving: Calories: 78; Total fat 2.6g; Sodium 20mg; Total carbs 12.3g; Fiber 4.2g; Sugars 6.9g; Protein 1.9g

Chocolate-Coconut Brownies

Prep time: 15 minutes | Cook time: 30–35 minutes | Serves: 16 brownies

½ cup gluten-free flour
¼ cup unsweetened alkalized cocoa powder
½ teaspoon sea salt
4 oz. semisweet chocolate, chopped

¾ cup unrefined coconut oil
1 cup raw cane sugar
4 eggs
1 teaspoon vanilla
4 oz. semisweet chocolate chips

1. At 350 degrees F, preheat your oven. Grease a 9-by-9-in baking pan and line with parchment paper. 2. Combine the cocoa powder, flour, and salt in a suitable bowl. 3. In a double boiler, melt the chopped chocolate and coconut oil. 4. Let it cool down slightly. Stir in the eggs, sugar, and vanilla, mix well. 5. Whisk in the flour mixture. Fold in the chocolate chips. Pour into the prepared pan. 6. Bake the food for almost 20 to 25 minutes. Cut into squares. Serve.
Per serving: Calories 179; Fat 11.9g; Sodium 30mg; Carbs 41.9g; Fiber 4.3g; Sugars 23.5g; Protein 7.9g

Hot Chocolate

Prep time: 5 minutes | Cook time: 8 minutes | Serves: 2

2 cups almond milk
1 tablespoon coconut oil
1 tablespoon collagen protein powder
2 teaspoons coconut sugar
2 tablespoons cocoa powder

1 teaspoon ground ginger
1 teaspoon ground cinnamon
1 teaspoon vanilla extract
½ teaspoon ground turmeric
Dash salt
Dash cayenne pepper

1. In a suitable saucepan, warm the almond milk and coconut oil for almost 7 minutes over medium heat, stirring often. 2. Add the protein powder, which will only properly dissolve in a heated liquid. Stir in the coconut sugar and cocoa powder until melted and dissolved. 3. Carefully pour the warm liquid into a blender. 4. Add the ginger, cinnamon, vanilla, turmeric, salt, and cayenne pepper. Blend for 15 seconds until frothy. 5. Serve immediately.
Per serving: Calories: 166; Total fat 16.2g; Sodium 15mg; Total carbs 5.6g; Fiber 1.9g; Sugars 3.1g; Protein 2.5g

Chocolate-Cherry Clusters

Prep time: 15 minutes | Cook time: 5 minutes | Serves: 10

1 cup dark chocolate, chopped
1 tablespoon coconut oil

1 cup roasted salted almonds
½ cup dried cherries

1. Layer a rimmed baking sheet with wax paper. Over a double boiler, stir together the chocolate and coconut oil until melted and smooth. 2. Remove this pan from the heat and stir in the almonds and cherries. 3. By the spoonful, drop clusters onto the wax paper. Refrigerate until hardened. 4. Transfer to an airtight container and refrigerate.
Per serving: Calories: 242; Total fat 17g; Sodium 17mg; Total carbs 18.8g; Fiber 2.9g; Sugars 14g; Protein 5.4g

Chocolate Fondue

Prep time: 20 minutes | Cook time: 5 minutes | Servings: 4

2 medium bananas, cut into 2" slices
2 medium kiwi, peeled, halved, and cut into 2" half-moons
8 medium strawberries, tops removed and cut in half lengthwise

8 kebab skewers
¼ cup 2 tablespoons whole milk
1 ¼ cups dark chocolate chips (cacao or higher)
1 teaspoon vanilla extract
1 teaspoon spice blend

1. Make fruit kebabs by skewering bananas, kiwi, and strawberries onto kebabs, alternating colors. Set aside. 2. In a small saucepot over medium-high heat, heat milk until just boiling. Reduce heat to low. 3. Add chocolate, vanilla, and sweet spice blend to milk. Stir until melted and well combined. 4. Place melted chocolate in a serving bowl or small individual bowls if for a group of kids. Dip fruit in and enjoy!
Per serving: Calories 271; Fat 11g; Sodium 8mg; Carbs 46.7g; Fiber 3.2g; Sugars 32.8g; Protein 4.2g

Chocolate Pots De Crème

Prep time: 15 minutes | Cook time: 5 minutes | Serves: 4–6

1 lb. silken tofu, drained
2 teaspoon vanilla extract
Kosher salt
1 ½ cups semisweet vegan

chocolate chips
1 teaspoon maple syrup
Chopped strawberries or blueberries for garnish

1. In a suitable saucepan, bring 2 in water to a simmer. 2. Place the tofu, vanilla, and ¼ teaspoon of salt in a blender and puree on low speed until smooth, scraping down the sides with a spatula if needed. 3. Add the chocolate chips in a suitable heatproof bowl that will fit in the saucepan over the simmering water without touching it. 4. Turn the heat to low and melt the chocolate, stirring, until smooth, 2 to 3 minutes. Allow the chocolate to cool slightly, and then pour into the blender. Puree until smooth. 5. Taste and add the maple syrup if desired. Taste once more and add a pinch of salt if needed. 6. Divide the mixture evenly among six ½-cup ramekin. Garnish with berries before serving.
Per serving: Calories: 127; Fat 3.5g; Sodium 54mg; Carbs 20.6g; Fiber 1g; Sugars 19.7g; Protein 3.9g

Mini Key Lime Bars

Prep time: 15 minutes | Freeze time: 2 hours | Serves: 8

For the Crust
¾ cup almond flour
¾ cup rolled oats
¼ cup coconut oil, melted
2 tablespoons coconut sugar

1 teaspoon ground cinnamon
½ teaspoon vanilla extract
Dash salt
Filtered water for mixing

For the Filling
2 cups coconut cream, chilled
¼ cup lime juice

1 tablespoon fresh lime zest
3 tablespoons honey

1. To make the crust: Layer the bottom of an 8-by-8-inch baking pan with parchment paper. 2. In a suitable food processor, add the almond flour, oats, coconut oil, coconut sugar, cinnamon, vanilla, and salt. 3. Pulse until a sticky dough forms, you can add 1 tablespoon of filtered water to help the ingredients combine fully, if necessary. 4. Press the crust mixture evenly on the bottom of the prepared pan. 5. To make the filling: In a suitable bowl, whip the coconut cream with an electric hand mixer until it resembles whipped cream. 6. Add the lime juice, lime zest, and honey. Continue to mix until the ingredients are well incorporated. 7. Spread the filling evenly over the crust. Cover and place the baking dish in the freezer for up to 2 hours. 8. Slightly thaw and slice the bars before serving.
Per serving: Calories: 271; Total fat 22.9g; Sodium 30mg; Total carbs 17.1g; Fiber 2.6g; Sugars 9.6g; Protein 3g

Seasonal Fruit Crisps

Prep time: 30 minutes | Cook time: 30–40 minutes | Serves: 8

2 cups rolled oats
1-½ cups flour
¾ cup brown sugar
½ teaspoon ground cinnamon
¼ teaspoon ground nutmeg
¼ teaspoon kosher salt

½ cup butter, diced
2 to 3 lbs. Apples, peeled, cored, and chopped
2 teaspoons raw cane sugar
Greek yogurt for serving
Honey for serving

1. At 350 degrees F, preheat your oven. Layer a baking sheet with parchment paper, and place eight 1-cup ramekins on the prepared sheet. 2. Combine the oats, flour, brown sugar, cinnamon, nutmeg, and salt in a suitable bowl. 3. Stir in the butter and use a pastry blender or fork to cut it into pea-size pieces. Refrigerate until ready to use. 4. Place the fruit in a suitable bowl and taste, adding the raw cane sugar only if necessary to sweeten. 5. Fill each ramekin to the top with fruit, then sprinkle with 3 tablespoons of the oat mixture. 6. Bake the food for 30 to 40 minutes until the tops are brown and bubbly. Set aside to cool for 20 minutes. 7. Top with a dollop of Greek yogurt, drizzle with honey and serve. 8. Make the topping ahead: The topping for the crisp freezes well in an airtight container or freezer bag, so make a big batch and bring it out whenever you're in the mood for dessert.
Per serving: Calories 213; Fat 12.1g; Sodium 60mg; Carbs 26.5g; Fiber 4.4g; Sugars 18g; Protein 2.4g

Strawberry-Lime Granita

Prep time: 1 hour 45 minutes | Cook time: 0 | Serves: 4–6

1 cup water
½ cup raw cane sugar

1 lb. strawberries, stems removed
½ cup lime juice

1. Fill a suitable bowl with ice water. 2. Combine the 1 cup water and sugar in a suitable saucepan. Warm over low heat until the sugar is dissolved. 3. Remove the simple syrup from the heat, place the pan in the ice-water bath, and stir to chill rapidly. 4. Alternatively, refrigerate the syrup for 3 hours or until chilled. Reserve four to six strawberries for garnish. 5. Place the remaining strawberries in a suitable blender. Blend until smooth, and then strain into a suitable bowl through a fine-mesh sieve to remove the seeds. 6. Add the lime juice and ½ cup of the simple syrup to the strawberry juice. Stir and taste, adding more simple syrup if desired. 7. Pour the strawberry mixture into a 13-by-9-by-2-in nonstick metal baking pan. Freeze the mixture for 25 minutes or until the mixture is icy around the edges. 8. Using a fork, stir the icy portions into the middle of the pan. Continue this process of stirring the icy edges into the center every 25 minutes for almost 1½ hours, or until the mixture has turned into flaky crystals.
9. To serve, scrape the granita into serving bowls or glasses and garnish with the reserved berries.
Per serving: Calories 284; Fat 23g; Sodium 14mg; Carbs 17.5g; Fiber 11.1g; Sugars 4g; Protein 6.1g

Brownies with Raspberry Sauce

Prep time: 10 minutes | Cook time: 20 minutes | Serves: 9 brownies

For the Raspberry Sauce
1 cup fresh raspberries
2 teaspoons coconut sugar

1 tablespoon filtered water

For the Brownies
Coconut oil for the pan
¾ cup almond butter
½ cup cocoa powder
¼ cup coconut sugar
1 egg yolk, whisked

1 ripe banana, mashed well
1 teaspoon vanilla extract
½ teaspoon baking soda
¼ teaspoon salt

1. To make the raspberry sauce: In a suitable saucepan over medium heat, stir together the raspberries, coconut sugar, and water, mashing the raspberries as they cook for 5 to 7 minutes, stirring often. Remove from the heat and set aside. 2. To make the brownies: At 350 degrees F, preheat your oven. Coat the bottom of an 8-by-8-inch baking pan with coconut oil. 3. In a suitable bowl, stir together the almond butter, cocoa powder, and coconut sugar. 4. Add the egg yolk, banana, vanilla, baking soda, and salt. Stir together until a smooth batter forms. Spread the batter evenly in the prepared pan. 5. Bake the food for 12 minutes. Remove it from oven and let cool for 5 minutes. Cut into 9 brownies. 6. Serve with the raspberry sauce drizzled over the top.
Per serving: Calories: 113; Total fat 2.8g; Sodium 139mg; Total carbs 24.3g; Fiber 2.7g; Sugars 19.2g; Protein 1.5g

Roasted Peaches with Raspberry Sauce

Prep time: 15 minutes | Cook time: 15 minutes | Serves: 4

4 peaches, ripe, halved
2 tablespoons coconut oil, melted
1 (10-ounce) bag frozen

raspberries, thawed
½ cup coconut cream
2 tablespoons chopped pistachios

1. At 400 degrees F, preheat your oven. 2. In a shallow baking dish, place the peaches and brush them with the melted coconut oil. 3. Place the dish in the preheated oven and roast the peaches for 10 to 15 minutes, or until they begin to brown. 4. While roasting the peaches, purée the raspberries in a suitable food processor. If you don't like seeds in your raspberry sauce, strain it through a fine-mesh strainer. 5. To serve, set the peaches on a serving platter, cut-side up. Top with coconut cream, drizzle with raspberry sauce and sprinkle with the pistachios.
Per serving: Calories: 106; Total fat 7.7g; Sodium 7mg; Total carbs 9.9g; Fiber 2.6g; Sugars 8.2g; Protein 1.4g

Chocolate-Avocado Mousse

Prep time: 10 minutes | Cook time: 5 minutes | Serves: 4-6

8 ounces bittersweet chocolate, chopped
¼ cup coconut milk
2 tablespoons coconut oil

2 ripe avocados
¼ cup raw honey or maple syrup
Pinch sea salt

1. In a suitable heavy saucepan, combine the chocolate, coconut milk, and coconut oil, cook them for 2 to 3 minutes over low heat, stirring constantly, or until the chocolate melts. 2. In a suitable food processor, combine avocado and honey. Add the melted chocolate and process until smooth. 3. Spoon the mousse into serving bowls and top each with a sprinkle of sea salt. Serve.
Per serving: Calories: 444; Total fat 31.2g; Sodium 75mg; Total carbs 40.4g; Fiber 6g; Sugars 31.7g; Protein 4.4g

Chai Pudding

Prep time: 5 minutes | Cook time: 0 minutes | Servings: 2

½ cup 2 tablespoons canned coconut milk
½ teaspoon sweet spice blend

1 teaspoon pure maple syrup
2 tablespoons chia seeds

1. In a small pot, over low heat, warm milk just until it achieves a liquid and uniform consistency. 2. In a suitable bowl or mason jar, combine milk, sweet spice blend, maple syrup, and chia seeds. Stir well to combine. 3. Place in refrigerator with a tight-fitting lid for at least 2 hours. 4. Remove from refrigerator and eat as is.
Per serving: Calories 284; Fat 23g; Sodium 14mg; Carbs 17.5g; Fiber 11.1g; Sugars 4g; Protein 6.1g

Oat and Fruit Bars

Prep time: 15 minutes | Cook time: 45 minutes | Serves: 16 bars

Cooking spray
½ cup maple syrup
½ cup almond or sunflower butter
2 medium ripe bananas, mashed
⅓ cup dried cranberries
1½ cups old-fashioned rolled oats

½ cup shredded coconut
¼ cup oat flour
¼ cup ground flaxseed
1 teaspoon vanilla extract
½ teaspoon ground cinnamon
¼ teaspoon ground cloves

1. At 400 degrees F, preheat your oven. Layer an 8-by-8-inch square pan with parchment paper, and coat the lined pan with cooking spray. 2. In a suitable bowl, combine the maple syrup, almond butter, and bananas. Mix until well blended. 3. Add the cranberries, oats, coconut, oat flour, flaxseed, vanilla, cinnamon, and cloves. Mix well. 4. Spoon this mixture into the prepared pan; the mixture will be thick and sticky. Use an oiled spatula to spread the mixture evenly. 5. Place the cake span in the preheated oven and bake for 40 to 45 minutes, or until the top is dry and a toothpick inserted in the middle comes out clean. 6. Cool completely before cutting into bars.
Per serving: Calories: 192; Total fat 6.6g; Sodium 5mg; Total carbs 30.7g; Fiber 4.2g; Sugars 16.3g; Protein 3.8g

Grilled Pineapple with Chocolate Ganache

Prep time: 30 minutes | Cook time: 15 minutes | Serves: 6

For the Ganache
½ cup coconut milk
1½ cups semi-sweet or bittersweet

chocolate morsels

For the Pineapple
1 pineapple, peeled, cored, and cut into 16 wedges
1 tablespoon coconut oil, melted

1 tablespoon coconut sugar
1 teaspoon chopped fresh rosemary

1. To make the ganache: In a suitable saucepan, add the coconut milk. Heat the milk over medium-high heat until it just begins to scald. 2. Remove this pan from the heat and add the chocolate. Let stand for 1 minute. 3. Whisk the mixture until it's smooth and satiny. 4. To make the pineapple: Preheat an indoor stove-top grill until very hot. Brush the pineapple wedges with melted coconut oil. 5. Grill the wedges for 1 to 2 minutes on each side or until grill marks appear. 6. Set the pineapple on a serving platter and sprinkle with coconut sugar and rosemary. 7. Serve with the ganache.
Per serving: Calories: 47; Total fat 1.7g; Sodium 5mg; Total carbs 8.5g; Fiber 0.5g; Sugars 6.7g; Protein 0.3g

Berry and Chia Yogurt

Prep time: 10 minutes | Cook time: 5 minutes | Serves: 4

1 (10-ounce) package frozen mixed berries, thawed
2 tablespoons lemon juice
½ vanilla bean halved lengthwise

2 tablespoons pure maple syrup
1 tablespoon chia seeds
4 cups unsweetened almond yogurt

1. Combine the mixed berries, lemon juice, vanilla bean, and maple syrup in a saucepan. 2. Bring to a boil over medium-high heat. Stir constantly. Reduce its heat to low and simmer for 3 minutes. 3. Turn off the heat, and then discard the vanilla bean. Mix in the chia seeds, then let sit for 10 minutes or until the seeds are thickened. 4. Divide them into four serving bowls, then pour 1 cup of yogurt in each bowl. 5. Serve immediately.
Per serving: Calories: 204; Total fat 2.5g; Sodium 35mg; Total carbs 46.4g; Fiber 1g; Sugars 37.3g; Protein 1g

Figs Apple Compote

Prep time: 1 hour | Cook time: 5 minutes | Servings: 8

4 cups apples, peeled and sliced
2 cups dried apricots, chopped
2 cups black figs, chopped

2 cups peaches, chopped
2 cups dates, chopped
Juice of 1 lemon

1. Put all the fruits in a suitable pot, then pour in enough water to cover. 2. Soak for an hour, then turn on the heat and bring to a boil. 3. Reduce its heat to low and simmer for almost 5 minutes. 4. Turn off the heat and drizzle with lemon juice. 5. Transfer them in a suitable bowl and serve immediately.
Per serving: Calories: 297; Fat 1.1g; Sodium 5mg; Carbs 75.1g; Fiber 11g; Sugars 46.8g; Protein 3.1g

Banana Cream

Prep time: 5 minutes | Cook time: 0 | Serves: 4

4 frozen, diced bananas

1. In a suitable food processor, blend the bananas for 3 to 5 minutes until they reach a whipped, creamy consistency. 2. Depending on how frozen the bananas are, it may take a bit longer. 3. Serve immediately.
Per serving: Calories: 70; Total fat 0.3g; Sodium 1mg; Total carbs 18g; Fiber 2.1g; Sugars 9.6g; Protein 0.9g

Peach-Raspberry Crumble

Prep time: 20 minutes | Cook time: 40 minutes | Servings: 10

5 medium fresh peaches, peeled and cut into ¼" slices
1 pint fresh raspberries
½ cup pure maple syrup
¾ cup 1 tablespoon whole-wheat

pastry flour
½ cup rolled oats (not instant)
½ cup chopped pecans
¼ teaspoon salt
5 tablespoons olive oil

1. At 350 degrees F, preheat your oven. 2. In a suitable bowl, combine peaches, raspberries, ¼ cup of maple syrup, and 1 tablespoon flour and mix well. Pour fruit mixture into a 9" round baking pan and set aside. 3. In a suitable bowl, combine the remaining ¾ cup flour, oats, pecans, and salt and mix well. 4. Add the remaining ¼ cup maple syrup and oil. Gently mix until flour and oats are evenly moist. 5. Toward end of mixing, your fingers can be used to press mixture into different-sized crumbles—some will be fine and other parts will be larger clumps. 6. Pour crumble topping loosely over fruit, covering evenly. Bake 40 minutes until crumble top is golden brown and fruit has bubbled up. 7. Remove from oven and let cool at least 30 minutes before serving.
Per serving: Calories 213; Fat 12.1g; Sodium 60mg; Carbs 26.5g; Fiber 4.4g; Sugars 18g; Protein 2.4g

Strawberry Granita

Prep time: 20 minutes | Cook time: 0 minutes | Servings: 8

4 cups hot water
2 medium pitted dates
2 white tea bags (decaffeinated if

children under twelve years old are served)
2 cups strawberries

1. Place hot water in a suitable bowl or pitcher. Add dates and tea bags. Steep 20 minutes. Remove tea bags. Cool. 2. Pour cooled tea and dates into blender. Add strawberries. Blend until smooth. 3. Pour blended mixture into a large glass casserole dish and place in freezer for almost 2 hours. (if frozen for much longer than that, it becomes harder to scrape.) 4. Remove from freezer and scrape thoroughly with a fork into small ice crystals. If bottom layers are not yet frozen enough to scrape, return to freezer for another hour and repeat scraping. 5. Serve in parfait cups.
Per serving: Calories 17; Fat 0.1g; Sodium 4mg; Carbs 4.3g; Fiber 0.9g; Sugars 3.1g; Protein 0.3g

Banana Pops

Prep time: 15 minutes | Cook time: 0 minutes | Servings: 4

¼ cup dark chocolate chips (cacao or higher)
2 large ripe bananas
4 popsicle sticks

½ cup plain, whole milk Greek yogurt
½ cup anti-inflammatory granola, crushed into small chunks

1. Prepare a baking sheet with parchment paper. Be sure tray will fit in a freezer. 2. Fill a medium saucepan ⅓ of the way with water. Place a suitable bowl on top of it. It should fit securely, but bottom of bowl should not touch bottom of pot. 3. Place chocolate in bowl and melt, while stirring occasionally. 4. Peel bananas and cut them in half crosswise. Insert sticks into cut ends of bananas. 5. Place yogurt in a small shallow bowl. Place granola on a flat plate. 6. To assemble, dip and roll banana in yogurt. Spread with back of a spoon or pastry brush to make sure it is well coated. 7. Then roll banana in granola until it is evenly coated. Use your fingers to gently help granola stick. 8. Place banana pops on sheet and drizzle melted chocolate evenly over them. 9. Place tray in freezer at least 2 hours or up to overnight to firm up toppings. Serve.
Per serving: Calories 179; Fat 11.9g; Sodium 30mg; Carbs 41.9g; Fiber 4.3g; Sugars 23.5g; Protein 7.9g

Chocolate Bark

Prep time: 10 minutes | Cook time: 5 minutes | Servings: 8

2 cups dark chocolate chips (cacao or higher)
½ cup chopped dried figs
½ cup chopped pecans
½ teaspoon orange zest
½ teaspoon fennel seeds, crushed or chopped

1. Layer a cookie sheet with parchment paper. 2. Fill a medium saucepan ⅓ of the way with water. Place a suitable bowl on top. It should fit securely, but bottom of bowl should not touch bottom of pot. 3. Place chocolate chips in bowl and melt, while stirring occasionally. (you can melt chocolate in the microwave.) 4. Once chocolate is smooth and melted, pour it onto cookie sheet. Spread with a spatula into a thin, even layer. 5. Sprinkle evenly with figs, pecans, orange zest, and fennel seeds, and place in refrigerator to set at least 2 hours or overnight. 6. Once set, break into pieces and serve.
Per serving: Calories 220; Fat 13.1g; Sodium 1mg; Carbs 29.1g; Fiber 2g; Sugars 22.2g; Protein 3.2g

Energy Bites

Prep time: 20 minutes | Cook time: 0 minutes | Servings: 24

½ cup sunflower seeds
¼ cup pumpkin seeds
20 medium whole dates, pitted and chopped
¾ cup shredded coconut
½ cup cacao powder
2 tablespoons coconut oil
⅛ teaspoon salt
1 ½ tablespoons water

1. Put seeds in a food processor and pulse until they are chopped (but not super fine like a powder). 2. Add dates, ½ cup shredded coconut, ¼ cup cacao, oil, salt, and water and process until ingredients are well mixed and mixture looks uniform. 3. Using a tablespoon, spoon out mixture and roll into balls. 4. Put the remaining ¼ cup shredded coconut and ¼ cup cacao on two separate flat plates. 5. Coat balls with cacao or coconut by rolling half of balls in one, and half in the other. Place completed balls on a parchment paper–lined baking sheet. 6. Refrigerate at least 30 minutes (or up to overnight) until they harden. They will keep in refrigerator in an airtight container or plastic bag up to 2 weeks.
Per serving: Calories 56; Fat 3.51g; Sodium 25mg; Carbs 6.53g; Fiber 3g; Sugars 4.07g; Protein 1.5g

Almond-Orange Torte

Prep time: 45 minutes | Cook time: 1 hr. 30 minutes | Servings: 16

3 large oranges
2 bay leaves
1 cinnamon stick
¾ cup sucanat
6 large eggs
½ teaspoon baking powder
3 ½ cups almond meal
1 cup hazelnut meal
¾ cup dark chocolate chips (cacao or higher)

1. At 350 degrees F, preheat your oven grease and flour a 9" × 13" pan. 2. In a medium pot, combine oranges, bay leaves, and cinnamon and cover with water. Bring to a boil and simmer over low heat 45 minutes until oranges are easily pierced with a fork. 3. Cut them in quarters and let cool. Take out seeds and blend in a food processor until mash is chunky but even. 4. In a suitable bowl, combine orange purée, sucanat, eggs, baking powder, and nut meals. Mix well, then fold in chocolate chips. 5. Pour batter into prepared cake pan. Bake the food for 40–45 minutes. 6. Let cool at least 30 minutes before serving.
Per serving: Calories 220; Fat 16.6g; Sodium 36mg; Carbs 13.4g; Fiber 3.9g; Sugars 7.6g; Protein 8.2g

Berry Pops

Prep time: 5 minutes | Cook time: 0 minutes | Servings: 4

1 cup blueberries, fresh or frozen
1 cup strawberries, fresh or frozen
2 tablespoons raw honey
2 cups plain whole-milk yogurt
1 teaspoon lemon juice
¼ cup filtered water

1. In your blender, add all the ingredients, then pulse to combine well until creamy and smooth. 2. Pour the prepared mixture in the ice pop molds, then place in the freezer to free for at least 3 hours. 3. Serve chilled.
Per serving: Calories 120; Fat 0.3g; Sodium 44mg; Carbs 26.4g; Fiber 1.7g; Sugars 21.1g; Protein 3.1g

Peach Cobbler

Prep time: 10 minutes | Cook time: 20 minutes | Servings: 8

1 teaspoon coconut oil plus ¼ cup, melted
2 cups sliced fresh nectarines
2 cups sliced fresh peaches
2 tablespoons lemon juice
¾ cup almond flour
¼ cup coconut sugar
¾ cup rolled oats
1 teaspoon ground cinnamon
½ teaspoon vanilla extract
Sea salt, to taste
Filtered water, for mixing

1. At 425 degrees F, preheat your oven. Grease a baking sheet with 1 teaspoon of coconut oil. 2. Combine the nectarines, peaches, and lemon juice in the sheet. Stir to mix well. Set aside. 3. Put the almond flour, coconut sugar, oats, cinnamon, vanilla, salt, and remaining coconut oil in a food processor. Pulse until a dry dough forms. Add a tablespoon of water if the dough is too dry. 4. Transfer the dough in a suitable bowl, then break the dough into chunks with your hands. Top the fruit in the baking sheet with the dough chunks. 5. Set the baking sheet in the preheated oven and bake for almost 20 minutes or until golden brown. 6. Serve warm.
Per serving: Calories 137; Fat 6.3g; Sodium 36mg; Carbs 16.9g; Fiber 3.2g; Sugars 8.4g; Protein 4g

Blueberry Cream Parfait

Prep time: 5 minutes | Cook time: 0 minutes | Servings: 4

For the Cream
2 (14-ounce / 397-g) cans coconut cream, chilled
1 tablespoon pure maple syrup
1 tablespoon fresh lemon zest
½ teaspoon vanilla extract
Sea salt, to taste
For the Parfait
2½ cups fresh blueberries

1. To make the cream: Whip the coconut cream in a suitable bowl with a hand mixer for almost 2 minutes or until the peaks form. 2. Then add the lemon zest, vanilla, maple syrup, and salt. Whip to combine well. 3. To make the parfait: Pour half of the cream mixture in the bottom of a serving glass, then top with 1 cup of blueberries. 4. Spread the cream mixture on top of the blueberries, then top the cream with remaining blueberries. 5. Serve immediately.
Per serving: Calories 460; Fat 32.4g; Sodium 61mg; Carbs 46.6g; Fiber 9.1g; Sugars 31.7g; Protein 5g

Coconut Hot Chocolate

Prep time: 5 minutes | Cook time: 7 minutes | Servings: 2

1 tablespoon coconut oil
2 cups coconut milk
1 tablespoon collagen protein powder
2 tablespoons cocoa powder
2 teaspoons coconut sugar
½ teaspoon ground turmeric
1 teaspoon ground ginger
1 teaspoon vanilla extract
1 teaspoon ground cinnamon
Sea salt, to taste
Cayenne pepper, to taste

1. Heat the coconut oil and almond milk in a saucepan over medium heat for 7 minutes. Stir constantly. 2. Mix in the collagen protein powder, then fold in the cocoa powder and coconut sugar. Stir to mix well. 3. Pour the prepared mixture in a suitable blender, then add the rest of the ingredients. Pulse until the prepared mixture is creamy and bubbly. 4. Serve immediately.
Per serving: Calories 559; Fat 55.8g; Sodium 54mg; Carbs 15.5g; Fiber 2.5g; Sugars 4.4g; Protein 9.2g

Chocolate Tofu Pudding

Prep time: 15 minutes | Cook time: 0 minutes | Servings: 8

2 cups dark chocolate chips (cacao or higher)
1-pound silken tofu
1 teaspoon vanilla extract

1. Fill a medium saucepan ⅓ of the way with water. 2. Place a suitable bowl on top. It should fit securely, but bottom of bowl should not touch bottom of pot. 3. Place chocolate in bowl and melt, while stirring occasionally. (a double boiler may be used or you can melt chocolate in the microwave.) 4. In your blender, add tofu, melted chocolate, vanilla and then blend until smooth. 5. Pour into a glass container, cover, and refrigerate at least 1 hour. Serve.
Per serving: Calories 177; Fat 9.5g; Sodium 20mg; Carbs 21.4g; Fiber 0.1g; Sugars 16.8g; Protein 5.9g

Brownies with Strawberry Sauce

Prep time: 10 minutes | Cook time: 20 minutes | Servings: 9 brownies

or the Strawberry Sauce:	
cup mashed fresh strawberries	1 tablespoon filtered water
teaspoons coconut sugar	
or the Banana Brownies:	
oconut oil, for greasing this pan	1 teaspoon vanilla extract
cup cocoa powder	½ teaspoon baking soda
cup coconut sugar	1 ripe banana, mashed
cup almond butter	¼ teaspoon sea salt
egg yolk, whisked	

. To make the strawberry sauce: Put the ingredients for the rawberry sauce in a saucepan and heat them for 6 minutes or until ickened and well combined, stirring instantly. 2. Turn off the heat nd set aside until ready to use. 3. To make the banana brownies: At 50 degrees F, preheat your oven. Grease a baking pan with coconut l. 4. Combine the cocoa powder, coconut sugar, and almond butter a suitable bowl. Stir to mix well. 5. Combine the egg yolk, vanilla, aking soda, banana, and salt in a separate bowl. Stir to mix well. 6. ake a will in the center of the cocoa powder mixture, then pour the repared egg mixture in the well. Stir to mix well until a batter forms. Pour the batter in the prepared baking pan, then level with a spatula. ake in the preheated oven for almost 12 minutes or until a toothpick serted in the center comes out clean. 8. Remove the brownies from e oven and allow to cool for almost 5 minutes. Glaze the brownies ith strawberry sauce and slice to serve.
er serving: Calories 118; Fat 5.6g; Sodium 281mg; Carbs 19.4g; iber 5g; Sugars 8.9g; Protein 3.8g

Chia Pudding with Cherries

Prep time: 10 minutes | Cook time: 0 minutes | Servings: 4

cups almond milk	½ cup chopped cashews
cup chia seeds	1 cup frozen no-added-sugar
teaspoon vanilla extract	pitted cherries, thawed, juice
cup pure maple syrup	reserved

In a suitable bowl, mix up the almond milk, chia seeds, vanilla, d maple syrup. 2. Refrigerate the mixture overnight. 3. Divide the mond milk mixture in four bowls, then serve with cashews and erries on top.
er serving: Calories 340; Fat 27.3g; Sodium 18mg; Carbs 22.9g; ber 5.5g; Sugars 12.7g; Protein 5.3g

Cranberry Ginger Compote

Prep time: 5 minutes | Cook time: 10 minutes | Servings: 4

cups fresh cranberries	¼ cup raw honey
tablespoon grated fresh ginger	Zest of 1 orange
ice of 2 oranges	

In a suitable pot, mix up all the ingredients. 2. Bring to a boil over edium-high heat, then cook for almost 10 more minutes or until it ickens and the cranberries pop. 3. Turn off the heat and allow to cool r a few minutes. 4. Pour them in a suitable bowl and serve warm.
er serving: Calories 160; Fat 0.2g; Sodium 1mg; Carbs 36.1g; Fiber 8g; Sugars 27.6g; Protein 0.8g

Blueberry Coconut Muffins

Prep time: 5 minutes | Cook time: 20 minutes | Servings: 4

cup fresh blueberries	1 tablespoon nutmeg, grated
egg whites	1 teaspoon baking powder
tablespoon coconut flour	1 teaspoon vanilla extract
cup chickpea flour	1 teaspoon stevia

At 325 degrees F, preheat your oven. Layer a 4-cup muffin tin with per muffin cups. 2. Combine all the ingredients in a suitable bowl. ir to mix well. 3. Divide the batter into the muffin cups, then set the uffin tin in the preheated oven. 4. Bake for almost 15 minutes or til a toothpick inserted in the center comes out clean. 5. Transfer the uffins on a cooling rack to cool for a few minutes before serving.
er serving: Calories 234; Fat 4.1g; Sodium 39mg; Carbs 37.2g; ber 11g; Sugars 8g; Protein 13.1g

Blueberry Cobbler

Prep time: 15 minutes | Cook time: 2 hours | Servings: 4 to 6

3 tablespoons coconut oil	1 tablespoon coconut sugar
2 cups frozen blueberries	½ teaspoon vanilla extract
3 large peaches, peeled and sliced	1 tablespoon pure maple syrup
1 cup rolled oats	1 teaspoon ground cinnamon
1 cup almond flour	Pinch ground nutmeg

1. Grease the slow cooker with 1 tablespoon of coconut oil. 2. Put the blueberries and peaches in the single layer in the slow cooker. 3. In a suitable bowl, mix up the rest of the ingredients. 4. Break the prepared mixture into chunks with your hands, then spread the chunks on top of the blueberries and peaches in the slow cooker. 5. Cover the slow cooker lid and cook on high for almost 2 hours or until golden brown. 6. Allow to cool for almost 15 minutes, then serve warm.
Per serving: Calories 300; Fat 16.9g; Sodium 8mg; Carbs 32.5g; Fiber 5.9g; Sugars 16.6g; Protein 6.9g

Spice Stuffed Apple Bake

Prep time: 15 minutes | Cook time: 2 hours | Servings: 5 apples

5 apples, cored	1 teaspoon ground cinnamon
½ cup water	¼ teaspoon ground cardamom
½ cup crushed pecans	½ teaspoon ground ginger
¼ teaspoon ground cloves	¼ cup melted coconut oil

1. Peel a thin strip off the top of each apple. 2. Pour the water in the slow cooker, then arrange the apples in the slow cooker, upright. 3. In a suitable bowl, mix up the rest of the ingredients in a suitable bowl. 4. Spread the prepared mixture on tops of the apples, then put the slow cooker lid on and cook on high for almost 2 hours or until the apples are tender. 5. Allow to cool for almost 15 minutes, then remove the apples from the slow cooker gently and serve warm.
Per serving: Calories 292; Fat 19.3g; Sodium 4mg; Carbs 33g; Fiber 6.9g; Sugars 23.6g; Protein 1.9g

Banana Cacao Brownies

Prep time: 15 minutes | Cook time: 3 hours | Servings: 4 to 6

3 tablespoons coconut oil	½ cup coconut sugar
2 ripe bananas, mashed	2 teaspoons vanilla extract
1 cup cacao powder	1 teaspoon baking soda
1 cup almond butter	½ teaspoon sea salt
2 large eggs	

1. Grease the slow cooker with 1 tablespoon of coconut oil. 2. In a suitable bowl, mix up the rest of the ingredients until a batter form. 3. Pour the batter in the greased slow cooker. Cover and cook on low for almost 3 hours or until lightly firmed and a toothpick inserted in the center comes out clean. 4. Remove the brownies from the slow cooker and slice to serve.
Per serving: Calories 181; Fat 12.8g; Sodium 391mg; Carbs 19.1g; Fiber 5.3g; Sugars 7.9g; Protein 5.8g

Quinoa with Raspberries

Prep time: 10 minutes | Cook time: 20 minutes | Servings: 4

1 cup quinoa, rinsed	2 tablespoons flaxseeds
2 cups water	1 teaspoon vanilla extract
¼ cup hemp seeds	Pinch sea salt
½ cup shredded coconut	¼ cup chopped hazelnuts
1 teaspoon ground cinnamon	1 cup fresh raspberries

1. In your saucepan, pour in the quinoa and water. Bring to a boil over high heat. 2. Reduce its heat to low and simmer for almost 20 minutes or until soft. 3. When the simmering is complete, mix in the hemp seeds, coconut, cinnamon, flaxseeds, vanilla, and salt. 4. Serve the quinoa with hazelnuts and raspberries on top.
Per serving: Calories 302; Fat 13.5g; Sodium 68mg; Carbs 35.3g; Fiber 7.8g; Sugars 2.4g; Protein 10.6g

Glazed Pears with Hazelnuts

Prep time: 10 minutes | Cook time: 15 minutes | Servings: 4

4 pears, peeled, cored, and quartered lengthwise
1 cup apple juice

1 tablespoon grated fresh ginger
½ cup pure maple syrup
¼ cup chopped hazelnuts

1. Put the pears in a suitable pot, then pour the apple juice over. Bring to a boil over medium-high heat. 2. Reduce its heat to medium-low, then cover and simmer for almost 15 minutes or until the pears are tender. 3. Meanwhile, put the ginger and maple syrup in a saucepan. Bring to a boil over medium-high heat. Stir constantly. 4. Turn off the heat and let stand until ready to use. 5. Transfer the simmered pears onto a large plate, then glaze with the gingered maple syrup. 6. Spread the hazelnuts on top and serve warm.
Per serving: Calories 286; Fat 3.4g; Sodium 9mg; Carbs 67g; Fiber 7.2g; Sugars 50.1g; Protein 1.6g

Apple Cinnamon Muesli

Prep time: 10 minutes | Cook time: 0 minutes | Servings: 4 to 6

2 cups rolled oats
¼ cup no-added-sugar apple juice
1¾ cups coconut milk

1 tablespoon apple cider vinegar
1 apple, cored and chopped
Dash ground cinnamon

1. In a suitable bowl, mix up the oats, apple juice, coconut milk, and apple cider vinegar. 2. Wrap the bowl in plastic and refrigerate the mixture overnight. 3. Remove the bowl from the refrigerator. Top with apple and sprinkle with cinnamon, then serve.
Per serving: Calories 384; Fat 32.2g; Sodium 20mg; Carbs 24.2g Fiber 5.5g; Sugars 9.2g; Protein 5.4g

Chapter 9 Sauce and Dressings

Worcestershire Caesar Dressing

Prep time: 5 minutes | Cook time: 0 | Servings: 1 ½ cups

2 tablespoons lemon juice	1 cup Anti-Inflammatory Mayo
2 small garlic cloves, minced	½ cup freshly grated Parmesan
1 teaspoon anchovy paste	cheese
1 teaspoon Dijon mustard	¼ teaspoon salt
1 teaspoon Worcestershire sauce	¼ teaspoon black pepper

1. In a suitable bowl, mix up the lemon juice, garlic, anchovy paste, mustard, Worcestershire sauce, mayo, Parmesan, salt and pepper until well combined. 2. Taste and adjust the seasoning to your liking. 3. Store in an airtight container in the refrigerator for up to 7 days.
Per Serving (2 tablespoons): Calories 19; Total Fat 0.27g; Sodium 132mg; Total Carbs 2.49g; Fiber 0.1g; Sugars 0.21g; Protein 1.79g

Basil Alfredo Sauce

Prep time: 5 minutes | Cook time: 10 minutes | Servings: 2 cups

½ cup (1 stick) unsalted butter	Parmesan cheese
4 garlic cloves, minced	1 teaspoon salt
1 cup whipping cream	1 teaspoon black pepper
4 ounces' cream cheese	⅓ cup chopped fresh basil
1½ cups freshly shredded	

1. Melt the butter over medium-low heat in a suitable saucepan, being careful not to burn it. 2. Stir in the garlic and sauté for almost 2 minutes. 3. Add the cream and cream cheese and whisk until melted and smooth. 4. Whisk in the Parmesan, salt, and pepper and Lower its heat to low. 5. Whisking constantly, cook for almost 4 minutes, until well combined and creamy. 6. Stir in the basil and serve warm.
Per Serving: Calories 149; Total Fat 15.4g; Sodium 313mg; Total Carbs 1.1g; Fiber 0.1g; Sugars 0.1g; Protein 2.2g

Keto Egg Sandwich

Prep time: 5 minutes | Cook time: 1 ½ minutes | Servings: 1

3 tablespoons almond flour	1 teaspoon everything bagel
1 large egg	seasoning
1 tablespoon olive oil	¼ teaspoon baking powder

1. In a microwave-safe 5-inch ramekin or small bowl, mix up the almond flour, egg, olive oil, everything seasoning and baking powder. 2. Microwave on high for almost 90 seconds. 3. Slide a knife around the edges of the ramekin and flip to remove the bread. Slice the round in half with a serrated knife to make two pieces for a sandwich.
Per Serving: Calories 261; Total Fat 18.58g; Sodium 219mg; Total Carbs 19.1g; Fiber 2.8g; Sugars 0.5g; Protein 5.8g

Lemon Turmeric Aioli

Prep time: 5 minutes | Cook time: 0 | Serving: 1 cup

1 cup Anti-Inflammatory Mayo	1 teaspoon ground turmeric
Grated zest and juice of 1 lemon	½ teaspoon cayenne pepper or red
2 garlic cloves, minced	pepper flakes (optional)
1 teaspoon monk fruit extract	

1. In a suitable bowl, mix up all the ingredients until smooth and creamy. 2. Cover the bowl and keep the aioli in the refrigerator for up to 7 days.
Per Serving: Calories 209; Total Fat 19.84g; Sodium 381mg; Total Carbs 7.24g; Fiber 0.4g; Sugars 3.06g; Protein 0.6g

Garlic Rosemary Butter

Prep time: 10 minutes | Cook time: 0 | Serving: ½ cup

½ cup (1 stick) unsalted butter	2 garlic cloves, minced
1 tablespoon chopped fresh	½ teaspoon salt
rosemary	

1. In a suitable bowl, use an immersion blender to blend the butter, rosemary, garlic and salt until smooth and creamy. 2. Using a spatula, transfer the butter mixture to a suitable glass container and cover. The mixture can be stored in the refrigerator for up to 1 month or in the freezer for up to 4 months.
Per Serving: Calories 143; Total Fat 15.46g; Sodium 301mg; Total Carbs 0.58g; Fiber 0.1g; Sugars 0.02g; Protein 1.03g

Easy Vinaigrette

Prep time: 5 minutes | Cook time: 0 | Serving: ¾ cup

½ cup avocado or olive oil	2 teaspoons dried rosemary, basil
¼ cup white or red wine vinegar	parsley, thyme, or oregano
1 tablespoon Dijon mustard	½ teaspoon salt
1 small garlic clove, pressed or	½ to 1 teaspoon red pepper flakes
minced	

1. Prepare a glass jar or a container with lid, mix up all the ingredients in it and shake until well combined. 2. Cover the jar or container with the lid and store the mixture in the refrigerator for up to 2 weeks. 3. Bring to room temperature and shake well before serving, as the oil and vinegar will naturally separate.
Per Serving: Calories 149; Total Fat 15.67g; Sodium 756mg; Total Carbs 0.82g; Fiber 0.3g; Sugars 0.08g; Protein 0.43g

Anti-Inflammatory Mayo

Prep time: 5 minutes | Cook time: 0 minutes | Serving: 1 cup

1 large egg	¼ to ½ teaspoon ground turmeric
2 teaspoons white wine vinegar	1 cup avocado oil
½ to 1 teaspoon salt	

1. Crack the egg into the bottom of a wide-mouth jar. 2. Add the vinegar, salt, and turmeric. 3. Gently add the oil, being careful not to disturb the egg. 4. Insert the immersion blender into the jar, allowing the blade casing to fully touch the bottom of the jar and sit flat. 5. Blend on low for almost 25 to 30 seconds without moving the blender, until the eggs emulsify. 6. Continuing to blend on low, slowly move the blender toward the top of the jar. 7. Move the blender up and down several times until the mayo is smooth and creamy. 8. You can store the mixture in the refrigerator for up to 2 weeks.
Per Serving: Calories 250; Total Fat 27.85g; Sodium 154mg; Total Carbs 0.12g; Fiber 0g; Sugars 0.03g; Protein 0.8g

Parmesan Basil Pesto

Prep time: 10 minutes | Cook time: 0 | Serving: 1 cup

4 cups packed whole fresh basil	1 teaspoon salt
leaves	½ teaspoon black pepper
½ cup freshly shredded Parmesan	½ cup olive oil
cheese	1 tablespoon freshly squeezed
¼ cup pine nuts	lemon juice
2 garlic cloves, peeled	

1. In a suitable food processor, add the basil, Parmesan, pine nuts and garlic and then blend them until very chopped. 2. Add the salt and pepper. 3. With the processor running, stream in the olive oil and lemon juice until well blended. If the mixture seems too thick, add warm water, 1 tablespoon at a time, until the texture is smooth and creamy. 4. Store the pesto in an airtight container in the refrigerator for up to 7 days.
Per Serving: Calories 168; Total Fat 16.65g; Sodium 349mg; Total Carbs 3.06g; Fiber 0.2g; Sugars 0.28g; Protein 2.66g

Easy Anti-Inflammatory Mayo

Prep time: 5 minutes | Cook time: 0 minutes | Servings: 4

1 large egg	¼ to ½ teaspoon ground turmeric
2 teaspoons white wine vinegar	1 cup avocado oil
½ to 1 teaspoon salt	

1. Crack the egg into a wide-mouth jar. Carefully add the vinegar, salt, and turmeric. Gently add the oil, being careful not to disturb the egg. 2. Carefully insert the immersion blender into the jar, allowing the blade casing to fully touch the bottom of the jar and sit flat. 3. Blend on low speed for almost 25 to 30 seconds without moving the blender, until the egg begins to emulsify and the prepared mixture starts to turn white and creamy. 4. Resume blending on low speed, then slowly move the blender toward the top of the jar, but remaining in the prepared mixture. 5. Move the blender up and down several times until the mayo is smooth and creamy. 6. The leftovers can be kept covered in the refrigerator for up to 2 weeks.
Per serving: Calories 93; Fat 8.4g; Sodium 311mg; Carbs 3.4g; Fiber 2.5g; Sugars 0.3g; Protein 2.3g

Homemade Guacamole

Prep time: 10 minutes | Cook time: 0 | Servings: 1 ½ cups

very ripe avocados, peeled, pitted	1 tablespoon chopped jalapeño
uice of ½ lemon	1 teaspoon salt
tablespoons olive oil	½ to 1 teaspoon ground turmeric
garlic clove, pressed or minced	½ teaspoon black pepper
tablespoon minced red onion	¼ to ½ cup chopped fresh cilantro (optional)

1. In a suitable bowl, mix up the avocados, lemon juice, olive oil, and garlic and mash well with a fork. Stir in the onion, jalapeño, salt, turmeric, pepper and cilantro until well combined. 2. Serve.
Per Serving: Calories 183; Total Fat 17.26g; Sodium 477mg; Total Carbs 8.37g; Fiber 5.6g; Sugars 0.76g; Protein 1.82g

Marinara Sauce with Basil

Prep time: 15 minutes | Cook time: 60 minutes | Servings: 8 cups

½ cup olive oil	tomatoes
2 tablespoons unsalted butter	2 tablespoons chopped fresh
1 red bell pepper, minced	oregano
½ small onion, minced	2 teaspoons salt
4 garlic cloves, minced	½ to 1 teaspoon red pepper flakes
2 (32-ounce) cans crushed	½ cup chopped fresh basil

1. In a suitable skillet, heat the butter and 2 tablespoons of olive oil over medium-low heat. 2. Add the bell pepper, onion and sauté for almost 5 minutes until just tender. Add the garlic and sauté for 2 minutes or until fragrant. 3. Stir in the tomatoes and their juices, oregano, salt, red pepper flakes, and the remaining olive oil and bring to boil. 4. Lower the heat to low and cover the skillet, and then simmer the food for almost 15 to 60 minutes, allowing the flavors to blend. The longer the sauce cooks, the more flavorful it will be, but it will be ready to eat after 15 minutes of simmering. 5. Remove the sauce from the heat and stir in the basil. Serve warm. 6. The leftovers can be stored in an airtight container in the refrigerator for up to 4 days.
Per Serving: Calories 183; Total Fat 16.09g; Sodium 860mg; Total Carbs 9.95g; Fiber 4.9g; Sugars 6.64g; Protein 2.33g

Avocado Cilantro Dressing

Prep time: 10 minutes | Cook time: 0 | Servings: 1 ½ cups

2 very ripe avocados, pitted and peeled	2 garlic cloves, peeled
1 cup packed fresh cilantro leaves	1 teaspoon salt
½ cup olive oil	½ teaspoon freshly ground black
¼ cup lime juice	pepper

1. In a suitable blender, add all the ingredients and then blend them until thick and creamy. If the mixture seems too thick, add warm water, 1 tablespoon at a time. 2. Store the prepared dressing in an airtight container in the refrigerator for up to 7 days.
Per Serving: Calories 163; Total Fat 16.71g; Sodium 237mg; Total Carbs 4.29g; Fiber 2.8g; Sugars 0.39g; Protein 0.92g

Almond Romesco Sauce

Prep time: 10 minutes | Cook time: 10 minutes | Serves: 2 cups

2 red bell peppers, chopped	1 cup blanched raw almonds
5 or 6 cherry tomatoes, chopped	¼ cup olive oil
3 garlic cloves, chopped	2 tablespoons apple cider vinegar
½ white onion, chopped	¼ teaspoon salt
1 tablespoon avocado oil	Black pepper

1. Preheat the broiler to high. Layer a baking sheet with aluminum foil. 2. Spread the bell peppers, tomatoes, garlic, and onion on the prepared sheet and drizzle with the avocado oil. Broil them for 10 minutes. 3. In a suitable food processor (or blender), pulse the almonds until they resemble bread crumbs. 4. Add the boiled vegetables, olive oil, vinegar, and salt, and season with pepper. Process them until smooth. Serve immediately. 5. Cover and refrigerate for up to 5 days, or freeze for 3 to 4 months.
Per serving: Calories: 102; Total fat 8.5g; Sodium 54mg; Total carbs 6g; Fiber 2.1g; Sugars 2.9g; Protein 2.4g

Riced Cauliflower with Basil

Prep time: 5 minutes | Cook time: 5 minutes | Servings: 6-8

1 small cauliflower head, broken into florets	½ to 1 teaspoon red pepper flakes
¼ cup olive oil	½ teaspoon ground turmeric
2 garlic cloves, minced	¼ to ½ cup chopped fresh basil, cilantro, or parsley
2 teaspoons salt	

1. In a suitable food processor, pulse the cauliflower several times, until it is the consistency of rice. 2. In the skillet, heat the olive oil over medium-high heat; add the cauliflower, garlic, salt, red pepper flakes, turmeric and sauté them for 5 minutes. 3. Transfer the cauliflower to a suitable bowl. Toss with the basil and serve warm.
Per Serving: Calories 70; Total Fat 6.87g; Sodium 593mg; Total Carbs 2.15g; Fiber 0.8g; Sugars 0.67g; Protein 0.76g

Dill Avocado Dressing

Prep time: 5 minutes | Cook time: 0 | Servings: 2 cups

1 very ripe avocado, pitted and peeled	1 tablespoon olive oil
½ cup Anti-Inflammatory Mayo	1 tablespoon freshly squeezed lemon juice
½ cup full-fat buttermilk	2 teaspoons chopped fresh dill, or
2 tablespoons chopped fresh parsley, or 1 teaspoon dried parsley	1 teaspoon dried dill
2 tablespoons chopped red onion	½ teaspoon garlic powder
	½ teaspoon salt
	¼ teaspoon black pepper

1. Blend the avocado, mayo, buttermilk, parsley, onion, olive oil, lemon juice, dill, garlic powder, salt, and pepper in the blender until thick and creamy, thinning out with additional lemon juice if necessary. 2. Store the prepared dressing in an airtight container in the refrigerator for up to 7 days.
Per Serving: Calories 83; Total Fat 6.55g; Sodium 150mg; Total Carbs 5.05g; Fiber 2.4g; Sugars 0.72g; Protein 2.49g

Garlic Tofu Sauce

Prep time: 10 minutes | Cook time: 0 | Servings: 2 cups

1 (12-ounce) package silken tofu	1 tablespoon fresh lemon juice
½ cup chopped fresh basil	1 teaspoon salt
2 garlic cloves, lightly crushed	¼ teaspoon black pepper
½ cup almond butter	

1. Add the tofu, basil, garlic, almond butter, lemon juice, salt, and pepper to the blender, blend them until smooth. If too thick, thin with a bit of water. 2. Refrigerate the sauce in an airtight container for up to 5 days.
Per Serving: Calories 130; Total Fat 10.73g; Sodium 295mg; Total Carbs 4.22g; Fiber 1.8g; Sugars 0.75g; Protein 6.82g

Lemon Dijon Dressing

Prep time: 10 minutes | Cook time: 0 | Servings: 1 ½ cups

1 cup extra-virgin olive oil	1 shallot, sliced
¼ cup fresh lemon juice	1 teaspoon grated lemon zest
1 tablespoon honey	1 teaspoon salt
1 teaspoon Dijon mustard	¼ teaspoon pepper

1. Add the olive oil, lemon juice, honey, Dijon, shallot, lemon zest, salt and pepper to the blender, then process them until smooth. 2. Refrigerate the dressing in an airtight container for up to 5 days.
Per Serving: Calories 155; Total Fat 15.53g; Sodium 707mg; Total Carbs 4.15g; Fiber 0.2g; Sugars 3.39g; Protein 0.3g

Spiced Ghee

Prep time: 2 minutes | Cook time: 5 minutes | Serves: ¼ cup

¼ cup ghee	2 ½ tablespoons basic spice blend

1. In a small saucepot, warm ghee until just melted for almost 1–2 minutes over low heat. 2. Add basic anti-inflammatory spice blend, stir to combine, and turn off the heat. 3. Keep in a suitable glass jar in the refrigerator until ready to use.
Per serving: Calories: 59; Total fat 4.3g; Sodium 0mg; Total carbs 5.8g; Fiber 0g; Sugars 5.8g; Protein 0g

Ginger Turmeric Dressing

Prep time: 10 minutes | Cook time: 0 | Servings: 1 ½ cups

1 cup extra-virgin olive oil
¼ cup apple cider vinegar
½ teaspoon Dijon mustard
1 garlic clove, sliced
½ teaspoon minced fresh ginger root

1 teaspoon salt
½ teaspoon ground turmeric
¼ teaspoon ground coriander
¼ teaspoon freshly ground black pepper

1. Process all the recipe ingredients in the blender until smooth. 2. Refrigerate the dressing in an airtight container for up to 7 days.
Per Serving: Calories 147; Total Fat 15.51g; Sodium 702mg; Total Carbs 1.63g; Fiber 0.1g; Sugars 1.01g; Protein 0.24g

Sesame Chives Dressing

Prep time: 5 minutes | Cook time: 0 | Servings: ¾ cup

½ cup canned coconut milk
2 tablespoons tahini
2 tablespoons freshly squeezed lime juice
1 teaspoon bottled minced garlic
1 teaspoon minced fresh chives
Pinch sea salt

1. In a suitable bowl, mix up the coconut milk, tahini, lime juice, garlic and chives until well blended. 2. Season with sea salt and transfer the prepared dressing to a container with a lid. Refrigerate the dressing for up to 7 days.
Per serving: calories 78; Total Fat 7.46g; Sodium 35mg; Total Carbs 2.75g; Fiber 0.9g; Sugars 0.79g; Protein 1.36g

Maple Vinegar Dressing

Prep time: 5 minutes | Cook time: 0 | Servings: 1 ¼ cups

1 cup canned full-fat coconut milk
2 tablespoons pure maple syrup

1 tablespoon Dijon mustard
1 tablespoon apple cider vinegar
Sea salt

1. Add the coconut milk, maple syrup, mustard and cider vinegar to the blender and then blend them until smoothly blended. Season with sea salt. 2. Refrigerate the prepared dressing in a sealed container for up to 7 days.
Per Serving: Calories 111; Total Fat 9.63g; Sodium 61mg; Total Carbs 6.86g; Fiber 1g; Sugars 5.4g; Protein 1.02g

Lemon Parsley Sauce

Prep time: 5 minutes | Cook time: 0 minutes | Servings: 1 cup

¾ cup chopped fresh parsley
Juice of 2 lemons
Zest of 2 lemons

2 tablespoons olive oil
2 teaspoons bottled minced garlic
¼ teaspoon sea salt

1. In a suitable bowl, mix up the parsley, lemon juice, lemon zest, olive oil, garlic and sea salt until well blended. 2. Refrigerate the mixture in a sealed container for up to 4 days.
Per serving: Calories 76; Total Fat 6.96g; Sodium 152mg; Total Carbs 4.49g; Fiber 0.5g; Sugars 1.32g; Protein 0.59g

Riced Cauliflower

Prep time: 5 minutes | Cook time: 10 minutes | Servings: 8

1 small cauliflower head, broken into florets
¼ cup olive oil
2 garlic cloves, minced
2 teaspoons salt

½ to 1 teaspoon red pepper flakes
½ teaspoon ground turmeric
¼ to ½ cup chopped fresh basil, cilantro, or parsley

1. In a suitable food processor, blend the cauliflower several times, until it is the consistency of rice. 2. In a suitable skillet, heat the olive oil over medium-high heat. Add the cauliflower, garlic, salt, red pepper flakes, and turmeric and sauté for no more than 5 minutes. 3. Remove the cauliflower from this skillet and place in a suitable bowl to stop the cooking. Toss with the basil and serve warm.
Per serving: Calories 59; Fat 6.3g; Sodium 585mg; Carbs 1.1g; Fiber 0.4g; Sugars 0.3g; Protein 0.3g

Lemon–Dijon Mustard Dressing

Prep time: 5 minutes | Cook time: 0 | Serves: 6 tablespoons

¼ cup olive oil
2 tablespoons lemon juice
1 teaspoon Dijon mustard
½ teaspoon raw honey

1 garlic clove, minced
¼ teaspoon dried basil
¼ teaspoon salt

1. In a suitable glass jar, combine the olive oil, lemon juice, mustard, honey, garlic, basil, and salt. 2. Cover and shake vigorously until the ingredients are well combined and emulsified. 3. Refrigerate for up to 1 week.
Per serving: Calories: 76; Total fat 8.5g; Sodium 107mg; Total carbs 0.8g; Fiber 0.1g; Sugars 0.6g; Protein 0.1g

Tahini-Lime Dressing

Prep time: 5 minutes | Cook time: 0 | Serves: ¾ cup

⅓ cup tahini (sesame paste)
3 tablespoons filtered water
2 tablespoons lime juice
1 tablespoon apple cider vinegar

1 teaspoon lime zest
1½ teaspoons raw honey
¼ teaspoon garlic powder
¼ teaspoon salt

1. In a suitable glass jar, combine the tahini, water, lime juice, vinegar, lime zest, honey, garlic powder, and salt. 2. Cover and shake vigorously until the ingredients are well combined and emulsified. 3. Refrigerate for up to 1 week.
Per serving: Calories: 100; Total fat 7.2g; Sodium 113mg; Total carbs 8.3g; Fiber 1.3g; Sugars 5.4g; Protein 2.3g

Paleo Caesar Dressing

Prep time: 10 minutes | Cook time: 0 | Serves: about ½ cup

¼ cup paleo mayonnaise
2 tablespoons olive oil
2 tablespoons lemon juice
½ teaspoon lemon zest
2 garlic cloves, minced

1 tablespoon white wine vinegar
½ teaspoon anchovy paste
¼ teaspoon salt
Black pepper

1. In a suitable bowl, whisk the mayonnaise, olive oil, lemon juice, lemon zest, garlic, vinegar, anchovy paste, and salt until well combined and emulsified. 2. Season the mixture with pepper. Cover and refrigerate for up to 7 days.
Per serving: Calories: 78; Total fat 9g; Sodium 139mg; Total carbs 0.4g; Fiber 0.1g; Sugars 0.1g; Protein 0.1g

Aioli

Prep time: 5 minutes | Cook time: 0 | Serves: about ½ cup

½ cup plain whole-milk yogurt
2 teaspoons Dijon mustard
½ teaspoon hot sauce

¼ teaspoon raw honey
Pinch salt

1. In a suitable bowl, stir together the yogurt, mustard, hot sauce, honey, and salt. 2. You can serve immediately or cover it and refrigerate for up to 3 days.
Per serving: Calories: 11; Total fat 0.1g; Sodium 37mg; Total carbs 1.9g; Fiber 0.1g; Sugars 1.4g; Protein 0.5g

Vegetable Stock

Prep time: 10 minutes | Cook time: 45 minutes | Serves: 9 cups

2 tablespoons olive oil
3 medium carrots, cut to 2" pieces
3 medium stalks celery, cut to 2" pieces
2 small onions
10 cups cold water

½ cup dried shiitake mushrooms
1 (3") piece dried kombu
2 bay leaves
1 bunch parsley stems, cut in half
1 teaspoon salt
½ teaspoon ground black pepper

1. In a suitable pot, sauté carrots, celery, and onions with oil for 5 minutes over medium heat. 2. Add water and all remaining ingredients. Bring to a boil and then reduce to a simmer 40 minutes. 3. Strain and discard solids, reserving liquid. Alternately, if desiring a stock that is more viscous and has a deeper flavor, purée about ⅓ of cooked vegetables in a suitable food processor or blender and add them back into the broth.
Per serving: Calories: 93; Total fat 7.1g; Sodium 632mg; Total carbs 7.9g; Fiber 1.9g; Sugars 3.7g; Protein 0.8g

Sweet Spiced Ghee

Prep time: 5 minutes | Cook time: 5 minutes | Serve: 1 cup

½ cup ghee
½ cup honey

2 ¼ tablespoons sweet spice blend

1. Combine all the recipe ingredients in a small, heavy-bottomed pot. 2. Warm over very low heat until honey and ghee have just melted. 3. Store them in a suitable glass jar.
Per serving: Calories: 59; Total fat 4.3g; Sodium 0mg; Total carbs 5.8g; Fiber 0g; Sugars 5.8g; Protein 0g

Sweet Spice Blend

Prep time: 5 minutes | Cook time: 0 | Serves: 2 ¼ tablespoons

1 tablespoon ground cinnamon
1 tablespoon ground cardamom

½ teaspoon ground clove
½ teaspoon ground star anise

1. Combine all the recipe ingredients in a suitable glass jar. 2. Mix well.
Per serving: Calories: 6; Total fat 0.1g; Sodium 1mg; Total carbs 1.7g; Fiber 0.9g; Sugars 0g; Protein 0.2g

Tex Mex Spice Blend

Prep time: 5 minutes | Cook time: 0 | Serve: ¼ cup

1 tablespoon sweet paprika
1 tablespoon ground cumin
1 tablespoon dried oregano

1 ½ teaspoon red chili flakes
¾ teaspoon ground black pepper

1. In a suitable glass jar, combine all the recipe ingredients. 2. Stir or shake well to mix.
Per serving: Calories: 8; Total fat 0.4g; Sodium 2mg; Total carbs 1.3g; Fiber 0.7g; Sugars 0.1g; Protein 0.3g

Avocado Dressing

Prep time: 10 minutes | Cook time: 0 | Serve: 1 cup

1 ripe avocado
¼ cup lime juice
2 garlic cloves, peeled
¼ cup fresh cilantro leaves, chopped

¼ cup water
2 tablespoons olive oil
¼ teaspoon salt
¼ teaspoon ground black pepper

1. In a blender, combine all the recipe ingredients. Blend until smooth. 2. Serve.
Per serving: Calories: 55; Total fat 5.6g; Sodium 52mg; Total carbs 1.6g; Fiber 1.1g; Sugars 0.1g; Protein 0.4g

Ranch Dressing

Prep time: 10 minutes | Cook time: 0 | Serves: 2 cups

1 cup plain Greek yogurt
½ cup buttermilk
¼ cup lemon juice
¼ cup fresh dill, chopped
1 tablespoon fresh thyme leaves

1 teaspoon onion powder
1 teaspoon garlic powder
½ teaspoon ground black pepper
½ teaspoon salt

1. In a suitable bowl, whisk together all the recipe ingredients. 2. Chill them for 30 minutes and they can be kept in the refrigerator for up to two weeks.
Per serving: Calories: 37; Total fat 0.7g; Sodium 190mg; Total carbs 4.7g; Fiber 0.4g; Sugars 3.3g; Protein 2.7g

Basic Spice Blend

Prep time: 5 minutes | Cook time: 0 | Serves: 2 ½ tablespoons

2 teaspoons ground turmeric
2 teaspoons ground cumin
2 teaspoons ground coriander

½ teaspoon ground black pepper
½ teaspoon dry mustard powder
½ teaspoon ginger powder

1. Combine all the recipe ingredients in a suitable glass jar. 2. Mix well.
Per serving: Calories: 6; Total fat 0.2g; Sodium 1mg; Total carbs 0.8g; Fiber 0.3g; Sugars 0g; Protein 0.2g

Nori Gomasio

Prep time: 10 minutes | Cook time: 0 | Serve: ½ cup

1 sheet nori
½ cup sesame seeds

½ teaspoon salt

1. Holding nori with tongs, pass the sheet over a low-medium gas flame or electric burner on your stove quickly four times on each side. 2. Break nori apart with your fingers and put it in a spice or coffee grinder. Pulse a few times until nori is broken down into small flecks. 3. Add sesame seeds and pulse a few more times until seeds are broken up. 4. Add salt, mix well, and keep in a suitable glass jar at room temperature for up to one month.
Per serving: Calories: 35; Total fat 3g; Sodium 98mg; Total carbs 1.4g; Fiber 0.8g; Sugars 0g; Protein 1.1g

Walnut Pesto

Prep time: 10 minutes | Cook time: 0 | Serve: 1 cup

2 cups fresh basil
¼ cup chopped walnuts
½ cup grated Parmiggiano cheese
2 garlic cloves, peeled

½ cup olive oil
½ teaspoon salt
⅛ teaspoon ground black pepper

1. Combine all the recipe ingredients in a suitable food processor. 2. Process, stopping to scrape down the sides until the mixture is very smooth and well blended. 3. Taste and adjust seasoning. Keep them in a suitable sealed container in the refrigerator for up to one week or frozen for six months.
Per serving: Calories: 119; Total fat 13.4g; Sodium 162mg; Total carbs 0.3g; Fiber 0g; Sugars 0g; Protein 1.1g

Creamy Coconut-Herb Dressing

Prep time: 5 minutes | Cook time: 0 minute | Serves: about 1 cup

8 ounces plain coconut yogurt
2 tablespoons lemon juice
2 tablespoons fresh parsley, chopped

1 tablespoon snipped fresh chives
½ teaspoon salt
Pinch black pepper

1. In a suitable bowl, whisk together the yogurt, lemon juice, parsley, chives, salt, and pepper. 2. Refrigerate in an airtight container.
Per serving: Calories: 15; Total fat 1.1g; Sodium 317mg; Total carbs 1.8g; Fiber 1.1g; Sugars 0.4g; Protein 0.1g

Pistachio Pesto

Prep time: 10 minutes | Cook time: 0 minute | Serves: 4 cups

2 cups tightly fresh basil leaves
1 cup raw pistachios
½ cup olive oil
½ cup shredded raw parmesan cheese

2 teaspoons lemon juice
½ teaspoon garlic powder
¼ teaspoon salt
Black pepper

1. In your food blender, combine the basil, pistachios, and ¼ cup of olive oil. Blend for 15 seconds. 2. Add the cheese, lemon juice, garlic powder, and salt, and season with pepper. 3. With the processor running, slowly pour in the remaining olive oil until all the recipe ingredients are well combined. 4. You can serve immediately or cover it and refrigerate for up to 5 days, or freeze for 3 to 4 months.
Per serving: Calories: 149; Total fat 16.2g; Sodium 116mg; Total carbs 2.2g; Fiber 0.8g; Sugars 0.6g; Protein 1.6g

Avocado and Herb Spread

Prep time: 10 minutes | Cook time: 0 | Serve: 1 cup

1 ripe avocado, peeled and pitted
2 tablespoons lemon juice
2 tablespoons fresh parsley, chopped

1 teaspoon fresh dill, chopped
½ teaspoon ground coriander
Sea salt, to taste
Black pepper, to taste

1. In a blender, pulse the avocado until smoothly puréed. 2. Add the lemon juice, parsley, dill, and coriander. Pulse until well blended. 3. Season with sea salt and pepper. 4. Refrigerate the spread in a suitable sealed container for up to 4 days.
Per serving: Calories: 3; Total fat 0.1g; Sodium 62mg; Total carbs 0.4g; Fiber 0.1g; Sugars 0.2g; Protein 0.2g

Dukkah

Prep time: 10 minutes | Cook time: 8 minutes | Serve: 1 cup

½ cup whole hazelnuts
2 tablespoons sunflower seeds
1 tablespoon cumin seeds
1 teaspoon fennel seeds
2 ½ tablespoons coriander seeds

2 tablespoons sesame seeds
½ teaspoon nigella seeds
1 teaspoon sweet paprika
½ teaspoon salt
¼ teaspoon ground black pepper

1. At 300 degrees F, preheat your oven. 2. Place hazelnuts and sunflower seeds on a sheet pan and toast for about 5 minutes until fragrant. 3. Transfer to a spice grinder and pulse just until they are ground. 4. Avoid getting to a flour stage; some pieces of nuts here and there are nice. Place in a suitable bowl. 5. Heat a suitable pan over medium heat for 1 minute. Then add cumin, fennel, and coriander (unless using already ground seeds). Toast them for 1 minute. 6. Place in spice grinder and pulse until seeds are broken down but not powdered. 7. Add spices to bowl with nuts. In the same pan, toast the sesame seeds and nigella seeds for 2 minutes. Add to bowl with nuts. 8. Add salt, paprika, and pepper to the bowl. Mix well. 9. Store them in an airtight glass container for up to one month.
Per serving: Calories: 67; Total fat 6.1g; Sodium 149mg; Total carbs 2.5g; Fiber 1.3g; Sugars 0.4g; Protein 1.9g

Berry Ginger Jam

Prep time: 10 minutes | Cook time: 30 minutes | Serves: 6 cups

8 cups berries, fresh or frozen
1 cup water
4 medium pitted dates

1 tablespoon grated fresh ginger
¼ cup lemon juice
¼ cup chia seeds

1. In a suitable pot over medium heat, combine berries, water, dates, ginger, and lemon juice. Mash berries slightly while mixing. 2. Bring to a simmer and cook for about 30 minutes. Add chia seeds and stir. Remove from heat and cool. 3. This jam may be stored in the refrigerator in an airtight jar for up to three weeks.
Per serving: Calories: 114; Total fat 0.4g; Sodium 2mg; Total carbs 29.6g; Fiber 3.7g; Sugars 23.7g; Protein 1.2g

Flax Eggs

Prep time: 5 minutes | Cook time: 0 | Serve: the equivalent of 1 egg

1 tablespoon ground raw flaxseed   2 ½ tablespoons water

1. In a suitable bowl, mix ingredients and let sit 5 minutes before using in a recipe.
Per serving: Calories: 45; Total fat 4g; Sodium 3mg; Total carbs 3.5g; Fiber 3g; Sugars 0g; Protein 2g

Tahini Maple Syrup

Prep time: 5 minutes | Cook time: 0 | Serve: ½ cup

¼ cup tahini   ¼ cup pure maple syrup

1. In a suitable bowl, whisk together tahini and maple syrup until combined. 2. If tahini is very thick, warming it gently over the stovetop will help to loosen it, making it easier to combine with the maple syrup. 3. You can store them in an airtight container in the refrigerator for up to 2 weeks.
Per serving: Calories: 70; Total fat 4.1g; Sodium 10mg; Total carbs 8.2g; Fiber 0.7g; Sugars 5.9g; Protein 1.3g

Lemon-Tahini Dressing

Prep time: 5 minutes | Cook time: 0 | Serves: 5 tablespoons

3 tablespoons tahini
1 ½ tablespoon lemon juice
¼ teaspoon salt

2 teaspoons honey
¼ cup hot water

1. Combine all the recipe ingredients in a suitable glass jar with a tight-fitting lid. 2. Shake vigorously until all the recipe ingredients come together and you have a smooth and uniform dressing. 3. You can store the dressing in an airtight container in the refrigerator for up to 2 weeks.
Per serving: Calories: 40; Total fat 3.1g; Sodium 81mg; Total carbs 2.7g; Fiber 0.5g; Sugars 1.5g; Protein 1g

Green Oil

Prep time: 5 minutes | Cook time: 0 | Serve: 1 cup

½ cup olive oil
½ cup chopped parsley
¼ cup rosemary leaves

¼ cup chopped chives
1 teaspoon salt
3 garlic cloves, peeled

1. In a suitable food processor, combine all the recipe ingredients and blend together until smooth. 2. Store them in a covered glass jar in the refrigerator for up to 7 days or freeze for up to six months.
Per serving: Calories: 17; Total fat 0.8g; Sodium 584mg; Total carbs 3.1g; Fiber 1.6g; Sugars 0g; Protein 0.3g

Nut Crumbs

Prep time: 10 minutes | Cook time: 0 | Serves: 1 ¼ cups

½ cup walnut pieces
⅔ cup almond flour
¼ cup cornmeal

2 teaspoons smoked paprika
1 tablespoon nutritional yeast
¼ teaspoon salt

1. Place walnuts in a mini blender and grind for about 1 minute until they are ground. 2. In a suitable bowl, combine ground walnuts with almond flour, cornmeal, paprika, yeast, and salt, mixing well. 3. Use immediately or keep in a suitable sealed container in the refrigerator.
Per serving: Calories: 17; Total fat 6g; Sodium 77mg; Total carbs 5.1g; Fiber 1.6g; Sugars 0.2g; Protein 3.3g

Apple-Raspberry Sauce

Prep time: 15 minutes | Cook time: 30 minutes | Serves: 2 cups

4 cups chopped medium red apples
1 cup water
2 tablespoons pure maple syrup

1 tablespoon apple cider vinegar
½ teaspoon ground cinnamon
¼ teaspoon ground ginger
1-pint raspberries

1. In a suitable pot over medium-low heat, combine apples, water, maple syrup, vinegar, cinnamon, and ginger. 2. Bring to a simmer. Cook them for about 20 minutes or until apples is tender. 3. Add raspberries and simmer for another 10 minutes. 4. Transfer to a suitable food processor and purée until slightly chunky. 5. Enjoy.
Per serving: Calories: 79; Total fat 0.3g; Sodium 2mg; Total carbs 20.1g; Fiber 4.3g; Sugars 12.2g; Protein 0.5g

Homemade Mild Curry Powder

Prep time: 5 minutes | Cook time: 0 | Serve: ¼ cup

1 tablespoon ground turmeric
1 tablespoon ground cumin
2 teaspoons ground coriander
1 teaspoon ground cardamom

1 teaspoon ground cinnamon
1 teaspoon ground ginger
½ teaspoon ground cloves

1. In a suitable bowl, stir together the turmeric, cumin, coriander, cardamom, cinnamon, ginger, and cloves until well blended. 2. Store the curry powder in an airtight container for up to 1 month.
Per serving: Calories: 9; Total fat 0.3g; Sodium 2mg; Total carbs 1.5g; Fiber 0.6g; Sugars 0.1g; Protein 0.3g

Avocado Ranch Dressing

Prep time: 5 minutes | Cook time: 0 minutes | Servings: 8

1 avocado, pitted and peeled
½ cup anti-inflammatory mayo
½ cup buttermilk
2 tablespoons chopped fresh parsley
2 tablespoons chopped red onion
1 tablespoon olive oil

1 tablespoon lemon juice
2 teaspoons chopped fresh dill, or
1 teaspoon dried dill
½ teaspoon garlic powder
½ teaspoon salt
¼ teaspoon black pepper

1. In a suitable blender or tall wide container, combine the avocado, mayo, buttermilk, parsley, onion, olive oil, lemon juice, dill, garlic powder, salt, and pepper and blend until thick and creamy, thinning out with additional lemon juice if necessary. 2. Store the dressing in an airtight container in the refrigerator for up to one week.
Per serving: Calories 53; Fat 4.7g; Sodium 108mg; Carbs 2.7g; Fiber 1g; Sugars 0.4g; Protein 0.5g

Marinara Sauce

Prep time: 15 minutes | Cook time: 70 minutes | Servings: 16

½ cup olive oil	tomatoes
tablespoons grass-fed butter	2 tablespoons chopped fresh
red bell pepper, minced	oregano
½ small onion, minced	2 teaspoons salt
garlic cloves, minced	½ to 1 teaspoon red pepper flakes
(32-ounce) cans crushed	½ cup chopped fresh basil

1. In a suitable skillet, heat 2 tablespoons of olive oil and the butter over medium-low heat. 2. Add the bell pepper and onion and cook for almost 5 minutes, until just tender. Add the garlic and sauté for almost 2 minutes until fragrant. 3. Stir in the tomatoes and their juices, oregano, salt, red pepper flakes, and the rest of the 6 tablespoons of olive oil and bring to boil. 4. Reduce its heat to low, cover, and simmer for almost 15 to 60 minutes, allowing the flavors to blend. 5. The longer the sauce cooks, the more flavorful it will be, but it will be ready to eat after 15 minutes of simmering. 6. Remove the sauce from the heat and stir in the basil. 7. Serve warm. If not using right away, allow the sauce to cool to room temperature before storing in an airtight container in the refrigerator for up to four days.
Per serving: Calories 119; Fat 7.8g; Sodium 519mg; Carbs 10.5g; Fiber 4.1g; Sugars 6.9g; Protein 3g

Chimichurri

Prep time: 5 minutes | Cook time: 0 | Serve: 1 cup

1 cup fresh parsley, chopped	2 tablespoons lemon juice
½ cup fresh mint leaves	2 teaspoons minced garlic
¼ cup olive oil	Pinch sea salt

1. In a suitable blender, combine the parsley, mint, olive oil, lemon juice, garlic, and sea salt. 2. Pulse until the herbs are very chopped, and the ingredients are well mixed. 3. Refrigerate the mixture in a suitable sealed container for up to 1 week.
Per serving: Calories: 78; Total fat 8.5g; Sodium 42mg; Total carbs 1.1g; Fiber 0.6g; Sugars 0.1g; Protein 0.4g

Lemon Gremolata Sauce

Prep time: 10 minutes | Cook time: 0 | Serve: 1 cup

¾ cup fresh parsley, chopped	2 tablespoons olive oil
Juice of 2 lemons	2 teaspoons minced garlic
Zest of 2 lemons	¼ teaspoon sea salt

1. In a suitable bowl, stir together the parsley, lemon juice, lemon zest, olive oil, garlic, and sea salt until well blended. 2. Refrigerate in a suitable sealed container for up to 4 days.
Per serving: Calories: 33; Total fat 3.5g; Sodium 62mg; Total carbs 0.6g; Fiber 0.2g; Sugars 0.1g; Protein 0.2g

Mediterranean Spice Rub

Prep time: 5 minutes | Cook time: 0 | Serve: ¾ cup

¼ cup coconut sugar	1 tablespoon dried tarragon
3 tablespoons dried oregano	1 teaspoon dried marjoram
leaves	1 teaspoon dried dill
2 tablespoons dried thyme leaves	1 teaspoon dried basil

1. In a suitable bowl, stir together the coconut sugar, oregano, thyme, tarragon, marjoram, dill, and basil until well blended. 2. Store the seasoning in a suitable sealed container for up to one month.
Per serving: Calories: 31; Total fat 0.5g; Sodium 2mg; Total carbs 7.5g; Fiber 2.1g; Sugars 4.2g; Protein 0.7g

Garlicky Gremolata Sauce

Prep time: 10 minutes | Cook time: 0 minutes | Servings: 8

¾ cup chopped fresh parsley	2 tablespoons olive oil
Juice of 2 lemons	2 teaspoons bottled minced garlic
Zest of 2 lemons	¼ teaspoon sea salt

1. In a suitable bowl, stir together the parsley, lemon juice, lemon zest, olive oil, garlic, and sea salt until well blended. 2. Refrigerate in a suitable sealed container for up to 4 days.
Per serving: Calories 22; Fat 2.4g; Sodium 41mg; Carbs 0.4g; Fiber 0.1g; Sugars 0g; Protein 0.1g

Spicy Vinaigrette with Parsley

Prep time: 5 minutes | Cook time: 0 | Serves: 1¼ cups

¾ cup olive oil	1 teaspoon minced garlic
¼ cup apple cider vinegar	1 teaspoon ground cumin
1 tablespoon lemon juice	¼ teaspoon ground coriander
¼ cup fresh parsley, chopped	Pinch sea salt

1. In a suitable bowl, whisk the olive oil, cider vinegar, and lemon juice until emulsified. 2. Whisk in the parsley, garlic, cumin, and coriander. Season them with sea salt. 3. Refrigerate the vinaigrette in a suitable sealed container for up to 2 weeks.
Per serving: Calories: 166; Total fat 19g; Sodium 2mg; Total carbs 0.5g; Fiber 0.1g; Sugars 0.1g; Protein 0.2g

Creamy Tahini Dressing

Prep time: 5 minutes | Cook time: 0 | Serve: ¾ cup

½ cup canned full-fat coconut milk	1 teaspoon minced garlic
	1 teaspoon minced fresh chives
2 tablespoons tahini	Pinch sea salt
2 tablespoons lime juice	

1. In a suitable bowl, whisk the coconut milk, tahini, lime juice, garlic, and chives until well blended. You can also prepare this in a blender. 2. Season with sea salt and transfer the dressing to a container with a lid. Refrigerate for up to 1 week.
Per serving: Calories: 34; Total fat 3g; Sodium 8mg; Total carbs 1.5g; Fiber 0.5g; Sugars 0g; Protein 1g

Jalapeno Guacamole

Prep time: 10 minutes | Cook time: 0 minutes | Servings: 4

2 avocados, pitted and peeled	1 tablespoon chopped jalapeño
Juice of ½ lemon	1 teaspoon salt
2 tablespoons olive oil	½ to 1 teaspoon ground turmeric
1 garlic clove, pressed or minced	½ teaspoon black pepper
1 tablespoon minced red onion	¼ to ½ cup chopped fresh cilantro

1. In a suitable bowl, combine the avocados, lemon juice, olive oil, and garlic and mash well with a fork. 2. Stir in the onion, jalapeño, salt, turmeric, pepper, and cilantro until well combined. 3. Serve immediately.
Per serving: Calories 179; Fat 17.8g; Sodium 392mg; Carbs 6.2g; Fiber 4.7g; Sugars 0.5g; Protein 1.3g

Keto Sandwich Round

Prep time: 5 minutes | Cook time: 2 minutes | Servings: 1

3 tablespoons almond flour	½ teaspoon salt
1 large egg	½ teaspoon garlic powder
1 tablespoon olive oil	¼ teaspoon baking powder

1. Prepare a suitable microwave-safe ramekin, add all the ingredients and mix well. 2. Microwave the mixture for 90 seconds. 3. When cooked, slide a knife around the edges of the ramekin and then flip to remove the bread. 4. Slice the round in half with a serrated knife to make 2 pieces for a sandwich.
Per serving: Calories 201; Fat 19.83g; Sodium 1173mg; Carbs 3.16g; Fiber 0.6g; Sugars 0.29g; Protein 3.72g

Rosemary Vinaigrette

Prep time: 5 minutes | Cook time: 0 minutes | Servings: 4

½ cup olive oil	minced
¼ cup white or red wine vinegar	2 teaspoons dried rosemary
1 tablespoon Dijon mustard	½ teaspoon salt
1 small garlic clove, pressed or	½ to 1 teaspoon red pepper flakes

1. In a glass jar with a lid, combine the avocado oil, vinegar, mustard, garlic, rosemary, salt, and red pepper flakes and shake until well combined. 2. Store, covered, in the refrigerator for up to two weeks. 3. Bring to room temperature and shake well before serving, as the oil and vinegar will naturally separate.
Per serving: Calories 45; Fat 3.8g; Sodium 337mg; Carbs 2.3g; Fiber 1.6g; Sugars 0.2g; Protein 0.6g

Maple-Mustard Dressing

Prep time: 5 minutes | Cook time: 0 | Serves: 1¼ cups

1 cup canned full-fat coconut milk	1 tablespoon Dijon mustard
2 tablespoons pure maple syrup	1 tablespoon apple cider vinegar
	Sea salt, to taste

1. In a suitable bowl, whisk the coconut milk, maple syrup, mustard, and cider vinegar until smoothly blended. Season them with sea salt. 2. Refrigerate the dressing in a suitable sealed container for up to 1 week.
Per serving: Calories: 41; Total fat 2.1g; Sodium 35mg; Total carbs 5.1g; Fiber 0.1g; Sugars 4g; Protein 0.4g

Turmeric Aioli

Prep time: 5 minutes | Cook time: 0 minutes | Servings: 8

1 cup anti-inflammatory mayo	1 teaspoon monk fruit extract
Grated zest and juice of 1 lemon	1 teaspoon ground turmeric
2 garlic cloves, minced	½ teaspoon cayenne pepper

1. In a suitable bowl, combine the mayo, lemon zest and juice, garlic, monk fruit extract, turmeric, and cayenne and whisk until smooth and creamy. 2. The aioli can be kept covered in the refrigerator for up to one week.
Per serving: Calories 16; Fat 1.1g; Sodium 24mg; Carbs 1.5g; Fiber 0.2g; Sugars 0.3g; Protein 0.2g

Garlic-Rosemary Butter

Prep time: 5 minutes | Cook time: 0 minutes | Servings: 4

½ cup grass-fed butter	2 garlic cloves, minced
1 tablespoon chopped fresh rosemary	½ teaspoon salt

1. In a suitable bowl, using an electric mixer on medium or using an immersion blender, blend the butter, rosemary, garlic, and salt until smooth and creamy. 2. Using a spatula, transfer the butter mixture to a small glass container and cover. 3. Store in the refrigerator for up to one month or in the freezer for up to four months.
Per serving: Calories 137; Fat 15.4g; Sodium 303mg; Carbs 0.3g; Fiber 0g; Sugars 0g; Protein 0.2g

Lime-Cilantro Dressing

Prep time: 5 minutes | Cook time: 0 minutes | Servings: 12

2 avocados, pitted and peeled	2 garlic cloves, peeled
1 cup packed fresh cilantro leaves	1 teaspoon salt
½ cup olive oil	½ teaspoon black pepper
¼ cup lime juice (about 4 limes)	

1. In a suitable blender or tall wide container, combine the avocados, cilantro, olive oil, lime juice, garlic, salt, and pepper and blend until thick and creamy. 2. If the prepared mixture seems too thick, add warm water, 1 tablespoon at a time. 3. Store the dressing in an airtight container in the refrigerator for up to 7 days.
Per serving: Calories 106; Fat 11.2g; Sodium 149mg; Carbs 2.3g; Fiber 1.7g; Sugars 0.1g; Protein 0.5g

Mild Curry Powder

Prep time: 5 minutes | Cook time: 0 minutes | Servings: 8

1 tablespoon ground turmeric	1 teaspoon ground cinnamon
1 tablespoon ground cumin	1 teaspoon ground ginger
2 teaspoons ground coriander	½ teaspoon ground cloves
1 teaspoon ground cardamom	

1. In a suitable bowl, stir together the turmeric, cumin, coriander, cardamom, cinnamon, ginger, and cloves until well blended. 2. Store the curry powder in an airtight container for up to 1 month.
Per serving: Calories 9; Fat 0.3g; Sodium 2mg; Carbs 1.5g; Fiber 0.6g; Sugars 0.1g; Protein 0.3g

Tarragon Spice Rub

Prep time: 5 minutes | Cook time: 0 minutes | Servings: 8

¼ cup packed coconut sugar	1 tablespoon dried tarragon
3 tablespoons dried oregano leaves	1 teaspoon dried marjoram
2 tablespoons dried thyme leaves	1 teaspoon dried dill
	1 teaspoon dried basil

1. In a suitable bowl, stir together the coconut sugar, oregano, thyme tarragon, marjoram, dill, and basil until well blended. 2. Store the seasoning in a suitable sealed container for up to 1 month.
Per serving: Calories 12; Fat 0.2g; Sodium 4mg; Carbs 2.8g; Fiber 0.7g; Sugars 1.3g; Protein 0.2g

Spicy Parsley Vinaigrette

Prep time: 5 minutes | Cook time: 0 minutes | Servings: 12

¾ cup olive oil	1 teaspoon bottled minced garlic
¼ cup apple cider vinegar	1 teaspoon ground cumin
1 tablespoon lemon juice	¼ teaspoon ground coriander
¼ cup chopped fresh parsley	Pinch sea salt

1. In a suitable bowl, whisk the olive oil, cider vinegar, and lemon juice until emulsified. 2. Whisk in the parsley, garlic, cumin, and coriander. 3. Season with sea salt. 4. Refrigerate the vinaigrette in a suitable sealed container for up to 2 weeks.
Per serving: Calories 150; Fat 12.3g; Sodium 409mg; Carbs 8.6g; Fiber 1.8g; Sugars 4.5g; Protein 3.4g

Tahini Dressing

Prep time: 5 minutes | Cook time: 0 minutes | Servings: 8

½ cup canned full-fat coconut milk	1 teaspoon bottled minced garlic
2 tablespoons tahini	1 teaspoon minced fresh chives
2 tablespoons lime juice	Pinch sea salt

1. In a suitable bowl, whisk the coconut milk, tahini, lime juice, garlic, and chives until well blended. You can also prepare this in a suitable blender. 2. Season with sea salt and transfer the dressing to a container with a lid. Refrigerate for up to 1 week.
Per serving: Calories 31; Fat 2.8g; Sodium 6mg; Carbs 1.1g; Fiber 0.4g; Sugars 0g; Protein 0.8g

Avocado Spread

Prep time: 10 minutes | Cook time: 0 minutes | Servings: 8

1 ripe avocado, peeled and pitted	1 teaspoon chopped fresh dill
2 tablespoons lemon juice	½ teaspoon ground coriander
2 tablespoons chopped fresh parsley	Sea salt, to taste
	Black pepper, to taste

1. In your blender, pulse the avocado until smoothly puréed. 2. Add the lemon juice, parsley, dill, and coriander. Pulse until well blended. 3. Season with sea black pepper and salt. 4. Refrigerate the spread in a suitable sealed container for up to 4 days.
Per serving: Calories 35; Fat 3.3g; Sodium 2mg; Carbs 1.6g; Fiber 1.2g; Sugars 0.1g; Protein 0.4g

Parsley Chimichurri

Prep time: 5 minutes | Cook time: 0 minutes | Servings: 8

1 cup chopped fresh parsley	2 tablespoons lemon juice
½ cup fresh mint leaves	2 teaspoons minced garlic
¼ cup olive oil	Pinch sea salt

1. In a suitable blender or food processor, combine the parsley, mint, olive oil, lemon juice, garlic, and sea salt. 2. Pulse until the herbs are very chopped and the ingredients are well mixed. 3. Refrigerate the prepared mixture in a suitable sealed container for up to 1 week.
Per serving: Calories 39; Fat 4.3g; Sodium 21mg; Carbs 0.5g; Fiber 0.3g; Sugars 0.1g; Protein 0.2g

The anti-inflammatory diet is one of the best and healthiest diets. If you want to stay healthy, follow an anti-inflammatory diet. You should eat fresh fruits, fresh vegetables, gluten-free foods, lean meat, fish, gluten-free grains, nuts, seeds, and many more in this diet. You can check parts of What to Eat and What Not to Eat in this cookbook. If you have any inflammatory symptoms, you should go to your doctor, who will accordingly give your food tips. And thus you can adjust your own diet with the assistance of this cookbook. Good diet habits should also be token, like drinking plenty of water, choose healthy snacks, consume healthy fats and proteins, and avoid fast, processed, and junk foods.

In this cookbook, you will find easy, healthy, and delicious recipes. In this book, anything you can imagine in a cookbook includes breakfast recipes, main dishes, meat, fish, soups, desserts, snacks recipes, and many more. It is a good option for your health. All recipes are simple to cook and easy to follow. You don't even need any special ingredients or equipment to make them. Thank you for choosing this cookbook and making us feel honored. Stay healthy, stay hydrated, and stay anti-inflammatory!

Appendix 1 Measurement Conversion Chart

WEIGHT EQUIVALENTS

US STANDARD	METRIC (APPROXIMATE)
1 ounce	28 g
2 ounces	57 g
5 ounces	142 g
10 ounces	284 g
15 ounces	425 g
16 ounces (1 pound)	455 g
1.5pounds	680 g
2pounds	907 g

TEMPERATURES EQUIVALENTS

FAHRENHEIT(F)	CELSIUS(C) (APPROXIMATE)
225 °F	107 °C
250 °F	120 °C
275 °F	135 °C
300 °F	150 °C
325 °F	160 °C
350 °F	180 °C
375 °F	190 °C
400 °F	205 °C
425 °F	220 °C
450 °F	235 °C
475 °F	245 °C
500 °F	260 °C

VOLUME EQUIVALENTS (DRY)

US STANDARD	METRIC (APPROXIMATE)
⅛ teaspoon	0.5 mL
¼ teaspoon	1 mL
½ teaspoon	2 mL
¾ teaspoon	4 mL
1 teaspoon	5 mL
1 tablespoon	15 mL
¼ cup	59 mL
½ cup	118 mL
¾ cup	177 mL
1 cup	235 mL
2 cups	475 mL
3 cups	700 mL
4 cups	1 L

VOLUME EQUIVALENTS (LIQUID)

US STANDARD	US STANDARD (OUNCES)	METRIC (APPROXIMATE)
2 tablespoons	1 fl.oz	30 mL
¼ cup	2 fl.oz	60 mL
½ cup	4 fl.oz	120 mL
1 cup	8 fl.oz	240 mL
1½ cup	12 fl.oz	355 mL
2 cups or 1 pint	16 fl.oz	475 mL
4 cups or 1 quart	32 fl.oz	1 L
1 gallon	128 fl.oz	4 L

Appendix 2 Recipes Index

Made in the USA
Middletown, DE
03 January 2023

21274406R00083